The Dialectical Path of Law

The Dialectical Path of Law

Charles Lincoln

LEXINGTON BOOKS
Lanham • Boulder • New York • London

Published by Lexington Books
An imprint of The Rowman & Littlefield Publishing Group, Inc.
4501 Forbes Boulevard, Suite 200, Lanham, Maryland 20706
www.rowman.com

6 Tinworth Street, London SE11 5AL, United Kingdom

British Library Cataloguing in Publication Information Available

Library of Congress Cataloging-in-Publication Data

Names: Lincoln, Charles (Charles Edward Andrew), IV, 1992– author.
Title: The dialectical path of law / Charles Lincoln.
Description: Lanham : Lexington Books, [2021] | Includes bibliographical references and index. | Summary: "The Dialectical Path of Law discusses the origin of law leading to the development of advanced corporate law intertwined with the formation of technical tax rules. Lincoln explores the recent developments of the OECD and United States tax rules within a hardly discussed context in legal academia—the Hegelian dialectic"—Provided by publisher.
Identifiers: LCCN 2021030771 (print) | LCCN 2021030772 (ebook) | ISBN 9781793632258 (cloth) | ISBN 9781793632265 (epub)
Subjects: LCSH: Law—Philosophy. | Taxation—Law and legislation—Philosophy. | Corporation law—Philosophy.
Classification: LCC K230.L55 A38 2021 (print) | LCC K230.L55 (ebook) | DDC 340/.1—dc23
LC record available at https://lccn.loc.gov/2021030771
LC ebook record available at https://lccn.loc.gov/2021030772

Contents

Preface

Holmes stated in *The Path of Law*[1] that he opposed deduction as the theoretical answer to legal questions, "[t]here is a concealed, half conscious battle on the question of legislative policy, and if anyone thinks that it can be settled deductively, or once for all, I only can say that I think he is theoretically wrong, and that I am certain that his conclusion will not be accepted in practice *semper ubique et ab omnibus*."[2] Here Holmes seems to oppose a theory of law existing as a logical construct.[3]

This is not to say, he opposed *a priori* or analytic judgments *per se* in Kantian sense,[4] but that law must have social constraints—and that law is not complete formalism but rather intuited and reasoned through social considerations.[5]

The genesis of these ideas began with anthropology. The notions of legal realism can be readily apparent through the lens of anthropology. Indeed, the creation of Franz Boas's new study of anthropology and the simultaneous inception of legal realism perhaps were markers of the general academic sentiment at the time—if not prescient of each other.

As an undergraduate, I wrote my senior thesis under the guidance and mentorship of an assistant Dean of Harvard Law School—Akiba Covitz. I argued that there existed a "Hegelian" dialectical movement in U.S. voting rights from exclusive to inclusive—that is, from white land owners to almost everyone, in theory, over time and even with setbacks on such expansions of the right to vote. This simplification of the *sublation,* as influenced by Fukuyama, led me to believe that law was a logical system that could be resolved through social interactions—the promise of equality and the lack thereof. This was the beginning of my thoughts of logic and social interactions.

In law school, I re-wrote my senior thesis as a punctuated and shortened law review article. At the same time, I worked on a critique of my former mentor's, Akiba Covitz's, Ph.D. dissertation. Covitz's Ph.D. is a work which I found to be one of the most inspirational pieces on the philosophical foundations of the U.S. government. As I interpreted it at the time, Akiba Covitz claimed that Plato's conception of the three-part soul in his *Republic* was represented in the U.S. government's three parts: judicial, executive, and legislative.[6] Covitz associates *thymos* with the judicial, the executive with *logos*, and the legislative with *eros*. I agreed entirely with the analysis but in conclusion rather saw the judicial was *logos*, the executive was *thymos*, and the legislative was *eros*. This shows my predilection—at least at the time—for legal formalism in the judiciary: the most logical of the three branches of government. In retrospect, perhaps Akiba Covitz had the more accurate formulation; but, the debate seems entirely relevant, perhaps even to the extent of seeing if the legislative could be *logos* or *thymos*.

Regardless of the correct formulation, in short, it seemed that there was an archetype of government that seemed suited for long-term existence that Plato had touched upon and perhaps Freud had illuminated upon in the individual sense through psychoanalysis. From a psychoanalytic Freudian sense, is it fair to say that the best government, at least in part, represents the individual or the psyche of the individual? Likewise, it seems fair to say that a Jungian archetype of government could exist.

Per Covitz's formulation and my re-interpretation of his formulation, I think the main counter arguments against the tripartite analysis of the U.S. system of government outlined in the Constitution is the concept of the administrative state and the overlay of the state governments. This is a counter argument that Covitz and I try to deal with in our independent publications. Perhaps, the best counter point to that counter argument is the concept that under the theory of Plato's soul in *The Republic* and in *Phaedrus* is that each individual—no matter what level or part of government—embodies some level of these souls. When problems occur individually or on the scale of government, as Plato predicted, they find their origin and follow from an imbalance of the interests of the soul as allegorically depicted in the *Phaedrus* with the charioteer.

In short, after I published the two law review articles on Hegelianism and the structure of the U.S. government from a Platonic perspective, it seemed to me that both the Hegelian dialectic and the idea of an archetypal government were commensurable. This in large part is and was the initial aim of this book. But as time progressed, the more important and relevant goal of the book appeared to me to deal with the difference of legal realism and legal formalism—that have lingered for over a century since Oliver Wendell Holmes Jr.'s critique of legal formalism in *The Common Law* and *The Path of Law*. Seemingly, Wittgenstein's later theories in his *Philosophical Investigations* bolster legal realism, because Wittgenstein argues that all language games and relations are social.[7]

At the same time, both the idea of the Hegelian dialectic and the archetypal system of government both seem lacking the ability to resolve the issue lingering between formalism (now seen as textualism) and legal realism. I had hoped this could be resolved through a combination of those two theories. Such a resolution was the initial dialectical goal I had envisioned. In some sense, the writing of a book can seem like a dialectical journey where the final result cannot be predicted.

Wittgenstein's language games and Gödel's incompleteness theory seem to provide each a refutation of legal realism and legal formalism. It seems neither theory of formalism or realism is fully comprehensive; yet at the same time, both complement each other and are entirely the same. The problem lies in a possible question of a new theory—or entirely a refutation of Wittgenstein's later thought and theory of language games from his *Philosophical Investigations* (if such a refutation exists).

Ultimately, the goal of this book is, and was, also to show a *sublation* of legal realism and legal formalism. If such a synthesis exists, then it could be helpful to set a standard for interpreting law from a different lens and could take a place in the market of ideas of legal textualism, formalism, or purposivism.

An analogous question to legal realism and legal formalism is the concept of whether mathematics exists independently of human existence or whether mathematics exists only because of human cognition.[8] This is a question that goes back to pre-Platonic thought and Greek antiquity. This book cannot answer this question, but it may provide an analogous system of analysis for approaching such questions in the philosophy of mathematics.

SUMMARY OF BOOK AND ARGUMENTS

The purpose of this book is not to answer questions that it presents but rather to frame questions in a compelling and useful manner. In large part, the frame of questions in a compelling, at times provocative, but useful way.

After the primary goal of fruitfully framing questions, overall, the book aims to demonstrate the existence of dialectic law and explore the consequences of the dialectic. The main argument is that the Hegelian dialectic and concept of *sublation* can be applied to the archetypal form of government to predict the future development of a government. This analysis turns on the *sublation* of legal realism and legal formalism. This *sublation* is dependent upon Wittgenstein's theory of language games—that language is a social construction.

The introduction and first chapter define and explore the origins of anthropological thought. These chapters are written with an aim of exploring law but attempt to not leave out the cultural values inherent in such approaches. The second chapter explores how anthropological theories' patterns explored in the first chapter provide various systems—among them Georges Dumézil's trifunctionalism. Such a trifunctional theory is not alone found in Dumézil's work but as explored in chapter 3, in Plato's work as well. Chapter 3 lays out my theory of the three part structure of the U. S. federal government based on the Constitution of 1787 as laid in contrast to Akiba Covitz's formulation.

Chapter 4 lays out how theoretical economics, capitalism, and international monetary policy—particularly in the role of taxation—play an essential role in the existence of the three part function of government.

The following chapters follow an Hegelian dialectical paradigm of the Universal, the particular, and *sublation* of solving legal issues: Chapter 4 discusses the Universal of international taxation, with the particulars of source and residence taxation. Chapter 5 provides the *sublation* hinted in chapter 4 of risk analysis. The risk analysis both is and is not source and residence taxation, yet at the same time provides the basis for both rules—a true Hegelian *sublation*. The later part of chapters 5 through 7 consider whether these rules would be adopted by the United States. Indeed, international organizations, such as the OECD, often propose rules. The OECD, an international organization, is consisted of multiple organizations, including the United States. In a crude Hegelian way, the OECD could be the Universal, the constituent countries the particulars. The *sublation* is the United States—neither the OECD nor *all* the constituent countries—yet is part of both. Likewise, it is worthwhile considering if it would adopt compelling rules from either the OECD or those other countries. It seems the answer is no, but recent case law may suggest otherwise. Chapters 8 and 9 discuss the particular instances of the U. S. case law approach to these issues. Chapters 10 through 11 provide suggested conclusions of how the United States will resolve these issues. But even as this book is written, administrative and statutory changes indicate that it is difficult to predict which way the United States will go on these issues. Chapter 12 addresses the difficulties of predicting the future but poses policy questions based on the current state of affairs.

Chapter 13 shifts from the concept of purely law and taxation to law and contractual relationships that form the foundations of taxation. To explore this, the chapter explores the origins of such laws and how they are portrayed in Shakespearean literature. Shakespearean literature is explored through a Hegelian and Lacanian psychological perspective.

Chapter 14 deals with some of the key issues the book has addressed in parts, specifically legal formalism and legal realism from the perspective of Gödel's incompleteness theorems and Wittgenstein's language games.

Chapter 15 pivots from Wittgenstein's language games and incorporates David Foster Wallace's writings on language into a theory of law as grammar.

The conclusion wraps up certain points and suggests questions for future inquiry.

Given the outline of the chapters in the book, the results and the purposes of the work can demonstrate the following several points. First, the efficacy of the Hegelian concept of *sublation* is demonstrated throughout each chapter's subject. In this sense, this is a field study showing the concept of dialectical negation in each of the following areas: anthropology, law, international taxation, Shakespearean literature, legal formalism, legal realism, Gödel's theories, and Wittgenstein's language games. Second, individually, the book proposes a theory that is a cross of legal formalism and legal realism. This theory could have implications for the political climate of conservativism and liberalism. Such political implications may not only apply in the United States but in countries, unions, such as the European Union, or entities, such as the United Nations, in which jurists choose to reject or adopt the existing varieties of legal formalism and realism. Third, solving part of the key aspects of source and residency, as well as risk allocation in international taxation. These aspects are key to the international economy, but also lend themselves well to the study of dialectic and *sublation* in law. Fourth, illuminating the psychological contours of law and literature, particularly through Shakespeare. This marries theories of literature, Hegelianism, and psychoanalysis together. Here, the theories of psychoanalysis are rooted in the traditional canon originating with Plato and Aristotle and ending specifically with Freud, Jung, and Lacan. Fifth, a dialectical analysis of theories on Hegel's theory of dialectics and theory of *sublation*. This fifth could be useful in exploring the various theories trying to sum up Hegelianism.

Overall, each chapter individually provides a summation of the theories addressed before they are analyzed. Specifically, these theories are summarized from the point of view of a legal treatise. The theories in the book could be referenced as if they were listed in an encyclopedia focused on philosophy, anthropology, law, and taxation. The theories listed are defined in a way that the author intends as "objective."[9] In case the analysis of the book is not useful, perhaps the theories, as examined and summarized before analysis, could be usefully cited for future reference. They are: key anthropological theories evolutionism, diffusionism, structuralism, functionalism, neo-evolutionists, materialism, memetic theories; Dumézilian trifunctionalism; Greek philosophy and specifically focusing on Plato's theories of the soul; economic risk and random simulations based in Zipf's law; tax treaties; transfer pricing; the structure and functions of the United Nations and OECD; monetary debt systems; Fukuyama's theory on the end of history; the OECD's BEPS project; U.S. Tax Court precedent on transfer pricing and risk allocation; Zizekian dialectics and psychoanalysis; Lacanian psychoanalysis; brief and perhaps useful psychoanalytic analysis of Shakespeare's plays *Richard II*, *Troilus and*

Cressida, *Comedy of Errors*, *Hamlet*; Gödel's Incompleteness Theorems; Wittgenstein's language games (as well as comparing them to his early theories in *Tractatus Logico-Philosophicus*); legal realism; and legal formalism; David Foster Wallace's theory of linguistics; and law as grammar.

NOTES

1. Holmes, Oliver Wendell. 1997. "The Path of the Law." *Harvard Law Review* 110 (5): 991–1009.

2. This phrase was even used in Holmes's judicial decision in "[o]therwise a constitution, instead of embodying only relatively fundamental rules of right, as generally understood by all English-speaking communities, would become the partisan of a particular set of ethical or economical opinions, which by no means are held *semper ubique et ab omnibus*."

"U.S. Reports: Otis v. Parker, 187 U.S. 606, 609 (1903)." n.d. Image. Library of Congress, Washington, D.C. 20540 USA. Accessed May 16, 2021. https://www.loc.gov/item/usrep187606/.

3. As to policy, in The Path of Law Holmes hints at a change in view toward strict liability, particularly in his thoughts on employer liability. In questioning why negligence is an element in employer liability, Holmes, in keeping with his anti-formalism, states that "if any one thinks it can be settled deductively . . . he is theoretically wrong." While not explicitly taking a position, Holmes, adopting a temporalist/relativist view, does juxtapose the state of society at the formation of tort law-one of "isolated, ungeneralized wrongs"-to the state of society at the time of The Path of Law-where most torts involve "certain well-known businesses."

Hackney, James R. "The Intellectual Origins of American Strict Products Liability: A Case Study in American Pragmatic Instrumentalism." *The American Journal of Legal History* 39, no. 4 (1995): 443, 445.

4. Discussed in more detail in the book. However, briefly, according to the German tradition of objectivism, "transcendental idealism is not the apotheosis of, but the antidote to, the Cartesian way of ideas. Nowhere is this antidote more apparent than in the Transcendental Deduction of the first *Kritik*, where Kant shows how the ideas of the knowing subject are determined by the intersubjective order of the a priori concepts of the understanding."

Beiser, Frederick C. 2002. *German Idealism: The Struggle against Subjectivism, 1781–1801*. Harvard University Press.

5. "First, in The Common Law, Holmes dealt a heavy blow to formalist thought in American law. Second, in The Path of Law, Holmes alluded to the way, given different social contexts (temporalism/relativism), that the perspective in The Common Law could lead to radically different legal policies than those he initially proposed."

Hackney, James R. 1995. "The Intellectual Origins of American Strict Products Liability: A Case Study in American Pragmatic Instrumentalism." *The American Journal of Legal History* 39 (4): 443, 445.

6. Covitz, Akiba. n.d. "The Soul of the Polity: Beginnings of American Constitutional Thought." Accessed May 16, 2021. https://repository.upenn.edu/dissertations/AAI9926112/.

7. § 201 Wittgenstein, Ludwig. 1968. *Philosophical Investigations*. Oxford: Basil Blackwell.

8. Many implications arise from the answer to such a question. Indeed, "[t]oday the movement toward universal datafication and knowledge discovery carries the tones of determinism and mathematical realism. Mathematical realism holds that humans do not invent mathematics but discover truth of the mathematical reality."

Ambrose, Meg Leta. n.d. "Lessons from the Avalanche of Numbers: Big Data in Historical Perspective." *Journal of Law & Policy for the Information Society* 11: 201, 232.

9. But such an attempt is often futile—the author readily admits this.

Introduction[1]

Why do different cultures and societies lead to different laws? After all, the way the law operates should be based in logic to be the best and most efficient way for the laws to govern human society to carry out their lives—if it were not so, we would change our patterns of existence and legal systems both through the political process or through anthropological cultural evolution.

As an extension of these questions, how can culture sufficiently act as a legal system without having been codified, written, or even actively acknowledged?

Culture is normative.[2] "Norms" are the socially mandated behavioral patterns which evolve into and are formalized, or formally expressed (i.e., linguistically) as law.[3] "Culture is [a] human extra-somatic adaptation,[4] dependent upon symbolling." Law is language.[5] Law is symbolic and a particularly ritualistic language.[6]

However, law often relies on definitions.[7] Yet, Wittgenstein argued that words are used without definitions and argued that definitions do not exist at all but only through relations in the way a word is used in language.[8]

Why do people around the world persist in continuing with different law structures contrary to the uniform law recommendations of the United Nations or Organisation for Economic Co-operation and Development recommendations? Or even on a national level of the United States through uniform law recommendations of the American Law Institute? And why do other international organizations expect other countries to conform to rules set out by the organizations in terms of basic contract, property, procedural laws, and so on? How can basic laws be replaced by different cultural practices? This introduction will take an anthropological approach to this inquiry and the ones above.[9] All social scientists try to answer such questions, but anthropologists work through contact with exotic societies and attempt to explain their behaviors.[10] Of course, by explaining the behavior of others, these scientists ultimately try to understand their own societies.[11]

Social scientists interested in the populations of the world have developed different answers to the basic questions: are all humans alike or are they different?[12] How are they alike, and how are they different? This is the fundamental problem in anthropology.[13] It is easy to see material and cultural differences when encountering different cultures.[14] Using the concepts of culture and cultural relatively that were popularized and made fundamental in anthropology by the students of Franz Boas, this "American School of Anthropology" emphasized the differences between populations.[15] At the same time, most European scholars accepted the psychological unity of mankind—the hypothesis that all humans think alike.[16]

Cultural relativity, the argument that all socially approved behavior can only be understood in the context of its own cultural setting, can be interpreted in a manner that discourages cross-cultural comparison and even negates the notion that all humanity uses the same thinking process.[17]

Although some credit Herodotus of Halicarnassus as the earliest precursor to anthropological studies,[18] one of the first encounters between the West and the Americas was recorded in the Franciscan friar Bernardino de Sahagún's *Historia general de las cosas de la Nueva España* or *Florentine Codex*—a bilingual Spanish and Nahuatl account of the practices of the Native Americans.[19] That volume earned Sahagún the title of the first Native American ethnographer. Another contrasting example is the great adventure story in Bernal Díaz del Castillo's *True History of the Conquest of New Spain.*[20] Díaz del Castillo was reacting to the "Black Legend," that is the Bishop of Chiapas Las Casas' accusation that the Spanish conquistadors slaughtered vast numbers of people in the name of the Catholic king of Spain, Charles, V.[21] The Spanish royal house was very preoccupied with this charge.[22] The supporters of the monarchy argued against Las Casas, but many church missionaries sided in his favor.[23] Díaz del Castillo—a soldier who participated in the conquest of Mexico with Hernán Cortés in 1519–1521—insisted that the account of the conquest by Francisco López de Gómara, Hernán Cortés's chaplain, was exaggerated.[24] Pro-government scholars emphasized Diaz del Castillo's descriptions of Aztec human sacrifices, including the dried blood on the walls of the temples and in the hair of the priests.[25] From this description, one can almost feel the visceral aspect of these temples. While, in Sahagún's description of the market at Tlatelolco,[26] when the conquistadors first entered Tenochtitlan—he describes the Spanish as brimming with admiration.[27] In comparison, Sahagún was sympathetic to the people he studied, while Bernal Díaz del Castillo seemed to have admired the natives only as worthy adversaries.[28]

NOTES

1. The ideas for this introduction began and originated in an article first published in Florida Coastal Law Review: Charles Lincoln, "A Brief Historical Sketch of an Anthropological Analysis of the Development of International and Comparative Law," *Fla. Coastal L. Rev.* 19 (2019): 221. As in that article, the author of this book is in great appreciation and thankfulness to the late Mayanist anthropologist Dr. Edward Barna Kurjack of Western Illinois University for his mentorship in anthropology. The author would also like to thank Dr. Charles Maier of Harvard University—whose Harvard College class titled "Global History 1920" taken by the author as an undergraduate provided the inspiration to explore ideas in this chapter and book.

2. Robert J. Cottrol, "Normative Nominalism: The Paradox of Egalitarian Law in Inegalitarian Cultures—Some Lessons from Recent Latin American Historiography." *Tulane Law Review* 81 (2007): 891–92 (noting that such an article needs a basis in definition of culture as a premise for use throughout the article).

[From a] historical sociology of law would presumably use law and its history not merely to illustrate the evolution of legal doctrine, or how the law resolved certain controversies, or even how it was influenced by the social currents of different eras. It would do these things of course, but it would presumably do something more. It would use the law as a window into the very civilization being studied. It would recognize that the law, both as stated and as actually applied, in the values expressed and in the promises unrealized, reveals a society and its culture in both its aims and its contradictions. This approach, I would argue, is an especially important one to bring to the study of legal history in Latin America. Many students of Latin-American law have long noted the gap between the law as stated and the law as actually applied. There has been in the history of law in Latin America what might be termed a kind of normative nominalism, a desire to use the law to make important normative statements, followed by often minimalist or nominal enforcement or application of legal norms.

3. Rene Reich-Graefe, "Deconstructing Corporate Governance: The Mechanics of Trusting." *Delaware Journal of Corporate Law* 38 (2013): 103, 124–25 (stating that law, social norms, and linguistics are intertwined in a unique way).

Social norms are powerful behavioral controllers within an overall hybrid and complex system of social control which relies on the interplay of legal, market, and social norm mechanisms for purposes of establishing efficient constraints on the future (in-)actions of individual participants in cooperative endeavors. Such a hybrid system, therefore, also casts a regulatory net over director decision-making behavior and, thus, allows for behavioral constraints on corporate directors for purposes of achieving sufficient levels of board accountability in corporate governance. This chapter starts the long-neglected analysis of the intersection of norms and director primacy with one of the central social norms and behavioral controllers in corporate governance and economic cooperation in this regard: trust.

4. Lawrence Lessig, "The New Chicago School." *The Journal of Legal Studies* 27, no. S2 (1998): 661–91, 662 (noting that this adaptation is based in the concept of

"trust" whereby "[t]he ultimate effect of the law is to provide entrustors with incentives to enter into fiduciary relationships, by reducing entrustors' risks and costs of preventing abuse of entrusted power, and of ensuring quality fiduciary services."); *see generally* Rene Reich-Graefe, "Deconstructing Corporate Governance: The Mechanics of Trusting." *Delaware Journal of Corporate Law* 38 (2013): 103, 190.

5. Steven D. Smith, "Law as Language." *Mercer Law Review* 63 (2011): 891, 893.

[The subtle] contention that law is language may reflect a more Wittgensteinian perspective one that aspires to be more attentive to the subtle, mysterious workings of language itself. Wittgenstein, after describing a straightforwardly referential account of language—this word refers to that object, and so forth—suggested that this simple referential account leaves out a good deal in the language. He famously offered a different analogy: Our language can be seen as an ancient city: a maze of little streets and squares, of old and new houses, and of houses with additions from various periods; this surrounded by a multitude of new boroughs with straight regular streets and uniform houses.

See § 18 and 8 Ludwig Wittgenstein, *Philosophical Investigations* (Oxford: Basil Blackwell, 1968).

Cf. Matthew D. Adler, "Expressive Theories of Law: A Skeptical Overview." *University of Pennsylvania Law Review* 148, no. 5 (2000): 1363–1501, 1376. https://doi.org/10.2307/3312747.

6. Jessie Allen, "A Theory of Adjudication: Law as Magic." *Suffolk University Law Review* 41 (2007): 773, 755.

(stating that the theory of legal magic is supported by early functionalist and structuralist theories).

[The] [e]arly functionalist and structuralist theories; "structural-functionalist" approaches that stress the social work of ritual and cultural analyses that interpret magic and ritual in terms of performance, language, and symbol all reject the necessary opposition of ritual magic and reason. Viewing law as magic from these perspectives produces two important challenges to the Realist view. First, it allows us to see that magic and ritual aspects of adjudication do not necessarily conflict with rational legal decision-making. Second, it suggests some ways that the legal magic the Realists criticized might actually enhance law's legitimacy and effectiveness.

Cf. Leon Green, "The Negligence Issue." *The Yale Law Journal* 37, no. 8 (1928): 1029–47, 1043.

("[A] 'scientific' statement of law has very little if any interest in how they shall treat these terms. The law provides the jury with no table or key by which they can translate these symbols into the terms of human conduct and human qualities. The law recites its ritual and stops.").

7. Though this proposition is often debated.

> We can now also see why the distinction between 'law' and 'the law' is not as fundamental as legal positivists assume. There is no question that we may speak about law in general. The question is whether the inquiry of understanding 'law' is fundamentally different from the inquiry of understanding 'the law' in particular cases. As we have seen, this view is closely tied to the validity-first view, in a sense, it is nothing but shorthand summary of it. But once the view that it is possible to identify individual valid legal norms separately

from their content is rejected, the theoretical distinction between 'law' and 'the law' goes with it. On the view that starts with the question of legitimacy, the latter is just the aggregate of the former, and the boundaries between norms (however those are defined) must be the outcome of looking at their content. Similarly, under the legitimacy-first framework, the separation between the question of what law is and how judges should decide cases becomes rather blurred. Given prevalent (albeit perhaps false) views on legitimacy, it is plausible that judges should decide cases by following 'the law.' It follows that to identify what the law is, what it requires, is (normally) also to identify how judges should decide cases." Dan Priel, "The Place of Legitimacy in Legal Theory.

McGill Law Journal / Revue de Droit de McGill 57, no. 1 (2011): 1–35, 29–30.

Cf. "In the first paragraph of his chapter 'Of Civill Lawes' in the *Leviathan*, Hobbes tells us that 'Civill Law' is sometimes used to refer to the received Roman law: 'But that is not what I intend to speak of here; my design being not to show what is Law here, and there; but what is Law; as *Plato*, *Aristotle*, *Cicero*, and divers others have done, without taking upon them the profession of the study of the Law.' Surely, one could not ask for a statement that is more in the mainstream of the definitional approach. Is it that Hobbes's definition itself is somehow lacking in terms of its positivist credentials?

James Boyle, "Thomas Hobbes and the Invented Tradition of Positivism: Reflections on Language, Power, and Essentialism." *University of Pennsylvania Law Review* 135, no. 2 (1987): 383–426, 391.

Indeed, even Richard Posner presents another idea, "The problem of definition is the old question of how to define 'what is literature?' or 'what is law?' According to Richard Posner, the question of what is law may have "little practical significance if, indeed, it is a meaningful question at all." I think the problem of defining law or literature is meaningful to the extent that it focuses on the relative significance of form and substance. We can differentiate a discourse from other discourses either through its form or substance. The question "what is law?" can be resolved either by identifying a legal statement as one made in legal form or as one bearing legal content. The problem of definition raises the question of whether anything we put in the box labeled "law" becomes law, or whether only certain intrinsically legal items may go into the box. If the latter is true, then we might have to ask how we identify intrinsically legal items in the first place, or, what makes legally appropriate content identifiable as such if there is not a formal trait which renders content perspicuous as a generically distinct type of content." Jeffrey Malkan, "Literary Formalism, Legal Formalism." *Cardozo Law Review* 19 (1997): 1393, 1417.

Yet again even Herbert Lionel Hart may contend with the analytic tradition, "Contemporary analytic jurisprudence, following Hart, sees the question, "What is law?" as the most important, though most perplexing, question it has to answer. This question is usually then paired with the question, "What is not law?," thereby raising what Brian Leiter (following Larry Laudan's work on the philosophy of science) calls the demarcation problem in jurisprudence20 (also referred to as the boundary problem). Traditional conceptual analysis in analytic jurisprudence has attempted to solve this problem by seeking necessary and sufficient features of law, although this attempt so far has been unsuccessful. Worse yet, Quinean holism has undermined faith in the distinctions between the necessary and the contingent and between the analytic and the synthetic that underpin the effort to identify and agree upon features of this sort." John T. Valauri, "Dialectical Jurisprudence: Aristotle and the Concept of Law." *Drexel Law Review* 3 (2010): 415, 420. *Cf.* But even one can see many criticisms of the analytical jurisprudence of law. "For criticisms of Dworkin from the perspective of "institutional legalism," see Francis Allen, "Rostow: Is Law Dead?" *Michigan Law Review* 70, no. 4 (1972): 766–72; Rostow, *The Rightful Limits of Freedom in a Liberal Democratic State: Of Civil Disobedience*, in id. at 60–66. Sanford Levinson, "Taking Law Seriously: Reflections on "Thinking Like a Lawyer." *Stan. L. Rev.* 30 (1978): 1071, 1109 fn. 126.

> 8. While exhibiting the logic of dialectic, the externalist puzzle is not in any respect suggestive of a dialectical progression. Wittgenstein saw it as a static dialectical movement—a circle—wherein the process of definitional reform continues *ad infinitum*. He believed externalism can offer no escape from this circle because few, if any, words conform to the standard of exactness required for a workable "real definition." For most words, there is "no one exact usage," "no one relation of name to object," no "strict" or "fixed" meaning, "no sharp boundary" marking off appropriate use. More importantly, the logical possibility of paradoxical application remains for even those words seemingly covered by complete definitions. So long as externalists search for meaning "by contemplating the expression itself," or by appealing to "higher order" principles, Wittgenstein contended they will remain enmeshed in the puzzle of definition, because "a word hasn't got a meaning given to it, as it were, by a power independent of us, so that there could be a kind of scientific investigation into what the word *really* means.

To Wittgenstein, "meaning" goes no further than use. "[T]he meaning of a word is its use in the language" and nothing more: "I t is the particular use of a word only which gives the word its meaning." Fruitful inquiry into the meaning of an expression consists solely in an examination of the "meaning someone has given to it" in "actual use." Wittgenstein cautioned against treating this inquiry as an invitation to extrapolate from use supposedly common elements for definitional purposes. Treating "use" as a synonym for "application," he perceived a "yawning gulf" between "illustration" through essentialist definitions—the necessary first step in the dialectical puzzle of definition—and "application" in particular cases." Douglas Lind, "Constitutional Adjudication as a Craft-Bound Excellence." *Yale Journal of Law & the Humanities* 6 (1994): 353, 363–65 (emphasis added by author). *See.* "Wittgenstein, Philosophical Remarks, § 15. See also ibid., § 82 ("It isn't a proposition which I put against reality as a yardstick, it's a system of propositions.") (emphasis in original); Wittgenstein, On Certainty, § 141 ("When we first begin to believe anything, what we believe is not a single proposition, it is a whole system of propositions. [Light dawns gradually over the whole.]") (emphasis in original); ibid., § 225 ("What I hold fast to is not one proposition but a nest of propositions.") (emphasis in original); Wittgenstein, *The Blue Book*, 5 ("The sign [the sentence] gets its significance from the system of signs, from the language to which it belongs.") Cf. Wittgenstein, *Remarks on the Philosophy of Psychology*, 2 vols., ed. G.H. von Wright and Heikki Nyman, trans. C.G. Luckhardt and M.A.E. Aue (Chicago: University of

Chicago Press, 1980), II:190 ("It seems therefore, that our concepts, the use of our words, are constrained by a factual framework.") *Id.* at fn. 70.

9. "Three Approaches to Law and Culture Symposium: The Future of Legal Theory: Essay 96 Cornell Law Review 2010-2011." Accessed May 18, 2021. 841–44 (2011) (explaining that, to answer this question and questions like it, there are essentially three major ways to interpret law and culture and nine altogether different categories).

> The first approach, the historical school, arose in German jurisprudence in the first half of the nineteenth century. It views law as a product of a nation's culture and as embedded in the daily practices of its people. According to the historical school, statutes are not meant to create law; rather, their function is to reflect existing social practices. And just as each group of nationals has its own language, expressing a unique national spirit, it also has its own distinctive law.

The second approach, the constitutive approach, developed in American jurisprudence in the 1980s. This approach views law as participating in the constitution of culture and thereby in the constitution of people's minds, practices, and social relations. It thus views the relationship between law and culture as working in an opposite direction from what the historical approach assumes; in both, however, law is an inseparable dimension of social relations.

The third approach, found in twentieth-century Anglo-American jurisprudence, views the law that the courts create and apply as a distinct cultural system. Law practitioners internalize this culture in the course of their studies and professional activity, and this internalization comes to constitute, direct, and delimit the way these practitioners think, argue, resolve cases, and provide justifications. In many cases, however, the legal culture allows for more than one possible solution. Therefore, while there may be objectivity in the law, there is also a degree of inconsistency in its application.

Beyond these three approaches concerning the relationship between law and culture, one can identify at least nine additional approaches in legal scholarship. The first, "law and anthropology," applies anthropological research methods to the study of law. The second, the "legal culture" approach, deals with people's views on the legal system and beliefs about the feasibility of taking legal action to promote their interests. The third, the "legal consciousness" approach, deals with the legal knowledge that people invoke in the course of their daily social interactions. The fourth, the "law and popular culture" approach, deals with law's representations in popular culture, its influence over popular culture, and the influence of popular culture on law. The fifth approach deals with the connection between law and the production of cultural artifacts, such as books and music, and naturally focuses on intellectual property law. The sixth approach, "law and multiculturalism," is a part of the voluminous literature published in the last four decades on multiculturalism and discusses the functions that law plays, and the normative solutions it should adopt, in culturally diversified countries. The seventh approach looks at the connection between law and culture from the perspective of particular legal branches or doctrines. The eighth approach, "law and culture in law and development," discusses the role of cultural change in legal and economic development processes that are taking place in developing countries. The ninth approach, "law as an autopoietic system," views law as an autonomous system whose contents and communications affect social reality in a unique manner, mutually influencing each other and creating law's contents from within. Menachem Mautner, "Three Approaches to Law and Culture." *Cornell L. Rev.* 96 (2011): 839, 841–44.

10. Lawrence Cohen, "003: Introduction to Social/Cultural Anthropology | Anthropology." Accessed May 18, 2021. https://anthropology.berkeley.edu/003-introduction-socialcultural-anthropology-0.

11. *Id.*

12. *See id.*

13. *See id.*

14. Neil Hamilton, and Jeff Maleska. "Helping Students Develop Affirmative Evidence of Cross-Cultural Competency." *Scholar: St. Mary's Law Review on Race and Social Justice* 19 (2017 2016): 187, 197. ("Bennett's three ethno-centric stages include denial, defense, and minimization. Denial is the stage in which one does not recognize any cultural differences and believes their own culture is 'correct.' Second, a person in the defense stage recognizes that other cultures exist, but does not acknowledge that these other cultures are valid. Third, those in the minimization stage tend to overemphasize the universality of their cultural and minimize the actual differences between different culture.")

15. Biography Editors. "Franz Boas." Biography. Accessed May 18, 2021. https://www.biography.com/scientist/franz-boas.

16. *See generally id.*

17. "Human Rights: An Examination of Universalism and Cultural Relativism: Journal of Comparative Social Welfare: Vol 22, 23-36 No 1." Accessed May 18, 2021. https://www.tandfonline.com/doi/abs/10.1080/17486830500522997.

18. Scott C. Littleton, *The New Comparative Mythology: An Anthropological Assessment of the Theories of Georges Dumézil* (1973) 27.

19. *See* Miguel León-Portilla, *Bernardino de Sahagún: First Anthropologist* (2012) 33; see also Diana Magaloni Kerpel, *The Colors of the New World: Artists, Materials, and the Creation of the Florentine Codex* (2014) 55.

20. Michael Palencia-Roth, "The Conquistadors: First-Person Accounts of the Conquest of Mexico. Edited and Translated by Particia de Fuentes. New World Encounters. Edited by Stephen Greenblatt." *Comparative Civilizations Review* 35, no. 35 (n.d.) (1997): 1, 7.

21. Susan Castillo, "Colonial Encounters in New World Writing, 1500-1786. Performing America—ProQuest," 2006 23–24. https://www.proquest.com/openview/a21a4fcf513a2219cc30b944cb5751e8/1?pq-origsite=gscholar&cbl=27448.

22. John Huxtable Elliott, *Imperial Spain* 1469–1716 (2002) 17; see also David A. Lupher, *Romans In a New World: Classical Models In Sixteenth-Century Spanish America* (2006) 55.

23. *See* History of Cuba. "Bartolomé De Las Casas." Accessed May 18, 2021. http://www.historyofcuba.com/history/oriente/LasCasas.htm.

24. Kimberle S. López, *Latin American Novels of the Conquest: Reinventing the New World* (2002) 44; *see also* Francisco Gonzáles-Hermosillo Adams, *El Sometimiento Del Señorío Indígena de Cholula Ante la Corona Española,* 3 Signos históricos (2001) 6, 6; Máximo José Rodríguez Navarri, *La Conquista de Méjico* (2016) 56.

25. Donald C. Briggs and Marvin Alisky, *Historical Dictionary of Mexico* (1981); Gerard Helferich, *Stone of Kings: In Search of the Lost Jade of the Maya* (2012) 330.

26. Miguel León Portilla, *The Broken Spears: The Aztec Account of the Conquest of Mexico* (2006) 44.

27. Nick Caistor, *Mexico City: A Cultural and Literary Companion* (2000) 4–6.

28. Lewis Hanke, *Bartolomé De Las Casas: An Interpretation of His Life and Writings* (2013) 6; see also Miguel León Portilla, *Native Mesoamerican Spirituality: Ancient Myths, Discourses, Stories, Doctrines, Hymns, Poems from the Aztec, Yucatec, Quiche-Maya and Other Sacred Traditions* (1980) 26.

Chapter 1

Anthropological Structuralism and Law

EVOLUTIONISM

Social evolutionism was the popular tradition in anthropology during the nineteenth century.[1] These scholars examined the history of humanity as a whole and divided that narrative into a series of stages.[2] Lewis Henry Morgan summarized human cultural evolution in three stages: savagery, distinguished by hunting and foraging economies;[3] barbarism, the stage of early agriculturalists living in villages; and civilization, the era of the first cities, writing, and metallurgy.[4]

Morgan lived in upstate New York in the 1800s, and thus had Iroquois neighbors.[5] He even started a literary club in 1841 called the "Order of the Iroquois," modeled after his understanding of Iroquois social organization at the time.[6] Certainly, Morgan's early work can be considered part of the James Fenimore Cooper and Henry Schoolcraft romantic tradition in the depiction of Native Americans.[7] Morgan's 1851 book *The League of the Iroquois* explained Iroquois society while at the same time laying the foundations for his theories on the stages of human cultural evolution.[8] As a lawyer, Morgan advocated for the Iroquois Indians trying to protect their lands.[9]

Meanwhile, some nineteenth-century evolutionists protested the clear record of atrocious behavior against natives, including Edward B. Tylor,[10] the first scholar to define culture.[11] Tylor insisted that the colonists were those who, after having been exposed to higher levels of morality, could treat native people in such horrible ways.[12] This exemplifies the social evolutionists' approach that believed in a linear hierarchy—the belief was that the Native Americans would ultimately ascend in the hierarchy. Morgan and Tylor were sympathetic to the native people they studied, but other evolutionists who considered themselves sociologists were not.[13]

I. SOCIAL DARWINISM

Herbert Spencer defined "survival of the fittest" in his *Principles of Biology*[14] and emphasized this idea in his concepts of social evolution.[15] Spencer felt that people suffering the consequences of their actions serve the future of society best;[16] for this reason, free education, public health measures such as compulsory vaccinations, and government welfare acted against the future evolution of humanity.[17] Spencer and his followers, known as Social Darwinists, had no sympathy for natives or even the lower classes of their own society.[18] Incidentally, the textbook used by John T. Scopes, of the famous "Monkey Trial," supported Social Darwinian ideas, such as eugenics, which are no longer considered in the realm of biology.[19]

The history of modern anthropology began with Franz Boas and his students in the late nineteenth and early twentieth centuries.[20] These scholars emphasized the related concepts of culture and cultural relativity.[21] They defined culture as the learned, shared behavior patterns characteristic of a society.[22] In other words, culture for the Boasians was a nonmaterial mental pattern for getting the work of life accomplished.[23] Cultural relativity argues that social acts and forms can only be understood in the context of their own cultural setting.[24]

Some scholars insist that carrying this relativist position to the extreme would maintain that cross-cultural comparisons are futile.[25] This Boasian, or "American School," perceived the human mind as a blank slate that became filled with the ideas that governed behavior through the process of enculturation—or in other words, education.[26] Ruth Benedict and Margaret Mead, both students of Boas,[27] continued the study of culture by considering early training of children to be a crucial part of the enculturation process;[28] Mead studied early child-rearing in many parts of the world,[29] pointing out differences and interpreting their significance.[30] On the other hand, Benedict's *Chrysanthemum and the Sword* is a national character study of Japan done at a distance during World War II.[31] The book acted as a manual for ranking officers and politicians explaining Japanese culture and thought.[32] Benedict's approach involved analyzing patterns of culture to explain how culture forms a system integrated by ideology.[33]

There were various responses to this "anti-scientific" approach of the Boas' American school. The nineteenth-century evolutionists had proposed a unilinear human history in a series of stages, and neo-evolutionists of the twentieth century affirmed this general viewpoint.[34] Today, archaeologists still employ the stages termed Paleolithic, Mesolithic, Neolithic, and Bronze Age civilizations to represent universal stages of human life.[35]

II. DIFFUSIONISM

Culture contact, as British, American, and German diffusionist schools insist, demolishes the veracity of any system of unilinear evolution;[36] that is, the notion that all human societies passed through the same stages of development (but perhaps at different times).[37] For diffusionists, the key feature of human history lies in the way cultural complexes are carried over land and sea from their places of origin to the areas where they are now found.[38] Many diffusionists were colonial administrators trying to defend their governments' policies.[39] Others were missionaries searching for the origins of civilization.[40] The racism and fantasy of most diffusionists, especially the idea that certain peoples were unequal to the task of assimilating the gift of civilization when it was brought to them,[41] has rendered much of their thinking obsolete.[42]

In Frazer's Golden Bough, we see the recurrence of the myth of Divine Kingship *All Over The World*—[43]but not everywhere in the world.[44] From the sixteenth-century time of the Spanish Conquest onward, first the Spanish and then Frazer realized the intimate formal and structural similarities between the Aztec Sacraments and the Christian Sacraments—[45]and between the divine Kingship of Tezcatlipoca and Jesus Christ—[46]and the annual celebration of the sacrifice and resurrection of the King.[47] Do the similarities between Aztec rites of Human Sacrifice and Good Friday/Easter result from diffusion or parallel evolution?[48]

Does Dumézilian Trifunctionalism (*idéologie tripartite*) of sociopolitical hierarchical formation, organization, and shape of Aztec, Maya, and Natchez (Mississippian) societies parallel Indo-European societies?[49] Do these formal, functional, and structural similarities result from diffusion or parallel evolution?[50]

All diffusion is subject to natural selection, even the diffusion of domesticated plants and animals, or non-domesticated species like rats and the fleas which carry the bubonic plague which wiped out the Aztec Civilization after the initial conquest was repulsed and repelled.[51]

III. STRUCTURALISM

Structuralists consider all humans to have the same "deep structures" under their cultural veneer; this explains the existence of cross-cultural similarities, such as language, reciprocity, and kinship systems, matching concepts of government and evidently closely related religious ideas.[52] In other words, they reaffirm Adolf Bastian's basic argument that all humans think alike.[53]

IV. FUNCTIONALISM

Functionalists argued that understanding how cultural complexes form systems is more useful than either evolution or diffusion in the study of society.[54] While Boaz and his students appear to view different societies to be entities that cannot be usefully compared,[55] Bronislaw Malinowski and A. R. Radcliffe-Brown conceived of two functional approaches in the study of societies.[56] Malinowski showed that the Kula Ring trade network of the Trobriand Islands, off of eastern New Guinea, is a system of trading partnerships[57] that involved dangerous voyages in outrigger canoes to meet with distant partners in order to present highly significant and valuable shell armbands in exchange for coral necklaces.[58] Despite the beliefs of the Trobriand Islanders, these Kula articles had no intrinsic value.[59] Malinowski observed that the fleet of canoes that set out on Kula expeditions carried secular goods for exchange as well.[60] This explained the function of the Kula Ring; as a practice that supports ordinary commerce.[61]

For Radcliffe-Brown, the Kula Ring had a deeper significance.[62] He noted that the relationships between leading individuals on islands in a large expanse of ocean constituted a substitute for an inter-island government.[63] The trading partnership of Kula Rings, based on reciprocity, allowed safe travel between islands in an area of endemic warfare.[64]

Previously, Marcel Mauss had explored reciprocity, insisting that all humans were programmed to give, receive, and repay gifts.[65] This approach anticipated later structuralist ideas.[66] Mauss argued that the purpose of this reciprocal gifting was to create social ties; in the case of the Trobriand Islands, the Kula Ring integrated the largest form of social organization known to the population there.[67] Malinowski, Mauss, and Radcliffe-Brown all explained the rationale for the dangerous and otherwise unintelligible Kula Ring, which started the study of other strange gift-giving practices,[68] the Potlach, and the frenzied gift buying at Christmas in the United States.[69]

V. NEO-EVOLUTIONISTS

Today we understand that all societies did not have to progress through all evolutionary stages because diffusion by cultural contact can change a society from a hunting and gathering base directly into civilization.[70] Another problem with nineteenth-century evolutionism is the linking of human physical development to cultural change.[71] Of course, the earliest physical anthropologists and archaeologists did not rely on genetic theory to the extent that contemporary students use these tools,[72] so erroneous ideas about the ancestry of early human populations being directly linked to specific contemporary people are associated with the social evolutionism of Herbert Spencer.[73] These scholars condemned social welfare as an act against nature; social evolution requires the "survival of the fittest."[74] Once again the purpose of the evolutionists was to explain human differences.[75]

Neo-evolutionists view human culture, as a whole, as constituting everything created by humanity through the use of language or symbolic logic;[76] thus, we can maintain that the way of life of *Homo sapiens* as a species did advance through Morgan's three stages.[77] Neo-evolutionists, especially V. Gordon Childe and Leslie A. White, emphasize this view.[78] White proposes that the evolution of society (human society as a whole) changed by the invention of new energy converters or tools that endowed populations of our species with the use of increased amounts of energy.[79] Childe described the archaeological evidence for a Paleolithic, Mesolithic (two successive stages of hunting and gathering), Neolithic (the stage of agricultural villages), and Bronze Age civilizations (characterized by cities, metallurgy, and writing).[80] Of course, individual cultures such as the foraging people of Australia, currently many of whom make their living as factory workers and teachers, made a quick leap from Mesolithic to contemporary civilization due to contact with the Western world.[81] However, the neo-evolutionists did not consider individual societies in their broadest formulations;[82] they argued that it was the entire human population during the past five million or more years that evolved to greater complexity due to progressively more efficient technology.[83] The answer to the very different behavior between evolved urban societies and other people is their variations in levels of technology.[84]

The neo-evolutionists, with this emphasis on technology, may be considered the forerunners of the Materialist School of Anthropology. Leslie A. White, a leading neo-evolutionist,[85] formulated a universal definition of culture: "Culture is an organization of phenomena—material objects, bodily acts, ideas, and sentiments—which consists of or is dependent upon the use of symbols,"[86] meaning culture relies on language.[87] Culture here means human culture—not Japanese or Trobriand Island but all culture through time.[88] Instead of mental templates for behavior, culture is a set of more or less material phenomena: acts, objects, ideas, feelings, and language.[89] White considers the things of the world to be either natural or cultural, and everything cultural takes its form due to the human use of language, which is universally human.[90] White emphasizes the role of technology in human evolution by arguing that culture changes because humans are more efficient in their use of energy.[91] In other words, energy converters (tools, such as windmills or cars) use more energy and are better at the use of energy.[92] This approach makes anthropology look more like a natural science and certainly makes White's approach similar to materialism. Furthermore, White's anthropology can help interpret elusive concepts, such as the idea of "capital" in economics, in terms of how much energy a person or entity can use.

VI. MATERIALISM

Materialists consider economics to be the key to understanding any human society.[93] Moreover, Marvin Harris, a leading materialist, insists that while the study of culture is important, anthropologists should stop accepting the informant's view of society as the best source of information.[94] Instead of talking with people, the materialist proposes to watch their behaviors and show how that conduct helps the population adapt to the environment.[95] Materialists are at their best when they present explanations of religious practices based on ecology.[96] These include Marvin Harris' summary discussions of the pork taboos of the Middle East, the great pig feasts of Melanesia, and the sacred cows of India.[97] Harris even suggests that the lack of care that leads to the death of unwanted infants in some parts of Brazil is justified by religious concepts affirming that some babies manifest a strong wish to return as angels to heaven.[98]

Claude Lévi-Strauss led the French structuralist attack on Boasian thinking.[99] The French school, together with its supporters in the United Kingdom and the United States, proposes that under the veneer of culture "deep structures"[100] exist, and due to these unconscious thought patterns, all humans think in the same way, specifically by manipulating permutations and combinations of opposing concepts.[101] They support this explanation of the way *Homo sapiens* think by analyzing myths and kinship structures to show basic combinations of contrasting thoughts.[102]

Although Lévi-Strauss praised and used the results of Franz Boas and his followers, such as Margaret Mead and Ruth Benedict, he viewed his work as a reinterpretation.[103] Nevertheless, his argument that "deep structures"[104] are universal throughout humanity and underlie cultural behavior attacks is the basic idea of the Boasian school that cultural forms can only be understood in the context of their own cultural setting.[105]

Another simple idea that has been emphasized and reinterpreted by social scientists is that humans alone are weak and puny, but in groups, they can shape their world.[106] To explain differences and similarities in human groups, the scientist must understand forms of social organization.[107] Most preindustrial social organization is based on different systems of kinship;[108] so many anthropologists focus on distinct forms of family and clan organization and their consequences for other areas of culture.[109] For example, in societies that are divided into kin groups based on descent through the mother's line (matrilineal), the child is in the same kin group of the mother's brother.[110]

This relieves the father of economic responsibility for the biological child and, to a certain degree, places the education of a child in the hands of the mother's kin group.[111] This results in a close relationship between the mother and her offspring.[112]

Living together with natives arouses the sympathy of anthropologists for the people they studied.[113] So understanding the point of view of a native became an important priority.[114] The American school promoted fieldwork and learning the language of the natives.[115] As Native American societies changed rapidly during the eighteenth and nineteenth centuries as their populations plummeted, many anthropologists used as informants those older individuals who could explain forgotten aspects of their cultures.[116] This focus on individuals and their life histories led some scholars to invent the field of cultural psychology.[117] Margaret Mead's study of infants and the ways mothers handle them as they grow up in different cultures results in the formation of personalities.[118] Mead's studies are early examples of cross-cultural psychology.[119]

The functionalism of Bronislaw Malinowski also derived from his situation as an enemy alien during World War I;[120] caught by the war in Australia, he was exiled to the Trobriand Islands for long enough to learn their language and observe their customs; through doing so, he learned that their behavior had a systemic quality and an internal rationale.[121] Prior to Malinowski, most people in the Western world considered the antics of native people to be unintelligible.[122] Popular anthropology resembled "Ripley's Believe it or Not" collections of strange customs sometimes explained by reference to Greek and Roman mythology.

NOTES

1. Alan Barnard and Jonathan Spencer, *Encyclopedia of Social and Cultural Anthropology* (1996) 213.
2. Gary A. Wright, "Origins of Food Production in Southwestern Asia: A Survey of Ideas." *Current Anthropology* 12, no. 4/5 (October 1, 1971): 447–477. https://doi.org/10.1086/201233.
3. *Id.*
4. Wright, *supra* note 27.
5. T. Britannica, Editors of Encyclopaedia. "Lewis Henry Morgan." *Encyclopedia Britannica*, December 13, 2020. https://www.britannica.com/biography/Lewis-Henry-Morgan.
6. Elisabeth Tooker, "The Structure of the Iroquois League: Lewis H. Morgan's Research and Observations." *Ethnohistory Tucson, Ariz* 30, no. 3 (1983): 141–154.
7. Scott Michaelsen, *The Limits of Multiculturalism: Interrogating the Origins of American Anthropology* (University of Minnesota Press, 1999). *See.* Curtis M.

Hinsley, "Scott Michaelson. The Limits of Multiculturalism: Interrogating the Origins of American Anthropology. xxviii+ 245 pp., bibl., index. Minneapolis: University of Minnesota Press, 1999. $49.95" (2003).

8. Robert Clark, "The Last of the Iroquois: History and Myth in James Fenimore Cooper's: The Last of the Mohicans." *Poetics Today* 3, no. 4 (1982): 115–134.

9. T. Britannica, Editors of Encyclopaedia. "Lewis Henry Morgan." *Encyclopedia Britannica*, December 13, 2020. https://www.britannica.com/biography/Lewis-Henry-Morgan.

10. Robert H. Lowie, "Edward B. Tylor." *American Anthropologist* 19, no. 2 (1917): 262–268.

11. Edward B. Tylor, "On a Method of Investigating the Development of Institutions; Applied to Laws of Marriage and Descent." *The Journal of the Anthropological Institute of Great Britain and Ireland* 18 (1889): 245–272.

12. Clifford Geertz, *Works and Lives: The Anthropologist as Author* (1988) 56–57.

13. Merwyn S. Garbarino, *Sociocultural Theory in Anthropology: A Short History* (1983) 32–34.

14. Robert L. Carneiro, "Herbert Spencer as an Anthropologist." *The Journal of Libertarian Studies* 5, no. 2 (1981): 153–210, 182–183.

15. Gregory Claeys, "The 'Survival of the Fittest' and the Origins of Social Darwinism." *Journal of the History of Ideas* 61, no. 2 (2000): 223–240, 227.

16. Herbert Spencer, *Social Statics* (1851) 19–20; *see also* K. R. Popper, *The Open Society and Its Enemies* (2012) 77–79.

17. Herbert Spencer, *A Plea for Liberty: An Argument Against Socialism and Socialistic Legislation. Murray* (1891) 15–17.

18. *Id.* at 214–215.

19. Randy Moore, *Creationism in the United States* (1998) 486–507.

20. George W. Stocking Jr, "Franz Boas and the Culture Concept in Historical Perspective 1." *American Anthropologist* 68, no. 4 (1966): 867–882, 867.

21. Geert Hofstede, "The Cultural Relativity of the Quality of Life Concept." *Academy of Management Review* 9, no. 3 (1984): 389–398, 389.

22. Yvan Allaire, and Mihaela E. Firsirotu. "Theories of Organizational Culture." *Organization Studies* 5, no. 3 (1984): 193–226, 195.

23. Bernhard J. Stern, "Concerning the Distinction between the Social and the Cultural." *Social Forces* 8, no. 2 (1929): 264–271.

24. Terence Turner, "Anthropology and Multiculturalism: What is Anthropology that Multiculturalists Should be Mindful of It?" *Cultural Anthropology* 8, no. 4 (1993): 411–429; *see also* Gumperz, John J., and Stephen C. Levinson. "Rethinking Linguistic Relativity." *Current Anthropology* 32, no. 5 (1991): 613–623, 614.

25. Ruth Macklin, *Against Relativism: Cultural Diversity and the Search For Ethical Universals in Medicine* (1999) 44; *see also* Alison Dundes Renteln, *International Human Rights: Universalism Versus Relativism* (2013) 77–79.

26. Roman Jakobson, and Franz Boas. "Franz Boas' Approach to Language." *International Journal of American Linguistics* 10, no. 4 (1944): 188–195.

27. There seems to be some debate and non-uniformity with whether or not "Boas" ended with an "s" or a "z." This article assumes "s" through seemingly common usage in articles, but with no clear citation.

28. Virginia Wolf Briscoe, "Ruth Benedict Anthropological Folklorist." *The Journal of American Folklore* 92, no. 366 (1979): 445–476.

29. Margaret Mead and Franz Boas, *Coming of Age in Samoa* (1973) 55.

30. Allison James, *Handbook of Ethnography* (2001) 246–257.

31. Federico Neiburg and Marcio Goldman, *Anthropology and Politics in Studies of National Character* (1998) 65; *see also* Ruth Benedict, *The Chrysanthemum and the Sword: Patterns of Japanese Culture* (1967) 450–454.

32. Sonia Ryang, *Chrysanthemum's Strange Life: Ruth Benedict in Postwar Japan* (2002) 87–116.

33. Daniel Rosenblatt, "An Anthropology Made Safe for Culture: Patterns of Practice and the Politics of Difference in Ruth Benedict." *American Anthropologist* 106, no. 3 (2004): 459–472.

34. Robert Chapman, *Archaeologies of Complexity* (2003) 6; see also Janet Richards and Mary Van Buren, *Order, Legitimacy, and Wealth in Ancient States* (2000) 3–6.

35. Christopher Hawkes, *Archeological Theory and Method: Some Suggestions From the Old World* (1954) 155–168; *see also* Wolfgang Wildgen, *The Paleolithic Origins of Art, Its Dynamic and Topological Aspects, and the Transition to Writing* (2004) 111–112.

36. Robert Layton, *An Introduction to Theory in Anthropology* (1997) 38.

37. Wilbur Zelinsky, "The Hypothesis of the Mobility Transition." *Geographical Review* (1971): 219–249, 219.

38. Morris J. Blaut, *The Colonizer's Model of the World: Geographical Diffusionism and Eurocentric History* (2012) 7, 7; *see also* Colin Renfrew, *Archaeology and Language: The Puzzle of Indo-European Origins* (1990) 13.

39. Jack Stauder, *The "Relevance" of Anthropology to Colonialism and Imperialism* (1974) 29–51.

40. Fiona Bowie, *The Anthropology of Religion* (2000) 18.

41. Jerry Gershenhorn, *Melville J. Herskovits and the Racial Politics of Knowledge* (2004) 93–94.

42. Herbert S. Lewis et al., *Current Anthropology* (2001) 381–406.

43. James George Frazer, *The Golden Bough* (1922).

44. "Archetype and myth have been studied particularly in literary criticism, depth psychology, and anthropology. See, e.g., James G. Frazer, *The Golden Bough: A Study in Magic and Religion* 412 (abr. ed. 1940) (studying personification of corn as (a goddess in various cultures); Northrop Frye, *Anatomy of Criticism* 136 (1957) (studying archetypes in the literary world); C.G. Jung, *The Archetypes and the Collective Unconscious* 4–5 (R.F.C. Hull trans., Princeton Univ. Press 2d ed., 1980) (1934) (studying archetypes as having existed since primordial unconscious)." Linda H. Edwards, "Once Upon a Time in Law: Myth, Metaphor, and Authority." *Tenn. L. Rev.* 77 (2009): 883, 916.

45. "Among the Hebrews, whose kingdom arose long after I-E [Indo-European] penetration of this region, the distinction between king and priest (e.g., Solomon) was by no means so clear as in Iran, India, or ancient Ireland. Even among the New World civilizations, distinctions between sacred and secular authority were generally absent: The Inca was, at the same time, both the chief-priest—indeed, the incarnation—of Viracocha and the supreme military commander of the empire; the Maya city-states were almost certainly theocratic in character, as was the Aztec empire, though in the latter there existed, to be sure, a somewhat wider cleavage between priestly and military authority." Scott C. Littleton, *The New Comparative Mythology: An Anthropological Assessment of The Theories of Georges Dumézil* (1973) 199. *See.* "But cf., for example, the position of *pulque* in Aztec religion and that of *chibcha* beer in Inca religion. Also, the ritual consumption of peyote among American Indians parallels, in many aspects, the assumed I-E festin." Scott C. Littleton, *The New Comparative Mythology: An Anthropological Assessment of The Theories of Georges Dumézil* (1973) 45 n. 3.

46. A common mythic thread is that of evil being portrayed as a trickster. This is true in the following Aztec myth of Quetzalcoatl, and in the Norse myth of Balder immediately thereafter. In the Aztec tradition, we find that the myth of Quetzalcoatl, in fact, maybe "a combination of fact and myth." In history, Quetzalcoatl may have been "Topilitzin (Our Prince)," who brought ethics and laws to the Toltec nation. In one version of the Quetzalcoatl myth, his counterpart, Tezcatlipoca, is not characterized as the Evil Twin of Quetzalcoatl, but for all intents and purposes he might as well be. Tezcatlipoca "represent[s] all the evils that test the moral fiber of human beings." Fittingly, "Tezcatlipoca is invisible" and has no corporeal presence. The themes of the principal Quetzalcoatl/Tezcatlipoca include the tensions between temptation and forbearance, temperance and excess, and reason and emotion. In this version, Tezcatlipoca holds a mirror to Quetzacoatl's face and persuades him that his image "is wrinkled like that of an ancient creature." Tezcatlipoca convinces the now insecure Quetzacoatl that he can regain his vitality and handsomeness by adopting a ridiculous raiment of quetzal bird feathers, a red and yellow painted face, a feathered beard, and a turquoise mask. He then urges Quetzacoatl to drink an inebriating beverage, of which he and his followers partake in excess. When he is again sober, Quetzacoatl realizes that among other immoral acts, he has committed incest with his sister. Even though he is ashamed, Quetzacoatl rationalizes temporarily that with his new wisdom of himself, he can lead his people. However, Tezcatlipoca continues his evil work by imposing illness and privation upon the tribe of Quetzacoatl, and ultimately Quetzacoatl leaves in a self-enforced exile and dies alone.

M. Stuart Madden, "Myth, Folklore, and Ancient Ethics." *Cumb. L. Rev.* 37 (2006): 43, 58–59.

47. "Sir James Frazer, in his classic The Golden Bough (1922), reviewing the practices of various cultures, explained that certain Mexican kings were made to swear an oath at the start of their reign to make the sun continue to shine, clouds to give rain, rivers to run and earth to give up its fruits." Paul S. Gillies, Esq., *Ruminations Mighty Oaths*, Vt. B.J., Spring 2005, at 17, 2005.

48. Indeed, to further illuminate this question, "Nagel says that our goal is to 'understand the whole world,' to have a gapless explanatory scheme for all phenomena, including

mental states. Nagel, supra note 16, at 6. Both Nagel and the early Wittgenstein believe that the world prefers to have itself described in some special way. As Wittgenstein wrote, "[i]t is obvious that an imagined world, however different it may be from the real one, must have *something*-a form-in common with it." Ludwig Wittgenstein, *Tractatus Logico-Philosophicus* § 2.022 (D.F Pears & B.F. McGuinness trans., 1974). Later, Wittgenstein came to regret such statements.

See Ludwig Wittgenstein, *Remarks on Frazer's Golden Bough at vi* (Rush Rees ed. & A.C. Miles trans., 1979) ("[W]hen I began in my earlier book [Tractatus] to talk about the 'world' (and not about this tree or this table), was I trying to do anything except conjure up something of a higher order by my words?"); Wittgenstein, supra note 13, § 97 ("[I]f the words 'language,' 'experience,' 'world,' have a use, it must be as humble a one as that of the words 'table,' 'lamp,' 'door'.").

This is pretty much the way pragmatists see things. Under Wittgenstein's later view, we will want to stop trying to give a totalizing account of the whole world, because "the whole world" describes nothing. As Rorty puts it,

[t]he notion of "the world" as used in a phrase like "different conceptual schemes carve up the world differently" must be the notion of something completely unspecified and unspecifiable-the thing-in-itself, in fact. . . .

To sum up this point, I want to claim that "the world" is either the purely vacuous notion of the ineffable cause of sense and goal of intellect, or else a name for the objects that inquiry at the moment is leaving alone: those planks in the boat which are at the moment not being moved about.

Richard Rorty, The World Well Lost, *in* Consequences of Pragmatism, supra note 12, at 3, 1415."

William G. Weaver, Richard Rorty and the Radical Left, *Va. L. Rev.* 78 (1992): 729, 757.

49. See generally. Scott C. Littleton, *The New Comparative Mythology: An Anthropological Assessment of the Theories of Georges Dumezil* (1973) 45 n. 3. *See.* Charles Edward Lincoln, *Ethnicity and Social Organization at Chichen Itza, Yucatan, Mexico* (Harvard University, 1990). (PhD dissertation, Department of Anthropology, Harvard University) Advisors Mathews, Peter, and Gordon R. Willey. (1990). *See.* Charles E. Lincoln, "The Chronology of Chichen Itza: A Review of the Literature." In *Late Lowland Maya Civilization: Classic to Postclassic*, edited by Jeremy A. Sabloff and E. Wyllys Andrews V, pp. 141–156 (Albuquerque: University of New Mexico Press, 1986).

50. Claude Lévi-Strauss, *Structural Anthropology* (C. Jacobson & B. Schoepf trans. 1963).

51. *See generally.* E. A. Storey, and Terry L. Jones. "Diffusionism in Archaeological Theory." *Polynesians in America: Pre-Columbian Contacts with the New World* (2011).

52. William H. Sewell Jr, "A Theory of Structure: Duality, Agency, and Transformation." *American Journal of Sociology* 98, no. 1 (1992): 1–29, 8; *see also* Jean Piaget, Structuralism (2015) 67.

53. Klaus-Peter Koepping, *Fieldwork and Footnotes: Studies in the History of European Anthropology* (1995) 75.

54. Robert Boyd and Peter J. Richerson, *Culture and the Evolutionary Process* (1988) 288–290.

55. Claude Lévi-Strauss, *Structural Anthropology* (1963) 35–36; *see also* Jerome Kirk and Marc L. Miller, *Reliability and Validity in Qualitative Research* (1986) 35.

56. Jonathan H. Turner, and Alexandra R. Maryanski. "Is 'Neofunctionalism' Really Functional?" *Sociological Theory* 6, no. 1 (1988): 110–121, 1120–1112.

57. Bernard Grofman and Janet Landa, *Social Networks* (1983) 347–348.

58. Martha Macintyre, "Warfare and the changing context of 'Kune' on Tubetube." *The Journal of Pacific History* 18, no. 1 (1983): 11–34, 11–12.

59. Annette B. Weiner, "Cultural Difference and the Density of Objects." *American Ethnologist* 21, no. 2 (1994): 391–403, 394–395.

60. Alexander Moore, *Cultural Anthropology: The Field Study of Human Beings* (1998) 272.

61. Andy Alaszewski, "Anthropology and Risk: Insights into Uncertainty, Danger and Blame From Other Cultures–A Review Essay." *Health, Risk & Society* 17, no. 3–4 (2015): 205–225, 205–210. *Cf.* John M. Conley, William M. O'Barr, "Back to the Trobriands: The Enduring Influence of Malinowski's Crime and Custom in Savage Society." *Law & Social Inquiry* 27, no. 4 (2002): 847–874, 858 (noting that one of the most important critiques and shortcomings of functionalism is epitomized by Malinowski's handling of the colonial authorities.)

> For most of the book they are virtually absent, lurking far in the background and exerting little if any influence on traditional Trobriand ways. But in the last twenty pages, we see glimpses of the Government Station (the local outpost of the colonial administration), magistrates, and prison sentences, all contaminating and compromising Trobriand law in at least a couple of memorable cases. In one instance, Malinowski reported, in a village "adjoining the Mission and the Government Station," a former chief's son had "completely ousted the real masters, supported in this by European influence." As in so much functionalist work, the reader is left wondering which is the rule and which is the exception.

This brings a general question to mind as to whether and to what extent anthropologists affect the environment they are reporting and observing. Can these be taken as objective opinion as if the observer were not present?

62. Bronislaw Malinowski, *Theories of Man and Culture* (1973) 272.

63. Glenn Petersen, "Indigenous Island Empires: Yap and Tonga Considered." *Journal of Pacific History* 35, no. 1 (2000): 5–27, 27 (noting that "[s]uch obligations were, of course, reciprocal in nature. A widow engaged in extended public mourning out of obligation to her husband's relatives; they reciprocated with gifts of food at later ceremonies. Even the epic, inter-island kula voyages gave dramatic emphasis to the 'sociological ties of an economic nature' between reciprocally obligated trading partners"); *see* Conley note 75, at 857.

64. *See* Conley *supra* note 75, at 858; Andrew James Connelly, *Counting Coconuts: Patrol Reports From the Trobriand Islands, Part I: 1907–1934* (2007) 9.

[More specifically, he argued that Trobriand civil law consisted of "a body of binding obligations, regarded as a right by one party and acknowledged as a duty by the other, kept in force by a specific mechanism of reciprocity and publicity inherent in the structure of their society." Underlying the enforcement of these obligations was economic reality: a "keen self-interest and watchful reckoning" a "rational appreciation of cause and effect." The psychological and cultural manifestations of reciprocity served as reinforcement, appealing to "social and personal sentiments such as ambition, vanity, pride, desire of self-enhancement by display, and also attachment, friendship, devotion and loyalty to kin." It is clear, though, that Malinowski saw material self-interest as the primary driving force, the chicken rather than the egg.

65. Timothy Christian Lind, *The Movement of Gift: Owning, Giving and Sharing in Religious Perspective* (2004) 43; *see also* Robert O. Keohane, "Reciprocity in International Relations." *International Organization* (1986): 1–27.

66. Filmer, Paul, Chris Jenks, Clive Seale, and David Walsh. "Developments in Social Theory." *Researching Society and Culture* 2 (2004): 33–46, 33; Henning Ritter, "The Ethnological Revolution: On Marcel Mauss." *Comparative Civilizations Review* 22, no. 22 (1990): 2.

67. Aafke Komter, "Gifts and Social Relations: The Mechanisms of Reciprocity." *International Sociology* 22, no. 1 (2007): 93–107, 96.

68. *See generally* Joseph M. Perillo, "Exchange, Contract and Law in the Stone Age." *Ariz. L. Rev.* 31 (1989): 17, 25–26.

69. Jean-Pascal Daloz, "Elite Distinction: Grand Theory and Comparative Perspectives." *Comparative Sociology* 6, no. 1–2 (2007): 27–74, 27–28.

70. Marvin Harris, *The Rise of Anthropological Theory: A History of Theories of Culture* (1968) 171; *see also* Lesser, Alexander. "Evolution in Social Anthropology." *Southwestern Journal of Anthropology* 8, no. 2 (1952): 134–146, 135.

71. Ronald Inglehart and Christian Welzel, *Modernization, Cultural Change, and Democracy: The Human Development Sequence* (Cambridge U. Press, 2005) 47, 47–48.

72. A. Sullivan Palincsar, "Social Constructivist Perspectives on Teaching and Learning." *Annual Review of Psychology* 49, no. 1 (1998): 345–375, 345, 354.

73. Christopher S. Henshilwood, Curtis W. Marean, Philip Chase, Iain Davidson, Clive Gamble, Trenton W. Holliday, Richard G. Klein et al. "The Origin of Modern Human Behavior: Critique of the Models and Their Test Implications." *Current Anthropology* 44, no. 5 (2003): 627–651, 636.

74. Thomas C. Leonard, "Origins of The Myth of Social Darwinism: The Ambiguous Legacy of Richard Hofstadter's Social Darwinism in American Thought." *Journal of Economic Behavior & Organization* 71, no. 1 (2009): 37–51, 39.

75. Harris, at 429.

76. Raoul Makarius, Harumi Befu, Gertrude E. Dole, Louis C. Faron, Stevan Harrell, Sue-Ellen Jacobs, Edmund Leach et al. "Ancient Society and Morgan's Kinship Theory 100 Years After [and Comments and Reply]." *Current Anthropology* 18, no. 4 (1977): 709–729, 709–711.

77. Leslie A. White, "Energy and the Evolution of Culture." *American Anthropologist* 45, no. 3 (1943): 335–356, 350.

78. Howard Brick, *Cold War Social Science* (2012) 157.

79. Spier Fred, "How Big History Works: Energy Flows and the Rise and Demise of Complexity." *Social Evolution & History* 4, no. 1 (2005): 30, 49.

80. V. Gordon Childe, "Social Evolution in the Light of Archaeology." *The Australian Journal of Anthropology* 4, no. 1 (1948): 175, 177.

81. Paul Shepard, *Limited Wants, Unlimited Means* (1998) 33.

82. Patrick C. West, *Theory of Liberty, Legitimacy and Power* (2013) 216.

83. Norman Yoffee, *Myths of the Archaic State: Evolution of the Earliest Cities, States, and Civilizations* (2005) 23, 93.

84. Albert Bandura, "Social Cognitive Theory: An Agentic Perspective," *Annual Review of Psychology* 52, no. 1 (2001): 1–26, 22–23; *see also* Kingsley Davis and Wilbert E. Moore, Kingsley Davis, "Some Principles of Stratification: A Critical Analysis: Reply." *American Sociological Review* 18, no. 4 (1953): 394–397, 247–248.

85. Abhik Ghosh, *Cultural Evolution* (2007) 16; *see* Peter Laska, *Left Curve* (2000) 24.

86. Leslie A. White, "Energy and the Evolution of Culture." *American Anthropologist* 45, no. 3 (1943): 335–356, 350.

87. Sue Savage-Rumbaugh et al., "The Emergence of Knapping and Vocal Expression Embedded in a Pan/Homo Culture." *Biology and Philosophy* 19 (2004): 541.

88. Christoph Brumann, "Writing For Culture: Why A Successful Concept Should Not Be Discarded." *Current Anthropology* 40, no. S1 (1999): S1–S27, 5.

89. Clifford Geertz and Michael Banton, *Religion as a Cultural System* (1966) 1.

90. John Tooby and Leda Cosmides, *The Adapted Mind: Evolutionary Psychology and the Generation of Culture* (1995) 24.

91. Benjamin S. Orlove, "Ecological Anthropology." *Annual Review of Anthropology* 9, no. 1 (1980): 235–273.

92. Murray J. Leaf, *Pragmatism and Development: The Prospect for Pluralist Transformation in the Third World* (1998) 20.

93. Frank W. Elwell, "Marvin Harris on the Universal Structure of Societies." *Socio-Cultural Systems*. Accessed May 18, 2021. http://www.faculty.rsu.edu/users/f/felwell/www/Theorists/Essays/Harris1.htm.; *see also* Steve Taylor, *The Madness of Materialism*, Psychol. Today 55 Accessed May 18, 2021. https://www.psychologytoday.com/blog/out-the-darkness/201203/the-madness-materialism.

94. Steve Taylor, *The Madness of Materialism, Psychol. Today* 55 Accessed May 18, 2021. https://www.psychologytoday.com/blog/out-the-darkness/201203/the-madness-materialism; *see Cultural Materialism,* All About Philosophy, Accessed April 13, 2018, https://www.allaboutphilosophy.org/ cultural-materialism.htm.

95. *See* Richard A. Lobban, "Pigs and Their Prohibition." *International Journal of Middle East Studies* 26, no. 1 (1994): 57–75, 58.

96. *See generally id.* (explaining the materialist view through religious mythology).

97. *Id.* at 57–59, 70.

98. Marvin Harris, *Theories of Culture in Postmodern Times* (1999) 46–47.

99. *See* Susan Hegeman, *Patterns for America: Modernism and the Concept of Culture* (1999) 9.

100. "Deep structures" used somewhat in the Jungian sense, but not conclusively.

"Such archetypes manifest themselves differently from country to country yet remain recognizable. For example, different constitutions invoke different national heroes, but the very act of invoking a hero by name in the constitution—be it a Bolivar, or a Mao, or a Kim Il Sung—is unmistakably characteristic of a particular kind of ideological narrative. In Jungian psychology, the hero is an archetype: it takes different forms across different cultures, but its meaning transcends any particular culture. Likewise, in constitutional drafting, the invocation of heroic figures is indicative of an ideological archetype: the names of the heroes vary from one constitution to the next, but the type of constitutional storytelling that invokes heroic figures is deeply familiar and resonates on multiple levels." David S. Law, "Constitutional Archetypes." *Tex. L. Rev.* 95 (2016): 153, 160–161.

Cf. Compare with this definition of Jungian archetype.

> A symbol is defined here as the means by which archetypes, of which we typically remain unconscious, communicate to consciousness. In Jung's framework, instincts, archetypes and symbols all stand in relation to each other. Instincts are physiological urges, and archetypes are the (typically unconscious) emotional and intellectual significance we give to instinctual urges. In Jung's framework, archetypes are the inclination to form pictures so that the unconscious can communicate with consciousness, and symbols are the means by which archetypes get communicated to consciousness. Symbols are not passed on by heredity; they are passed on by acculturation. Thus in the terms of this framework, the law, as a distinct culture, could indeed have its own symbols for expressing information. Symbols impart information to the consciousness, but their strength is at least made clear (if not diminished) by bringing them to consciousness for examination. See *Encountering Jung: Jung on Mythology* 39–40 (Robert A. Segal, ed., 1998) [hereinafter Encountering Jung]; see also Martha C. Nussbaum, *Poetic Justice: The Literary Imagination and Public Life* 53–72 (1995), exploring the tension between "emotions" (which symbols invoke by communicating the power of the archetype which in turn explains the power of the instinctual) and "reason."

Jo Carrillo, "Disabling Certitudes: An Introduction to the Role of Mythologies of Conquest in Law." *U. Fla. JL & Pub. Pol'y* 12 (2000): 13, 31 fn. 24.

101. Stuart Ewen, *All Consuming Images: The Politics of Style in Contemporary Culture* (1999) 4.

102. *Id.*

103. *See id.*

104. Aside from Jungian psychoanalysis, there seems to be a pattern of connecting morality with deep structures from a philosophical perspective.

"The term 'obligatum' may sound odd at first, and perhaps even overly technical, but it resonates with two terms that will help to clarify what exactly is being proposed. First, the term 'obligatum' resonates with the adjective 'obligato,' which means 'indispensable' or 'not to be left out'—as in an obligato accompaniment, which is an integral part of a larger musical performance. For reasons that will become clear below, the idea that each part of an obligatum is an integral and indispensable part of the functioning whole is an idea that the term itself should vividly connote. Second, the term 'obligatum' brings to mind the idea of an obligation. This is also an appropriate connotation because obligata are—on the view elaborated here—part of the normal psychological background in which obligations can be said to arise and exist. Obligata are in fact the very attitudes we employ when we sustain conventions, the phenomena that David Hume famously described."

Robin Bradley Kar, "The Deep Structure of Law and Morality." *Tex. L. Rev.* 84 (2006) 877, 903 (2006).

105. *See* William H. Sewell Jr., "A Theory of Structure: Duality, Agency, and Transformation." *American Journal of Sociology* 98, no. 1 (1992): 1–29, 1, 7, 12.

106. *See generally* Stanley R. Barrett, *Culture Meets Power* (2002) (discussing the social structure of power and the relationship of power to humans).

107. See Blake E. Ashforth and Fred Mael, "Social Identity Theory and the Organization." *Academy of Management* 14 (1989) 20, 20.

108. Arthur L. Stinchcombe, *Social Structure and Organizations,* Handbook of Organizations (James G. March ed., 1965) 142, 142–193.

109. *See* William G. Ouchi and Alan L. Wilkins, "Organizational Culture." *Annual Review of Sociology* 11 (1985): 457, 458, 461–464, 471.

110. William Davenport, "Nonunilinear Descent and Descent Groups." *American Anthropologist* 61 (1959): 557, 560.

111. Rebecca Sear and Ruth Mace, "Who Keeps Children Alive? A Review of the Effects of Kin on Child Survival." *Evolution and Human Behavior* 29 (2008): 1, 5–15.

112. Martin Daly et al., "Kinship: The Conceptual Hole in Psychological Studies of Social Cognition and Close Relationships." *Evolutionary Social Psychology* (Jeffry A. Simpson & Douglas T. Kenrick eds., Lawrence Erlbaum Associates, Inc. 1997) 265–296, 272.

113. Diane Lewis, "Anthropology and Colonialism." *Current Anthropology* 14 (1973): 581, 586–588.

114. Kathleen L. Gregory, "Native-View Paradigms: Multiple Cultures and Culture Conflicts in Organizations." *Administrative Science Quarterly* 28 (1983): 359, 359–376.

115. John U. Ogbu, "Cultural Discontinuities and Schooling." *Anthropology & Educ. Quarterly* 13 (1982): 304, 290–307.

116. H. Russell Bernard et al., "The Construction of Primary Data in Cultural Anthropology." *Current Anthropology* 27 (1986): 382, 383–384.

117. Patricia M. Greenfield, "Three Approaches to the Psychology of Culture: Where do They Come From? Where Can They Go?" *Asian Journal of Social Psychology*, 3 (2000) 223, 228.

118. Robert A. LeVine, and Karin Norman, "The Infant's Acquisition of Culture: Early Attachment Reexamined in Anthropological Perspective." *The Psychology of Cultural Experience* (Carmella C. Moore & Holly F. Mathews eds., Cambridge University Press, 2001), 83–104.

119. Nancy Chodorow, *Family Structure and Feminine Personality, reprinted in* Feminism in the Study of Religion (Darlene Juschka ed., Continuum 2001), 81, 81–105; *see also* Charles M. Super and Sara Harkness, "The Developmental Niche:

A Conceptualization at the Interface of Child and Culture." *International Journal of Behavioral* 9 (1986): 545, 547.

120. Michael W. Young, *Malinowski: Odyssey of an Anthropolgist* (Yale Univ. Press, 2004), 1884–1920 xx.

121. Adam Kuper, *Anthropology and Anthropologists: The Modern British School* (3rd ed. 1996), 1–34.

122. Steven Conn, *History's Shadow: Native Americans and Historical Consciousness in the Nineteenth Century* (The University of Chicago Press, 2004), 215.

Chapter 2

Toward More Memes[1] of Theories

I. TRIFUNCTIONALISM

The question of tri-partite-like theories is whether the form of trifunctionalism influences societal structure or if societal structure informs observers of the form?[2]

The concept of trifunctionalism is deeply embedded in numerous historical examples, such as in classical antiquity and Roman social order.[3] This in turn influenced Montesquieu's writings. "Mingling patriarchal ideals from Roman antiquity with feudal 'trifunctionalism,' the 'noirs' inherited from Montesquieu a fundamental belief in an umbilical link between the "intermediate powers" of a society of orders, and political and individual liberty."[4]

Montesquieu's writings in turn influenced the drafters of the U.S. Constitution in 1787. For example, in Federalist No. 47 by James Madison under the pseudonym of Pubilis states, "[t]he accumulation of all powers, legislative, executive, and judiciary, in the same hands, whether of one, a few, or many, and whether hereditary, self-appointed, or elective, may justly be pronounced the very definition of tyranny."[5] Madison further writes, "[t]here can be no liberty where the legislative and executive powers are united in the same person or body."[6] This is a direct quote to Montesquieu.[7] Furthermore, this is picked up in Federalist No. 48 where Madison continues, "[a]ll the powers of government, legislative, executive, and judiciary, result to the legislative body. The concentrating these in the same hands is precisely the definition of despotic government." This quote from Madison illustrates the importance and relevance of trifunctional government.[8]

II. TOWARD A NEW THEORY OF ANTHROPOLOGY[9]

A new anthropological theory that could contend with the former paradigms would have to distinguish itself from the former robust theories, but also—possibly—sublate them into a new theory. Perhaps, this can be done in the same way that Dumézilian trifunctionalism[10] is distinguishable from the tripartite Freudian paradigm of Sigmund Freud's psychoanalysis; or, how the three parts of Plato's soul espoused in *The Republic* and *Phaedrus* are different from the former two examples, but also related. The relatedness[11] is in the sense of the sublated fashion whereby the former theories are incorporated through assimilation with the former and build off each other.

III. RISK AND RANDOMNESS: ZIPF'S LAW AND POLITICAL POWER THROUGH TREATIES AND MONTE CARLO SIMULATIONS[12]

Legal realism can often be interpreted through the lens of psychology[13] and anthropology.[14] But theoretical statistics and new modes of logic could be applicable as well. In some sense, the new sets of logic from Aristotle's *Organon* to Francis Bacon's *Novum Organon* can provide the means to analyze such issues.[15]

Such analysis could be analogous to using Jungian archetypes of empirical mathematical theory—such as Zipf's law[16]—to try to predict how the words, and thus effects, of tax treaties, will change in the future. Distributions of word hierarchies and the frequency of certain words occurring could also be described in tax laws as well through jurimetrics analysis.[17] This type of analysis could be amplified through Monte Carlo simulations—as such computer-generated simulations that are now readily usable for analysis of contractual agreements between private parties.[18] Arguably, the conjunction and use of Zipf's law and mathematical Jungian archetypes[19] could be used to predict the future of tax law through Monte Carlo simulations.[20]

An example of the theories in action could be the separate paradigms for discerning uniformity in national laws—specifically a technical aspect of international taxation.[21] However, technical issues of law—especially tax law—have origins in the expropriation of nations and states in history. This, too, can be interpreted through anthropological lenses and perspective.

In an anthropological spirit, analyzing the European territorial and colonial interests may present a useful method for interpreting domestic European technical tax law. It is vital to consider what the colonial interests were of European countries and how those interests influenced their tax systems—a vital means of gaining revenue for government expenditures.

The convention of considering colonial relations and tax systems has not been widely explored but is likely a large reason for how the international current tax system—which largely emerged before former European colonies gained independence—came into effect.[22] Indeed, the first tax treaties emerged in the German states of the Holy Roman Empire, before it was unified by Otto Von Bismarck in 1871.[23] However, the paradigm of empires and colonies is especially relevant given that the League of Nations put out its first model tax treaties in the 1920s when most former European imperial (especially British) colonies were still territories of the primarily European-based empires.[24] These treaties largely remained as paradigms for tax treaties even after the formation of the United Nations in 1942 with the "Declaration of United Nations" by the Allies of World War II.[25]

There existed a confluence of events that changed who had precedence in writing model tax treaties. The United Nations absorbed the existing mandate of the League of Nations both in tax and other international matters. At the time, primarily European countries that had empires made up the League of Nations and the United Nations itself. The member European countries and specifically those with empires were made up of states that were not yet independent countries. Thus, those independent states' revenue and tax interest was not as represented as they later would be in the League of Nations. These territories of the empires at the time were considered "source" states for taxation purposes—meaning that income and resources originated there. This paradigm of "source" did not largely change even after the countries gained independence from the empires.

On the other hand of this confluence, the economic destruction of Europe in World War II necessitated the creation of the OECD (Organisation for Economic Co-operation and Development (OECD; French: *Organisation de coopération et de développement économiques*, OCDE). Initially, the OECD originated in name as the Organisation for European Economic Co-operation (OEEC) in 1948 along with other plans, such as the Marshal Plan, to rebuild Europe with primarily American funding.[26]

However, the OEEC was for European cooperation, not necessarily "source" country development where the colonies were. This is because the source countries in large part did not gain independence until the 1950s and 1960s after the death of UN General Secretary Dag Hammarskjöld[27] when the goal of the UN shifted to help gain independence for colonized countries.[28] Before this, the UN and the OEEC had a similar goal of helping European empire colonizers—"residence"—countries expand their interests over the interests of source countries.[29]

Gradually as colonies gained independence, the UN became an important factor in voicing the needs of "source" jurisdictions that were no longer colonies.[30]

Overall, in essence, the combination of anthropological thought with the connection of legal realism can explain in large part the rise of these supranational international organizations that function to establish global peace and provide paradigms for tax treaties. At the same time, these theories can explain how the legal construction shift of sourcing taxation rights changed over time.

NOTES

1. "Memetics" is the study of how memes—informational units that carry ideas and cultural information—evolve and spread. Francis Heylighen and Klaas Chielens, *Evolution of Culture, Memetics, in* Encyclopedia of Complexity and System Science 3205, 3205 (Robert Meyers ed., 2009). The term "meme " (pronounced "meem") was coined by Richard Dawkins: "We need a name for the new replicator, a noun that conveys the idea of a unit of cultural transmission, or a unit of imitation. 'Mimeme' comes from a suitable Greek root, but I want a monosyllable that sounds a bit like 'gene,'" he explained, "I hope my classicist friends will forgive me if I abbreviate mimeme to meme. If it is any consolation, it could alternatively be thought of as being related to 'memory', or to the French word même. It should be pronounced to rhyme with 'cream'." Richard Dawkins, The Selfish Gene 192 (1989). Memes can be any distinct memorable unit, such as a melody, a catch phrase, or the design of a building or clothing article. *See Examples of Memes*, Memetics, http://memetics.chielens.net/memetics/examples.html [http://perma.cc/n9uu-rzjq]. Given the Internet's ability to quickly proliferate information, memes are particularly prevalent in cyberspace. *See* Paul Gil, *What Is a "Meme"? What Are Examples of Modern Internet Memes?*, ABOUT TECH, http://netforbeginners.about.com/od/weirdwebculture/f/What-Is-an-Internet-Meme.htm [http://perma.cc/lfg4-nmjn]. Videos and graphic images like the "Rickroll," *Rickroll*, Know Your Meme, http://knowyourmeme.com/memes/rickroll [https://perma.cc/wze7-q9m3], the "Numa Numa Guy," *Numa Numa*, Know Your Meme, http://knowyourmeme.com/memes/numa-numa [https://perma.cc/y4mx-rjg4], and "Someecards," *Your Ecards/Someecards.com*, Know Your Meme, http://knowyourmeme.com/memes/sites/your-ecards-someecardscom [https://perma.cc/2dr9-8cgh], are common examples. *See generally* Know Your Meme, http://knowyourmeme.com/ [https://perma.cc/ca3w-buua] ("a website dedicated to documenting Internet phenomena: viral videos, image macros, catchphrases, web celebs, and more"). One quintessential type of meme features a frequently used, interchangeable picture with white words in the same font: Impact. Phil Edwards, *The Reason Every Meme Uses That One Font*, VOX (July 26, 2015), http://www.vox.com/2015/7/26/9036993/meme-font-impact [https://perma.cc/k2dr-xw3e]."

Robert T. Sherwin, "# HaveWeReallyThoughtThisThrough: Why Granting Trademark Protection to Hashtags Is Unnecessary, Duplicative, and Downright Dangerous." *Harv. JL & Tech.* 29 (2015): 455, 493 n. 195. *Cf.* "Benjamin gives voice to the idea of convolution in his 1929 essay on Marcel Proust, whose massive memoir, *À la Recherche du Temps Perdu*, is famously launched from a fold of pastry—a '*petite madeleine*'—that is simultaneously a fold of time." Christopher Tomlins, "Revolutionary Justice in Brecht, Conrad, and Blake." *Law & Literature* 21, no. 2 (2009): 185–213, 188.

2. Perhaps, the concept of "trifunctionalism" is imposed by humans' rationalization of observed phenomena. Or perhaps the trifunctionalism is an endemic paradigm.

3. Georges Dumézil, *Archaic Roman Religion* (Baltimore: Johns Hopkins University Press, 1970).

4. Kent Wright, *Jacques De Saint Victor, La Premiere Contre-rèvolution (1789–1791)* (Paris: Presses Universitaires De France, 2010), pp. 504. é30 (Isbn 978-2-130-57077-6), 30 *Law & Hist. Rev.* 319, 320–321 (2012).

5. Victoria Nourse, "Toward a Due Foundation for the Separation of Powers: The Federalist Papers as Political Narrative." *Tex. L. Rev.* 74 (1995): 447, 521 fn. 330.

6. Victoria Nourse, "Toward a Due Foundation for the Separation of Powers: The Federalist Papers as Political Narrative." *Tex. L. Rev.* 74 (1995): 447, 521 fn. 330.

7. R. Shackleton, "Montesquieu." *Encyclopedia Britannica*, February 6, 2021. https://www.britannica.com/biography/Montesquieu.

8. Victoria Nourse, "Toward a Due Foundation for the Separation of Powers: The Federalist Papers as Political Narrative." *Tex. L. Rev.* 74 (1995): 447, 521 fn. 330. ("For this reason that convention which passed the ordinance of government laid its foundation on this basis, that the legislative, executive, and judiciary departments should be separate and distinct, so that no person should exercise the powers of more than one of them at the same time" (quoting Thomas Jefferson); id. at 313 ("[A] mere demarcation on parchment of the constitutional limits of the several departments is not a sufficient guard against those encroachments which lead to a tyrannical concentration of all the powers of government in the same hands.") (Emphasis added throughout). *Id.*

9. To be thoroughly contrasted with: Slavoj Žižek, *Absolute Recoil: Towards a New Foundation of Dialectical Materialism* (2015). *Cf.* Slavoj ŽIžek, *Less Than Nothing: Hegel and the Shadow of Dialectical Materialism* (2012).

10. Cf. The concept of trifunctionalism is deeply embedded in numerous historical examples, such as in classical antiquity and Roman social order. This in turn influenced Montesquieu's writings. "Mingling patriarchal ideals from Roman antiquity with feudal "trifunctionalism," the "noirs" inherited from Montesquieu a fundamental belief in an umbilical link between the "intermediate powers" of a society of orders, and political and individual liberty." Kent Wright, *Jacques De Saint Victor, La Premiere Contre-rèvolution (1789–1791)* (Paris: Presses Universitaires De France, 2010), pp. 504. é30 (Isbn 978-2-130-57077-6), 30 *Law & Hist. Rev.* 319, 320–321 (2012).

Montesquieu's writings in turn influenced the drafters of the U.S. Constitution in 1787. "See The Federalist No. 47, at 301 ("The accumulation of all powers, legislative, executive, and judiciary, in the same hands, whether of one, a few, or many, and whether hereditary, self-appointed, or elective, may justly be pronounced the very definition of tyranny."); id. at 302 ("There can be no liberty where the legislative and executive powers are united in the same person or body" [quoting Montesquieu]); The Federalist No. 48, at 310-11 ("All the powers of government, legislative, executive, and judiciary, result to the legislative body. The concentrating these in the same hands is precisely the definition of despotic government" [quoting Thomas Jefferson]); id. at 311 ("For this reason that convention which passed the ordinance of government laid its foundation on this basis, that the legislative, executive, and judiciary departments should be separate and distinct, so that no person should exercise the powers of more than one of them at the same time" [quoting Thomas Jefferson]); id. at 313 ("[A] mere demarcation on parchment of the constitutional limits of the several departments is not a sufficient guard against those encroachments which lead to a tyrannical concentration of all the powers of government in the same hands.") (Emphasis added throughout)." Victoria Nourse, "Toward a Due Foundation for the Separation of Powers: The Federalist Papers as Political Narrative." *Tex. L. Rev.* 74 (1995): 447, 521.

11. The concept of relatedness is found in Plato's theory of the forms and in the concept of dialectic.

"After all, dialectic, as the art of differentiating rightly, is really not some kind of secret art reserved for philosophers. Whoever is confronted with a choice must decide. Being confronted with choices, however, is the unalterable circumstance of human beings. Their having to make choices removes them from the realm of the rest of living things, which unquestioningly follow their animal desires (therion erotes) wherever these—like forces of nature—may drive them. To be a human being means always to be confronted with choices. As Aristotle puts it, human beings 'have' prohairesis (choice). They must choose. Having to choose, however, entails wanting to know, that is, to know what is best, to know what is good. And that means knowing reasons why, knowing grounds, and using grounds to differentiate. Socrates' partners in the discussion experience this: they learn that concern for a life of justice and rectitude necessarily leads to giving justification for the good.100 Dialectic, then, is not a techne, but is like what Aristotle called a hexis, a disposition. There is a moral dimension here in that what is at stake is not simply the exercise of judgment as technique, about matters scientific or technical; rather, dialectic exercised in the practical, social, realm is concerned with the good, and is related to one's 'way of being'. As noted above, in a different context, it is the role of every citizen to exercise practical judgment. Gadamer focuses on the fact that giving justification is not simply applied to technical matters or the decisions in the art of making (handwork). Rather, the exercise of judgment takes place in the everyday social domain, without specialized knowledge. Yet, that there is no specialized knowledge to guide one's actions and judgments does not mean that the everyday, status quo, views prevail."

Ingrid Scheibler, "Gadamer, Heidegger, and the Social Dimensions of Language: Reflections on the Critical Potential of Hermaneutical Philosophy." *Chi.-Kent L. Rev.* 76 (2000): 853, 888. *See.* "Gadamer, The Idea of the Good, supra note 94 at 37-38. Note also, in a similar vein, Gadamer writes of Plato that, Now it strikes me as significant that Plato holds fast to this characteristic of practical knowledge, and that he distances himself from technical knowledge. Dialectic is not general and teachable knowledge, even if Plato often follows customary language usage and also speaks of it as techne or episteme. It is not in the least surprising, however, that he can call dialectic 'phronesis' too. Dialectic is not something that one can simply learn.

It is more than that. It is 'reasonableness'." Ingrid Scheibler, "Gadamer, Heidegger, and the Social Dimensions of Language: Reflections on the Critical Potential of Hermaneutical Philosophy." *Chi.-Kent L. Rev.* 76 (2000): 853, 892 fn.98.

12. Part of the idea for this chapter came from one of the theses that I submitted for a thesis project that I did at Boston University under the direction of Professor Richard Ainsworth. This was in part fulfillment of my Masters (LL.M.) degree in tax law at Boston University.

13. Psychological and behavioral economics can play a large part in the theories of legal realism. "Each of the varieties of new legal realism builds from what came before in different, revitalizing ways. For example, psychology was central to the old legal realism. For Judge Frank, "[o]ur law schools must become, in part, schools of psychology applied to law in all its phases," because "the judge should be not a mere thinking-machine but well trained, not only in rules of law, but also in the best available methods of psychology." Those working in behavioral law and economics now state the same. They import cognitive psychology's more sophisticated methods, which have advanced greatly since Judge Frank's references to Sigmund Freud and "father-worship." Victoria Nourse, and Gregory Shaffer. "Varieties of New Legal Realism: Can a New World Order Prompt a New Legal Theory." *Cornell L. Rev.* 95 (2009): 61, 90.

14. For a holistic account of both psychology and anthropology, Brian Leiter discusses old waves and new waves of legal realism. "Scholars from Sweden, Denmark, the United States, Canada, Britain, Romania, France, and South Africa were all there as 'legal realists'—or, at least sympathizers with legal realism—and represented disciplinary backgrounds in law, anthropology, psychology, sociology, and philosophy. But what does it mean to be a 'legal realist'? What unites the two most famous 'old' Legal Realisms—the American and the Scandinavian—with the 'new legal realism' invoked, variously, by sociologists, anthropologists, and political scientists, among others? There are, of course, other 'legal realisms,' old and new, from the 'free law' movement in Germany more than a century ago, to the Italian Realism of the Genoa School today. My focus, however, shall be on the old and new Realisms that are probably most familiar. Is there anything they all share?" Brian Leiter, "Legal Realisms, Old and New." *Valparaiso University Law Review* 47, no. 4 (2014): 67–81, 949–950.

Cf. "See, for example, Llewellyn, 44 *Harv L Rev* at 1224 . . . (describing how legal realism attempts to expose the role of psychology in judicial action); Max Radin, Statutory Interpretation, 43 *Harv L Rev* 863, 885 (1930) (arguing that non-value-based methods of interpretation such as legislative history, purpose, and canons of construction cannot sufficiently explain statutory interpretation by courts). It would be a mistake, however, to suggest that realists as a whole believed that the values or commitments of particular judges explained outcomes. For a superb discussion, see generally Leiter, American Legal Realism." Thomas J. Miles, and Cass R. Sunstein. "The New Legal Realism." *U. Chi. L. Rev.* 75 (2008): 831, 851 n. 21.

15. "The Data-Accounting method bears a venerable pedigree. It is, indeed, akin in critical respects to the 'Socratic method' of conceptual or doctrinal clarification via acceptable and unacceptable particular entailments familiarly found in the

Platonic dialogues and in many American law school classrooms. And it is a staple of much modern philosophic writing. The method also bears transparent parallels to 'the scientific method'—and to its statistical-theoretic counterpart, the isolation of more or less critical factors in multi-factoral regression analysis—as popularly exposited by many self-styled 'scientists,' philosophers of science, legal pedagogists, statisticians, and laypersons alike. Indeed, Professor Rawls, whose influential method of 'reflective equilibrium' in assessing conceptions of justice is a somewhat more nuanced form of Data-Accounting, draws explicit analogy between his own method and the accounts of scientific theory-assessment advocated by Professors Goodman and Quine, an account traceable to, nearly a century earlier, the philosopher-scientist Pierre Duhem." Robert Hockett, "The Deep Grammar of Distribution: A Meta-Theory of Justice." *Cardozo L. Rev.* 26 (2004): 1179, 1190–1191 (2005).

16. "This is important because word frequency roughly follows a power law distribution known as Zipf's law." Barton Beebe, and Jeanne C. Fromer. "Are We Running Out of Trademarks: An Empirical Study of Trademark Depletion and Congestion." *Harv. L. Rev.* 131 (2017): 945, 975. "See Steven T. Piantadosi, Zipf's Word Frequency Law in Natural Language: A Critical Review and Future Directions, 21 *Psychonomic Bull. & Rev.* 1112 (2014)." *Id.* at fn. 135.

17. "A special case of power-law distributions is known as Zipf's law, after George Kingsley Zipf, a Harvard linguistics professor, who sought to determine the 'size' (or frequency of use) of the most common words in the English language. Zipf's law states that the size of the rth largest occurrence of an event is inversely proportional to its rank. Zipf's law is generally approximated by the rank-size rule, which states that the second most frequently used word should appear half as often as the most frequently used word, the tenth most common word would occur about one-tenth as often as the most popular word, and so on.8 If a power-law distribution follows Zipf's law, one can plot the data on log-log graph paper and the resulting series of points will reveal a line with a slope of-1." Thomas Bak, "Power-Law Distributions and the Federal Judiciary." *Jurimetrics* (2006): 139–160, 141–142.

18. "This Article has two main components: methodological and substantive. Methodologically, it develops a new way of measuring and coding the economic impact of contractual, statutory, and regulatory variables as well as judicial opinions and general institutional practices through Monte Carlo simulations. The simulation approach creates a cardinal measure of value by putting a hypothetical party in a realistic environment and asking how much this party stands to gain or lose from specific changes in contractual or legal provisions. More specifically, I use simulations to quantify the penalties that venture capital partnership agreements impose on venture fund investors who default on their contractual obligation to supply capital when requested by the fund." Kate Litvak, "Monte Carlo Simulation of Contractual Provisions: An Application to Default Provisions in Venture Capital Limited Partnership Agreements." *Cornell L. Rev.* 98 (2012): 1495, 1496.

19. "See Robin Robertson, Jungian Archetypes, Jung, Gödel and the History of Archetypes 186 (1995)." Collin O'Connor Udell, "Parading the Saurian Tail: Projection, Jung, and the Law." *Ariz. L. Rev.* 42 (2000): 731, 776.

20. Arguably, the ways of cognition—such as those explored in Douglas R. Hofstadter, Gödel, Escher, Bach: An Eternal Golden Braid (1979)—are the basis of Plato's forms that ultimately lead to the decisions of tax treaties. The author has a work in progress on this issue. (On file with author).

See. "In Plato's most radical formulations, the poet always misrepresents the truth. In the Republic, Plato describes the existence of immutable, abstract, and invisible Forms. These Forms are the ideals to which Plato seeks to anchor the state and the human soul, which is the microcosm of the state. The highest Platonic aspiration for human beings is to bring us closer to these Forms. The difficulty is that our ordinary modes of perception—such as our senses—cannot seize these ideas. Only right reason, as exercised through dialectic, can do so in any systematic way." Kenji Yoshino, "The City and the Poet." *Yale LJ* 114 (2005): 1835, 1842–1843. *Cf.* Lincoln, Charles. "A Structural Etiology of the US Constitution." *J. Legis.* 43 (2016): 122.

21. See. Charles Edward Andrew Lincoln IV, *Can Sovereign Nations Achieve Uniformity of Transnational Tax Laws?*, A Thesis Submitted in partial fulfillment of the requirements of the degree of Master of Laws in Tax at Boston University by Charles Edward Andrew Lincoln IV Adviser: Richard T. Ainsworth (2018). On file with author.

This was written as the second master's thesis for the same program (that is the second master's thesis for Boston University: two masters' theses for one program). Charles Edward Andrew Lincoln IV, *Are International Tax Treaties Compatible with Controlled Foreign Corporation (CFC) Rules? A Technical and a Political History Approach for a Normative Result*, A thesis Submitted in partial fulfillment of the requirements of the degree of Master of Laws in Tax at Boston University by Charles Edward Andrew Lincoln IV Adviser: Richard T. Ainsworth (2018). On file with author.

Cf. Not to be confused with author's first master's thesis at the University of Amsterdam. Charles Edward Andrew Lincoln, IV, *Amazon Inc., BEPS, and the New Method of Risk Allocation Comparing U.S. Jurisprudence and OECD Approaches To Risk Allocation In The Post-BEPS Era Of Transfer Pricing*, University Of Amsterdam LL.M. Thesis For Advanced Masters in International Tax Law Final Version—July 27, 2017 Supervisors: Hein Vermeulen And Rutger Hafkenscheid.

22. "Developed countries, however, often ignore their role as source countries in promoting tax competition. They can more readily sacrifice source taxation, bilaterally and unilaterally, because they have strong residence systems. At the same time, they often have somewhat effective systems for the taxation of nonresident business income at least where such business activity requires a substantial presence in that country. They can even be somewhat aggressive in taxation because they provide significant markets for the consumption of the foreign enterprises' products and services. Emerging economies do not share the same economic factors. Most rely on territorial taxation and are only slowly adopting residence principles. This was often because territorial taxation was the heritage of colonial rule. For example, the English mandate for its colonies was that only income arising in the colonies came within the 'colonial jurisdiction' to tax. South Africa, which, as a former British colony, had adopted strict territorial tax principles, did not adopt the residence principle until 2000 after

the overthrow of apartheid. Because most developing economies have been slow to adopt residence principles, some have been victimized by the flight of capital of their residents. Their principle character is that of a capital-importing nation, however, whose primary tax emphasis is the source taxation of both residents and nonresidents alike." William B. Barker, "An International Tax System for Emerging Economies, Tax Sparing, and Development: It Is All about Source." *U. Pa. J. Int'l L.* 29 (2007): 349, 360–361.

23. This unification was the result of the Franco-Prussian War (1870–1871). "The German theory of Bundestreue has roots in the conservative political ideology that Chancellor Otto von Bismarck and others deployed to protect the unity of the newly created German Reich of 1871." Daniel Halberstam, "Of Power and Responsibility: The Political Morality of Federal Systems." *Virginia Law Review* (2004): 731–834, 740.

Cf. Though—arguably incorrectly—others have written "[t]he governments of Austria-Hungary and Prussia concluded a convention on June 21, 1899, which is recognized as being the first general international tax treaty; see Skaar, *Permanent Establishment: Erosion of a Tax Treaty Principle* (Netherlands: Aspen Publishers, 1991)" Dale Pinto, "'Conservative' and 'Radical' Alternatives for Taxing E-Commerce (PART 1)." *Journal of International Taxation* 16, no. 8 (2005): 14, 64. This is simply, because—again arguably—Prussia ceased to exist when it conquered most of the German territory to the Rhine Province and Cologne by 1871. But this treaty of 1899 was based off how German states made arrangements within the German Empire.

Otto Von Bismarck's Prussian Empire was proclaimed in the Hall of Mirrors at Versailles, France. A Famous depiction of this is seen in "Anton von Werner's patriotic, much-reproduced depiction of the proclamation of Wilhelm I as German emperor in the Hall of Mirrors at Versailles. Focus is on Bismarck, center, wearing white uniform. (1885)" Wikipedia contributors, "Otto von Bismarck," *Wikipedia, The Free Encyclopedia*, https://en.wikipedia.org/w/index.php?title=Otto_von_Bismarck&oldid=1023682217 (accessed May 20, 2021).

24. "See generally William B. Barker, Optimal International Taxation and Tax Competition: Overcoming the Contradictions, 22 *Nw. J. Int'l L. & Bus.* 161, 182–183 (2002) (describing the historical development of source taxation); Michael J. Graetz & Michael M. O'Hear, The 'Original Intent' of U.S. International Taxation, 46 *Duke L.J.* 1021, 1023 (1997) (explaining the importance of the League of Nations' 1928 model bilateral income tax treaties); Reuven S. Avi-Yonah, The Structure of International Taxation: A Proposal for Simplification, 74 *Tex. L. Rev.* 1301, 1303 (1996) (explaining the 1920s movement to avoid international double taxation)." William B. Barker, "An International Tax System for Emerging Economies, Tax Sparing, and Development: It Is All about Source." *U. Pa. J. Int'l L.* 29 (2007): 349, 389 fn. 3.

25. "In 1942, President Franklin D. Roosevelt coined the term 'United Nations' in the 'Declaration by United Nations,' 23 signed by twenty-six Allied Powers in confirmation of their commitment to fight together against the Axis Powers of World War II." Britta A. Schnoor, "International Law, the Power of the Purse, and Speaking

with One Voice: The Legal Cacophony Created by Withholding US Dues from the United Nations." *Iowa Law Review* 92, no. 3 (2007): 1133, 1138–1139.

26. "The foreign policy of the United States in the post–World War II era fashioned a new order in Europe. The United States wished to coordinate the administration of aid under the European Recovery Programme[*sic*]—the Marshall Plan as it is commonly known. In response, the sixteen recipient countries formed an intergovernmental body, the Organization for European Economic Cooperation (the 'OEEC') in April of 1948. The OEEC immediately focused on the European Recovery Programme in an attempt to identify an efficient method of allocating American aid among the recipient countries. Although the OEEC remained an intergovernmental body whose primary concerns were cooperation and coordination rather than union, the OEEC fostered new modes of thinking and laid a solid foundation for future developments. By 1959, the OEEC's original objectives had, for the most part, been met." John P. Flaherty, and Maureen E. Lally-Green. "The European Union: Where is it Now." *Duq. L. Rev.* 34 (1995): 923, 930.

27. "The death of Secretary General Dag Hammarskjold in a plane crash occurred on September 17, 1961 en route to meetings with the belligerents in the Congo." Joseph C. Sweeney, "The Just War Ethic in International Law." *Fordham Int'l LJ* 27 (2003): 1865, 1903.

28. This occurred during his trip to negotiate peace during the complicated political event surrounding the Siege of Jadotville in the breakaway State of Katanga.

29. "The Organization for Economic Cooperation and Development (OECD) was formerly organized as the Organization for European Economic Cooperation (OEEC) as a public international organization in which the United States participated under authority of the Economic Cooperation Act of 1948 (62 Stat. 137), as amended." Rev. Rul. 72-183, 1972-1 C.B. 213 (1972).

30. "The UN Model was the product of a series of discussions and meetings of an Ad Hoc Group of Experts formed in 1967 to address concerns that the OECD Model (and, by association, the U.S. Model) was not appropriate for tax treaties involving non-reciprocal cross border activity." Allison D. Christians, "Tax Treaties for Investment and Aid to Sub-Saharan Africa a Case Study." *Brook. L. Rev.* 71 (2005): 639, 660. *See.* "The Group of Experts included members from Latin American, North American, African, Asian, and European countries. The group also had observers from the IMF, the International Fiscal Association, the OECD, the Organization of American States, and the International Chamber of Commerce. See United Nations, Commentary on the Articles of the 1980 United Nations Model Double Taxation Convention Between Developed and Developing Countries 2 (Jan. 1, 1980); *see also* United Nations Dep't of Economic and Social Affairs, United Nations Model Double Taxation Convention Between Developed and Developing Countries viii (2001)." *Id.* at fn. 78. *See also.* "Leif L. Mutén, Double Taxation Conventions Between Industrialised and Developing Countries, in *Double Taxation Treaties Between Industrialised and Developing Countries*; Oecd And Un Models, A Comparison 3 (Kluwer Law and Tax'n Pubs. 1990)." *Id.* at fn. 79.

Chapter 3

Is there a "Jungian Archetype" of Government?

Structuralism and Constitutional Forms of Government in a Postmodern World[1]

It is often difficult to bridge the theoretical to the technicalities of law. For example, connecting the more mundane issues about offer, acceptance, and consideration theories of contract law to John Locke's philosophy on the social contract may present some difficulties. It may daunt a theoretician and practitioner to communicate a clear and effective argument that is also compelling and valid at the same time.

One such bridge may present itself in interpreting constitutions and specifically the U.S. Constitution. At the same time, the document has been the subject of intense technical debate on the technicalities of the Commerce Clause to the philosophical foundations of the government to even social issues in the United States today.

As discussed in the prologue, many of the theories surrounding the development of the ideas in this book began with an exploration of the structure of the U.S. Constitution.

This chapter offers an interpretation of the problems addressed by, and the eventual purpose of, the U. S. government. Simultaneously, it seeks to analyze and explain the continued three-part structure of the U. S. federal government as outlined in the constitution. Subsequently, this chapter defines the three parts of the federal government—judiciary, executive, and legislative—as explained through the lens of the Platonic paradigm of (*logos* = word = law), (*thymos* = external driving spirit = executive), and (*eros* = general welfare = legislative) as extrapolated from Plato's dialogues.

First, this chapter establishes Plato's theory of the three-part Platonic soul as a major premise, as in a syllogism. Second, the chapter lays out the generally accepted division of the U.S. Constitution as creating three parts to the federal government as a minor premise. Third, the syllogism completes by weaving in the major premise of Plato's soul into the minor premise of the three parts of the U. S. federal government. This third step of this application suggests a possible future evolution of the structure.

This chapter fits into the wider issue of the functionally efficient and naturally adaptive structure of the U.S. federal government. Providing a historical and philosophical context to this structural analysis will serve as a framework for future research on the operation of the federal government. When the branches of the federal government step out of their roles, the balance of the structure of the federal government becomes disrupted occurring in liminal periods of paradigmatic change.

INTRODUCTION TO THE PLATONIC PARADIGM

This chapter argues that the tripartite system of the federal government in the United States can be viewed through the Platonic concept of the soul (ψυχή).[2] The major premise is that the U. S. federal government has three major parts, the judiciary, the executive, and the legislative. The minor premise of this chapter is that the Platonic soul is divided into three parts the *logos* (λογιστι κόν),[3] the *thumos* (θυμοειδές),[4] and the *eros* (ἐπιθυμητικόν).[5] The syllogism and argument of this chapter is that the three federal parts of government represent the Platonic soul: the judiciary being the *logos*, the executive being the *thumos*, and the legislative being the *eros*. This chapter will explore these concepts in greater depth. As a corollary, when the soul of the polity[6] becomes unbalanced, then people become dissatisfied with the government because the government does not fulfill its function administratively—as in acting in opposition to the laws—and in promoting justice. However, sometimes overstepping a role in the Platonic soul of the polity is a necessary change.[7]

I. PREMISES AND STRUCTURES OF ANALYSIS

Presumed throughout this chapter is that the world has order based on reason that reflects nature.[8] In Plato's *Timaeus*, the interlocutor suggests that nature is organized and is thus intelligible.[9] The alternative to this presumption is that there is no order to the universe or world and humans try to impose order to it.[10] Lucretius in his *On the Nature of the Universe* introduced such a view.[11] Consequently, nature can represent itself in the structure of law, specifically the law of the United States.[12]

A. Why a Structured Approach at All? An Anthropological-Philosophical Explanation.

To understand why it is appropriate to analyze and compare the structure of the U.S. federal government—as outlined by the U.S. Constitution of 1789—with the Platonic concept of the soul, it is helpful to have some understanding of the context of philosophical-anthropological thought related to it. The following paragraph is a brief overview of relevant historical analysis to provide context related to structural and "trifunctionalist" analysis. Indeed, many anthropological-philosophical theories exist for understanding the basic structures of societies and governments, from Claude Lévi-Strauss's structuralism theories,[13] to Michel Foucault on the impetus behind government function,[14] and Marvin Harris on the gift-giving incentives in a society's structure.[15] Concurrently, the idea of a "tripartite" structure of society being inherent to human cultures is not new, but has been written about extensively by George S. Dumézil,[16] and has been written by Sigmund Freud's division of psychoanalysis.[17] Indicative of the universal nature of the "trifunctionalist" Dumézilian approach has even been applied to Pre-Columbian Yucatán Mayan societies.[18] Poetically, in the Homeric Greek account of the Judgment of Paris—before the beginning of the Trojan War in Homer's *Iliad*—Paris of Troy is given a Dumézilian "choice," a beauty contest among three goddesses Hera, Athena, and Aphrodite.[19] It seems fitting to apply the Ancient Greek concept of the Platonic Soul to governmental structure, because the "trifunctionalist" approach has origins in Ancient Greece but can also be seen in non-Western civilizations as well.

A balanced view of government may exist in the separation of powers as Montesquieu laid out "that of enacting laws, that of executing the public resolutions, and of trying the causes of individuals."[20] Exploring this thought "[i]n The Federalist No. 47, Madison explained that while Montesquieu was correct in saying that the separation of the legislative, executive, and judicial powers was essential to liberty, that conclusion did not purport to tell us how strict the resultant separation had to be."[21] Based on their education, the framers of the constitution may have even had Plato's Soul in mind when they framed the constitution.[22] Even if the framers did not have Plato in the back of their minds, the idea of Plato's Soul is arguably inherent in humans regardless of how it is defined.[23] Moreover, a structured approach to the philosophical underpinnings to a government can be assumed to have been in the framer's mind—whether consciously or subconsciously.

B. Why Plato? Truth and Justice in Plato

If one accepts the premises that structured and philosophical approaches are a reasonable mode of analysis, then why should one use Plato's approach specifically?

This idea of comparing the Platonic soul to the U. S. federal system of government has previously been written about by Akiba Covitz in *The Soul of the Polity*.[24] Covitz argued the syllogism as the judiciary is the *thumos*, the executive is the *logos*, and the legislative is the *eros*. This chapter greatly appreciates and gains much inspiration from Covitz's theory, but switches correspondences from *thumos* to *logos* for the judiciary, *logos* to *thumos* for executive and maintains Covitz's conception of legislative as *eros*.[25] However, Covitz uses a different terminology of (1) artifice; (2) nature; and (3) history/divinity/myth in lieu of *logos*, *eros*, and *thumos*, respectively.[26] Covitz argues that the constitution had a psychoanalytic dimension, and these Platonic elements in large part represented this psychoanalysis.[27]

Professor Covitz sincerely wanted to explore what a constitution is. He asked "*ti esti* or 'what is?'" translated from Greek.[28] This is a classic question that drove the Greeks as a purely innocent love for searching for knowledge. This chapter has a sourced inspiration from such an inquiry. Covitz asks, "[w]hy, then, have I chosen Plato's *Republic* along with the Constitution of the United States as the two main texts that I will analyze?"[29] He answers, "My broadest goal is to seek the beginnings of American constitutional thought, and my related, narrower goal is to respond to the question of why the American Constitution is seen to be such a success." Indeed, this represents a variation of the two-pronged endeavor, which this chapter searches to solve: what does it mean for the three parts of the government to interact with one another? The second is: Why has the American Constitution lasted so long? Indeed, with relatively few amendments.

Covitz suggests an easy answer to these questions would be to "provide satisfying answers to my questions would be to choose the Constitution of the United States and a more contemporary and more straightforward text (at least in terms of form) such as Locke's Second Treatise on Government, or Montesquieu's Spirit of the Laws." But Professor Covitz sought a "more than a deeper understanding of the American Constitution; [he sought] its beginnings."

Professor Covitz quotes an introduction to an edition of Plato's works by Erich Segal where Segal quotes "Spanish neo-Kantian social theorist, José Ortega y Gassett," that succinctly indicates Professor Covitz's and this chapter's focus on the *Republic*. Covitz writes, "Ortega y Gassett describes Plato's influence on Western thought in the following manner: 'It is impossible to tell [to] what deep levels of the Western mind Platonic notions have penetrated. The simplest sort of person regularly employs expressions and portrays views which are derived from Plato (Plato 1986, vii).'"

Covitz lays out the great appeal to using Plato's work, "[p]ut more simply, Plato has provided for the West a fertile image, founded on a complex theory of psychology and politics, of how the soul is seen as working and how it is intimately connected with politics and constitutions." However, Covitz admits there is a darker—more tyrannical and dictatorial—side to Plato's works. Specifically, "according to [Karl] Popper, Plato's Republic is the handbook of tyranny and the guide to constructing a society closed to all change and freedom. Plato's use of lies, myths, and the powers of divinity as aspects of constitutional life, are indicative for Popper of Plato's falsity and duplicity (see Popper 1945)." This is a relevant argument because, despite the appeal of Plato's work for positive ideas, there has also been a more evil side to the works going to support fascism and Nazism.[30]

However, if one is to understand the beginning of the U.S. Constitution, one must be familiar with—not only the circumstances that gave its birth—but also the great books that the authors of the constitution read. Covitz supports this standpoint by writing "if one is to search out the theoretical beginnings of American constitutional thought, one must come to grips with the textual beginnings of the Western constitutional thought in which the American experience is itself framed," this can be interpreted as the books and laws the framers were most familiar, "regardless of our views of Plato's tyrannical or democratic qualities. Important, underlying aspects of this broader realm of Western constitutional thought began in the dialogic pages and the constitutional theory of Plato's Republic."

1. Truth and Plato's Forms

Indeed, it must be mentioned that Plato's soul has a special connection to truth and Plato's "Forms" in his philosophy, as explained by Kenji Yoshino.[31] Unlike, "the poet [who] always misrepresents the truth," Yoshino claims, "[i]n the Republic, Plato describes the existence of immutable, abstract, and invisible Forms."[32] Yoshino states that "[t]hese Forms are the ideals to which Plato seeks to anchor the state and the human soul, which is the microcosm of the state. The highest Platonic aspiration for human beings is to bring us closer to these Forms. The difficulty is that our ordinary modes of perception—such as our senses—cannot seize these ideas." However, Yoshino interestingly writes, "Only right reason, as exercised through dialectic, can do so in any systematic way."[33]

Plato's—and Professor Yoshino's—intersection of truth, as represented by the forms and justice compels one to look further into why the two are related.

Professor Yoshino's formulation of "right reason"[34] sounds akin to the concept of natural law. Natural law exists in religion and higher ethics, which may or may not exhibit themselves in statutes and case law. Natural can be defined as that which is not positive law, but it can also be defined as follows, "[n]atural law refers to the ethic of justice, fairness, or right. Although denominated 'law,' it is not positive law at all, but rather is a sense derived from God-given or rational sources."[35] Such a definition emphasizes the importance of religion as a base for natural law. But, it can also be based on rational reason or right reason as Professor Yoshino or St. Thomas Aquinas would argue.[36] This means natural law can come from secular sources, and an atheist could believe in natural law through right reason or rational sources.

Although an all-encompassing definition of natural law would not only contrast itself with positive law, but would rather show how it, "relates to positive law by serving as a standard against which positive law can be judged. Natural law is frequently cited as the 'ought' and positive law as the 'is,' meaning that natural law is what should be done and positive law is what exists as the rule established by the sovereign."[37]

Alternatively, positive law is commonly referred to as law passed by legislatures or case law. For a succinct definition, "positive law, or every law simply and strictly so called, is set by a sovereign person, or a sovereign body of persons, to a member or members of the independent political society wherein that person or body is sovereign or supreme."[38] Moreover, "[e]very positive law, or every law simply and strictly so called, is set by a sovereign person, or a sovereign body of persons, to a member or members of the independent political society wherein that person or body is sovereign or supreme."[39]

2. *Justice and Plato*

In regards to the Platonic Soul, a person acts justly if the soul acts in concordance with each constituent part without overstepping its reach and unjustly if the soul acted in an unbalanced manner.[40] Likewise, an unbalanced soul may follow any means necessary in Machiavellian fashion to reach a desirable goal.[41] Choosing between what is viewed as natural law and positive law can depend on the balance of the soul.[42] Indeed, in Sophocles' play *Antigone*, the eponymous character suffered such a choice between following positive law or natural law when deciding to follow the edicts of King Creon not to bury her brother or her religious beliefs to bury her brother.[43] Perhaps this choice between natural law and positive law—also phrased as choosing between what is "right" and following the law—is one of the fundamental cruxes of jurisprudence.[44] An informed viewpoint on the Platonic conception of the soul can help analyze choices between positive and natural law, understand the structure of the constitution, and explain why former choices had been made, as well as why some decisions in the Supreme Court and Congress are made the way they are.

3. *Truth, Justice, and Plato*

Thus, Plato intimately intertwines truth and justice. The Platonic forms—eternal ideals—represent truth.[45] Concurrently, justice represents human activity carrying out and adhering to the truth of the forms. However, how can human activity carry truth to achieve justice? This requires the elements of the Platonic soul to exist in a balance. But what is the Platonic soul? What are its elements? How can they exist in harmony?

II. Three Parts of the Federal Government

1. The Judiciary

The role of the judiciary in large extent is to follow syllogistic and logical application of the law as found in the idea of *stare decisis et non quieta movere*[46] to provide a system of legitimacy and predictability.[47] As the Ninth Circuit Court of Appeals stated, "[s]tare decisis is the policy of the court to stand by precedent; the term is but an abbreviation of stare decisis et non quieta movere—'to stand by and adhere to decisions and not disturb what is settled.'"[48]

However, pure syllogistic thinking manifested in *stare decisis* does not always occur. Although Justice Rehnquist—writing for the majority in the *Payne v. Tennessee* case—admits, "*Stare decisis* is the preferred course because it promotes the evenhanded, predictable, and consistent development of legal principles, fosters reliance on judicial decisions, and contributes to the actual and perceived integrity of the judicial process"[49] (emphasis in original). Moreover, regarding policy, Rehnquist writes, "[a]dhering to precedent 'is usually the wise policy, because in most matters it is more important that the applicable rule of law be settled than it be settled right.'"[50] However, he claims "when governing decisions are unworkable or are badly reasoned, 'this Court has never felt constrained to follow precedent,'" meaning in other words, "*Stare decisis* is not an inexorable command; rather, it "is a principle of policy and not a mechanical formula of adherence to the latest decision."[51] He further indicates that not using *stare decisis* is "true in constitutional cases, because in such cases 'correction through legislative action is practically impossible.'"[52]

Rehnquist's opinion on *stare decisis* has been affirmed and restated in several Supreme Court opinions, even more recently in *Johnson v. United States*, where Justice Scalia's majority opinion, "[t]he doctrine of stare decisis allows us to revisit an earlier decision where experience with its application reveals that it is unworkable," showing how experience can inform application of *stare decisis*.[53]

At first, this move away from purely logical toward using "experience" may seem like a contradiction of the purely logical aspect of the *logos* in the Platonic soul. Indeed, this is not akin to the *elegantia juris* using pure logic in law as envisioned by the Romans.[54] Rather it is more similar to Oliver Wendell Holmes's legal realism where he writes in his book *The Common Law*, "[t]he life of the law has not been logic: it has been experience."[55] Indeed, Holmes criticized the purely scientifically logical methods proposed by Professor Christopher Columbus Langdell[56] that he "could be suspected of ever having troubled himself about Hegel, we might call him a Hegelian in disguise, so entirely is he interested in the formal connection of things, or logic, as distinguished from the feelings which make the content of logic, and which have actually shaped the substance of the law."[57]

Indeed this mode of realism could come into action in judicial decisions specifically with "sociological jurisprudence"—proposed by Roscoe Pound—whereby courts could consider social factors in decision-making.[58] Furthermore, Holmes wrote that even decisions that appear to be based on firm logical deductions are decisions of policy by stating "[p]erhaps one of the reasons why judges do not like to discuss questions of policy, or to put a decision in terms upon their views as law-makers, is that the moment you leave the path of merely logical deduction you lose the illusion of certainty which makes legal reasoning seem like mathematics."[59] But declared that choosing the premises—being the choice of policy—then using logical deductions from there for "certainty is only an illusion, nevertheless."[60]

2. *Executive*

A prime example of the outline of the definition of the Executive branch's power is seen in *Youngstown Sheet & Tube Co. v. Sawyer*.[61] The case rose as a result of the steel strikes during the Truman Administration during the Korean War, President Truman sought to take executive control over the steel producers under the inherent powers doctrine. *Youngstown Sheet & Tube Co. v. Sawyer*.[62]

Writing for the majority opinion Justice Black stated the Presidential and Executive power "must stem either from an act of Congress or from the Constitution itself." *Youngstown Sheet & Tube Co. v. Sawyer*.[63]

The court's majority opinion stated that the court could not "with faithfulness to our constitutional system hold that the Commander in Chief of the Armed Forces has the ultimate power as such to take possession of private property in order to keep labor disputes from stopping production. This is a job for the Nation's lawmakers, not for its military authorities" *Youngstown Sheet & Tube Co. v. Sawyer*, 343 U.S. 579, 587.

Furthermore, the court declared that "[i]n the framework of our Constitution, the President's power to see that the laws are faithfully executed refutes the idea that he is to be a lawmaker."[64] This means that the constitution limits the executive's rulemaking force. Instead the court continues interpreting the constitution so as to give power to the legislature to make rules, "'[a]ll legislative Powers herein granted shall be vested in a Congress of the United States . . . .' After granting many powers to the Congress, Article I goes on to provide that Congress may "make all Laws which shall be necessary and proper for carrying into Execution the foregoing Powers, and all other Powers vested by this Constitution in the Government of the United States, or in any Department or Officer thereof."[65]

Specifically in terms of taking of private property for public use, the court stated only Congress is authorized for "the taking of private property for public use."[66]

Finally—perhaps in an originalist interpretation fashion—the court declared "[t]he Founders of this Nation entrusted the lawmaking power to the Congress alone in both good and bad times. It would do no good to recall the historical events, the fears of power and the hopes for freedom that lay behind their choice. Such a review would but confirm our holding that this seizure order cannot stand."[67]

As a result of the case, in the concurring opinion Justice Frankfurter wrote, "[l]oose and irresponsible use of adjectives colors all nonlegal and much legal discussion of presidential powers. 'Inherent' powers, 'implied' powers, 'incidental' powers, 'plenary' powers, 'war' powers and 'emergency' powers are used, often interchangeably and without fixed or ascertainable meanings."[68]

Discussing the Separation of Powers, a concurring opinion written by Justice Frankfurter stated, "[t]he doctrine of the separation of powers was adopted by the Convention of 1787, not to promote efficiency but to preclude the exercise of arbitrary power. The purpose was, not to avoid friction, but, by means of the inevitable friction incident to the distribution of the governmental powers among three departments, to save the people from autocracy."[69]

In relation to the *thumos*, *Youngstown Sheet & Tube Co.* represents how the executive branch is limited in its functions of making laws, but it carries out these laws. The executive may resolve conflicts through agencies.

Specifically through the Chevron deference doctrine whereby the Supreme Court decided that "considerable weight should be accorded to an executive department's construction of a statutory scheme it is entrusted to administer, 14 and the principle of deference to administrative interpretations."[70]

Justice Stevens wrote the case involved that "[i]n the Clean Air Act Amendments of 1977, Pub. L. 95-95, 91 Stat. 685, Congress enacted certain requirements applicable [840] to States that had not achieved the national air quality standards established by the Environmental Protection Agency (EPA) pursuant to earlier legislation."[71] He continued stating that "[t]he amended Clean Air Act required these 'nonattainment' States to establish a permit program regulating 'new or modified major stationary sources' of air pollution."[72] Furthermore, the EPA required that plants comply with a certain level of conditions.[73] The issue of the case was "whether EPA's decision to allow States to treat all of the pollution-emitting devices within the same industrial grouping as though they were encased within a single 'bubble' is based on a reasonable construction of the statutory term 'stationary source.'"[74]

The court reasoned when reviewing an agency's construction of a statute, it must ask two questions.[75] The first question is "whether Congress has directly spoken to the precise question at issue. If the intent of Congress is clear, that is the end of the matter; for the court, as well as the agency, must give effect to the unambiguously expressed intent of Congress."[76] The second question arises if "Congress has not directly addressed the precise question at issue, . . . the question for the court is whether the agency's answer is based on a permissible construction of the statute," meaning the court defers to an agency's interpretation.[77] Concurrently, if the agency does not have an interpretation, the court would interpret the statute.[78]

The court reasoned and "justified this new general rule of deference by positing that Congress has implicitly delegated interpretive authority to all agencies charged with enforcing federal law."[79] Indeed, the decision "the decision [made] administrative actors the primary interpreters of federal statutes and relegate courts to the largely inert role of enforcing unambiguous statutory terms."[80]

3. *The Legislative*

With the example of the Eighteenth Amendment, the Congress passed a law that represented a *will* of portions of the country to not allow alcohol. But it took the Twenty-first Amendment to realize that the Eighteenth Amendment did not accurately represent what people desired. In a sense, the Eighteenth Amendment represented the soul of the polity going out of control. This was initially an unjust result (although deemed just at the time), and then Congress repealed it deciding that the Twenty-first Amendment was just (meaning the Eighteenth was deemed unjust).

The need to have rules of statutory interpretation indicates that there is a need to interpret often difficult to understand laws.[81] This could be the effect of many reasons, such a quick drafting or function of political maneuvering to gain enough votes or lack thereof.[82] Professor Gluck has pointed out that a large part of the problem about public outcry against the courts and the legislature is because we do not have a clear idea of what they should be doing:

> These moves have been grounded in a spectacular lack of theory about the role that courts should play in the legislative process itself—which is, after all, the fundamental constitutional question of the Court-Congress relationship in statutory cases. Should courts try to understand how Congress works, or is Congress too complex to understand? Should courts be "tough" on Congress, perhaps to incentivize Congress to draft better the next time, or should courts cut Congress some slack, and even

> correct enacted imperfections? Perhaps courts are best conceived as guardians of the U.S. Code, obligated to shape increasingly imperfect statutes into a more coherent product for the public, no matter how disconnected that result may be from Congress's own intentions. The court has long resisted definitively answering these basic questions, even as the most difficult statutory cases turn on them.[83]

Indeed, the problem of the legislature or courts not conforming to what it's theoretical role within the three branches of government has occurred in other branches as well, including the judiciary with the Supreme Court. Even, "[t]he Warren Court understood the problems and the promises of politics from its own experience. The Court numbered among its members former senators, representatives, and state legislators, a former governor and a former mayor, and former cabinet members."[84]

Moreover, there does not seem to be a uniform system of interpreting statutes even despite its large importance for courts upholding the rules.[85] Others argue for adopting a uniform system of statutory interpretation.[86] Indeed, there could be problems using different types of statutory analysis within courts, because one method may work in one case, but not in another case; yet, the subsequent courts would be urged to use precedent from the former case.[87] Alternatively, others argue against a uniform system of statutory interpretation, because such a system could lead to a rigid system of *stare decisis* for interpreting statutes.[88] However, despite several states having adopted "methodological" and "formalistic" *stare decisis*,[89] it is unclear whether the method produces equitable results.[90]

Although the legislatures have utmost formality, such as with Robert's *Rules of Order*[91] or Thomas Jefferson's *Manual of Parliamentary Practice*,[92] statutes that come from Congress are often unclear.

III. Plato's Soul

1. *Welcome to Plato's Soul*[93]

Before an understanding of how the Platonic soul functions within the U. S. federal government, a brief outline of Plato's conception of the soul is required. Plato wrote that the soul (ψυχή) consists of three parts; the λογιστικόν (logical), the θυμοειδές (thymotic/spirit), and the ἐπιθυμητικόν (appetitive/erotic).[94] Concurrently, a person has all three parts within herself or himself and acts justly if all the parts of the soul act as it is supposed to act.[95] If each part of the soul and each part of the city conduct their activities according to their "nature" or part of the soul, then all three parts of both city and individual will produce justice.[96]

2. Logos

Logos (λογιστικόν)[97] in the Platonic sense represents the part of the soul that loves knowledge and the search for knowledge.[98] The word in itself has a unique concept behind it: "λογιστικόν is one of Plato's many synonyms for the intellectual principle. Cf. 441 C, 571 C, 587 D, 605 B. It emphasizes the moral calculation of consequences, as opposed to blind passion."[99] This idea can be compared to the section in the *Phaedrus* where "Socrates compares the soul to a charioteer who controls two horses—one white and docile, the other black and intemperate. These three figures echo the division of the soul into reason, emotion, and appetite in Book IV of the Republic."[100] The charioteer is *logos* keeping control of the two horses.

3. Eros

Eros (ἐπιθυμητικός)[101] in the Platonic sense represents what Socrates says is "that with which it loves, hungers, thirsts, and feels the flutter and titillation of other desires, the irrational and appetitive—companion of various repletions [sic] and pleasures."[102]

4. *Thumos*

Thumos (θυμοειδές)[103] in the Platonic sense represents the "spirit"[104] of unifying with the logos but resisting the erotic part of the soul.[105] James Adams wrote in regards to this part of the Platonic soul that,

> [t]here is also a third element or part of soul, that which we call the element of Spirit. It is distinct from the Appetitive element, with which, indeed, it frequently contends. Its function is to support the Rational part of the soul. In a man of noble character the spirited element is quiescent or the reverse in accordance with the commands of Reason. It must not however be identified with Reason; for it is present in children and the lower animals, whereas Reason is not. Homer also recognizes that the two elements are distinct.

ff. The analogy between the righteous city and the righteous soul is continued throughout this section. It should be noted however that the parallel is no longer quite exact. The difference between θυμοειδές and λογιστικόν in the soul is greater than that between auxiliaries and rulers in the state: for the λογιστικόν is not a select part of the θυμοειδές—as the rulers are of the soldiers—but something generically distinct from it. Otherwise, the analogy holds (with the reservations mentioned on 435 A).[106]

Furthermore, this key concept of *thumos*/spirit (θυμός) can be described as in the distinctively Platonic sense of θυμός as the power of noble wrath, which, unless perverted by a bad education, is naturally the ally of the reason, though as mere angry passion it might seem to belong to the irrational part of the soul, and so, as Glaucon suggests, be akin to appetite, with which it is associated in the mortal soul of the *Timaeus* 69 D. In *Laws* 731 B-C, Plato tells us again that the soul cannot combat injustice without the capacity for righteous indignation. The Stoics affected to deprecate anger always, and the difference remained a theme of controversy between them and the Platonists. Cf. Schmidt, *Ethik der Griechen*, ii. pp. 321 ff., Seneca, De ira, i. 9, and *passim*. Moralists are still divided on the point. Cf. Bagehot, *Lord Brougham*: "Another faculty of Brougham . . . is the faculty of easy anger. The supine placidity of civilization is not favorable to animosity [Bacon's word for θυμός]." Leslie Stephen, *Science of Ethics*, pp. 60 ff. and p. 62, seems to contradict Plato: "The supposed conflict between reason and passion is, as I hold, meaningless if it is taken to imply that the reason is a faculty separate from the emotions," and so on. But this is only his metaphysics. On the practical ethical issue, he is with Plato.[107]

5. The Platonic Soul Overall

Essentially, the Platonic soul (ψυχή) consists of three parts; the λογιστικόν (logical), the θυμοειδές (thymotic/spirit), and the ἐπιθυμητικόν (appetitive/erotic). Each part represents an integral part to how a human functions. But there must exist a balance between the parts for justice to exist.

IV. COMPARING THE STRUCTURE OF THE FEDERAL GOVERNMENT TO THE PLATONIC SOUL

A. Judiciary as *Logos*

1. *Explaining Why the Judiciary is Not* Thumos

The judiciary[108] in this chapter's paradigm represents logos. *Logos* is part of the Platonic part of the soul that represents logic.[109] This contrasts with Professor Covitz's formulation of the judiciary representing the *thumos*. His argument is compelling. However, in the *Republic*, Socrates states, that a person "watering and fostering the growth of the rational principle [logos] in his soul and the others the appetitive and the passionate [two representing eros]," and this specific person "is not by nature of a bad disposition but has fallen into evil communications," meaning this person has not become evil but just in between the pull of *logos* and *eros*.[110] Socrates says this tension will resolve in "a compromise and turns over the government in his soul to the intermediate principle of ambition and high spirit and becomes a man haughty of soul and covetous of honor [meaning a turn to the *thymotic* part of the soul]."[111]

This indicates that one will likely turn to politics while in the tension of logos and *eros*, and in other words has become *thymotic*. This is more akin to the president, a politician, who in all likelihood is in search of honor, much like other politicians. Because if the executive of the country did not seek honor or maintain some "haughtiness," other politicians and world leaders would take advantage of us. She must be a decisive president, not merely logical. Yet, logic—as well as *eros*—may exist within her, but she must as president have a prevailing *thymotic* element.

This is in sharp contrast to the Article III judges especially. These judges—as intended by the framers of the constitution—were not and are not politicians seeking re-election.[112] But rather they are aloof from the political system seeking to interpret and apply the law.[113] This logical analysis—which can be informed with the other elements of the soul—is the guiding principal of the judiciary. The judiciary represents *logos*.

2. *Cases and Examples Showing Why the Judiciary Represents Logos*

In the *Phaedrus*, Socrates designates the charioteer as *logos* keeping control of the *eros* and *thumos*. Likewise, Chief Justice Marshall said, "it is emphatically the province and duty of the judicial department to say what the law is."[114] The Supreme Court uses judicial review and interprets the constitution and legislatively passed statutes to keep them in check much like the charioteer in Plato's *Phaedrus*.

When constituent parts of the soul become imbalanced, then unjust results arise, such as *Plessy v. Ferguson*.[115] However, imbalance and stepping out of a role in the separate powers may lead to more just and fair results, such as *Brown v. Board of Education*.[116]

In Plessy *v. Ferguson*,[117] the Supreme Court stepped out of its judicial authority and took on a legislative function, but with an unjust result. The court declared that a "State, shall provide equal but separate accommodations" for members of different races.[118]

In *Brown v. Board of Education*,[119] the Supreme Court stepped out of its judicial authority and took on a legislative function, but with a just result. In *Brown v. Board of Education*,[120] the court noted that "[t]he doctrine of 'separate but equal' did not make its appearance in this Court until 1896 in the case of *Plessy v. Ferguson* . . . involving not education but transportation," showing that the court in *Plessy* stepped out of its mode of *stare decisis* and made law based on no previous law. *Brown v. Bd. of Educ.*[121]

Most recently, in *Obergefell v. Hodges*,[122] many in the United States appreciate the decision, but others see it as a violation of natural law. Either way, the Supreme Court took on a legislative role in deciding the case as Professor Kenji Yoshino writes,

> [w]hile Obergefell's most immediate effect was to legalize same-sex marriage across the land, its long-term impact could extend far beyond this context. To see this point, consider how much more narrowly the opinion could have been written. It could have invoked the equal protection and due process guarantees without specifying a formal level of review, and then observed that none of the state justifications survived even a deferential form of scrutiny. The Court had adopted this strategy in prior gay rights cases.[123]

Professor Laurence Tribe supports this position by stating, Professor Kenji Yoshino's splendid comment makes clear just how misguided these glib detractions are and eloquently elaborates the important doctrinal work done by Justice Kennedy's decision, which represents the culmination of a decades-long project that has revolutionized the court's fundamental rights jurisprudence. As Yoshino demonstrates, *Obergefell* has definitively replaced *Washington v. Glucksberg's* wooden three-prong test focused on tradition, specificity, and negativity with the more holistic inquiry of Justice Harlan's justly famous 1961 dissent in *Poe v. Ullman*, a mode of inquiry that was embodied in key opinions from the mid-1960s to the early 1970s.[124]

Over time, society may come to a consensus of whether the court decided the case correctly. But it currently serves as an example of a court decision stepping out of the bounds of the role of the judiciary and acting in a way to solve aspects that the legislature could not fix in terms of Constitutional guarantees.[125]

Although ideally the court would follow *logos*, the catch is that the members of the court are not purely guided by *logos*—as to be expected—because all humans, according to Plato, have three aspects of the soul within themselves. The idea of a three-part soul may be intended to understand the basic functions of an aspect of government, each member has an entire soul (ψυχή) governing their aspects of existence. This leads to more nuanced decisions, not only in the judiciary but all three branches of the government.

In terms of judiciary, stepping out the bounds of the separate powers or the role in the soul of the policy can have bad and good outcomes.

Justice from the charioteer comes from consistency, as many philosophers have defined justice. In this case, the *logos* as seen through the Supreme Court and judiciary, applying and saying what the law is.

B. Executive as *Thumos*

In this chapter, the executive[126] represents *thumos*. *Thumos* represents the spirit of the soul as represented by the white horse in the *Phaedrus*.[127] The white horse is spirited but controlled with a sense of potential shame.[128]

1. *Explaining Why the Executive is Not Logos*

However, in Professor Covitz's formulation, the executive represents *logos*. As mentioned previously, Socrates states in the *Republic* that a person "watering and fostering the growth of the rational principle [logos] in his soul and the others the appetitive and the passionate [two representing eros]," and this person "is not by nature of a bad disposition but has fallen into evil communications," meaning this person has not become evil, but just in between the pull of *logos* and the pull of *eros*, but is otherwise unable to make a decision.[129] Socrates says this tension will resolve in "a compromise and turns over the government in his soul to the intermediate principle of ambition and high spirit and becomes a man haughty of soul and covetous of honor [meaning a turn to the *thymotic* part of the soul]."[130]

This indicates that one will likely turn to politics while in the tension of logos and *eros*, and in other words has become *thymotic*. This is more akin to the president—rather than a member of the judiciary—who in all likelihood is in search of honors much like other politicians. This is not a negative aspect of the executive necessarily. Because if the executive of the country did not seek honor or maintain some "haughtiness," other politicians and world leaders would take advantage of us. She must be a decisive president, not merely logical. Yet, logic—as well as *eros*—may and must exist within her, but she must as president have a prevailing *thymotic* element.

2. *Cases and Examples Showing Why the Executive Represents* Thumos

Here, the *thumos* manifests itself where a part of the executive branch of government—such as the EPA—would interpret a statute from the legislature and implement it. This occurs through the rules laid out by the Supreme Court and the judiciary as seen in the *Chevron* case.

Through 2013–2015, the Obama administration issued executive orders relating to immigration.[131] By November of 2015, the Fifth Circuit Court of Appeals declared the executive orders unconstitutional.[132] Regardless whether the executive orders are eventually upheld as constitutional or not, they represent the executive branch of government conducting actions with the administration's justification that they are the most "thymotic" solution to the immigration problem. If the orders are upheld to be constitutional after all, then the judiciary or the legislature will deem them to have been the most effective approach at the time to avoid a greater disaster later. If the orders are not upheld to be constitutional, then the judiciary or the legislature will have deemed them not the most effective approach at the time. In an ironic sense, the immigration orders—if deemed constitutional—will be seen as a way to unify the country in a spirited "thumotic" way to avoid a greater catastrophe.[133]

Because the executive—and the legislature as well—are charged with the carrying out the daily activities of the nation, international relations appears to be of paramount importance with spirited leadership.

Thus, the leadership and executive actions that may not or may be based in *logos* and *eros*, but through a combination of the two as is the Platonic paradigm for *thumos*, which this chapter argues fits into the paradigm of the executive branch of government in the U.S. Constitution.

C. The Legislature as Eros

In this chapter, the legislature[134] represents *eros*. *Eros* represents the basic instincts and desires of the soul as represented by the black horse in the *Phaedrus*. The black horse can wear down the white horse and charioteer.

The Patient Protection and Affordable Care Act Patient Protection and Affordable Care Act[135] (Obamacare) as passed by the Congress and signed into law in 2010.[136] According the Supreme Court, "the Act aims to increase the number of Americans covered by health insurance and decrease the cost of health care. The Act's 10 titles stretch over 900 pages and contain hundreds of provisions."[137]

This example shows how the concept of justice is inconsistent. At the time it may be clear what the *eros*, the legislature, sees as justice. Overtime, this may become clear and unclear.

CONCLUSION

To reiterate, this chapter has demonstrated that to interpret the problems and the eventual purpose of the U. S. government while simultaneously explaining its continued existence by analyzing the three-part structure of the U. S. Federal government as outlined in the constitution—and subsequently interpreted by all three parts of the government—through the lens of the Platonic paradigm of *logos*, *thumos*, and *eros* as explained in Plato's dialogues. The major premise of the chapter is Plato's three-part soul. The minor premise is the three-part structure of the U. S. government. The syllogism is the analysis in the chapter attempts to show how each part of the Platonic soul represents itself in the three parts of judiciary for *logos*, executive for *thumos*, and legislature for *eros*.

Overall, this Platonic analysis of the constitution's structure and function could add to the dialogue of constitutional analysis. Indeed, there are arguments for originalist, textualist, evolving constitutional doctrine, but there seems to be a basis for a Platonic interpretation of the constitution.

In line with a balanced soul of the polity and a balanced government, it would seem that each part of government would not reach into another's duties.[138]

As fate would have it, each person—in the Platonic paradigm—has the three parts of the Platonic soul. Although an individual may act in one part of the federal government, each person has all three parts. Thus, it is to be expected that different parts of the soul would manifest in a different part of the federal government.

NOTES

1. This chapter is largely based on an article published by the author and cited to as Charles Lincoln, "A Structural Etiology of the U.S. Constitution." *J. Legis.* 43 (2016): 22. That article was a continuation of research done as a senior at Harvard University under the direction of Akiba Covitz (who was at the time assistant dean at Harvard Law School) and a response to his dissertation at the University of Pennsylvania—*The Soul of the Polity*.

2. This can perhaps be better understood for purposes of this chapter as "aspects of existence." Also, consider the similarity to Sigmund Freud's psychoanalysis. Sigmund Freud, *The Ego and the Id* (1923), in *The Standard Edition of the Complete Psychological Works of Sigmund Freud* (James Strachey ed. & trans., 1961) 3, 25.

The Liddell & Scott's A Greek-English Lexicon defines the word as, "ψυχή ψύχω I.breath, Lat. anima, esp. as the sign of life, the life, spirit." "Henry George Liddell, Robert Scott, An Intermediate Greek-English Lexicon, Ψυχή." Accessed May 19, 2021. http://www.perseus.tufts.edu/hopper/text?doc=Perseus%3Atext%3A1999.04.0058%3Aentry%3Dyuxh%2F.

3. Plato, *The Republic of Plato* (Allan Bloom ed. & trans., 2d ed. 1991) [hereinafter Plato, Republic]. 435e–442a.

4. Plato, Republic, supra note [ORIGINAL REPUBLIC FOOTNOTE], at 439a, 439e3-4.

5. Id. at 439d5-436a1-3.

6. "A particular form of government or political organization."

7. In the dialogue, Socrates suggested the three parts of the soul should not prevent the other parts from functioning appropriately. *Id.* at 433a.

8. Cicero, *De Republica* (Cambridge, MA: Loeb Classical Library, 1928), 3.22.33.

9. Plato, *Timaeus* (Oxford: Oxford University Press, trans Robin Waterfield, 2008) at 30a-31b. The page numbers used throughout this chapter (and book) to refer to Platonic texts are in accord with the Stephanus pagination.

Substantively, are randomness or patterns provable or real? How do we even decide what is random if not through statistical or other mathematical analysis? Philosophically speaking, there could be a discrepancy between a series following a mathematical rule or being truly random. Ludwig Wittgenstein in his *Philosophical Investigations* explained how randomness *can* really be explained in terms of increasing complexity of following a rule, but paradoxically if everything can be shown to be following a rule, it can also at the same time be shown to not follow a rule.

> 201. This was our paradox: no course of action could be determined by a rule, because every course of action can be made out to accord with the rule. The answer was: if everything can be made out to accord with the rule, then it can also be made out to conflict with it. And so there would be neither accord nor conflict here. It can be seen that there is a misunderstanding here from the mere fact that in the course of our argument we give one interpretation after another; as if each one contented us at least for a moment, until we thought of yet another standing behind it. What this shows is that there is a way of grasping a rule which is not an interpretation, but which is exhibited in what we call "obeying the rule" and "going against it" in actual cases. Hence, there is an inclination to say: every action according to the rule is an interpretation. But we ought to restrict the term "interpretation" to the substitution of one expression of the rule for another. Ludwig Wittgenstein, Philosophical Investigations (G.E.M. Anscombe & R. Rhees eds., G.E.M. Anscombe trans., 1972) § 201.

This makes one question whether randomness really exists or does everything follow a set rule? See, for example, Ahilan T. Arulanantham, "Breaking the Rules?: Wittgenstein and Legal Realism." *Yale L.J.* 107 (1998): 1853, 1869–1871. Dennis Patterson, "Wittgenstein and Constitutional Theory." *Tex. L. Rev.* 72 (1994): 1837, 1851. Scott Hershovitz, "Wittgenstein on Rules: The Phantom Menace." *Oxford J. of Leg. Stud.* 22 (2002): 619, 639–640.

10. Such an example can be seen in literature,

> Borges's *The Library of Babel* implicitly undercuts all the written structures—religion, science, art—through which human beings strive to impose order on an unruly world. It consists of a fantastic monologue in which a Librarian, who lives in a Library which is also the universe, tries unsuccessfully to describe the chaotic infinity (or near infinity) that surrounds him. According to the Librarian, the Library may or may not be endless; but it is certainly meaningless, being made up of numberless books in a Babel of tongues. Because it contains all the possible combinations of letters in all languages, many of the books contain only an intelligible word or two, or are only partially true copies of books contained in their proper form elsewhere in the library. The librarians spend their time, among other ways, searching for the true catalogue that would bring order and meaning to their incomprehensible collection.

Susan Mann, "The Universe and the Library: A Critique of James Boyd White as Writer and Reader." *Stan. L. Rev.* 41 (1989): 959, 965.

11. *Lucretius: On the Nature of Things* (H. A. J. Munro trans.), reprinted in 12 *Great Books of the Western World* (Robert Maynard Hutchins ed., 1952) 1, 12.

Concurrently, directly contrasting the Platonic theory of order the universe,

> The contrary materialist view characterizes archetypes as speculative constructs. Aristotle and Plato had their ancient Greek materialist counterparts in Epicurus, Democritus, and Lucretius, who in his On the Nature of the Universe wrote that all things began from "the purposeless congregation and coalescence of atoms." There are uniform and entirely natural causes in a closed system not ordered or otherwise affected by the presence of a higher mind capable of recognizing and ordering information. Thus, Epicurus could hold that morality was merely a sensual matter of seeking pleasure and avoiding pain, not a sensitivity issue to any particular purpose or design. Aristotle's teleological universe was rejected for an atomistic universe without purpose or form in which biological forms and

> the ordered universe in which they exist were not the fixed product of information, intelligence, or design but of random accretion. Nobel Prize winning biologist George Wald, physicist Freeman [26] Dyson, and astronomer George Greenstein explain the improbability of the universe's remarkable order by suggesting either that the universe did not exist until humans observed it and (in Wald's words) that "[t]he universe wants to be known."

Marion Hilligan, Nelson P. Miller, Don Petersen and Chris Hastings, "SYMPOSIUM ISSUE: WORLD VIEWS COLLIDE: A Dialogue on State-Authored Embryonic Stem-Cell Research, Human Enhancements, Physician-Assisted Suicide and the Value of Life: SUPERHUMAN-BIOTECHNOLOGY'S EMERGING IMPACT ON THE LAW." *T.M. Cooley L. Rev.* 24 (2007): 1, 25–26.

12. Such as the interlocutor suggests nature represented itself in Athens. Timaeus 90b-c. *See.* Recent work suggesting there is an order to the world's structure. "About fifty years ago a physicist called Paul Dirac asked himself why the number ten to the fortieth power keeps occurring. The square of this number, ten to the eightieth power, is the mass of the visible universe, measured in terms of the mass of the proton. The number itself, ten to the fortieth, is the present age of the universe, expressed in units of time it takes light to travel across a proton. And, get this, the constant that measures the strength of gravity in terms of the electrical force between two protons is ten to the fortieth times weaker! Also, ten to the fortieth to the one-fourth, or ten to the tenth, just about equals the number of stars in a galaxy, the number of galaxies in the universe, and the inverse of the weakfine structure constant! John Updike, Roger's Version 23-24 (1986); George Johnson, *A Fire in the Mind: Science, Faith, and the Search for Order* 308–316 (1996)." Robert Birmingham, "Proving Miracles and the First Amendment." *Geo. Mason L. Rev.* 5 (1996): 45, 60.

13. "To illustrate the nature of structuralist theory, this discussion will concentrate on the work of Claude Levi-Strauss. Levi-Strauss has made the search for the fundamental properties of human thought the focus of his work. His basic objective is uncovering the universal, basic structure of human thought, which is deep below the surface but is manfested [*sic*] in myth, language, cooking, table manners, and the general structures of social life. This basic structure, which is termed 'deep structure,' will identify cross-cultural similarities." Donald H. J. Hermann, "Phenomenology, Structuralism, Hermeneutics, and Legal Study: Applications of Contemporary Continental Thought to Legal Phenomena." *U. Miami L. Rev.* 36 (1982): 379, 390–391.

14. "Michel Foucault's compelling and poetic methodological manifesto describes the nature of 'critique' and, thereby, the proper role of the critic. For Foucault, 'critique' was more than a means to an end; criticism was itself an act of resistance and refusal. Toward this end, Foucault sought to decouple criticism from positive programs for social and political change. Criticism is, according to this view, a negative operation—'essays in refusal'—resisting and rejecting 'what is' without regard for 'what needs to be done.' For this reason, Foucault's views have occasionally been labeled 'rejectionist.' Such 'rejectionist' claims, in turn, exemplify the most feared aspects of a new challenge to traditional legal thought: postmodernism." Derek P. Jinks, "Essays in Refusal: Pre-Theoretical Commitments in Postmodern Anthropology and Critical Race Theory." *Yale L.J.* 107 (1997): 499, 499–500. *See also.* For a discussion on Foucault's ideas on law and sovereignty: Tom Frost,

"Agamben's Sovereign Legalization of Foucault." *Oxford J. Legal Studies* (2010): 30 (3): 545.

15. Marvin Harris, *The Rise of Anthropological Theory* (1968). *See*. Perry Dane, "Jurisdictionality, Time, and the Legal Imagination." *Hofstra L. Rev.* 23 (1994): 1, 94. See. "The reciprocity concept justifies the assumption that one who gives will receive in return, though there are no hard promises as to timing, quality, or quantity." Ragsdale Jr, John W. "The Rise and Fall of the Chacoan State." *UMKC L. Rev.* 64 (1995): 485, 528. *See*. Perry Dane, "Jurisdictionality, Time, and the Legal Imagination." *Hofstra L. Rev.* 23 (1994): 1, 94. *See*. In regards to gift-giving cultures. Bronislaw Malinowski, *Argonauts of the Western Pacific* (Routledge 1961) (1922) 72–76.

16. According to Dumézil, the division of society—government—into three parts was inherent in all Indo European societies. The trifunctional pattern (and implicit political separation of powers) is manifest among the Hindus in the original castes: Brahmana (teachers, priests, keepers of the law), Ksatriya (warrior kings), and Vaisya (farmers, producers, merchants, and doctors). "For classic development of this so-called 'tripartite hypothesis' concerning the division of social roles in Proto-Indo-European societies, see generally Georges Dumézil, Flamen-Brahman (1935); Georges Dumézil, *Mitra-Varuna: An Essay on Two Indo-European Representations of Sovereignty* (Derek Coltman trans., 2d ed. 1988)." Robin, Bradley Kar, "Western Legal Prehistory: Reconstructing the Hidden Origins of Western Law and Civilization." *U. Ill. L. Rev.* (2012): 1499, 1525 n. 71. *See*. Georges Dumézil, *Archaic Roman Religion* (1966) 585. *See also*. For critiques of the Trifunctional Hypothesis: Wouter W. Belier, *Decayed Gods: Origin and Development of Georges Dumézil's "Ideologie Tripartie"* (1991) 17–20.

17. David S. Caudill, "Freud and Critical Legal Studies: Contours of a Radical Socio-Legal Psychoanalysis." *Ind. L.J.* 66 (1991): 651, 658–659. *See* S. Freud, The Ego and the Id, in 19 *The Standard Edition of the Complete Psychological Works of the Complete Psychological Works of Sigmund Freud* (J. Strachey ed. 1951) 3.

18. Charles E. Lincoln, *Ethnicity and Social Organization at Chichen Itza, Yucatan, Mexico* (PhD dissertation, Department of Anthropology, Harvard University) Advisors Mathews, Peter, and Gordon R. Willey (1990). *See*. Charles E. Lincoln, "The Chronology of Chichen Itza: A Review of the Literature." In *Late Lowland Maya Civilization: Classic to Postclassic*, edited by Jeremy A. Sabloff and E. Wyllys Andrews V, pp. 141–156 (Albuquerque: University of New Mexico Press, 1986).

19. The Iliad of Homer 14:28–30 (Richmond Lattimore trans., 25th reprint ed. 1976) (1951). *See* "[T]he well known Judgment of Paris, which Homer apparently knew. Although it is not directly recounted in the Iliad, there is a clear reference to it in Book 14, where Hera's displeasure with the other gods (i.e., gods who were urging Achilles to treat Hector's corpse with respect) was attributed to the Judgment of Paris: 'because of the delusion of Paris / who insulted the goddesses when they came to him in his courtyard / and favoured her who supplied the lust that led to disaster.' The myth of the Judgment of Paris began when Peleus and Thetis did not invite Eris, the goddess of discord, to their wedding. Eris, feeling snubbed, concocted one of literary history's most evil schemes. She procured a golden apple and inscribed it 'For the fairest.' She then crashed the wedding feast and tossed the apple onto the table. Three

goddesses, Hera, Athena, and Aphrodite, each argued that it should be her's. They asked Zeus to decide. He refused because he feared his wife's anger in the event that he did not choose her. He passed the buck and suggested that the Trojan prince Paris, the son of Priam, act as arbiter." Russ VerSteeg, "A Contract Analysis of the Trojan War." *Ariz. L. Rev.* 40 (1998): 173, 192.

20. Montesquieu, *The Spirit of the Laws* (Thomas Nugent trans., Hafner Pub. 1949) (1748) bk. XI, ch. 6, at 152.

21. John F. Manning, "Separation of Powers as Ordinary Interpretation." *Harv. L. Rev.* 124 (2010): 1939, 2004 (2011).

22. James J. Walsh, *Education of the Founding Fathers of the Republic: Scholasticism in the Colonial Colleges* (1970) 104–105.

23. Jean-Francois Pradeau, *Plato and the City* (University of Exeter Press, Exeter, 2002), 129.

24. As far as the author knows, Akiba Covitz is the only person to have written on this subject.

25. As well as long-term personal correspondence with Professor Akiba J. Covitz discussing the dissertation's ideas. Professor Covitz was the author's mentor during the author's undergraduate studies.

26. Covitz, xxii–xxv.

27. Covitz, xviii–xx.

28. Covitz, iv.

29. This chapter will too focus on the constitution and Plato's *Republic*, but also other works that have interpreted the two of them.

30. Arthur Herman, The Cave And The Light (2013).

31. Kenji Yoshino, "The City and the Poet." *Yale L.J.* 114 (2005): 1835, 1842.

32. *Id.*

33. *Id.* 1842–1843.

Conversely, Plato's idea of the soul is similar but different from Aristotle's view, Aristotle's use of the vocabulary of *dunamis* is unusually complex and requires clarification. A typical example of the first meaning ("innate") is found at Aristotle, Ethica Nicomachea, supra note 13, at 1105b20-28, which contrasts *dunamis* with a developed capacity. But in other passages, *dunamis* is clearly used in the sense of a developed capacity. Id. at 1094b2, 1101b13, 1143a28. Finally, the term is sometimes used when the capacity is already active, and thus the conditions for its activation must be present. See Aristotle, De Anima 412a1-413a10 (W.D. Ross ed., 1956) (defining *psuche* as the active organization of a body that has life, potentially, or *dunamei*). Of course, as Aristotle immediately points out, one is alive only when the body is actually alive, thus meeting all the "external" conditions for the presence of psuche. See id.; see also Martha C. Nussbaum, Commentary on Aristotle, *De Motu Animalium* 271, 363–364 (Martha Craven Nussbaum trans., 1978) (discussing Aristotle, *De Motu Animalium* 702a30-31, 703b29-32).

Martha Nussabaum, "The Supreme Court: 2006 Term: Foreword: Constitutions And Capabilities: "Perception" Against Lofty Formalism." *Harv. L. Rev.* 121 (2007): 4, 34.

34. *Id.*

35. Bruce D. Fisher, "The Ethical Consumer: A Rejecter of Positive Law Arbitrage." *Seton Hall L. Rev.* 25 (1994): 230, 245.

36. Natural law can find its roots as far as the Ancient Greeks and Aquinas. Martin Rhonheimer, "Natural Law as a Work of Reason: Understanding the Metaphysics of Participated Theonomy." *Am. J. Juris.* 55 (2010): 41, 47, 50. See generally, Philip A. Hamburger, "Natural Rights, Natural Law, And American Constitutions." *Yale Law Journal* (1993): 907–960.

37. *Id.*

38. Linda Meyer, "'Nothing We Say Matters': Teague and New Rules." *The University of Chicago Law Review* 61, no. 2 (1994): 423–492, 460.

39. *Id.*

The author goes on to explain how,

> [Positive law] . . . is set by a monarch, or sovereign number, to a person or persons in a state of subjection to its author. John Austin, The Province of Jurisprudence Determined (1832), reprinted in John Austin, The Province of Jurisprudence Determined and The Uses of the Study of Jurisprudence 132 (Noonday, 1954). See also Frederick Schauer, Constitutional Positivism, 25 *Conn L Rev* 797, 799 (1993) (Legal positivism takes the position that the law "is not derived necessarily from fundamental moral principles, but rather is simply posited by human beings and human institutions"), and the bibliography of major theorists cited therein. Id at 799 n 3.

However, Professor Nonet discusses the essence of positive law in relation to Nietzsche's philosophy, "What is positive law? We may begin with the familiar account that the word 'positive' suggests immediately: positive law (Nietzsche calls it Gesetz) is law that exists by virtue of being posited (gesetzt), laid down and set firmly, by a will empowered so to will. Such law 'exists' in the sense that it has validity (Geltung). It has validity if the will (Wille) from which it issues has the power (Macht) to impose it, to demand and secure obedience to its command." Philippe Nonet, "What is Positive Law?" *The Yale Law Journal* 100, no. 3 (1990): 667–699, 667–668.

40. Plato, Republic, supra note [ORIGINAL REPUBLIC FOOTNOTE], at 608c-621d.

41. Niccolo Machiavelli, The Prince (Luigi Ricci and E.R.P. Vincent trans.), reprinted in *Social and Political Philosophy: Readings from Plato to Ghandi* (John Somerville & Ronald E. Santoni eds., 1963) 123.

42. Cf. Christopher Bobonich, "Persuasion, Compulsion, and Freedom in Plato's 'Laws'," in *Plato*, ed. Gail Fine (Oxford: Oxford University Press, 2000), 884.

43. Albert Grande, "Education as a Natural Right." *John's J. Legal Comment* 21 (2006): 53, 53–56. "Antigone, with clear conscience, deliberately violates King Creon's law that denies her brother a decent burial. Her brother had been a rebel and was thereby denied the honor of a proper burial. Antigone appeals to the higher unwritten laws of God, the eternal natural laws. While it is unknown when those laws originated, Antigone's act of defiance violates written laws in favor of natural law, which respects a sister's right to bury her brother, despite the king's prohibition." *Id.*

44. Cicero, De legibus, 1.18, at 316–317 (Clinton Walker Keyes trans., 1928) ("Law is the highest reason, implanted in Nature, which commands what ought to be done and forbids the opposite.") It's interesting to consider how positive law is rooted in nature.

45. Discuss Cave Analogy.

46. "*Stare decisis* is short for *stare decisis et non quieta movere*, which means 'stand by the thing decided and do not disturb the calm.' *Stare decisis* attempts to balance two competing considerations: the need of the community for stability in legal rules and decisions and the need of courts to correct past errors. This doctrine has been part of the American legal landscape since the country's formation." *Petersen v. Magna Corp.*, 484 Mich. 300, 314 (Mich. 2009). The court further noted "[t]he doctrine can be traced back to medieval England." *See.* Thomas Healy, "Stare Decisis as a Constitutional Requirement." *W. Va. L. Rev.* 104 (2001): 43, 56–62. *Petersen*, 484 Mich. at 314.

However, the article itself notes that very few cases were recorded during the Anglo-Saxon period. However, there were many records of Anglo-Saxon and Norman history such as the "Anglo-Saxon Chronicle," 1067 AD, version D (B. L. Cott, Tiber B. iv), *English Historical Documents*, 2nd Ed., Vol. 2, Ed. David C. Douglass and G. W. Greenaway (London: Oxford University Press, 1981) 150. Indeed, there are even visual representations, such as the Bayeux Tapestry. See *The Bayeux Tapestry, A Comprehensive Survey*, Ed. Sir Frank Stenton (New York: Phaidon, 1957).

But earlier Roman law was itself a compilation of cases in digests, which Roman lawyers would reference. Shael Herman, "Legacy and Legend: The Continuity of Roman and English Regulation of the Jews." *Tul. L. Rev.* 66 (1991): 1781, 1797. Even as early as the 1st Century B.C. "Cicero praised his friend, the jurist Servius Sulpicius Rufus for using dialectic and treating law as [a science]," indicating that—much like the modern method of using case law—Romans treated like cases alike. James Gordley, "The Method of the Roman Jurists." *Tul. L. Rev.* 87 (2012): 933, 947 fn. 73 (2013). *See generally* Peter Stein, *Regulae Iuris: From Juristic Rules to Legal Maxims* (1966).

By 1256 Henry de Bracton wrote of the importance of using past precedent he experienced previously to decide current cases before him, "if any new and unusual matters arise, which have not before been seen in the realm, if like matters arise let them be decided by like since the decision is a good one for proceeding a similibus ad similia." Thomas Healy, "Stare Decisis as a Constitutional Requirement." *W. Va. L. Rev.* 104 (2001): 43, 56–57.

47. Henry Paul Monaghan, "Stare Decisis and Constitutional Adjudication." *Columbia Law Review* 88, no. 4 (1988): 723–773, 749–752.

48. *United States IRS v. Osborne (In re Osborne)*, 76 F.3d 306, 309 (9th Cir. 1996).

Moreover, the court unpacked the etymology of *stare decisis* writing, "[c]onsider the word 'decisis.' The word means, literally and legally, the decision. Nor is the doctrine stare dictis; it is not 'to stand by or keep to what was said.' Nor is the doctrine stare rationibus decidendi—'to keep to the rationes decidendi of past cases.' Rather, under the doctrine of stare decisis a case is important only for what it decides—for the 'what,' not for the 'why,' and not for the 'how.' Insofar as precedent is concerned, stare decisis is important only for the decision, for the detailed legal consequence following a detailed set of facts." *United States IRS v. Osborne (In re Osborne)*, 76 F.3d 306, 309 (9th Cir. 1996).

49. *Payne v. Tennessee*, 501 U.S. 808, 827, 737–738 (1991).

50. *Id.* at 738.

51. *Id.*

52. *Id.*

53. *Johnson v. United States*, 135 S. Ct. 2551, 2562 (2015).

54. Thomas C. Grey, "Holmes and Legal Pragmatism." *Stan. L. Rev.* 41 (1989): 787, 861.

55. Oliver Wendell Holmes, Jr., *The Common Law* (Mark DeWolfe Howe ed., Harvard Univ. Press, 1963) (1881), p1.

56. Andrew P. Morriss, "Codification and the Right Answers." *Chi.-Kent L. Rev.* 74 (1999): 355.

Compare with *Id.* n. 161 "The Civil Code of the State of New York (pt. 1), 2 *Alb. L.J.* 385, 385 (Nov. 19, 1870). This was the idea behind the case method introduced by Christopher Columbus Langdell at Harvard Law School in 1870, where Carter had trained. See Wiecek, supra note 10, at 92-93."

Indeed, many legal scholars have long viewed Christopher Columbus Langdel l, the Dean of Harvard Law School from 1870 to 1895, as the prototypical American jurist of the late nineteenth century. He portrayed the common law as a conceptually ordered scientific system in which rigorous logical reasoning trumped concerns about the just resolution of particular cases. In Langdell's Orthodoxy, probably the most influential modern article on Langdell, Thomas Grey dubbed this system of legal thought "classical orthodoxy." Others have labeled it "mechanical jurisprudence," "classical legal thought," "liberal legal science," or "Langdellian formalism." Whatever term they have preferred, scholars have long agreed that Gilded Age legal thinkers viewed the common law as a rigidly logical, amoral system.

Lewis A. Grossman, "Langdell Upside-Down: James Coolidge Carter and the Anticlassical Jurisprudence of Anticodification." *Yale J. L. & Human.* 19 (2007): 149, 150.

57. Oliver Wendell Holmes, Jr., *The Common Law* (Mark DeWolfe Howe ed., Harvard Univ. Press, 1963) (1881), p1. Holmes continued a sentence later, "[t]he form of continuity has been kept up by reasonings [*sic*] purporting to reduce every thing to a logical sequence; but that form is nothing but the evening dress which the new-comer puts on to make itself presentable according to conventional requirements. The important phenomenon is the man underneath it, not the coat; the justice and reasonableness of a decision, not its consistency with previously held views . . . As a branch of anthropology, law is an object of science; the theory of legislation is a scientific study; but the effort to reduce the concrete details of an existing system to the merely logical consequences of simple postulates is always in danger of becoming unscientific, and of leading to a misapprehension of the nature of the problem and the data." *Id.*

58. Roscoe Pound, "Mechanical Jurisprudence." *Columbia Law Review* 8 (1908): 605, 606.

59. "Holmes, Privilege, Malice, and Intent." *Harv. Law Rev.* 8 (1894): 1, 7.

60. *Id.* at 7.

61. 343 U.S. 579 (1952).

62. 343 U.S. 579, 582–585 (1952).

63. 343 U.S. 579, 585.

64. *Youngstown Sheet & Tube Co. v. Sawyer*, 343 U.S. 579, 588.

65. *Youngstown Sheet & Tube Co. v. Sawyer,* 343 U.S. 579, 589.

66. *Youngstown Sheet & Tube Co. v. Sawyer*, 343 U.S. 579, 588.

67. *Youngstown Sheet & Tube Co. v. Sawyer*, 343 U.S. 579, 589.

68. *Youngstown Sheet & Tube Co. v. Sawyer*, 343 U.S. 579, 647 (1952).

69. *Youngstown Sheet & Tube Co. v. Sawyer*, 343 U.S. 579, 629 (1952).

70. *Chevron, U.S.A., Inc. v. NRDC, Inc.*, 467 U.S. 837, 844 (1984).

71. Chevron, U.S.A., Inc. v. NRDC, Inc., 467 U.S. 837, 839–840.

72. *Id.* at 840.

73. *Id.*

74. *Id.*

75. *Chevron, U.S.A., Inc. v. NRDC, Inc.*, 467 U.S. 837, 843.

76. *Chevron, U.S.A., Inc. v. NRDC, Inc.*, 467 U.S. 837, 843–844.

77. *Chevron, U.S.A., Inc. v. NRDC, Inc.*, 467 U.S. 837, 844.

78. *Id.*

79. Thomas W. Merrill, "Judicial Deference to Executive Precedent." *Yale L.J.* 101 (1992): 969.

80. Thomas W. Merrill, "Judicial Deference to Executive Precedent." *Yale L.J.* 101 (1992): 969, 969–970.

81. Abbe R. Gluck, "Imperfect Statutes, Imperfect Courts: Understanding Congress's Plan in the Era of Unorthodox Lawmaking." *Harv. L. Rev.* 129 (2015): 62, 63.

82. Cristina Marcos, and Sarah Ferris. "House Votes to Repeal ObamaCare | TheHill." Accessed May 19, 2021. https://thehill.com/policy/healthcare/231638-house-votes-to-repeal-obamacare.

83. *Id.*

84. Pamela S. Karlan, "Foreword: Democracy and Disdain, The Supreme Court 2011 Term." *Harv. L. Rev.* 126 (2012): 1–45, 5.

85. Carlos E. Gonzalez, "Reinterpreting Statutory Interpretation." *NCL Rev.* 74 (1995): 585, 586.

86. "Methodological *stare decisis*—the practice of giving precedential effect to judicial statements about methodology—is generally absent from the jurisprudence of mainstream federal statutory interpretation, but appears to be a common feature of some states' statutory case law." Abbe R. Gluck, "The States as Laboratories of Statutory Interpretation: Methodological Consensus and the New Modified Textualism." *The Yale Law Journal* (2010): 1750–1862, 1754.

87. Brian G. Slocum, "Overlooked Temporal Issues in Statutory Interpretation." *Temp. L. Rev.* 81 (2008): 635, 637–638 (Scolum's article illustrates some of the

problem of using different types of statutory analysis with courts, because one method may work in one case, but not in another.)

88. Glen Staszewski, "The Dumbing Down of Statuary." *B.U.L. Rev.* 95 (2015): 209, 217–219. (Staszweski argues against a uniform system of statutory interpretation throughout the article.)

89. Professor Gluck expands on these terms methodological and formalistic.

> By "formalistic," I mean clearly defined, ex ante interpretive rules arranged to be applied in a consistent order. But the characteristics of the particular rules chosen (for instance, whether and when legislative history may be consulted) need not themselves be rigid. Cf. Cass R. Sunstein, Must Formalism Be Defended Empirically?, 66 *U. Chi. L. Rev.* 636, 638 (1999) ("Formalist strategies . . . entail three commitments: to promoting compliance with all applicable legal formalities (whether or not they make sense in the individual case), to ensuring rule-bound law . . . and to constraining the discretion of judges . . .").

Abbe R. Gluck, "The States as Laboratories of Statutory Interpretation: Methodological Consensus and the New Modified Textualism." *The Yale Law Journal* (2010): 1750–1862, 1754 fn. 8.

90. Sydney Foster, "Should Courts Give *Stare Decisis* Effect to Statutory Interpretation Methodology?" *Geo. L.J.* 96 (2008): 1863.

91. H. Robert, *Robert's Rules of Order Newly Revised* (1970). Saul Levmore, "Parliamentary Law, Majority Decision-making, and the Voting Paradox." *Virginia Law Review* (1989): 971–1044.

92. Thomas Jefferson, Jefferson's Manual of Parliamentary Practice (1801), reprinted in Rules of the House of Representatives, H.R. Doc. No. 279, 99th Cong., 2d Sess. (1987).

93. A secondary account must be limited inherently to espouse the entire idea, but also to capture the rhetorical and poetic qualities inherent in Plato's writings. In some sense, this is a reflection or hyperreality simulacra of the "real" represented in Plato's corpus. See Jean Baudrillard, *The Precession of the Simulacra, in Simulacra and Simulation* (Sheila Faria Glaser trans., University of Michigan Press, 1997) (1981).

See "This is closely related to Žižek's assertion that 'we lack the very language to articulate'" ideas and knowledge surrounded by ideology. Slavoj Žižek, *Welcome to the Desert of the Real* 2 (2002). See generally Sorajjakool, infra note 67 (It is extremely difficult to articulate conditions you refuse to believe or accept)." Nick J. Scuillo, "Žižek/Questions/Failing." *Willamette L. Rev.* 47 (2011): 287, 325 n. 55.

94. Republic, 443c-e.

95. Republic, 441d12-e2.

96. Republic, 433a, where Socrates states "[a]nd what we did lay down, and often said, you recall, was that each one man must perform one social service in the state for which his nature is best adapted." Likewise, if this does not happen, then there would be injustice (ἀδικία).

97. Etymologically speaking, The Liddell & Scott's A Greek-English Lexicon defines the word as, "λογιστικός from λογιστής 1 I.skilled or practised in calculating, Xen., Plat.:—ἡ λογιστική (sc. τέχνη), arithmetic, Plat. II.endued with reason, rational, Arist.:—τὸ λ. the reasoning faculty, Plat. 2.using one's reason, reasonable,

Xen." "Henry George Liddell, Robert Scott, An Intermediate Greek-English Lexicon, Λογιστικός." Accessed May 19, 2021. http://www.perseus.tufts.edu/hopper/text?doc=Perseus%3Atext%3A1999.04.0058%3Aentry%3Dlogistiko%2Fs.

98. Republic, 435 e.

99. This can be compared to "*Crito* 46 B (one of the passages which the Christian apologists used to prove that Socrates knew the λόγος), *Theaetetus* 186 C ἀναλογίσματα πρός τε οὐσίαν καὶ ὠφέλειαν, and *Laws* 644 D. Aristotle *Eth.* 1139 a 12 somewhat differently."

"Plato, Republic, Book 4, Section 439d." Accessed May 19, 2021. http://www.perseus.tufts.edu/hopper/text?doc=Perseus%3Atext%3A1999.01.0167%3Abook%3D4%3Asection%3D439d.

100. Kenji Yoshino, "The City and the Poet." *Yale L.J.* 114 (2005): 1835, 1841–1868.

101. Etymologically speaking, the Liddell & Scott's A Greek-English Lexicon defines the word as, "ἐπιθυμητικός from ἐπιθυμέω [select] desiring, coveting, lusting after a thing, c. gen., Plat., etc.:—adv., ἐπιθυμητικῶς ἔχειν τινός ~ ἐπιθυμεῖν." Citing Liddell and Scott. *An Intermediate Greek-English Lexicon* (Oxford: Clarendon Press, 1889). "Henry George Liddell, Robert Scott, An Intermediate Greek-English Lexicon, Ἐπιθυμητικός." Accessed May 19, 2021. http://www.perseus.tufts.edu/hopper/text?doc=Perseus%3Atext%3A1999.04.0058%3Aentry%3De)piqumhtiko%2Fs.

See other references to Liddell & Scott's famous lexicon in legal secondary sources: Randall Baldwin Clark, "Platonic Love in a Colorado Courtroom: Martha Nussbaum, John Finnis, and Plato's Laws in Evans v. Romer." *Yale J. L. & Humanities* 12 (2000): 1, 5–6.

102. Republic, 439 d.

103. The Liddell & Scott's A Greek-English Lexicon defines the word as, "θυμοειδής 1 εἶδος 1.high-spirited, courageous, Lat. animosus, Plat., Xen. 2.hot-tempered, restive, id=Xen." "Henry George Liddell, Robert Scott, An Intermediate Greek-English Lexicon, Θυμοειδής." Accessed May 19, 2021. http://www.perseus.tufts.edu/hopper/text?doc=Perseus%3Atext%3A1999.04.0058%3Aentry%3Dqumoeidh%2Fs.

104. This spirit has been described in a distinctively Platonic sense of θυμόςas the power of noble wrath, which, unless perverted by a bad education, is naturally the ally of the reason, though as mere angry passion it might seem to belong to the irrational part of the soul, and so, as Glaucon suggests, be akin to appetite, with which it is associated in the mortal soul of the Timaeus 69 D. In Laws 731 B-C Plato tells us again that the soul cannot combat injustice without the capacity for righteous indignation. The Stoics affected to deprecate anger always, and the difference remained a theme of controversy between them and the Platonists. Cf. Schmidt, Ethik der Griechen, ii. pp. 321 ff., Seneca, De ira, i. 9, and passim. Moralists are still divided on the point. Cf. Bagehot, Lord Brougham: "Another faculty of Brougham . . . is the faculty of easy anger. The supine placidity of civilization is not favorable to animosity [Bacon's word for θυμός]." Leslie Stephen, Science of Ethics, pp. 60 ff. and p. 62, seems to contradict Plato: "The supposed conflict between reason and passion is, as I hold, meaningless if it is taken to imply that the reason is a faculty separate from the

emotions," etc. But this is only his metaphysics. On the practical ethical issue, he is with Plato.

105. "James Adam, The Republic of Plato, Book 4, Section 439E." Accessed May 19, 2021. http://www.perseus.tufts.edu/hopper/text?doc=Perseus%3Atext%3A1999.04.0094%3Abook%3D4%3Asection%3D439e.

106. *Id.*

107. "Plato, Republic, Book 4, Section 439e." Accessed May 19, 2021. http://www.perseus.tufts.edu/hopper/text?doc=Perseus%3Atext%3A1999.01.0168%3Abook%3D4%3Asection%3D439e.

108. "The judicial Power of the United States shall be vested in one supreme Court, and in such inferior Courts as the Congress may from time to time ordain and establish." U.S. Const. art. III, 1.

Further, Chief Justice Marshall in *Marbury v. Madison* stated, "the particular phraseology of the constitution of the United States confirms and strengthens the principle, supposed to be essential to all written constitutions, that a law repugnant to the constitution is void; and that courts, as well as other departments, are bound by that instrument." 5 U.S. (1 Cranch) at 180.

109. W.K.C. Guthrie, *A History of Greek Philosophy* (Cambridge Univ. Press, 1962): 419–434.

110. Republic, 550b.

111. *Id.*

112. Saikrishna Prakash, and Steven D. Smith. "How to Remove a Federal Judge." *Yale LJ* 116 (2006): 72 87–88.

113. Saikrishna Prakash, and Steven D. Smith. "How to Remove a Federal Judge." *Yale LJ* 116 (2006): 72 87–88, 136–137.

114. *Marbury v. Madison*, 5 U.S. (1 Cranch) 137, 177 (1803); accord *United States v. Nixon*, 418 U.S. 683, 703–705 (1974).

115. 163 U.S. 537 (1896).

116. 349 U.S. 294 (1955).

117. 163 U.S. 537.

118. 163 U.S. 537, 541 (1896).

119. 349 U.S. 294.

120. 349 U.S. 294 (1955).

121. 347 U.S. 483, (1954).

122. 576 U.S. ___ (2015).

123. Kenji Yoshino, "The Supreme Court, 2014 Term—Comment: A New Birth of Freedom?: Obergefell v. Hodges." *Harv. L. Rev.* 129 (2015): 147, 147.

Illustrating the differences of originalist and evolutionary document theories of interpreting the constitution, Andrew W. Schwartz writes discussing the *Obergerfell* case, "[t]he majority and dissenting opinions in *Obergefell v. Hodges*, the Supreme Court's recent decision finding that same-sex marriage is a constitutional right, offer a lucid comparison of originalism with evolutionary document theories of interpretation. The majority point out that the institution of marriage 'has evolved over time'. *Obergefell v. Hodges*, No. 14-556, slip op. at 6 (U.S. June 26, 2015). Finding that the right to marry the person of one's choice, regardless of their gender, was compelled by the due process clause of the Fourteenth Amendment, the majority described its task as interpreting a constitutional provision that sets forth broad principles rather than specific requirements. History and tradition guide and discipline this inquiry but do not set its outer boundaries. That method respects our history and learns from it without allowing the past alone to rule the present. The nature of injustice is that we may not always see it in our own times. The generations that wrote and ratified the Bill of Rights and the Fourteenth Amendment did not presume to know the extent of freedom in all of its dimensions, and so they entrusted to future generations a charter protecting the right of all person to enjoy liberty as we learn its meaning. When new insight reveals discord between the constitution's central protections and a received legal stricture, a claim to liberty must be addressed. *Id.* at 10-11 (citations omitted). In sharp contrast, Chief Justice Roberts and Associate Justice Alito, in their dissenting opinions, refused to recognize contemporary views of marriage, asserting that the notion of marriage as solely between a man and a woman is 'deeply rooted in this Nation's history and tradition.' *Id.* at 14 (Roberts, C.J., dissenting); *id.* at 2 (Alito, J., dissenting) (quoting *Washington v. Glucksberg*, 521 U.S. 701, 720–721 (1997)). Justice Scalia, in a separate dissent, relied on the public understanding of the meaning of marriage at the time the due process clause was ratified in 1868, which, he argued, universally confined marriage to a man and a woman. *Id.* at 4 (Scalia, J., dissenting)." Andrew W. Schwartz, "No Competing Theory of Constitutional Interpretation Justifies Regulatory Takings Ideology." *Stan. Envtl. L.J.* 34 (2015): 247, 25.

124. Laurence Tribe, "Equal Dignity: Speaking Its Name." *Harv. L. Rev. F.* 129 (2015): 16, 16.

125. "For me, the 'living Constitution' is not a convenient slogan for transforming our very imperfect constitution into something better than it is. While the effort to make the constitution into something truly wonderful is an ever-present temptation, the problem with this high-sounding aspiration is obvious: there are lots of competing visions of liberal democratic constitutionalism, and the constitution shouldn't be hijacked by any one of them. The aim of interpretation is to understand the constitutional commitments that have actually been made by the American people in history, not the commitments that one or another philosopher thinks they should have made. On this key point, I am closer to Justice Scalia than to Professor Ronald Dworkin. I part company when Scalia joins Alfarabi in assuming that the formal text contains the complete constitutional canon, thereby cutting himself off from the last seventy-five years of constitutional achievement."

Bruce Ackerman, "The Living Constitution." *Harv. L. Rev.* 120 (2007): 1737, 1754–1755.

126. With its source of power from U.S. Const. art. II, § 1, cl. 1.

127. Plato, Phaedrus 248d-e (Christopher J. Rowe trans., 1986) [hereinafter Phaedrus].

128. *Id.* at 247e–248e.

129. Republic, 550b.

130. *Id.*

131. National Archives. "Executive Orders Disposition Tables," August 15, 2016. https://www.archives.gov/federal-register/executive-orders.

132. "The Fifth Circuit Court of Appeals Rules Against Obama's Executive Actions on Immigration—The Atlantic." Accessed May 19, 2021. https://www.theatlantic.com/politics/archive/2015/11/fifth-circuit-obama-immigration/415077/. and "Obama to Appeal Immigration Ruling to Supreme Court—The New York Times." Accessed May 19, 2021. https://www.nytimes.com/2015/11/11/us/politics/supreme-court-immigration-obama.html.

133. "Catastrophe" used here in the Ancient Greek sense of "cata" and "strophe," meaning under turned or overturning. Oxford English Dictionary (2d ed. 1989).

"Etymology: < Greek *καταστροφή* overturning, sudden turn, conclusion, < *κατα-στρέφειν* to overturn, etc., < *κατά* down + *στρέφειν* to turn." *Id.*

134. With its power generally emanating from U.S. Const. art. 1.

135. 124 Stat. 119.

136. "Obama Signs Health Care Overhaul into Law - The New York Times." Accessed May 19, 2021. https://www.nytimes.com/2010/03/24/health/policy/24health.html.

137. *Nat'l Fed'n of Indep. Bus. v. Sebelius*, 132 S. Ct. 2566, 2580.

138. The Federalist No. 47, at 301 (James Madison) (Clinton Rossiter ed., 1961).

Chapter 4

What Is Money? The Debt–Promise to Pay–Answer to Anthropological Legal and Historical Analysis

Thomas Hobbes wrote in his *Leviathan* that the money exchanging hands, monetary policies, activities, and similar transactions were the blood of the "Leviathan"—the eponymous subject of the book.[1] Hobbes writes that this "blood" of the Leviathan includes the "collectors, receivers, and treasurers" and a separate set of treasures to pay public and private ministers.[2] Hobbes analogizes the financial transactions to the veins and arteries of a living man, stating that this "artificial man [the Leviathan] maintains his resemblance with the natural [man]; whose veins, receiving the blood from the several parts of the body, carry it to the heart; where, being made vital, the heart by the arteries sends it out again, to enliven and enable for motion all the members of the same."[3] In other words, the ability to have private exchanges of money as well as public supervised government exchanges of money allows the "Leviathan" to survive and function in the same way veins carry blood to different parts of the body to allow a human to live.

I. THE CURRENT MECHANISMS IN THE U.S.—AND MOST OF THE WORLD—FOR MONETARY POLICY

Historical Analysis of Tax Treaties and International Monetary Legal Framework: The U.S. Federal Reserve in the Post-Bretton Woods World

Ultimately, the mechanisms of finance in the United States are really the accumulation of historical precedents—both legal and non-legal (such as economic, but also social) —that lead to and have led to the current system, on a continuing and settled basis.

The legal and economic systems merging for the best system for an international monetary order can represent a balance of legal realism and legal formalism.

"Money" is printed by the U.S. government, designated as an official note. Value comes from how many of those printed pieces of paper exist. This is the basic concept of inflation. This concept of value and inflation is said to be connected to a commodity, such as how much gold or silver existed in the federal reserve physical locations or Fort Knox. Such systems have been in place since at least Mesopotamia where clay tablets were used to represent credit, or at least contracts that seem to resemble modern forms of fiat currency.[4]

The Federal Reserve System is made up of twelve regional banks,[5] a board of governors appointed by a president and confirmed by Senate.[6] But they are not under the executive branch of government.[7] The duty of the Federal Reserve in part is to control inflation.[8] Some inflation is key to economic success.[9] Inflation is a concept of value.[10] Deflation is the inverse.[11] The question is whether in a post-Bretton Woods system, is the key to a little bit of inflation, economic success? In other words, does inflation cause economic success or does economic success cause inflation?

Historically, much of the concepts of finance came from Mesopotamia. Indeed, "[m]uch evidence from Mesopotamia, Egypt, and Ugarit supports the notion that ancient kings commonly did impose general taxes to help finance the provision of royal services."[12] Per taxation, Ancient Mesopotamians had to pay taxes throughout their long history.[13] In Mesopotamia, around the years c.a. 2500–2000 BCE, many of these taxes were applied to various types of property, "income" or imposed through import duties[14] These taxes aimed to support governmental functions that included royal activities, religious temples, and other similar services.[15]

The Mesopotamian paradigm is notable because it indicates that Bronze Age society found such systems relevant—as we do today. Indeed, the system of commerce and taxation in Mesopotamia does not reflect the graduated income tax system that is currently in existence in the world, but it sounds surprisingly familiar.

Although much change has occurred between now and then, the modern system of finance and taxation started changing into its modern form in the 1800s. Taking an example from the "frontier" in Canada in the 1830s, the evolution of legal structures cannot be easily understood without understanding the historical, political, and economic situation in the Canadian territories.[16] In the 1830s, reformers attacked governmental officials, "over a variety of issues, including banking reform, taxation, educational policy, and the collection of quit rents to pay the costs of government."[17] Reformers ultimately mobilized support in various Canadian territories, such as Nova Scotia, to reform such policies.[18]

Interestingly, the United States simultaneously had similar issues to Canada but resolved them in a different fashion.[19] Debates in the United States were not limited to specific states' finances but over the role of gold and silver as a currency as opposed to credit as lent by banks.[20] Moreover, bank panics, deflation, and the rhetoric of Jacksonian Democrats and President Jackson's war against the Bank of the United States did not add to trust of banks and credit.[21] Jacksonian Democrats pushed for gold and silver to be the method of payment for land.[22]

This system of banking that was highly localized after Jackson's presidency changed during the Civil War under President Abraham Lincoln's administration. The contentious banking issues that existed in the 1830s returned during the Civil War under the Lincoln administration when the U. S. federal government actively sought funds to support the war—this caused Lincoln to sign the Legal Tender Act on February 25, 1862.[23] The concept of Legal Tender Act was that it allowed for the United States to issue "notes" and designate them legal tender for public and private debts—this replaced the specie system Jacksonian Democrats argued for in the 1830s.[24] At the time, Democrats from the remaining northern states during the Civil War opposed the Act, but found the unity of the Union more important and did not stage a large debate against the passage of the Act in Congress.[25]

Following the Civil War, the Lincolnian system changed over time from Reconstruction to World War I and World War II. After the collapse of the League of Nations and the post–World War II era, the United Nations started changing the monetary system as technology changed the global system of finance and taxation.

The system changed after World War II. It should be noted currently, the global system of finance is the largest it has been on average in history.[26] Indeed, this massive size is due to international trade and financial investment activity being global in nature.[27] This system resembles the concepts of the market as it originated in Bronze Age Egypt and Mesopotamia. The legal groundwork of the modern global foreign exchange markets has their origins in the Bretton Woods Agreement in 1944.[28] The Bretton Woods system sought to promote a uniform global monetary system, reductions in tariffs, and removal of trade barriers.[29]

Between WWII and 1971, the United States federal government's ability to pay its debts, concerned various stakeholders.[30] Despite concerns over the United States's ability to repay its debt and to maintain the creditworthiness of the United States, the U.S. dollar remained the world's "reserve currency."[31] Throughout the United States it was largely understood that the US dollar possessed particular strength and came with a reliable security plan enabling its exchange for gold.[32,33] However, in 1961 such belief was put into action when there was a major run on gold and gold supplies on Fort Knox and the federal reserve.[34] As a result, the federal reserves were severely depleted.[35]

At the time, the U.S. government thought its international tax policy could help improve its ability to gain revenue.[36] Using tax revenue to pay debts could possibly replace the American federal government's reliance on gold reserves.[37] The notion was comprised of a restructuring of the US tax system which offered greater incentives to invest within the US versus abroad.[38] Indeed, speaking to Congress, Secretary of the Treasury Clarence Douglas Dillon urged Congress to end the tax deferral regime because it would allow and encourage repatriation and U.S. corporations' investments in the United States.[39]

After WWII, the Bretton Woods convention seemed to address the seemingly unstable financial system.[40] The instability of the interwar period was marked by "the collapse of the gold standard, the Great Depression, the rise of protectionist" domestic measures, and the apparent connections all these failures had with each other.[41] Regarding pre-WWII finance, governments embraced the so-called "Beggar-Thy-Neighbour" policies to address the economic effects of the Great Depression.[42] These "Beggar-Thy-Neighbour" policies included increased tariffs, "currency devaluations", and "discriminatory trading blocs".[43] However, these policies did not improve the overall economic environment for most countries, even domestically.[44] Moreover, such policies added to the instability of international affairs.[45]

On the other hand, the benefit was that the Bretton Woods Agreement created a system of fixed exchange rates directly correlating to the U.S. dollar.[46] This fixed exchange rate allowed free trade to occur and for a commensurate standard at which currencies could compare themselves— the standard of the U.S. dollar.[47] Moreover, those agreeing to the Bretton Woods system also agreed to abstain from trade wars through lowering the value of their currencies—as had been done during the Great Depression.[48] It should be noted that Bretton Woods allowed for countries to regulate currencies to the extent that their domestic economies would otherwise be destabilized.[49]

The reform of the Bretton Woods system was a response to the "international monetary crisis of August 1971".[50] This monetary crisis was brought about when U.S. President Richard Nixon suspended the ability to convert U.S specie dollars into gold.[51] As a result of Nixon's suspension, floating fiat "exchange rates became the normal standard for industrialized liberal democracies".[52] This change in 1971 meant that no currency had a fixed value relating to another currency in place of the U.S. dollar.[53] In other words, all currencies had a floating value.[54] This change shaped the current "global foreign exchange market.[55] Since the 1970s, the global legal structure changed as the volume and intricacy of the global market changed and communications technologies made the execution of contracts and agreements easier to more effectively complete.[56] In conjunction with this complexity, the regulatory oversight of the foreign exchange market system has increased significantly as well as the risk and capital requirements for entering into such markets.[57]

Considering the theoretical perspective of economics, Keynesian policies historically governed those of most countries.[58] From the mid-20th century until the 1970s, Keynesian theory was used to justify "capital controls to protect domestic economic policies."[59] This was particularly true in developed countries using such theories to regulate capital flows.[60]

Ultimately, the post-Bretton Woods system after 1971 has removed the connection of currency to a tangible commodity. Now, it is a fiat system of currency. Akin to an 1830s dialectic is the synthesis of the Lincoln Administration to a full post-Bretton Woods system of fiat currency.

Should there be calls for a "New Bretton Woods" system?

The question remains: should there be a call for a "New Bretton Woods" system based on a dialectical connection of an understanding of legal realism and legal formalism? The answer is unclear, but perhaps a system based on a further understanding of the balance between economic and legal theory based on logic would be beneficial.

II. WHAT, THEN, IS OWNERSHIP?

Ownership is a concept that exists in law from a social perspective. Without a social context, ownership would not exist. From a legal formalistic point of view, ownership readily avails itself in law and contract. However, from a legal realistic point of view, formalism sometimes falls short of defining and articulating what ownership is. Is ownership separate from law or is ownership dependent on the existence and acceptance of law in a social context? In other words, does ownership exist independent of law? Likewise, does ownership exist independent of humans? Or does it exist only with the conception of humans' projection of what they determine as ownership?

In a search for definitions that are not readily apparent, analogous authority is more persuasive if it can be substantiated through example and demonstration of how the theory is related—specifically in this case, as related to the concept of ownership. There are various examples of the bifurcation of ownership, such as trust ownership delineating legal and equitable title.[61] Exploring the history and different types of ownership recognized in law can illuminate a clearer definition of ownership of property that is imperative for understanding "anthropology" —the *logos* of humans.

In a direct sense, Medieval and feudal law has influenced the common law English system that the United States has inherited. But this common law system that originated in the Anglo-Saxon Heptarchy had roots in the Roman codified system of law.[62] Though, the Code of Justinian (Codex

Justinianus)[63]—which is often cited as the basis for Roman law[64]—compiled in 529 CE was a conglomeration of previously decided cases, which is arguably case law—a type of judge-made law.[65] It can be argued civil or codified law is the compilation of judge-made law. In the Anglo-American tradition, judge-made law is now referred to as common law. If this is so, this is another way to say there is no difference between common law and civil law.

In a Medieval law sense,[66] ownership is control and possession of all beneficial—or destructive—uses of the property to the exclusion of all other peers and inferiors. The sovereign guarantees private "fee" (faith) possession. This means that the sovereign in a European Feudal can take property and the right to property away (*i.e,* nullify private fee ownership). By contrast, Sovereign ownership only exists by force supported by mystical ritual acceptance either through divine right or "the consent of the governed."

Although the historical origin of property rights is vital for understanding ownership, seeing how ownership affects practical use and other rights can analogously set the stage and clarify what ownership is. Ownership of property can be seen analogously through where it has significant importance: the world of tax. Who has ownership of property is the starting point for whom to tax.

The U.S. Supreme Court has ruled that in determining the question of ownership in relation to taxation that "no one fact is normally decisive but that all considerations and circumstances of the kind [the Court had] mentioned are relevant to the question of ownership and are appropriate foundations for findings on that issue."[67] In the same case, the court went on to say, "where . . . the benefits directly or indirectly retained blend so imperceptibly with the normal concepts of full ownership . . . To hold otherwise would be to treat the wife as a complete stranger; to let mere formalism obscure the normal consequences of [social] solidarity; and to force concepts of ownership to be fashioned out of legal niceties which may have little or no significance in such [cultural] arrangements."[68]

In this case, the court had a "substance over form approach," whereby it stated, "[s]o far as his dominion and control were concerned it seems clear that the trust did not effect any substantial change. In substance his control over the corpus was in all essential respects the same after the trust was created, as before. The wide powers which he retained included for all practical purposes most of the control which he as an individual would have."[69] This case seems to stand for the proposition that "legal"—that is title ownership over property—is likely not enough, on its own, to amount to ownership over property. In some sense, this seems to indicate that physical control over property is salient for determining ownership of property. Legal substantiation is not enough—economic substance must exist as well.[70]

Regarding a similar issue, the U.S. Tax Court, in its search for a definition of ownership, suggested that a benefit-and-burden test would be applicable for ownership of sale of property for tax purposes.[71] Indeed, how could a sale occur without ownership?[72] To find out if a sale took place, the court looked at several factors to determine if a benefits or burdens that would lead to the conclusion of a sale existed.[73] These factors were: "(1) Whether legal title passes; (2) how the parties treat the transaction; (3) whether an equity was acquired in the property; (4) whether the contract creates a present obligation on the seller to execute and deliver a deed and a present obligation on the purchaser to make payments; (5) whether the right of possession is vested in the purchaser; (6) which party pays the property taxes; (7) which party bears the risk of loss or damage to the property; and (8) which party receives the profits from the operation and sale of the property."[74] Like seeing various examples of what is sought, this does not give us the Platonic "form" of ownership.[75]

III. BUT IF WE KNOW WHAT MONEY "IS," WHAT ARE COMPANIES? MULTINATIONALS AND FUKUYAMA

It is a long-held legal idea in the United States that corporations are "persons."[76] But this is a fiction. Corporations are not people. Indeed, the concept of a corporation is a "fiction," in the sense that it is a human agglomeration. For that matter, all of law is a fiction.

Francis Fukuyama in his seminal book *The End of History and the Last Man* did not argue for an end to humanity as such, but a teleological goal for human development. He argued—in part—that history's teleology does not need to be interpreted only through an *a priori* perspective.

Fukuyama builds off Hegelian[77] thinking that employs Kantian terminology in his works on classical liberalism and *The End of History and the Last Man*.[78] Such terminology relates a vital part of Hegelian and Fukuyama's thinking.[79]

Indeed, "[m]ost currently trenchant ideas of liberalism may be reduced to the moral individual of Kant's *Groundwork to a Metaphysics of Morals*, *Metaphysics of Morals*, and *Critique of Moral Reason*, largely familiar from John Rawls' *A Theory of Justice* and the economic individual of Hobbes's *Leviathan* and Adam Smith's *The Wealth of Nations*."[80] But at the same time, "[t]his is a bit unfair, both to the fonts of the liberal tradition and to contemporary scholarship" because Fukuyama in his *The End of History and the Last Man* uses Hegelian ideas intertwined with liberalism but distinguishes them from Kant and Hobbes's writings.[81] Moreover, one of the often cited forms of these theories in Ronald Dworkin's *Law's Empire* (1986) does not fit into what scholars classify as liberalism; "[n]onetheless, . . . [Fukuyama and Dworkin] are the scholarly exceptions that prove the political rule."[82]

It is worthwhile discussing the contours of Hegelian—and its predecessor Kantian philosophical analysis that influenced Hegelian thought. *A priori* is making a judgment without reference to the outside world; they are inherently abstract thoughts and arguments.[83]

It may be useful to summarize Kant's epistemology and metaphysics as it relates to Idealism, which Hegel himself substantially changed. Indeed, in Kant's *Critique of Pure Reason*, he in large part rejects empiricism. Empiricism was the theory that information is received through our senses.[84] In rejecting empiricism, Kant's *Critique of Pure Reason* followed up on Hume's critique of inductive reasoning and causality.[85] In this endeavor, Kant states that Hume awoke him from his "dogmatic slumbers."[86] David Hume's skepticism demonstrates that a "cause" is not necessary for every perceived event.[87] For example, just because a cue stick appears next to some billiard balls does not prove the cue stick caused the balls to reach their place. This is not to say there may have been another force, such as a human arranging the balls in a certain way on the billiard table but rather a source that is wholly unavailable to human understanding through our senses. Kant goes to show—whereby he explores the ramifications of Hume's skepticism—stating that there could be forces entirely beyond the human capacity to understand what put the billiard balls in their place. Kant's *Critique of Pure Reason* argues that there is a *transcendental* reality that is independent of the human capacities for sensation.[88] Kant names these aspects only available to the mind through *a priori*[89]

Moreover, "[a]ccording to Kant, *a priori* concepts are part of a mental apparatus which orders the physical world into comprehensible form." It would be helpful to explore a few examples to clarify Kant's notion. Julio Thompson writes, "[o]ne example of a priori knowledge is space. We cannot see space. Nor can we perceive it by any of the other senses."[90] Rather, it should be noted, "space is an 'intuition' that our mind applies to the sensory data it receives." Thompson goes on to write, "[i]n Kant's view, unless we apply these a priori concepts, which he divides into various categories … the world is an incomprehensible jumble of stimuli, which have no inherent order of their own." [91]

J. Watson's table of Kantian *a priori* categories is an excellent summation:

An example of *a priori* thinking is that of all of mathematics; that is, the world completely within the minds of humans.[92] A posteriori positions are based on experience of the world. An example of a posteriori thinking is a person perceiving rain because the qualia[93] indicating it is raining. Synthetic judgments are judgments that are made by combining two ideas; this would be the observations that led to the development of Newtonian physics.[94] These synthetic judgments are not inherent in their premises.[95] Analytic judgments are judgments that are inherent in the abstract definitions provided.[96] Analytic judgments are inherent in their premises.[97]

Table 4.1 J. Watson's table of Kantian a priori categories.

Quantity	Quality
Unity	Reality
Plurality	Negation
Totality	Limitation
RELATION	**MODALITY**
Inherence and Subsistence	Possibility and Impossibility
Cause and Effect	Existence and Non-Existence
Community	Necessity and Contingency

Source: Julio A. Thompson, *Essays on Kelsen. Edited by Richard Tur and William Twining. New York: Oxford University Press. 1986. Pp. VIII, 345. $44.00*, 86 Mich. L. Rev. 1470, 1474 n.9 (1988).

Then, there is a way to combine all four terms. There can be analytic *a priori*. This would be demonstrated by a statement, such as "all kangaroos are animals." The idea of "animal" is contained in the idea of "kangaroo." Synthetic *a priori* is Kant's main interest in the *Critique of Pure Reason*.[98] That is judgments that are known to be true independent of experience but that gives us knowledge of the world.[99] An example of this is mathematics in general and Newtonian physics that is informative about the world.[100]

Fukuyama's theory of the "end of history" posits "using Hegel's historical analysis, optimistically called the post-Cold War period 'The End of History,'" in which Fukuyama means "that the direction in which we," that is, the world, "were heading was making it clear that democracy and liberty were our destiny, given their obvious superiority as systems of governance."[101] Henry Hansmann has argued an extension of Fukuyama's thesis of political history to the history and ultimate teleological goals of corporate law; "to put it differently, one's faith in reaching the end of history for corporate law may be closely tied to one's faith in achieving Fukuyama's original End of History in politics."[102] Although one can argue that corporate law and politics are separate in terms of their progression in history,[103] it seems that the two affect one another.

Though Fukuyama's thesis[104] may not be fulfilled in the modern-day,[105] it does present a compelling paradigm to interpret history and human society from an anthropological lens. Fukuyama focused his argument on the politics of society but did not contemplate the often unwritten, unsung, history of corporations, and corporate law. The effects of corporate law can be seen from the Dutch free state of Amsterdam issuing the first stocks,[106] or yet the related Tulip crisis in the Dutch city,[107] to the financial speculation leading to the Mississippi Bubble in the 1700s,[108] to the inflation in the U.S. Civil War,[109] the Economic Crisis in the U.S. in 1877,[110] to the collapse of the Bretton Woods system in the 1970s,[111] and even more recently the financial crisis of 2007/2008.[112] All of these events have in common that they were in part due to the accounting and legal structure of their respective jurisdictions and that they affected the political outcome in the years to follow.

However, the singular concept of "one law" or one regulation[113] that leads to the change does not take into account the vast magnitude and multifarious array of the memes[114] in existence affecting society.[115] This is why it is difficult to limit a theory of society through anthropology to one singular idea; there are many competing often compelling, non-contradictory, and contradictory ideas that equivocally substantiate a series of phenomena and events. This is not simply chaos theory. But an admission that one theory often is not enough to fully account for human affairs.[116]

One example of corporate history that tips Marxist theories of dialectical materialism on its head is Malcom Gladwell's description of the corporate proxy voting wars that led to the development of Joseph Flom building Skadden, Arps, Slate, Meagher, & Flom. Historically, "white-shoe" law firms consisted of white Anglo-Saxon Protestants (WASPS).[117] Specifically, the white-shoe firms had teamed with the management of multinationals corporations.[118] Indeed, when Flom was entering the legal market, the major law firms in New York operated like private social clubs—arguably akin to the private social clubs that existed in New York at the time.[119] These firms were known as "white-shoe" law firms.[120] These firms at the time sought only to hire individuals that had the following qualities: "lawyers who are Nordic, having pleasing personalities and 'clean-cut' appearances, are graduates of the 'right schools,' have the 'right' social background and experience in the affairs of the world, and are endowed with tremendous stamina."[121] If one did not fit into the foregoing "white-shoe" criteria, one would join a smaller firm or set up one's own firm.[122]

Flom instead of siding with the management and the gentlemen agreements—because such work was not given to him—but rather he "became the preeminent attorney handling proxy fights, and the white-shoe law firms were regularly outsourcing clients to him. While white-shoe firms disdained proxy fights in the 1950s and 1960s, by the 1970s and 1980s hostile takeovers had become big business,[123] and all firms wanted to get into the game. According to Flom, '[The white-shoe firms] thought hostile takeovers were beneath contempt until relatively late in the game, and until they decided that, hey, maybe we ought to be in that business, they left me alone. And once you get the reputation for doing that kind of work, the business comes to you first.'"[124]

One interesting caveat of the Flom story is that it seems to show that the Marxist theory of historical progression was not played out. Indeed, Flom did not side with management or the working side of the corporations, but he found another situation where the proxy legal attribute of the legal system allowed him to use his expertise. But his proxy war in it of itself does not seem to fit into the Marxist theory of dialectical materialism, because he neither sided with management nor the working force. He changed the socioeconomic paradigm on several layers of society completely.

The story of Flom is just one story of multiple memes functioning simultaneously. Indeed, Flom can fit into the "great man" theory of history. Yet, apart from Malcolm Gladwell's account, such stories do not often make their way to the sociological and anthropological—much less the public image—for thinking how society functions. In that sense, Flom's story is half "great man" theory of history and simultaneously, perhaps even dialectically—which is why it is such a good example of societal historically progression—he is also fitting into Tolstoy's theory of the "man" leading history featured in his second epilogue in *War and Peace*.[125] This is because Flom functions as one of many people working as a person in history.

Although individuals play unique roles as memes, law, and the systems it creates are the memes less subject to change.[126] Law ensures ownership, ownership leads to the legally satisfied functioning of sales. Once, legal structures have evolved sufficiently enough, then taxation seems to arise. That is to say, once a system of contracts exists, then a system of corporations has the base to inherently rise as an advanced form of contract. Thereafter, basic taxation superimposed on this form of corporate law causes the modern challenges of advanced taxation.[127] Indeed, prior to the nineteenth century, the modern form of taxation had never existed, and thus the challenges of such taxation had never been dealt with.[128] It affects the societal structure unlike any other system. Indeed, today there are hardly any philosophical or theoretical approaches to taxation and accounting.[129]

IV. THE FUTURE OF CORPORATE LAW: SHIFTING AGENCY AND PRINCIPLES' LENSES ANTHROPOLOGICALLY:

However, hitherto has been shown the history of corporations, the point is to use it to interpret present and future possibilities.

Examining a corporation is analogous to examining a contract or what the concept of ownership is from a legal realistic and legal formalistic point of view. Moreover, examining the concepts of ownership and a contract from an anthropological perspective could help give a sense of why the legal concept of agency exists in its current legal formulation. Such a perspective on agency would inform the preferable mechanisms of taxation.

V. THE LEGAL STRUCTURE OF DEBT AND MARKET CAPITALISM

Now, that a history and the possible futures of corporations and their ontology has been explored, it would help to examine how corporations and the legal structure of debt facilitates money. Examining the things that corporations create and produce is not engaging in floccinaucinihilipilification of dividends and interest. Rather, it is necessary to distinguish dividends from interest in a philosophical sense. Indeed, a Lockean analysis—given that it is the basis of Constitutional and property right interpretation—in the United States would be vital.

According to the United States Internal Revenue Code, a dividend is: (1) a distribution, (2) of property, (3) made by a corporation, (4) to its shareholders, (5) out of its earnings and profits in a taxable year.[130]

The payment of "dividends" constitutes a distribution of a corporation's (or partnership's) earnings to its stockholders (or partnership "shareholders," as in many American jurisdictions as a "Licensed Limited Partnership").[131] Dividends arise only from the fairly calculated profits or "surplus income" of a corporation.[132]

Income from dividends earned is unearned, even if the payee is an officer, director, or employee of the corporation, because even officers, directors, and employees who receive dividend payments are "sharing" in the profits of another legal entity, a collective but "incorporated" effort rather than "merely" each individuals' effort.

It is absurd to assert that the only value of a product is the manual labor that creates it. The skills of a metallurgist, an engine specialist, leather specialist, and rubber specialist are all essential to make a car. However, it is essential to unify and efficiently direct, coordinate, and organize these skills. Management and planning groups bring these skilled specialists together. The investor puts up capital by means of a risk. It is a sacrifice of daily pleasures and comfort by the investor. Putting up the money is an investment of putting up money that could be put up valuably elsewhere. The investors are those who fund unity of the manual labor skills. It is preposterous to say that manual laborers are the only ones who bring worth. Without the risk of investment funding the planning and management, the car would not be made. The investment of capital is the sine qua non of capitalism. Dividends are an essential aspect. Without the investor, there is no management, planning, or workers.

Dividends are the justly earned compensation for the most careful kind of gambling. Every investor accepts the risk of losing everything he has gambled, but he would not engage in such aleatory behavior if there were no incentives of a return in excess of his investment. The shareholder's equity ownership is the body of his investment. The dividend is his compensation for the time value sacrifice he has made for the creation of a greater or entirely new and unique good for the world. It is this use and redirection of economic surplus to creativity which advances civilization.

This is antithetical to the Lockean analysis.[133] "[I]n order to pay dividends to stockholders, corporations must pay employees a sum that is less than the full market value of what they produce. This is true if we accept John Locke's argument that the value of a good is completely due to the labor that was expended to create it."[134] In other words, Locke only sees the value in the time and work put into a product and would not recognize the investor's risk.

The OECD Model Convention on Income and on Capital defines dividends as "income from shares, 'jouissance' shares or 'jouissance' rights, mining shares, founders' shares or other rights, not being debt/claims, participating in profits, as well as income from other corporate rights which is subjected to the same taxation treatment as income from shares by the laws of the State of which the company making the distribution is a resident."[135]

The payment of interest on bonds and other debt constitutes direct expenses of, and to, any corporation, such as a loan.[136] The OECD Model Convention on Income and on Capital defines interest as, "income from debt-claims of every kind, whether or not secured by [a] mortgage and whether or not carrying a right to participate in the debtor's profits, and in particular, income from government securities and income from bonds or debentures, including premiums and prizes attaching to such securities, bonds or debentures."[137]

Such a discussion of dividends and interest would be lacking without a brief mention of their converse of royalties and professional services.

According to the United States Code Annotated, royalties are payments made for the license or use of property, such as mineral rights, copyrights, patents, etc.[138] Royalties act as a type of consideration for the use of a specialized aspect of intellectual property.[139]

The OECD Model Convention on Income and on Capital defines royalties as "payments of any kind received as a consideration for the use of, or the right to use, any copyright of literacy, artistic or scientific work including cinematograph films, any patent, trade mark, design or model, plan, secret formula or process, or for information concerning industrial commercial or scientific experience."[140]

The two definitions for royalties are similar, except that the OECD Model does not contain mention of mineral rights.[141] This is likely due to the phenomena that many countries do not consider minerals to be private property, but the United States does consider mineral rights to be private property.[142] Thus, often royalties are referred to as mineral royalties for the right to use the land.[143]

Fees for services—fees for technical services—involve the fruit of technical labor.[144] There is no set technical definition of these services, but they may include computer services, accounting, law, and agriculture.[145]

There is a difference from royalties because royalties involve the non-continuing creation and use of the specialized skill.[146] These are fees for technical services that are continually in use.[147]

VI. QUESTION: WILL THE U.S. TAX COURT APPLY ACTION 9 OF OECD BEPS?[148]

Will the U. S. Tax Court apply Action 9's recommendations regarding risk allocation for transfer pricing purposes?

In short, no.

The explicit non-stated—that is to say, the known unknown—reason is the balance of legal realism over legal formalism. In this case, the system of law in the United States in regard to tax law—a relatively new and fascinating system compared to contract law or corporate law —will weigh more toward formalism on the concept of risk allocation.

Tax law is a unique field not only because it is new but because it provides a clear angle to examine the concepts of legal formalism and legal realism.

The U.S. Tax Court will not apply the OECD BEPS Action 9 Recommendation regarding risk allocation for three reasons. (1) Two Constitutional reasons: (a) the Constitutional cavalcade of hierarchy regarding international law in the United States—much less the precedential value of a secondary source, such as OECD reports. (b) The concept of *stare decisis* that is embedded in the common law system of the Anglo-American tradition relies on cases being decided as they have been decided in the past. The tradition of upholding prior precedent is not easily broken—except for egregious reason.

(2) Given the status of international law and international secondary sources in the United States in addition to the concept of *stare decisis*, the U.S. Tax Court—as all courts in the United States—consistently build on judicial application of law. Four key transfer pricing cases since the 1986 transfer pricing tax reforms in the United States will be shown to support the concept of *stare decisis*.

(3) Finally, the most recent transfer pricing case—Amazon—shows that the court still upholds the prior precedential cases through *stare decisis*. Moreover and perhaps more importantly, in the international context regarding other countries' decision to implement Action 9, had the IRS brought the argument of Action 9 forward, not only would the entire case have been analyzed differently, but the prospect of bringing Action 9's reasoning forward, the IRS would have forfeited all claims to the pricing of the transferred intellectual property (IP) to the "empty company"—as will be shown later.

The OECD and the U.S. Tax Court of the United States diverge radically in their adherence to or derogation from the language of contracts as the basis for assessing the pecuniary income consequences of differential risk allocation by and through transfer pricing arrangements as featured in BEPS Actions 8–10, specifically Action 9.

Two polar opposites define the alternative approaches to the proper appraisal of income for purposes of taxation for transfer pricing. On the one hand, the U. S. Tax Court has focused on contractual language and terms of agreement. On the other hand, the OECD through BEPS jurisdictions (most of the rest of the world where policies have been formulated) choose to analyze actual economic behavior and reality, independent of the mere words chosen by the parties.

Globalization and technology have greater importance in our daily lives. As technology and industrial processes grow, technology leads to greater globalization, and, in turn, greater globalization of supply chains leads to more efficient technology. For example, years ago, heart problems would lead to death, but now small "battery" type instruments (pacemakers) can prevent heart attacks. The examples of the health benefits from technology are endless.

As technology becomes more efficient, globalization has also created supply chains and industrial production processes that are no longer local. As global supply chains increase in complexity, profits need to be properly allocated to certain jurisdictions for taxation purposes[149]—to raise revenue[150] support government functions for society's benefit.[151] This is a fundamental issue of international taxation.[152] The leading principle for the allocation is the arm's length principle, according to which related enterprises must charge prices that would have been charged in the open market. Although the principle goal aims at avoiding profit shifting, multinational enterprises for years used to shift profits to low tax jurisdictions to avoid taxes in high tax jurisdictions. In the early part of the twenty-first century, increased attention to these tax avoidance phenomena has led to the OECD's BEPS project to combat this harmful tax competition.[153] This is the most groundbreaking change to the international tax treaty[154] framework since the 1920s[155]—that was initially set up to facilitate cross-border trade.[156] This BEPS project has led to fundamental proposals—as a type of model law—to change the international tax system.[157]

One of the proposed changes in BEPS is the Action Plan 9 interpretation of conduct. The OECD seems to be indicating that for application of the arm's length principle, contractual arrangements should still be followed as long as they conform to actual economic reality. But, at a second glance—as will be explored more in-depth in this chapter—this is not the case. The OECD claims that the contracts will be looked at as long as they reflect what "should" (i.e., there was enough financial capacity to assume the risks)[158] have been contracted.

In the midst of this change, the U.S. Tax Court, and the other key parts of the U.S. tax structure—both domestic and international—runs contrary to the BEPS project's recommendations. There are many examples of these differences, such as the Republican Tax Reform Proposal by the Ways and Means Committee or the Trump tax proposal.[159] One example is especially evident in the U.S. Tax Court's recent case *Amazon* (2017) relating to transfer pricing.

Given these differences, there are many implications, such as a prospect of a political battle over the different jurisdictions' rights to tax certain revenue streams and bases[160] or a decrease in the importance of BEPS.[161]

The present rules can predict the future with a high degree of probability in regards to tax consequences, such as tax deductions or credits and their results.[162] However, the rough overall view of the present and the contradictions in the international tax system cannot determine the entire future clearly.[163]

The dichotomy between the U.S. Tax Court's decisions—especially the *Amazon* (2017) case—compared to the OECD proposals in Action Points 8–10 in regard to transfer pricing.

VII. PIVOT OF RISK AND TAXATION AND SUMMARY OF ARGUMENT

The pivot of this thesis revolves around BEPS Action Plan 9's proposed analysis of risk. Action Plan 9 seems to say that contracts are still first to be examined.[164] However, step (5) of the "Analysis of risks in commercial or financial relations," indicates that the OECD wants to look at what should—by OECD standards—have been contracted based on the financial capacity to assume such risks.[165]

Rutger Hafkenscheid's[166] article *The BEPS Report on Risk Allocation: Not So Functional* examines the BEPS Report on Transfer Pricing and risk allocation. Hafkenscheid argues that although Action 9 seems to purport that contractual allocations should still be examined, yet he demonstrates that "[i]f a company lacks the functionality, but has the capital to bear risks, the risks and remuneration—according to the OECD—should be allocated to the related party that does have the functionality." Functionality is the key factor and "contractual allocation may be followed only if the contract allocates the risks to where the OECD wants the risks to be allocated."

In short, the *two prongs* of step 5 in the new risk allocation analysis provide for (1) "*control over risk*" and (2) "whether the party assuming risk . . . has the *financial capacity to assume risk*"—each with its own definition provided by BEPS—both trump contracts.

However, in the end, this two-pronged analysis leads to different results comparing an affiliate within a corporate group and a stand-alone company. But, the purpose of the arm's length principle was to lead to the same results when comparing an affiliate within a corporate group and a stand-alone company—even if both companies conduct the exact same actions. Thus, step 5 of the new risk allocation analysis, paradoxically, takes the cake of the arm's length and eats it as well—creating uncertainty in the fiction of the arm's length principle.

Hafkenscheid's article seems most prescient given the results of two transfer pricing cases—especially the *Amazon* case. In those cases, the U.S. Tax Court decided to first look at the contractual arrangements, and then examine whether they conform to economic reality.[167] Indeed, the court found the contracts to conform to economic reality.

The main difference in the U.S. Transfer Pricing approach for risk allocation is that the United States has expressed—through the U.S. Tax Court—the intention to look at the contracts—and then see if they conform to economic reality.[168] While, on the other hand, the OECD through BEPS has stated in a disguised manner—and as uncovered by Hafkenscheid—that contracts will only be considered if they are what "should" have been contracted under the functional analysis whereby a party has the control to bear risk and remuneration accordingly.

NOTES

1. Leviathan, Thomas Hobbes Chapter xxiv of the Nutrition and Procreation of a Commonwealth.
2. Leviathan, Thomas Hobbes Chapter xxiv of the Nutrition and Procreation of a Commonwealth.
3. Leviathan, Thomas Hobbes Chapter xxiv of the Nutrition and Procreation of a Commonwealth.
4. Kathryn E. Slanski, "The Law of Hammurabi and Its Audience." *Yale J.L. & Human.* 24 (2012): 97, 98–99.
5. Board of Governors of the Federal Reserve System. "Federal Reserve Board - Federal Reserve Banks." Accessed May 20, 2021. https://www.federalreserve.gov/aboutthefed/federal-reserve-system.htm. *See.* Jessica Bulman-Pozen, "Our Regionalism." *U. Pa. L. Rev.* 1 66 (2018): 377, 442.
6. Indeed, saying there is gold or silver in Fort Knox as an exchangeable asset for fiat currency is no longer valid. "Such language may have been appropriate in earlier eras, when the U.S. dollar was legally backed by or convertible into real assets such as gold and silver, and thus the funds available for spending by the Treasury were limited by external resource considerations. Nevertheless, it is clearly inapplicable

today, as the modern U.S. dollar is a floating, fiat currency, whose nominal value is not tied to any fixed commodity or commitment to maintain a certain amount of real purchasing power. In place of stacks of gold bars in a vault deep underground at Fort Knox, the modern symbolic manifestation of America's monetary power is a computer at the Federal Reserve, where, in Chairman Bernanke's words, bank accounts are simply "mark [ed] up" as necessary in a manner tantamount to printing money." Rohan Grey, *Administering Money: Coinage, Debt Crises, and the Future of Fiscal Policy*, Ky. L.J. 109 (2021): 229, 259–60. *See*. United States Mint Public Enterprise Fund 31 U.S.C.A. § 5136 (West).

7. *See*. Peter J. Boettke, and Daniel J. Smith. "Federal Reserve Independence: A Centennial Review." *The Journal of Prices & Markets* 1, no. 1 (2012): 2013, 31–48. *Cf.* "Is the Federal Reserve Truly Independent from Executive Pressure?" Kevin Morrissey, "IV. Executive Influence on the Federal Reserve." *Rev. Banking & Fin. L.* 38 (2018): 37, 47.

8. "The Federal Reserve uses interest rates to strike a balance in monetary policy: interest rates that are too high will increase unemployment, but interest rates that are too low risk sparking rapid inflation." Harry Stein, "America Can Still Do Big Things: Dispelling the Fiscal Hysteria That Thwarts Good Public Policy." *Harv. L. & Pol'y Rev.* 11 (2017): 141, 153.

9. Indeed, "if one measures the economic success of wartime financing by focusing on the state's ability to extract tax revenue from a broad base of citizen/taxpayers while limiting the costs of inflation." Ajay K. Mehrotra, "Lawyers, Guns, and Public Moneys: The U.S. Treasury, World War i, and the Administration of the Modern Fiscal State." *Law & Hist. Rev.* 28 (2010): 173, 183.

10. Bernard Black and Reinier Kraakman, "A Self-Enforcing Model of Corporate Law." *Harv. L. Rev.* 109 (1996): 1911, 1981 n. 42. *See*. Richard S. Markovits, "On the Economic Efficiency of Using Law to Increase Research and Development: A Critique of Various Tax, Antitrust, Intellectual Property, and Tort Law Rules and Policy Proposals." *Harv. J. on Legis.* 39 (2002): 63, 92.

11. Richard S. Markovits, "Why Kaplow and Shavell's 'Double-Distortion Argument' Articles Are Wrong." *Geo. Mason L. Rev.* 13 (2005): 511, 619 n. 152.

12. Ajay K. Mehrotra, *Lawyers, Guns, and Public Moneys: The U.S. Treasury, World War One, and the Administration of the Modern Fiscal State*, Law & Hist. Rev. 28 (2010): 173, 183. Indeed, "if one measures the economic success of wartime financing by focusing on the state's ability to extract tax revenue from a broad base of citizen/taxpayers while limiting the costs of inflation." *Id.*

13. Russ VerSteeg, "Early Mesopotamian Commercial Law." *U. Tol. L. Rev.* 30 (1999): 183, 212–213.

14. Russ VerSteeg, "Early Mesopotamian Commercial Law." *U. Tol. L. Rev.* 30 (1999): 183, 212–213.

15. Russ VerSteeg, "Early Mesopotamian Commercial Law." *U. Tol. L. Rev.* 30 (1999): 183, 212–213.

16. Jim Phillips and Bradley Miller, "'Too Many Courts and Too Much Law': The Politics of Judicial Reform in Nova Scotia, 1830–1841." *Law & Hist. Rev.* 30 (2012): 89, 91.

17. Jim Phillips and Bradley Miller, "'Too Many Courts and Too Much Law': The Politics of Judicial Reform in Nova Scotia, 1830–1841." *Law & Hist. Rev.* 30 (2012): 89, 91.

18. Jim Phillips and Bradley Miller, "'Too Many Courts and Too Much Law': The Politics of Judicial Reform in Nova Scotia, 1830–1841." *Law & Hist. Rev.* 30 (2012): 89, 91.

19. Hon. Randall T. Shepard and Douglas Fivecoat, *Indiana's Supreme Court in the Civil War: How Can the Constitution Be Unconstitutional?*, Res Gestae, April 2006, at 29, 32.

20. Hon. Randall T. Shepard and Douglas Fivecoat, *Indiana's Supreme Court in the Civil War: How Can the Constitution Be Unconstitutional?*, Res Gestae, April 2006, at 29, 32.

21. Hon. Randall T. Shepard and Douglas Fivecoat, *Indiana's Supreme Court in the Civil War: How Can the Constitution Be Unconstitutional?*, Res Gestae, April 2006, at 29, 32.

22. Hon. Randall T. Shepard and Douglas Fivecoat, *Indiana's Supreme Court in the Civil War: How Can the Constitution Be Unconstitutional?*, Res Gestae, April 2006, at 29, 32.

23. Hon. Randall T. Shepard and Douglas Fivecoat, *Indiana's Supreme Court in the Civil War: How Can the Constitution Be Unconstitutional?*, Res Gestae, April 2006, at 29, 32.

24. Hon. Randall T. Shepard and Douglas Fivecoat, *Indiana's Supreme Court in the Civil War: How Can the Constitution Be Unconstitutional?*, Res Gestae, April 2006, at 29, 32.

25. Hon. Randall T. Shepard and Douglas Fivecoat, *Indiana's Supreme Court in the Civil War: How Can the Constitution Be Unconstitutional?*, Res Gestae, April 2006, at 29, 32.

26. David T. Bloom, "The Legal Underpinnings of the Global Foreign Exchange Market." *N.C. Banking Inst.* 23 (2019): 27, 28.

27. David T. Bloom, "The Legal Underpinnings of the Global Foreign Exchange Market." *N.C. Banking Inst.* 23 (2019): 27, 28.

28. David T. Bloom, "The Legal Underpinnings of the Global Foreign Exchange Market." *N.C. Banking Inst.* 23 (2019): 27, 28.

29. David T. Bloom, "The Legal Underpinnings of the Global Foreign Exchange Market." *N.C. Banking Inst.* 23 (2019): 27, 28.

30. Paul W. Oosterhuis, "The Evolution of International Tax Policy-What Would Larry Say?" *Ohio N.U. L. Rev.* 33 (2007): 1, 2–3.

31. Paul W. Oosterhuis, "The Evolution of International Tax Policy-What Would Larry Say?" *Ohio N.U. L. Rev.* 33 (2007): 1, 2–3.

32. Paul W. Oosterhuis, "The Evolution of International Tax Policy-What Would Larry Say?" *Ohio N.U. L. Rev.* 33 (2007): 1, 2–3.

33. Paul W. Oosterhuis, "The Evolution of International Tax Policy-What Would Larry Say?" *Ohio N.U. L. Rev.* 33 (2007): 1, 2–3.

34. Paul W. Oosterhuis, "The Evolution of International Tax Policy-What Would Larry Say?" *Ohio N.U. L. Rev.* 33 (2007): 1, 2–3.

35. Paul W. Oosterhuis, "The Evolution of International Tax Policy-What Would Larry Say?" *Ohio N.U. L. Rev.* 33 (2007): 1, 2–3.

36. Paul W. Oosterhuis, "The Evolution of International Tax Policy-What Would Larry Say?" *Ohio N.U. L. Rev.* 33 (2007): 1, 2–3.

37. Paul W. Oosterhuis, "The Evolution of International Tax Policy-What Would Larry Say?" *Ohio N.U. L. Rev.* 33 (2007): 1, 2–3.

38. Paul W. Oosterhuis, "The Evolution of International Tax Policy-What Would Larry Say?" *Ohio N.U. L. Rev.* 33 (2007): 1, 2–3.

39. Paul W. Oosterhuis, "The Evolution of International Tax Policy-What Would Larry Say?" *Ohio N.U. L. Rev.* 33 (2007): 1, 2–3. *See.* Revenue Act of 1962, Hearings before the Committee on Finance, U.S. Senate, 87th Cong. 2d Sess., on H.R. 10650, pt. I, p. 447–448; see also S. Rep. No. 87-1881, at 3662 (Dissenting Views).

40. David T. Bloom, "The Legal Underpinnings of the Global Foreign Exchange Market." *N.C. Banking Inst.* 23 (2019): 27, 28.

41. David T. Bloom, "The Legal Underpinnings of the Global Foreign Exchange Market." *N.C. Banking Inst.* 23 (2019): 27, 28.

42. David T. Bloom, "The Legal Underpinnings of the Global Foreign Exchange Market." *N.C. Banking Inst.* 23 (2019): 27, 28.

43. David T. Bloom, "The Legal Underpinnings of the Global Foreign Exchange Market." *N.C. Banking Inst.* 23 (2019): 27, 28.

44. David T. Bloom, "The Legal Underpinnings of the Global Foreign Exchange Market." *N.C. Banking Inst.* 23 (2019): 27, 28.

45. David T. Bloom, "The Legal Underpinnings of the Global Foreign Exchange Market." *N.C. Banking Inst.* 23 (2019): 27, 28.

46. David T. Bloom, "The Legal Underpinnings of the Global Foreign Exchange Market." *N.C. Banking Inst.* 23 (2019): 27, 28.

47. David T. Bloom, "The Legal Underpinnings of the Global Foreign Exchange Market." *N.C. Banking Inst.* 23 (2019): 27, 28.

48. David T. Bloom, "The Legal Underpinnings of the Global Foreign Exchange Market." *N.C. Banking Inst.* 23 (2019): 27, 28.

49. David T. Bloom, "The Legal Underpinnings of the Global Foreign Exchange Market." *N.C. Banking Inst.* 23 (2019): 27, 28.

50. David T. Bloom, "The Legal Underpinnings of the Global Foreign Exchange Market." *N.C. Banking Inst.* 23 (2019): 27, 28.

51. David T. Bloom, The Legal Underpinnings of the Global Foreign Exchange Market, 23 *N.C. Banking Inst.* 27, 28 (2019).

52. David T. Bloom, "The Legal Underpinnings of the Global Foreign Exchange Market." *N.C. Banking Inst.* 23 (2019): 27, 28.

53. David T. Bloom, "The Legal Underpinnings of the Global Foreign Exchange Market." *N.C. Banking Inst.* 23 (2019): 27, 28.

54. David T. Bloom, "The Legal Underpinnings of the Global Foreign Exchange Market." *N.C. Banking Inst.* 23 (2019): 27, 28.

55. David T. Bloom, "The Legal Underpinnings of the Global Foreign Exchange Market." *N.C. Banking Inst.* 23 (2019): 27, 28.

56. David T. Bloom, "The Legal Underpinnings of the Global Foreign Exchange Market." *N.C. Banking Inst.* 23 (2019): 27, 28.

57. David T. Bloom, "The Legal Underpinnings of the Global Foreign Exchange Market." *N.C. Banking Inst.* 23 (2019): 27, 28.

58. Philip J. MacFarlane, "The Imf's Reassessment of Capital Controls After the 2008 Financial Crisis: Heresy or Orthodoxy?" *UCLA J. Int'l L. & Foreign Aff.* 19 (2015): 167, 180.

59. Philip J. MacFarlane, "The Imf's Reassessment of Capital Controls After the 2008 Financial Crisis: Heresy or Orthodoxy?" *UCLA J. Int'l L. & Foreign Aff.* 19 (2015): 167, 180.

60. Philip J. MacFarlane, "The Imf's Reassessment of Capital Controls After the 2008 Financial Crisis: Heresy or Orthodoxy?" *UCLA J. Int'l L. & Foreign Aff.* 19 (2015): 167, 180. *Cf.* "Prior to an examination on the impact of neoliberalism on the policics of the IMF and World Bank, it is worth discussing the evolution of political economics. During a time when government regulations were desired Keynesian economics became the most popular. From the Great Depression until the end of World War II, Keynesian economics had its primary influences on economic policies. Keynes presumed that in order to correct market imperfections, state intervention had to be implemented. One of the most important lessons which Keynes helped teach was that markets are not self-correcting and government intervention is required to ensure recovery and a return to full employment." Mark J. Wolff, "Failure of the International Monetary Fund & World Bank to Achieve Integral Development: A Critical Historical Assessment of Bretton Woods Institutions' Policies, Structures & Governance." *Syracuse J. Int'l L. & Com.* 41 (2013): 71, 96–97.

61. Ganesh Sitaraman, "Economic Structure and Constitutional Structure: An Intellectual History." *Tex. L. Rev.* 94 (2016): 1301, 1315.

However, Harrington was the first theorist to make explicit--even more so than Aristotle—that the forms of government were based on property ownership. "If one man be sole landlord of a territory," he wrote, "his empire is absolute monarchy." If the few or a nobility, or a nobility with the clergy, be landlords . . . the empire is mixed monarchy. . . . And if the whole people be landlords, or hold the lands so divided among them, that no one man, or number of men, within the compass of the few or aristocracy, overbalance them, the empire . . . is a commonwealth."

Id.; Cf. Linda R. Hirshman, "The Virtue of Liberality in American Communal Life." *Mich. L. Rev.* 88 (1990): 983, 1000–01.

Although Aristotle did not elaborate on the role of the particular virtue of liberality in the public realm, the Politics reveals his assumptions about moderation in the pursuit of money and the objects of moderation in its retention. For example, in describing the household, Aristotle makes the point that wealth is limited to the resources necessary for its subsistence. He distinguishes the accumulation of wealth obtained by trade, which is potentially unlimited, and concludes that people pursue the accumulation of excessive wealth due to anxiety about their livelihoods, an anxiety so great that they neglect their moral well-being. In response to this problem, Aristotle reiterates the theme of moderation. Disputing Plato's scheme in the Republic of common ownership of property, Aristotle distinguishes between the love of money, which he accepts as universal, and the "excess" of such love, which he condemns. Immediately thereafter, he reminds the reader that the function of the form of goodness he calls liberality "consists in the proper use which is made of property."

Id. See also Maxwell M. Garnaat, "The Republic of Virtue: The Republican Ideal in British and American Property Law." *Cornell Int'l L.J.* 51 (2018): 731, 735. "Property ownership in Aristotle's republicanism mirrors his larger conception of politics: it encourages a middle ground that avoids both 'rule of the people in its extreme form,' a crude and destructive anarchy, or 'unmixed oligarchy' that—without the restraint of a mixed government—results in 'tyranny.'" *Id.*

62. Thornton M, Hinkle, "Magna Charta." *Yale L. J.* 8 (1899): 262, 264–65.

> Who were the people that gave to all time this model for bills of rights and constitutions? The prior history of the island is that of a series of conquests, beginning with that of the Romans, who found a rude, savage people, whom they left four centuries later, more civilized, but less brave and warlike, to become an easy prey to foreign invasion. To protect themselves from the Picts and Scots of the north they called in the aid of the Anglo-Saxons, who drove out not only the Picts and Scots, but the majority of those who had invited them there. They founded the Heptarchy, which 450 years of Danish invasion and other exciting causes gradually welded into one kingdom, whose people were to remain the same Anglo-Saxon people through Danish invasions and Norman Conquest. *Id.*

63. Code of Justinian, The Encyclopedia Britannica, (Nov. 12 2014), http://www.britannica.com/topic/Code-of-Justinian (last visited Oct. 15, 2018).

64. "Numerous codifications or collections of the law preceded the 533 A.D. Code of Justinian. A collection of Imperial statutes was prepared by the jurist Papirius Justus in the latter part of the second century AD203 Under Diocletian, there was prepared a Codex Gregorianus which recorded constitutions from Hadrian to the approximate date of 295 AD. There followed a Codex Hermogenianus that compiled constitutions up to approximately 365 AD, and then a Codex Theodosianus under the auspices of Theodosius II that pertained to the Eastern Empire and was completed in 439 AD at the instance of Valentinian III for the Western Empire.

The later Roman law of delict derived from the Twelve Tables, and of course the customary law that preceded the Twelve Tables, as further designed at the warp and woof of jurists and Praetors to produce as complete as possible structure of civil liability. It is recognized now as a major development "from archaic formalism to rationalism." Of the sources of later Roman law the Institutes of Justinian (483–562 AD) proclaim: "Our law comes either from written or unwritten sources, just as among the Greeks; some laws are written, others unwritten. Written law comprises legislation, legis (enactments of the comitia), plebiscites, resolutions of the Senate, the will of the Emperor (in its various manifestations), the edicts of magistrates and the answers of the learned."

M. Stuart Madden, "The Graeco-Roman Antecedents of Modern Tort Law." *Brandeis L.J.* 44 (2006): 865, 901.

65. "Rather, Justinian's committees of jurists provided basically two reference works containing collections of past laws and extracts of the opinions of the great

Roman jurists." Code of Justinian, Encyclopedia Britannica, https://www.britannica.com/topic/Code-of-Justinian (last visited March 8, 2020).

66. Roscoe Pound, "Fifty Years of Jurisprudence." *Harv. L. Rev.* 50 (1937): 557, 582 fn. 129. Medieval law in this sense as a combination of "canon and feudal law," particularly in Anglo-Saxon Heptarchy that would later be united under Alfred the Great in 800 A.D. into England.

> Vol. 1 (1920). Vol. 2, The Jurisprudence of the Greek City (1922), deals with the second of six types of law, as determined by types of society, of which he had proposed to treat. He projected an ideological study of law as related to those types, namely, (1) origins in totemic society, (2) tribal law, (3) civic law, i.e., a type of legal order determined by the 'social tie of the city state', (4) medieval law in its combination as canon and feudal law, (5) 'individualist jurisprudence', i.e., the law as determined by a competitive individualist organization of society, and (6) the beginnings of socialistic jurisprudence. True to the tradition of historical jurisprudence, it is a survey of social control as a whole. True to the British tradition it is a political interpretation or better political-sociological. Philosophically its pluralist idealism has some affinity to Kohler's neo-Hegelian "complex idea". Indeed Kohler might unify Vinogradoff's six types by the idea of civilization.

67. *Helvering v. Clifford*, 309 U.S. 331, 336–337, 60 S. Ct. 554, 557, 84 L. Ed. 788 (1940).

68. *Helvering v. Clifford*, 309 U.S. 331, 336–337, 60 S. Ct. 554, 557, 84 L. Ed. 788 (1940). Author replaced the word "family" with "social" and the word "household" with "cultural."

69. *Helvering v. Clifford*, 309 U.S. 331, 335, 60 S. Ct. 554, 556, 84 L. Ed. 788 (1940). See. *Comm'r v. Sunnen*, 333 U.S. 591, 595, 68 S. Ct. 715, 718, 92 L. Ed. 898 (1948).

70. "We think the Board justifiably concluded from its findings that the transaction between the taxpayer and the trustee bank, in written form a transfer of ownership with a lease back, was actually a loan secured by the property involved. General recognition has been given the 'established doctrine that a court of equity will treat a deed, absolute in form, as a mortgage, when it is executed as security for a loan of money.' In the field of taxation, administrators of the laws and the courts are concerned with substance and realities, and formal written documents are not rigidly binding. Congress has specifically emphasized the equitable nature of proceedings before the Board of Tax Appeals by requiring the Board to act 'in accordance with the rules of evidence applicable in courts of equity of the District of Columbia.' Revenue Act 1928, s 601, 26 U.S.C. s 611, 26 U.S.C.A. Int. Rev. Acts, page 456." *Helvering v. F. & R. Lazarus & Co.*, 308 U.S. 252, 255, 60 S. Ct. 209, 210–211, 84 L. Ed. 226 (1939).

71. *Calloway v. Comm'r*, 691 F.3d 1315, 1327 (11th Cir. 2012).

72. *Calloway v. Comm'r*, 691 F.3d 1315, 1327 (11th Cir. 2012).

73. *Calloway v. Comm'r*, 691 F.3d 1315, 1327 (11th Cir. 2012).

74. *Calloway v. Comm'r*, 691 F.3d 1315, 1327 (11th Cir. 2012). See. "Grodt & McKay Realty, 77 T.C. at 1237–38 (internal citations omitted); see also Anschutz, 664 F.3d at 324–25." *Id.*

75. Defining Plato's forms, Kenji Yoshino writes: "In the Republic, Plato describes the existence of immutable, abstract, and invisible Forms. These Forms are the ideals to which Plato seeks to anchor the state and the human soul, which is the microcosm of the state. The highest Platonic aspiration for human beings is to bring us closer to these Forms. The difficulty is that our ordinary modes of perception—such as our senses—cannot seize these ideas. Only right reason, as exercised through dialectic, can do so in any systematic way." Kenji Yoshino, "The City and the Poet." *Yale L.J.* 114 (2005): 1835, 1843.

76. Historically the history of corporations derives from the medieval concept of a university; whereby, universities, such as the University of Paris, were the first corporations. "City Making consists of four large parts. The first is an intellectual history of Anglo-American local government law. Frug traces the city as a legal concept from its origins in the medieval law of corporations. The medieval municipal corporation was formally a type of chartered corporation, governed by the same law that covered business enterprises and universities: All of these entities were voluntary associations of citizens—private enterprises—and agents of government in the sense that they operated according to charters granted by the state and were required to serve the public interest. The corporation was a hybrid of what we now think of as public and private; it was an agent of government and an association of citizens. A radical turning point in Frug's history comes with the development of a sharp public/private divide in the nineteenth century that redefined American cities as purely public governmental entities or 'creatures of the state'. The public/private division of corporations initiated a change in local government doctrine that deprived cities of much of the formal autonomy they enjoyed as chartered corporations and submerged the associational aspects of cities in favor of their more technocratic, governmental qualities." Richard Thompson Ford, "Bourgeois Communities: A Review of Gerald Frug's City Making." *Stan. L. Rev.* 56 (2003): 231, 232.

77. Fukuyama adopts Alexandre Kojève's approach to Hegelian concepts.

78. Historically the history of corporations derives from the medieval concept of a university; whereby, universities, such as the University of Paris, were the first corporations.

"City Making consists of four large parts. The first is an intellectual history of Anglo-American local government law. Frug traces the city as a legal concept from its origins in the medieval law of corporations. The medieval municipal corporation was formally a type of chartered corporation, governed by the same law that covered business enterprises and universities: All of these entities were voluntary associations of citizens—private enterprises—and agents of government in the sense that they operated according to charters granted by the state and were required to serve the public interest. The corporation was a hybrid of what we now think of as public and private; it was an agent of government and an association of citizens. A radical turning point in Frug's history comes with the development of a sharp public/private divide in the nineteenth century that redefined American cities as purely public governmental entities or "creatures of the state." The public/private division of corporations initiated a change in local government doctrine that deprived cities of much of the formal autonomy they enjoyed as chartered corporations and submerged the associational aspects of cities in favor of their more technocratic, governmental qualities."

Richard Thompson Ford, "Bourgeois Communities: A Review of Gerald Frug's City Making." *Stan. L. Rev.* 56 (2003): 231, 232, quoting Gerald E. Frug, *City Making: Building Communities Without Building Walls* 39–50 (1999).

79. David A. Westbrook, "Liberal Environmental Jurisprudence." *U.C. Davis L. Rev.* 27 (1994): 619, 712 fn. 161.

80. David A. Westbrook, "Liberal Environmental Jurisprudence." *U.C. Davis L. Rev.* 27 (1994): 619, 712 fn. 161.

81. David A. Westbrook, "Liberal Environmental Jurisprudence." *U.C. Davis L. Rev.* 27 (1994): 619, 712 fn. 161.

82. David A. Westbrook, "Liberal Environmental Jurisprudence." *U.C. Davis L. Rev.* 27 (1994): 619, 712 fn. 161.

83. According to Kant, a priori concepts are part of a mental apparatus which orders the physical world into comprehensible form. A few examples should clarify this notion. One example of a priori knowledge is space. We cannot see space. Nor can we perceive it by any of the other senses. Instead, space is an "intuition" that our mind *applies* to the sensory data it receives. In Kant's view, unless we apply these a priori concepts, which he divides into various categories, *see* note 10 *infra*, the world is an incomprehensible jumble of stimuli, which have no inherent order of their own.

It may be helpful to consider a rather American application of this German philosophy. Mom places her famous apple pie in the refrigerator and closes the door. Our sensory data tell us that this time-honored delicacy has disappeared. Yet this observation never develops into a thought because we apply the a priori concept that the world has continuity to it. Thus, Kant concludes, what we consider reality is really a *synthesis* of a priori concepts and the constant flow of sensory data. Scholars differ over whether Kant believed the light went out when the refrigerator door was closed.

Having reviewed Kant's basic stance, the notion of *causality* as an a priori concept is easier to comprehend. Just as the a prior concept of space operates as a lens through which we view the jumbled physical world in spatial terms, so does the a priori concept that events have causes render our view of reality in causal terms. *See* I. KANT, CRITIQUE OF PURE REASON *189–211. For a concise exegesis of the six proofs Kant employed to establish is theory, see N. SMITH, A COMMENTARY TO KANT'S 'CRITIQUE OF PURE REASON' 363–81 (1918)." Julio A. Thompson, *Essays on Kelsen*. Edited by Richard Tur and William Twining (New York: Oxford University Press, 1986), pp. VIII, 345. $44.00, 86 *Mich. L. Rev.* 1470, 1474 fn. 9 (1988).

84. Julio A. Thompson, *Essays on Kelsen*. Edited by Richard Tur and William Twining (New York: Oxford University Press, 1986), pp. VIII, 345. $44.00, 86 *Mich. L. Rev.* 1470, 1474 fn. 9 (1988).

85. Steven D. Smith, "Believing Like a Lawyer." *B.C. L. Rev.* 40 (1999): 1041, 1111–1112. *See*. Julio A. Thompson, *Essays on Kelsen*. Edited by Richard Tur and William Twining (New York: Oxford University Press, 1986), pp. VIII, 345. $44.00, 86 *Mich. L. Rev.* 1470, 1474 fn. 9 (1988).

86. F.S.C. Northrop, "Law, Language and Morals." *Yale L.J.* 71 (1962): 1017, 1028. *See.* Chapter I. the General Concept of Rights, *Stan. L. Rev.* 58 (2006): 2000, 2006.

87. "Kant's system arose somewhat as an historical accident. Hume had arrived at scepticism in dealing with the concept of causation. Kant sought to solve Hume's problem (i.e., to show a necessary connection *a priori* between cause and effect) and in that effort (that he succeeded is doubtful) found a single principle for the deduction of concepts of pure understanding. He developed a system of *a priori* synthetical principles which are the basis of possible experience but which can not be referred to things in themselves. Mind was set apart from outward things. Kant's principal work appeared before the discovery of the conservation of matter and energy, the doctrine of evolution, the laws of thermodynamics, the electronic theory of matter, and the more recent theories of special and general relativity. The newer ideas do not abolish the Kantian system, but, on the whole, they have tended to diminish its influence. Kant formulated his ideas with amazing confidence in his own position and with extraordinary care and skill, but yet as one attempts to follow him into the transcendental atmosphere where his reasoning leads, and as one contemplates the luxuriant manifoldness of all that which lies beyond the mind, the reflection intrudes itself that *subtilitas naturae subtilitatem argumentandi multis partibus superat.*" A. Kocourek, Lezioni Di Filosofia Del Diritto. by Giorgio Del Vecchio. Città Di Castello, Società Anonima Tipographica "Leonardo Da Vinci," 1930. Pp. IV, 351, 40 *Yale L.J.* 1129, 1130 (1931).

88. *See generally* Frederick C. Beiser, *German Idealism: The Struggle Against Subjectivism 1781–1801* (2002).

89. Julio A. Thompson, *Essays on Kelsen.* Edited by Richard Tur and William Twining (New York: Oxford University Press, 1986), pp. VIII, 345. $44.00, 86 *Mich. L. Rev.* 1470, 1474 fn. 9 (1988).

90. Julio A. Thompson, *Essays on Kelsen.* Edited by Richard Tur and William Twining (New York: Oxford University Press, 1986), pp. VIII, 345. $44.00, 86 *Mich. L. Rev.* 1470, 1474 fn. 9 (1988).

91. Julio A. Thompson, *Essays on Kelsen.* Edited by Richard Tur and William Twining (New York: Oxford University Press, 1986), pp. VIII, 345. $44.00, 86 *Mich. L. Rev.* 1470, 1474 fn. 9 (1988).

92. This is an arguable point.

93. "Qualia" used here David Hume's sense of the world. Kant wrote in his *Prolegomena to Any Future Metaphysics* "I freely admit that it was the remembrance of David Hume which, many years ago, first interrupted my dogmatic slumber and gave my investigations in the field of speculative philosophy a completely different direction." Immanuel Kant, *Prolegomena to Any Future Metaphysics [1783]*, Lewis W. Beck, ed. and trans. (Bobbs-Merrill: Indianapolis, 1985).

94. Indeed, "[t]he 'synthetic a priori'—Kant's technical term for a basis of knowledge that is given rather than derived—thus removes from Newtonian physics any experiential constraints. As Kant himself makes clear, this nonempirical form of knowledge is not adequate to physics; he insists, however, that it is adequate to ethics. Natural science 'may accept many propositions as universal on the evidence

of experience', Kant says, '[b]ut it is otherwise with Moral Laws. These, in contra-distinction to Natural Laws, are only valid as Laws, in so far as they can be rationally established à priori and comprehended as necessary'. The moral universe is a universe unindebted to empirical observations. In its preassigned domain, it can enjoy that loftiest of privileges, the privilege of 'apodeictic certainty'." Wai Chee Dimock, "Rethinking Space, Rethinking Rights: Literature, Law, Science." *Yale J.L. & Human.* 10 (1998): 487, 493–494. *See.* "Immanuel Kant, *The Philosophy of Law* 15 (W. Hastie trans., Edinburgh, T. & T. Clark 1887). This is a translation of Kant's Metaphysische Anfangsgrunde der Rechtslehre (1796), also translated as The Metaphysical Elements of Justice." *Id.* at fn. 29.

95. In terms of inferential philosophical syllogistic logic, "a synthetic judgment, in Kantian terms--that cannot be reduced to a logical, syllogistic form solely on the basis of premises." André LeDuc, "Making the Premises About Constitutional Meaning Express: The New Originalism and Its Critics." *BYU J. Pub. L.* 31 (2016): 111, 199.

96. "This distinction is similar to Kant's distinction between analytic and synthetic judgments. For Kant, an analytic judgment is one that breaks a concept down into its constituent parts. For example, all bachelors are unmarried. On the other hand, Hedge is using these terms to describe not just statements but a method. For example, an analytic method is one that focuses on a single conception and lays out its constituent parts." Catharine Pierce Wells, "Langdell and the Invention of Legal Doctrine." *Buff. L. Rev.* 58 (2010): 551, 618 fn. 152.

97. See André LeDuc, "Making the Premises About Constitutional Meaning Express: The New Originalism and Its Critics." *BYU J. Pub. L.* 31 (2016): 111, 199. In terms of inferential philosophical syllogistic logic, "a synthetic judgment, in Kantian terms—that cannot be reduced to a logical, syllogistic form solely on the basis of premises." *Id.*

98. Angelica Nuzzo, "The Critique Of Judgment: Reflective Judgment, Determinative Judgment, And The Problem Of Particularity." *Wash. U. Jur. Rev.* 6 (2013): 7, 21. For an in depth discussion of Kant's idea of synthetic a priori see the follwing,

In the first *Critique* a *priori* principles and judgments make experience possible insofar as—and precisely because—they are *synthetic*. In the horizon of the *Critique of Judgment*, Kant contends that those synthetic a priori principles contain that which all our empirical cognitions "*have necessarily in common*"; hence that on the basis of the synthetic *a priori* principles (the transcendental laws of nature), "the *analytic* unity of all experience" first becomes possible. Strikingly, however, Kant now admits that the synthetic *a priori* principles still do not make possible "that *synthetic* unity of experience as a system that connects under one principle empirical laws *also according to that in which they differ*." Clearly, in this passage, Kant presents as analytic what the first *Critique* claims instead to be synthetic (i.e., the unity of nature--whereby the ambiguity of "nature" once taken as nature in general, once taken as nature in its empirical laws should be underscored), thereby advancing the further need to guarantee the *synthetic* unity of the manifold empirical forms of experience. Those same transcendental principles that the first *Critique* demonstrates to be synthetic are recognized here as a merely analytic function. Although logically their synthetic nature is not repealed, Kant now assesses their transcendental role within the process of our *empirical* cognition of nature. The focus has changed from the order of nature in general to the manifold of nature's empirical forms. With regard to this further problem, those transcendental principles provide (only) the *analytic* unity of experience in general by expressing that which all experiences have in common. Yet, since they cannot say anything regarding how different empirical laws actually differ from each other, they cannot ground the *synthetic* unity of empirical cognitions or the system of empirical laws of nature. *Id.*

99. Wai Chee Dimock, "Tenth Anniversary Symposium: New Direction: Rethinking Space, Rethinking Rights: Literature, Law, Science." *Yale J.L. & Human.* 10 (1998): 487, 493–94. Providing a definition of synthetic a priori in a Kantian sense see the following within the context of ethics,

> The "synthetic a priori"—Kant's technical term for a basis of knowledge that is given rather than derived—thus removes from Newtonian physics any experiential constraints. As Kant himself makes clear, this nonempirical form of knowledge is not adequate to physics; he insists, however, that it is adequate to ethics. Natural science "may accept many propositions as universal on the evidence of experience," Kant says, "but it is otherwise with Moral Laws. These, in contradistinction to Natural Laws, are only valid as Laws, in so far as they can be rationally established a priori and comprehended as necessary." The moral universe is a universe unindebted to empirical observations. In its preassigned domain, it can enjoy that loftiest of privileges, the privilege of "apodeictic certainty. *Id.*

100. Id. Cf. Jeffrey M. Lipshaw, "The Epistemology Of The Financial Crisis: Complexity, Causation, Law, And Judgment." *19 S. Cal. Interdisc. L.J.* 299, 314 n.53 (2010). Lipshaw compares and contrasts a priroi knowelldge in Kant's thinking and Hume's thinking.,

> What we can know a priori was a subtle move on Kant's part. He criticized Hume first for failing to acknowledge that mathematics involves synthetic a priori knowledge, i.e., concepts not otherwise self-evident that can be derived purely through the exercise of reason. The question then is not whether synthetic a priori knowledge is possible (because it is with respect to mathematics), but how, and whether we might have synthetic a priori knowledge beyond the examples of mathematics. Prolegomena, supra note 20, at 21–24. The answer is a cautious "yes." We can have metaphysical knowledge of synthetic a priori concepts like substance or causality "on which alone experience is possible, but never of the laws to which things may in themselves be subject, without reference to possible experience.

Id. at 53–54. Kant emphasized this point later in the Prolegomena, supra note 20, at 72–73:

Hence if the pure concepts of the understanding do not refer to objects of experience but things in themselves (noumena), they have no significance whatever. They serve, as it were, only to decipher appearances, that we may be able to read them as experience. The principles which arise from their reference to the sensible world, only serve our understanding for empirical use. Beyond this they are arbitrary combinations, without objective reality, and we can neither cognise their possibility a priori, nor verify their reference to objects, let alone make it intelligible by any example… ." *Id.*

101. Max M. Kampelman, "Entering New Worlds: A Challenge." *Colum. J. Transnat'l L.* 32 (1995): 457, 458 (1995).

102. Henry Hansmann, "How Close Is the End of History?" *J. Corp. L.* 31 (2006): 745, 749 (2006).

Cf. "Henry Hansmann, How Close Is the End of History?" *J. Corp. L.* 31 (2006): 745, 745, 749 (stating that one's faith in reaching the end of history for corporate law may be closely tied to one's faith in achieving Fukuyama's original End of History in politics). Curiously, Hansmann's commentary could be seen to parallel that expressed in Francis Fukuyama, *The End of History and the Last Man* (1992), which served as the inspiration for the title of Hansmann and Kraakman's article, The End of History for Corporate Law. See Hansmann & Kraakman, supra note 1, at 439. Francis Fukuyama, *Our Posthuman Future: Consequences of the Biotechnology Revolution* (2002), qualifies Fukuyama's original "end of history" thesis, much like Hansmann may be seen to have qualified the strength of the original "end of history for corporate law" prediction that he and Kraakman made in 2001." Leonard I. Rotman, "Debunking the 'End of History' Thesis for Corporate Law." *B.C. Int'l & Comp. L. Rev.* 33 (2010): 219, 272 fn. 45.

103. Leonard I. Rotman, "Debunking the "End of History" Thesis for Corporate Law." *B.C. Int'l & Comp. L. Rev.* 33 (2010): 219. Rotman discusses alternate theories of the "end" of history. Perhaps a better way to phrase this would be the "goal" as in the teleological goal of history. Rotman discusses this "end" within the concept of jurisprudence and law,

> This Article debunks Hansmann and Kraakman's "end of history" thesis on both U.S. and Canadian corporate law grounds. A critical examination of high-profile U.S. corporate law jurisprudence indicates that the shareholder primacy norm cannot be supported, even by cases such as *Dodge v. Ford and Revlon, Inc. v. MacAndrews & Forbes Holdings, Inc.*, which exist at the foundation of shareholder primacy arguments. Further, Canadian corporate law jurisprudence and the structure of Canadian corporate law statutes reveal the complete lack of support for shareholder primacy arguments north of the forty-ninth parallel, further impeding Hansmann and Kraakman's claim. This state of affairs demonstrates that Hansmann and Kraakman's "end of history" thesis is, at best, premature and, at worst, incorrect.

104. "Fukuyama's definitive thesis of his work is that the capitalist liberal democracy paradigm is the teleological last, or end form, of political economy; meaning that political economies have reached their end form—teleologically speaking." Charles Edward Andrew Lincoln IV, "Hegelian Dialectical Analysis of U.S. Voting Laws." *U. Dayton L. Rev.* 42 (2017): 87, 111 fn. 31.

105. "Recent events in the United States and abroad have caused many to speculate as to whether Fukuyama or Huntington has accurately set forth the appropriate paradigm for viewing the post-Cold War era. As just discussed, the debate brings with

it not only broader issues regarding international politics, but also issues regarding the role that Western capitalism, consumer culture, and materialism play in the post-Cold War era. With the latter set of issues comes the connection between globalization and the domain of domestic contract law.

Law, including contract law, is a significant force that has aided in the creation of the Western consumer society and that advances Western capitalism. Domestic commercialism does have a cultural dimension, a point that both Fukuyama and Huntington recognize, and sterile assumptions that markets are not impacted by culture simply are not sustainable. Domestic contract law, in other words, is as much an expression of American culture and economic beliefs as it is an expression of ostensibly neutral, universal market principles."

Brooke Overby, "Contract, in the Age of Sustainable Consumption." *J. Corp. L.* 27 (2002): 603, 626.

106. The modern period saw the introduction of many new devices to permit intermediated investment. The Muscovy Company, which was founded in 1553, is believed to have issued the first modern equity instrument. It was followed by the East India Company in 1600 and the first permanent joint-stock company, the Dutch East India Company, in 1602. What is believed to have been the first negotiable bond, the 'Grand Parti', was issued by the French government in 1555. Unlike earlier bond-like instruments, the Grand Parti could be purchased by almost anyone, not just the large banking houses. Secondary trading of securities was formalized with the opening of the Amsterdam Bourse in 1611, and the negotiation of options and futures contracts were conducted soon thereafter. The first stock exchange in London specifically built for that purpose was opened in 1802. 99Link to the text of the note However, in the United States, stock trading transactions were conducted literally on the streets of New York City prior to the creation of the New York Stock Exchange in 1817. Convertible securities and preferred stock were developed and popularized in the seventeenth and eighteenth centuries." Charles R. P. Pouncy, "Contemporary Financial Innovation: Orthodoxy and Alternatives." *SMU L. Rev.* 51 (1998): 505. *Cf.*

> The gestation and birth of what would become the modern corporation can be observed in the history of the East India Company. The early voyages of the East India Company were treated as individual ventures in which investors subscribed, and, if the voyage was profitable, received their principal and profit upon the voyage's conclusion. This process would soon become unwieldy as it became increasingly difficult to strictly segregate the accounts attributable to each individual voyage, so in 1613, the East India Company stopped selling shares in individual voyages, but sold four-year subscriptions. Permanent capital stock was established in 1657. Shares became freely transferable at prices periodically established by the company. In 1661, the company began distributing dividends rather than divisions of profits and assets.

See Jonathan Baskin & Paul J. Miranti, Jr., A History of Corporate Finance 313 (1997). and Michael Chatfield, A History of Accounting Thought 5 (photo. reprint 1979) (1977).

This has a parallel history with the Dutch religious expansion into what is modern New York "First settled by the Swedes in 1638 in an effort to compete with Dutch trade, Delaware (originally named "New Sweden") was home to the first Lutheran minister in America. The colony was small and poorly supported by Sweden. Survival consumed the attention of the settlers, eliminating any substantial development in the nature of church expansion. The irritation of the Dutch governor in New Amsterdam just to the north culminated in an attack on tiny New Sweden in 1655 and its surrender to Dutch authority. The governor would have only nine years to savor his victory. In 1664, the surrender of New Amsterdam to England placed control of all modern New York, Pennsylvania, and Delaware in the hands of James, Duke of York (soon to be James II). When William Penn asked Charles II for a grant in the New World, he was given control of Pennsylvania in 1681, and Delaware was ceded by James to Penn in 1682. Thus, territory which had already passed from Swedish Lutheran to Dutch Reformed to Anglican control was now under the jurisdiction of a Quaker proprietor. So ended any further flirtation in Delaware with a church established by law."

Furthermore, "Concerning the attitude of the Dutch governor in New Amsterdam, Munroe records: The death blow to New Sweden came from the very people who had inspired its birth; Dutch it had been, and to the Dutch it was returned. Peter Stuyvesant, who became governor of New Netherland in 1647, was annoyed by the Swedish presence on the Delaware. He was experienced in colonial affairs through service in the West Indies, where armed combats were frequent and islands passed back and forth between the European powers like pieces in a game. He had also become crippled in such service, losing a leg in battle with the French on the island of St. Martin.

Id. Concerning the surrender, Munroe relates: On September 15, 1655, near Fort Christina, Stuyvesant and [Johan] Rising met to sign the capitulation, and at three o'clock on that afternoon the Swedes marched out of the fort with drums beating, fifes playing, banners flying. In ensuing days Rising did his best to urge all Swedes to return to their homeland, but he had little influence. In the end only thirty-seven people comprised his party when he left New Amsterdam for Europe on October 23." *Id.*

107. It has been noted, "[n]o discussion of financial speculation can begin without taking note of the tulip mania that gripped Holland in the seventeenth century. Mark Frankel, in his review of Mike Dash's 1999 book, Tulipomania: The Story of the World's Most Coveted Flower & The Extraordinary Passions It Aroused, tells the story. Tulips had been prized since the mid-1550s for their extraordinary beauty, purity and sharpness of colors, and extravagant presentation. The fact that it took seven years to grow a tulip from seed to bulb only added to its allure. By the beginning of the seventeenth century, Holland was at the peak of its power, with the merchants in Amsterdam making 400% profits on their East Indies trading. These wealthy Dutch displayed their riches by building grand estates surrounded by elaborate flower gardens that featured rare and exquisite tulips. In 1624, a man in Amsterdam who owned the only twelve bulbs of a midnight blue tulip topped by a band of pure white and accented by crimson flares was offered as high as 3,000 guilders for one bulb. By comparison, Rembrandt received only half that amount when he painted his masterpiece, the Night Watch. Prices rose steadily throughout the 1630s and speculators entered the marketplace. In the winter of 1636-37, one rare tulip bulb that was about to split in two was sold at auction for 5,200 guilders. Some bulbs were changing

hands in the marketplace ten times a day. Then came the crash. All it took was one buyer in Haarlem who refused to pay for a bulb that he had purchased at auction. Panic struck, and within days, the marketplace had all but vanished. Bulbs, which had routinely commanded 5,000 guilders days before, began to trade for fifty guilders. Great fortunes evaporated overnight." Marvin N. Bagwell, "Unsettling Mortgage Law: Implications for Practitioners and title Insurers: Can't Live Without Air: Title Insurance and the Bursting of the Real Estate Bubble." *Pace L. Rev.* 30 (2009): 180, 200–201.

Indeed, although Amsterdam may have some of the roots of the modern form of capitalism and corporate legal entities, it also has shown the beginning of one of the first modern economic crashes. This has been explained in different ways before. "Efficient Capital Market Hypothesists and other classical economists have a difficult time explaining phenomena like 'tulipmania', Amsterdam's 17th century frenzy of trading in tulip bulbs. See Charles Mackay, *Extraordinary Popular Delusions and the Madness of Crowds* 1–97 (1980). Also, the 18th century's Mississippi and South Sea Bubbles present similar puzzles. But see Robert Flood and Peter Garber, *Speculative Bubbles, Speculative Attacks and Policy Switching* (1994) (endeavoring to 'rationalize' these seemingly irrational market behaviors)." Hon. Richard D. Cudahy, "Retail Wheeling: Is This Revolution Necessary?" *Energy L. J.* 15 (1994): 351, 356. *Cf.* Jan Sitmaartensdijk and Yfke Nijland, *Operatie Black Tulip: De uitzetting van Duitse burgers na de oorlog* (Amsterdam: Boom, 2009).

Such examinations of economic crises are vital to the understanding of the world history and economy in terms of corporate law, which is really an advanced form of agency law. Exploring the history of the British Empire in relation to economics and law's confluence with currency, Ronen Palan has noted, "The argument is that hegemonic states go through historical cycles, known as the hegemonic cycle theory. According to the theory, hegemonic states rise to power on the back of a vibrant manufacturing sector; they then develop a strong commercial sector; and finally they end up with a strong financial sector. The result is that during a period of decline, a hegemonic power tends to maintain a disproportionately bloated, politically powerful commercial and financial sector. This was true of the declining Dutch, as well as the British hegemonic, states. Nevertheless, while Amsterdam was the largest financial center of its day, and experienced the first serious financial crises (the Tulip mania), Holland was still largely a trading state and as a result was dominated during and after its decline by commercially oriented elites. London, by contrast, emerged as a truly global financial center during the heyday of the British Empire, and as a result, the British state has been dominated politically by a financial elite. This theory may then explain the specific British link discussed in this article." Ronen Palen, "Money Matters: The Law, Economics, and Politics of Currency: International Financial Centers: The British-Empire, City-States and Commercially Oriented Politics." *Theoretical Inq. L.* 11 (2010): 149, 154.

108. The Mississippi Company bubble has been explained in terms of printing and currency credit crises.

"Law's money-printing (credit-creating) operations were used to support the price of the Mississippi Company shares at a high level through late February, 1720.

That allowed the French ruler to sell his shares at that level and, in a rather personal version of public finance worthy of Henry VIII, to book a nice profit. Thinking that his credit creation might have gone too far, Law then stopped supporting the share price. When it plunged by 25 percent in a few days, shareholders protested against the measures that had caused the drop, so Law reinstituted the share price-support program, fixing the price at 9,000 livres. That meant that Law had to buy Mississippi Company shares at that price if it threatened to slip any lower. Effectively, shares and paper banknotes became one and the same. By May, if not earlier, all of the money creation produced financial overheating and price inflation. Law then decided to try to cool the overheated economy by having the government announce that Mississippi share prices would undergo a phased reduction totaling 44 percent of their value, and banknotes would undergo a similar phased reduction to 50 percent of their face value by December 1720. As a result of the announcement, Mississippi Company shares lost half of their value in the market in a few days. Although the Regent, against Law's wishes, revoked the phased-reduction edict, the market price of Mississippi shares never recovered enough to reach even the prices proposed in the phased reduction. Confidence in the value of both paper money and shares had been irreparably damaged. At the same time, though, the French state had greatly reduced the burden of its debts."

Richard Sylla, "Economy of Supplying Money to a Growing Economy: Monetary Regimes and the Search for an Anchor to Stabilize the Value of Money." *Theoretical Inq. L.* 11 (2010): 1, 23.

The Mississippi Crisis in 1720 is compared with the risks of having a centralized banking and monetary reserve system in relation to the desideratum of identifiable monetary regimes.

"The power of a central bank to create money in the modern fiat money regime is vastly greater than it was under a commodity-based standard, and the money can be supplied at a far lower cost. That was John Law's great insight long ago, one demonstrated again in the panic of 2008 when the U.S. central bank expanded its balance sheet by a factor of more than two in just a few months. But Law in practice failed to answer the question regarding how much fiat money should be created. Instead, in an effort to implement another part of his plan, conversion of France's public debt to equity shares in the Mississippi Company, he oversaw the creation of far too much fiat paper money. As a result, both he and his money lost credibility. Law left France, and his fiat money—banknotes and shares in the company, which were equivalent at the height of his system in May 1720—lost almost all of its value by the end of the year. Paradoxically, the French state that sent Law into exile benefited from his failure: 'Law's System certainly bankrupted the creditors of the state; the state, however, as debtor, was a net gainer'."

Richard Sylla, "Economy of Supplying Money to a Growing Economy: Monetary Regimes and the Search for an Anchor to Stabilize the Value of Money." *Theoretical Inq. L.* 11 (2010): 1, 23.

109. Indeed, the story of the Civil War's costs from an economic perspective is embedded in the introduction of the IRS and the first tax—a shift from the former economic base of tariffs and bonds that the U.S. government used to rely on—to the.

110. "From 1873 to 1877, land speculation and bank failures caused an economic crisis; three million workers lost their jobs and thousands of farmers lost their farms. With President Hayes's promise to remove federal troops from the South, Reconstruction ended. As Cruikshank signaled in 1876, the Court intended to end Reconstruction by denying federal protection through the Fourteenth Amendment and the Due Process Clause to blacks attempting to exercise their rights to peaceably assemble and bear arms. The Court's language in Cruikshank broadly conceptualized due process, but the Court avoided asserting the protections of due process by characterizing the violation as private rather than state action." Natalie M. Banta, "Substantive Due Process in Exile: The Supreme Court's Original Interpretation of the Due Process Clause of the Fourteenth Amendment." *Wyo. L. Rev.* 13 (2013): 151, 179.

111. "The collapse of the Bretton Woods System did not abrogate the Bretton Woods Agreement.102 The method of indexing currencies to gold, and the U.S. dollar, changed to a floating exchange rate system. Despite conversion to a floating system, the BIS maintained a gold pool until 1986, ensuring that prices on private markets corresponded to official gold prices according to the directives issued by the Governors of G-10 central banks. However, during the post Bretton Woods era, the actions of the BIS can be characterized as reactive rather than preventative measures. The shift to floating exchange rates in March of 1973 highlighted the need for coordination among central banks of major trading countries, and for regular exchanges of information about the exchange markets and about central banks' interventions in those markets." G. Boyd Tarin, "The Bank for International Settlements: Keeping A Law Profile?" *Transnat'l Law.* 5 (1992): 839, 851–852.

112. "The global financial crisis that began in summer 2007 has continued to wreak devastating loss and damage across all markets, all economies, and all countries.1 An initial liquidity contraction in the financial markets was transformed into a full solvency crisis following the collapse of Lehman Brothers on September 15, 2008, which was a precursor to the most savage global recession since the Great Depression during the 1930s. This crisis was almost wholly unpredicted and led to a massive collapse in growth and investment across the world. Leading emerging markets were not immune as any possible decoupling or separation evaporated. It was not until the end of the second quarter of 2009 that some stabilization in the financial sector was detected. Any full recovery within the real economy would be postponed until 2010 or later." George A. Walker, "Financial Crisis-U.K. Policy and Regulatory Response." *Int'l Law.* 44 (2010): 751, 751–752.

113. Indeed, it is often difficult to single out one law. Is it one section? One code? One entire U.S. Title?

114. "Legal theorists have long invoked evolution as a metaphor for the development of the law, particularly for the common law system that is the hallmark of Anglo-American jurisprudence. Few, however, have applied the principles of natural selection as a tool for legal analysis. Moreover, apparently none has considered the impact of Dawkins' meme-based theory upon an evolutionary analysis of the law. This Article undertakes such a study. Part I discusses the mechanism of natural selection. Part II applies the principles of natural selection to certain nonbiological

entities. Dawkins' concept of the meme is explored and critiqued, and similarities and differences between memetic and genetic evolution are discussed. Part III surveys the literature of the evolutionary tradition in jurisprudence and concludes that the memetic perspective has much to offer that tradition. This Part also demonstrates that the difficulties inherent in developing a science of memetics are greatly reduced in the context of the law." Michael S. Fried, "The Evolution of Legal Concepts: The Memetic Perspective." *Jurimetrics J.* 39 (1999): 291, 292.

115. *Cf.* Leo Tolstoy, *War and Peace, Epilogue, pt. II* (Rosemary Edmonds trans., Greenwich House, 1982) (1868). Tolstoy provides an alternate interpretation of history that focuses on many multifarious factors and individuals rather than solely on "great men" that guide history.

116. "Chaos theory provides that causes have effects, and a small cause can generate a large impact. While what is taking place in the universe may not be predictable, the system is nonetheless not random. The appearance of disorder is a masquerade for what is in fact an orderly process. Under chaos theory, a butterfly flapping its wings in Brazil might, by generating a large series of steps, cause a typhoon in the Pacific Ocean. In the tax world chaos theory has comparable application. The Crane case is the butterfly. Everything else is the typhoon." Walter D. Schwidetzky, "The Partnership Allocation Rules of Section 704(b): To Be or Not to Be." *Va. Tax Rev.* 17 (1998): 707, 739.

117. *Id.* at fn. 2. "According to Malcolm Gladwell, white-shoe law firms were those traditional, old-line law firms that populated downtown Manhattan. The nickname, white-shoe is a reference to the type of shoe favored by those attorneys who staffed the traditional law firms." *Id. See also* Eli Wald, "The Rise and Fall of the Wasp and Jewish Law Firms." Stan. L. Rev. 60 (2008): 1803, 1812.

Nor was the religious identity of the large firms superficial. While the merit-based hiring and promotion criteria of the Cravath System purported to ignore irrelevant considerations such as social standing and religious affiliation, its "carefully prescribed path" was never based on merit alone. Rather, "[i]n addition to academic credentials [the young men] were expected to possess 'warmth and force of personality' and 'physical stamina." These hard-to-quantify and difficult-to-assess qualities were a cover for, or at least directly correlated with, certain religious, socioeconomic, and cultural characteristics. In other words, large firms used the "warmth of personality" standard to systematically exclude candidates who satisfied their merit-based criteria but nonetheless were not considered among the "best men"—young, white, Anglo-Saxon Protestant men from affluent socioeconomic backgrounds.

Id. See also "Justice Crucified: The Story of Sacco and Vanzetti by Roberta Strauss Feuerlicht." *Harv. L. Rev.* 92 (1979): 781.

To Feuerlicht, the two great villains of the case are A. Lawrence Lowell, president of Harvard and chairman of the Governor's advisory committee which approved the death sentences, and Justice Oliver Wendell Holmes, who refused to grant a stay of execution and bring the case before the full Supreme Court (p. 431). Although her venom seems more justifiably directed against the former than the latter, both are representatives of the author's ultimate bogeyman, the White Anglo-Saxon Protestant. In the first third of the book, in which Feuerlicht offers a caustic survey of American history, the "WASPs' sting" is the dominant force, bringing injustice wherever it strikes.

In fact, while making a casual digression to current events, the author goes so far as to blame the WASP's for the Boston busing crisis, since they allegedly taught the Irish how to persecute others. In case any reader has missed the point, she makes her focus explicit while fixing a place in history for Sacco and Vanzetti: "But the reach of the WASPs exceeded their grasp; in winning the case they lost their souls, and their moral authority passed to immigrants like Sacco and Vanzetti." *Id.*

118. Andrew Bolson, Lessons from an Outlier What Young Lawyers Can Learn from the Story of Joe Flom, *N.J. Law.*, August 2013, at 57.

119. Andrew Bolson, Lessons from an Outlier What Young Lawyers Can Learn from the Story of Joe Flom, *N.J. Law.*, August 2013, at 57.

120. Andrew Bolson, Lessons from an Outlier What Young Lawyers Can Learn from the Story of Joe Flom, *N.J. Law.*, August 2013, at 57.

121. Andrew Bolson, Lessons from an Outlier What Young Lawyers Can Learn from the Story of Joe Flom, *N.J. Law.*, August 2013, at 57.

122. Andrew Bolson, Lessons from an Outlier What Young Lawyers Can Learn from the Story of Joe Flom, *N.J. Law.*, August 2013, at 57.

123. For a story about one of the most notable takeovers in the form of a leveraged buyout in the 1980s see *Bryan Burrough and John Heylar, Barbarians at the Gate: The Fall of RJR Nabisco* (1990); and the film based on the book Barbarians at the Gate (Glenn Jordan 1993).

124. Andrew Bolson, Lessons from an Outlier What Young Lawyers Can Learn from the Story of Joe Flom, *N.J. Law.*, August 2013, at 57.

125. "Although Bobbitt is careful to disclaim that he has "discovered an historical law of general application," there is a feeling of historic inexorability in his narrative. It is true, he observes, that crucial decisions were made at certain junctures—usually by the great men of history he focuses on—and those choices did influence the course of events. Bobbitt's chronicle thus blends Leo Tolstoy's historic egoism and Bruce Ackerman's theory of "constitutional moments" as applied to state systems. When Bobbitt rhetorically asks, "[b]iogenetic evolution is punctuated; why can't the evolution of states also be?" he invokes the sense of decisive, but somehow historically predetermined, junctures in history.

In truth, Bobbitt is really a Hegelian metaphysician. His is a history of sweeping movements caught in a dialectic of conflict and change. Sometimes he clearly embraces this view, as when he observes (in the context of the Westphalian confirmation of the legitimacy of the kingly state): "the triumph of one constitutional order . . . germinates the form that will ultimately vanquish it."

> Such statements evoke our old friends, thesis and antithesis and synthesis. Bobbitt's metaphysic is to take bundles of strategic, legal, and historical phenomenon and distill their first principles. With a keen eye to categories and types, almost Linnaean in its attention to detail, Bobbitt succeeds in fashioning the empiric database that supports those first principles. And despite his protestations to the contrary, make no mistake: Bobbitt offers a unified field theory of the fate of nations. What plate tectonics did for our understanding of geology or Freudian psychology for our insights into human behavior, this book makes a powerful case for a single set of explanations for the rise and fall of different kinds of state regimes.

David J. Bederman, *The New International Law in an Old Age of Indeterminacy The Shield of Achilles: War, Peace, and the Course of History* by Philip Bobbitt (New York: Alfred A. Knopt, 2002), pp. Xxxiii, 919. (Fnd1), 81 *Tex. L. Rev.* 1521, 1533–1534 (2003).

Cf. Michael Clifford, "Hegel and Foucault: Toward a history without man." *Clio* 29, no. 1 (1999): 1. *See.* "The story of its ruin is simple and obvious; and, instead of inquiring why the Roman empire was destroyed, we should rather be surprised that it had subsisted so long. The victorious legions, who, in distant wars, acquired the vices of strangers and mercenaries, first oppressed the freedom of the republic, and afterwards violated the majesty of the purple. The emperors, anxious for their personal safety and the public peace, were reduced to the base expedient of corrupting the discipline which rendered them alike formidable to their sovereign and to the enemy; the vigour of the military government was relaxed, and finally dissolved, by the partial institutions of Constantine; and the Roman world was overwhelmed by a deluge of Barbarians." Edward Gibbon. *The Decline and Fall of the Roman Empire*, Chapter 38 General Observations on the Fall of the Roman Empire in the West.

126. "While the underlying laws governing the natural selection of memes are identical to those that apply in genetics, important differences between the two replicators create practical difficulties in developing a rigorous memetic science. These difficulties have led some theorists to question whether memetics could feasibly be developed into a practicable tool for prediction and control. These problems are, however, greatly reduced for memes in the legal system." Michael S. Fried, "The Evolution of Legal Concepts: The Memetic Perspective." *Jurimetrics J.* 39 (1999): 291, 300–301.

127. "The entity classification debate began a century ago with the passage of the Revenue Act of 1894, which, in addition to levying a tax on the income of wealthy individuals, imposed an entity level tax on corporate income. The imposition of a tax on corporations raised the issue of Congress' intent in singling out this class of business entities rather than imposing a broad-based tax on all business organizations. As it turns out, Congress based its decision more on an effort to soothe the psyche of the American public than on any theoretical underpinnings." Patrick E. Hobbs, "Entity Classification: The One Hundred-Year Debate." *Cath. U. L. Rev.* 44 (1995): 437, 441.

128. "Commentators also frequently refer to the concepts of horizontal and vertical equity as components of the 'ability to pay' tax fairness concept. As generally understood, horizontal equity requires that taxpayers with the same ability to pay be taxed alike, while vertical equity requires that people with different abilities to pay be taxed differently. Vertical equity supports a progressive tax system that imposes graduated rates ranging from 0% (an exemption from tax) for those at the bottom to relatively high rates applicable at the top of the scale. As with the ability-to-pay concept generally, horizontal and vertical equity both require an answer as to what 'counts as' the same ability to pay. Is income the appropriate measure, or should we also consider wealth? The decision as to what items to include may predetermine the equity conclusion. The uncertainties, and the related debate over progressivity, go back to the origins of the federal income tax in the 1860s, when Congress considered whether to have a flat rate system or a graduated rate structure. In spite of periods of

stronger opposition, Congress has consistently treated progressivity as a fundamental aspect of the federal tax system, and scholars who take seriously the need to define the normative foundations of tax policy continue to explore this ongoing consensus in favor of progressivity. For example, in a recent article, Thomas Griffith suggests that a redistributively progressive tax increases people's happiness because of the primary importance of relative, rather than absolute, incomes." Linda M. Beale, "Congress Fiddles While Middle America Burns: Amending the Amt (and Regular Tax)." *Fla. Tax Rev.* 6 (2004): 811, 820–821.

129. Though accounting has had a longer history.

130. "(a) General rule.—For purposes of this subtitle, the term "dividend" means any distribution of property made by a corporation to its shareholders—(1) out of its earnings and profits accumulated after February 28, 1913, or(2) out of its earnings and profits of the taxable year (computed as of the close of the taxable year without diminution by reason of any distributions made during the taxable year), without regard to the amount of the earnings and profits at the time the distribution was made." 26 U.S.C.A. § 316 (West).

131. "Interim distributions are similar to dividends in the sense that they often involve surplus money or assets and are paid before an LLC dissolves and winds up its business." 2 Advising Small Businesses § 23:1 (2016).

132. "Most corporation statutes contain some type of balance sheet test. Earned surplus statutes provide that dividends may be declared and paid in cash or property only out of the unreserved and unrestricted earned surplus of the corporation." 11 Fletcher Cyc. Corp. § 5329.15.

133. Speaking of supple forms of antithetical Lockean ideals: "Under the instrumentalist version of Lockean theory discussed above, the reason for allowing an individual to reap the rewards of effort is to provide an incentive for that effort. If enough incentive is left in place after taxation, the effort should still occur under this theory. Taxing the product of labor, however, reduces the incentive to engage in productive labor, at least in theory. Thus taxes, which remove some of the incentive, seem to be antithetical to the instrumentalist form of Lockean labor theory. This is only true, however, if there is no windfall inherent in the rewards to labor. Windfalls by definition are unexpected and unpredicted and should have no effect on incentives. The windfall portion of market prices is analogous to economic rent—that part of, say, an individual's salary that exceeds the price the individual could command in the next best activity. If a lawyer is willing to work for $45,000 a year, the lawyer will probably be delighted to work for $200,000 a year. The additional $155,000 per year does not perform the instrumentalist function of inducing the lawyer to practice law; it is more like a windfall or a bonus. To the extent that taxes are taken out of this "windfall" amount, there should be little or no effect on the lawyer's willingness to engage in the practice of law. Of course, at least some of the lawyers working for $200,000 would, at least in theory, not work for less." Donna M. Byrne, "Locke, Property, and Progressive Taxes." *Neb. L. Rev.* 78 (1999): 700, 724–725.

134. Randy Beck, "The Faith of the 'Crits': Critical Legal Studies and Human Nature." *Harv. J.L. & Pub. Pol'y* 11 (1988): 433.

135. OECD Model Convention, Art. 10.3. It is unclear whether the American term for mineral rights would fall into the definition of dividends or royalties.

136. Interest expenses and their underlying debt are allocated according to the use of the debt proceeds. *Chapman v. C.I.R.*, 107 T.C.M. (CCH) 1433 (T.C. 2014).

137. OECD Model Convention, Art. 11.3.

138. U.S.C.A. § 543 (West).

139. "A patent licensor may require the licensee to pay a royalty for the privilege of practicing the invention.1 The obligation to pay such a fee is founded on the agreement between the patentee and licensee.2 The right to collect royalties owed on a patent licensing agreement can be assigned without also assigning the underlying patent rights.3 Ordinarily, mere use of a patented article, even with knowledge of the patentee, raises no implied promise to pay royalties thereon."

60 Am. Jur. 2d Patents § 925.

140. OECD Model Convention, Art. 12.2.

141. OECD Model Convention, Art. 12.2.

142. This is speculation by the author. Other countries may have private mineral rights for subeterranenan minerals. Although it may be fair to say that private—rather than private—ownership of mineral rights however distributed promotes economic growth.

"If Texas courts are willing to acknowledge the economic perspective on this analysis rather than just the narrow, premises-based perspective, they may likely find, as the alternatives become economically viable for oil and gas producers, that reasonable alternatives do exist."

Andrew D. Lewis, "The Ever-Protruding Stick in the Bundle: The Accommodation of Groundwater Rights in Texas Oil and Gas." *Tex. A&M L. Rev.* 2 (2014): 79, 86–87.

Also, it may be fair to say that private ownership of mineral rights could also mean more tax revenue for the state.

143. "To understand the impact of an oil and gas lease, imagine an individual receiving a fee simple absolute grant of land under a land patent. Under the common law ad coleum doctrine, that person would own the surface of the land, all of the space above it, and everything below it, including the mineral estate.3 Before the execution of an oil and gas lease, the owner would possess the entire 'bundle of sticks' in the mineral estate, i.e., the rights to: (1) execute an oil and gas lease; (2) receive bonus for executing a lease; (3) receive delay rental payments; (4) receive royalty payments; and (5) produce oil and gas from the property (including necessary rights of ingress and egress)."

Derek Cook and Jennie K. Martin, "Oil and Gas Basics Understanding the Sticks to Avoid Stones and Broken Bones." *Tex. B.J.* 76 (2013): 319.

See. See 2 William Blackstone, *Commentaries on the Law of England 18* (William Draper Lewis ed., 1902).

144. IBFD, Glossary, Technical Assistance Fees. Accessed September 27, 2016 at 6:07 PM.

145. *Id.*

146. "[T]here is no justification for applying a royalty source rule to certain types of services income (e.g., technical services) and not to other types of services income

(e.g., marketing, legal, or accounting services), particularly when the services may have nothing to do with any royalty payment." Richard L. Doernberg, "The U.S.-India Income Tax Treaty: Breaking New Ground in Taxing Services Income from Licensing Technology." *Tax Law.* 44 (1991): 735.

147. "Fees for technical services" means any consideration (including any lump-sum consideration) for rendering any managerial, technical, or consultancy services (including the provision of services of technical or other personnel), but does not include consideration for any construction, assembly, mining, or similar project undertaken by the recipient or consideration that would be under the heading "Salaries." ¶ 18.09 INDIAN TAX CONSIDERATIONS FOR U.S. INVESTMENTS, U.S. Tax. Foreign Cont. Bus. ¶ 18.09.

148. Much of the structure and ideas of this chapter and the chapters dealing directly with the U.S. tax court come directly from my advanced LL.M. master's thesis submitted to the University of Amsterdam. Moreover, I re-published some of these ideas in a new format in a Lexis Nexis treatise on international taxation and transfer pricing with my mentor—William Byrnes, IV—who has shepherded and guided me through the tax world since I was a J.D. student at Texas A&M University. Indeed, much of the text comes directly from my thesis at the University of Amsterdam for the degree I attained in 2017.

149. "When a foreign taxpayer generates income in the United States, both the United States (the source country) and the foreign taxpayer's country of residence (the residence country) generally have jurisdiction to tax that income. The overriding objective of the U.S. system of international taxation is to equitably resolve these competing claims in a way that stimulates global commerce while simultaneously mitigating risks of multiple taxation and tax avoidance." Brianne N. De Sellier, John M. Kelleher, Revisiting Nexus Standards: Establishing U.S. Jurisdiction to Tax Cross-Border Commerce, *Fla. B.J.*, April 2014, at 31.

150. "Daniel Shaviro, The Financial Transactions Tax Versus (?) the Financial Activities Tax 21–22 (N.Y.U. Law and Econ. Working Papers, Working Paper No. 292, Mar. 2012), http://lsr.nellco.org/nyu_lewp/292; Thornton Matheson, Financial Sector Taxation and the Ongoing Financial Crisis, in *Taxing the Financial Sector: Financial Taxes, Bank Levies and More* 203 (Otto Marres & Dennis Weber eds., 2012)" Carlo Garbarino and Giulio Allevato (FNaaa1), "The Global Architecture of Financial Regulatory Taxes." *Mich. J. Int'l L.* 36 (2015): 603, 648.

151. "The basis for these rules is in the observation that society requires taxation (revenue) so it can thrive beyond subsistence, yet taxation is economically inefficient and wasteful." Yariv Brauner, "Value in the Eye of the Beholder: The Valuation of Intangibles for Transfer Pricing Purposes." *Va. Tax Rev.* 28 (2008): 79, 82. See, for example, Richard A. Musgrave and Peggy B. Musgrave, *Public Finance in Theory and Practice* 303 (3rd ed., 1980).

152. "In this respect, there are two fundamental approaches to resolving competing claims to tax the same income: 1) residence-based taxation; and 2) source-based taxation." *Id.*

153. "On the corporate tax avoidance front, the OECD and G20 launched the Base Erosion and Profit Shifting (BEPS) project in 2013, culminating with the release of

a series of action reports in October 2015." Reuven S. Avi-Yonah and Haiyan Xu, "Evaluating BEPS: A Reconsideration of the Benefits Principle and Proposal for Un Oversight." *Harv. Bus. L. Rev.* 6 (2016): 185, 188.

154. Pasquale Pistone, General Report, in *The Impact of the OECD and UN Model Conventions on Bilateral Tax Treaties* 2 (Michael Lang et al. eds., 2012).

155. "The BEPS project is the most extensive attempt to change international tax norms since the 1920s." Itai Grinberg, "The New International Tax Diplomacy." *Geo. L.J.* 104 (2016): 1137, 1140. *Cf.* Indeed, this is true of the transfer pricing rules as well. "Bret Wells and Cym Lowell, "Tax Base Erosion: Reformation of Section 482's Arm's Length Standard." *Fla. Tax Rev.* 15 (2014): 737, 745 (noting that the arm's-length standard has been the global standard since the 1920s). This Article focuses on the U.S. transfer pricing rules, which are similar in many respects to the transfer pricing rules of other countries." Orly Mazur, "Transfer Pricing Challenges in the Cloud." *B.C. L. Rev.* 57 (2016): 643, 693.

156. "Sunita Jogarajan, Stamp, Seligman and the Drafting of the 1923 Experts' Report on Double Taxation, 5 *World Tax J.* 368 (2013) (exposing the history of the League of Nations tax treaty work and the centrality of double taxation to this work)." Yariv Brauner, "Treaties in the Aftermath of Beps." *Brook. J. Int'l L.* 41 (2016): 973, 1041 fn. 50. *See . . . Report on Double Taxation Submitted to the Financial Committee by Professors Bruins, Einaudi, Seligman, and Sir Josiah Stamp*, League of Nations Doc. E.F.S. 73.F.19 (1923)." Yariv Brauner, "Treaties in the Aftermath of Beps." *Brook. J. Int'l L.* 41 (2016): 973, 1041 fn. 51.

157. *See generally*. For a discussion on the origins of BEPS and its intricacies, a unique article by Pascale Saint-Amans who is leading the OECD's tax division through the BEPS era. "On BEPS, see, e.g., Pascal Saint-Amans and Rafaelle Russo, The BEPS Package: Promise Kept, 70 IBFD Bulletin for International Taxation 4 (2016); Hugh J. Ault, "Some Reflections on the OECD and the Sources of International Tax Principles." *Tax Notes Int'l* 70 (2013): 1195; Itai Grinberg, *Breaking BEPS: The New International Tax Diplomacy*, Geo. L. J. (forthcoming), http://ssrn.com/abstract–2652894; Adam H. Rosenzweig, "Building a Framework for a Post-BEPS World." *Tax Notes Int'l* 74 (2014): 1077; Richard J. Vann, "Policy Forum: The Policy Underpinnings of the BEPS Project—Preserving the International Corporation Income Tax." *Can. Tax J.* 62 (2014): 433; Hugh J. Ault et al., *Base Erosion and Profit Shifting: A Roadmap for Reform* (Bos. Coll. Law Sch., Working Paper No. 324, 2014), http://ssrn.com/abstract=2459646; Yariv Brauner, *What the BEPS?* (Univ. of Fla. Coll. of Law, Legal Studies Working Paper No. 15-40, 2014), http://ssrn.com/abstract=2408034; Dhammika Dharmapala, *Base Erosion and Profit Shifting: A Simple Conceptual Framework* (Univ. of Chi. Law Sch. Coase-Sandor Inst. for Law & Econ., Working Paper No. 703, 2015), http://ssrn.com/abstract =2497770; Dhammika Dharmapala, *What Do We Know About Base Erosion and Profit Shifting? A Review of the Empirical Literature* (Univ. of Chi. Law Sch., Coase-Sandor Inst. for Law & Econ., Working Paper No. 702, 2014), http://ssrn.com/abstract =2373549; Daniel Shaviro, *The Crossroads Versus the Seesaw: Getting a 'Fix' on Recent International Tax Policy Developments* (N.Y. Univ. Sch. of Law, Pub. Law & Legal Theory Research Paper Series, Working Paper No. 15-20, 2015), http://ssrn

.com/abstract=2605144." Reuven S. Avi-Yonah and Haiyan Xu, "Evaluating BEPS: A Reconsideration of the Benefits Principle and Proposal for UN Oversight." *Harv. Bus. L. Rev.* 6 (2016): 185, 238 fn. 5.

158. *See generally* for risk assessment. *OECD Draft Handbook on Transfer Pricing Risk Assessment* (OECD 2013). Discussing who is in the best position to assess risks and by what methodology. *Cf.* R. Hafkenscheid, "The BEPS Report on Risk Allocation: Not so Functional." *Intl. Transfer Pricing J.* 24 (2017): 1, Journals IBFD.

159. A Better Way: Our Vision for a Confident America, GOP TAX REFORM TASK FORCE (November 30, 2016), https://abetterway.speaker.gov/_assets/pdf/abetterway-tax-policypaper.pdf [perma.cc/G6B3-YMT3].

160. "The waste that our transfer pricing rules represent is considered necessary, since without such rules, MNEs could essentially escape taxation, and countries could find themselves in fierce and impossible competition for revenue. An arm's length based transfer pricing regime, such as ours, permits relatively peaceful division of revenues between countries." Yariv Brauner, "Value in the Eye of the Beholder: The Valuation of Intangibles for Transfer Pricing Purposes." *Va. Tax Rev.* 28 (2008): 79, 83.

161. Cliff Taylor, *Chances of US tax reform high under Donald Trump, PwC says*, Irish Times (Last accessed April 17, 2017), http://www.irishtimes.com/business/economy/chances-of-us-tax-reform-high-under-donald-trump-pwc-says-1.2944744.

162. "Chaos theory provides that causes have effects, and a small cause can generate a large impact. While what is taking place in the universe may not be predictable, the system is nonetheless not random. The appearance of disorder is a masquerade for what is in fact an orderly process. Under chaos theory, a butterfly flapping its wings in Brazil might, by generating a large series of steps, cause a typhoon in the Pacific Ocean. In the tax world chaos theory has comparable application." Walter D. Schwidetzky, "The Partnership Allocation Rules of Section 704(b): To Be or Not to Be." *Va. Tax Rev.* 17 (1998): 707, 739. *Compare With.* Jack Manhire, "Tax Compliance as a Wicked System." *Florida Tax Review* 18 (2016): 235, Texas A&M University School of Law Legal Studies Research Paper No. 16-29.

163. *Id. See.* Professor Erwin Chemerinsky's discussion of how U.S. court decisions can seem neutral or arbitrary, but in the end, do have some structure. "A successful challenge to its legitimacy will lead the Court to provide a more open justification for its rulings, one that more explicitly identifies and defends its value choices. Alternatively, if the U.S. Supreme Court's decision making is actually based on the quest for neutrality, revealing the misguided nature of such a quest facilitates the development of theories of constitutional interpretation." Erwin Chemerinsky, "The Vanishing Constitution." *Harv. L. Rev.* 103 (1989): 43, 61.

164. The goal of Action Plan 9 is to "[d]evelop rules to prevent BEPS by transferring risks among, or allocating excessive capital to, group members." This process involves "adopting transfer pricing rules or special measures to ensure that inappropriate returns will not accrue to an entity solely because it has contractually assumed risks or has provided capital." Following this statement, Professors Avi-Yonah and Xu summarize the new goals as stating "[t]he rules must align returns with value creation. Under Action 9, contractual allocations of risk are respected only when they

are supported by actual decision-making and thus exercising control over these risks." Reuven S. Avi-Yonah and Haiyan Xu, "Evaluating BEPS: A Reconsideration of the Benefits Principle and Proposal for UN Oversight." *Harv. Bus. L. Rev.* 6 (2016): 185, 225.

165. *See*. Actions 8-10, Paragraphs 1.56–1.70.

166. Tax adviser, practicing at Loyens & Loeff, Amsterdam, The Netherlands. Rutger Hafkenscheid was also one of my thesis advisors at the University of Amsterdam along with Hein Vermeulen that supervised my work and research of the thesis. My thesis at the University of Amsterdam has greatly influenced chapters 5 through 12 of this book.

> 167. The Final Transfer Pricing Report includes three important revisions to the Transfer Pricing Guidelines with respect to their application to related-party transactions involving intangible assets. The first set of revisions focuses on policing contractual allocations of risks. The final report views written contracts between related enterprises as 'the starting point' in determining the allocation of responsibilities, risks and anticipated outcomes. But these contractual allocations of responsibilities, risks, and anticipated outcomes must reflect economic reality—which requires consideration of the functions performed by the parties, considering the assets used and risks assumed; the characteristics of the property transferred or services provided; the economic circumstances of the parties and the relevant market in which they operate; and the parties' business strategies. Under the Final Transfer Pricing Report, the key to deserving a return from ownership of an asset is actual control and decision-making ability. Thus, if a party is contractually allocated a risk, the party must have not only the financial capacity to assume the risk, but also the functional ability to control the risk—which means that the party must have the actual ability to make decisions with respect to the risk. But if the entity is a so-called 'Cash Box'—possessing capital, but no functional ability to exercise control over the final risks—the Final Transfer Pricing Report opines that the entity should receive 'no more than a risk-free return, assuring that no premium returns will be allocated to cash boxes without relevant substance'. Or, depending on the facts, the entity might be entitled to a risk-adjusted return.

¶ 14.11 INTERNATIONAL TRANSACTIONS INVOLVING INTANGIBLE ASSETS AMONG RELATED PARTIES (INTERNATIONAL TRANSACTIONS), 1998 WL 1038740, 9.

168. "An interesting aspect of the taxing powers of the United States government, is the fact that the IRS Commissioner appears to have the power to choose the best of both worlds, as the Commissioner's view of economic reality dictates. Thus, on the one hand, with respect to a contract between two parties, even though there remain obligations to be performed, the Service can determine that the economic reality underlying the transaction is such that the income is deemed received by a party which the Service wishes to tax. While on the other hand, as we shall see in the context of § 482, the Commissioner has the authority indefinitely to review the economic reality underlying a contract to determine if the price, indeed, reflects the economic reality consistent with the commensurate with income standard, regardless of the parties' honest effort to fix contractual obligations at arm's length." Karl William Viehe, "The Legal and Economic Realities of Transfer Pricing: An Analysis of the Draft Revenue Procedure on Advance Transfer Price Rulings." *Transnat'l Law.* 4 (1991): 1, 5 (1991).

Chapter 5

An Example Discussed

SITUATION: SUMMARY OF OECD—BEPS ACTION 9 ON VALUATION OF INTANGIBLES AND SUPPLY CHAIN—TRANSFER PRICING METHODS

Introduction to Chapter 5

Chapter 4 is divided into two substantive sections. The first deals specifically with the changes of BEPS relating to risk allocation. The second deals with the concept of the functions, assets, and risk analysis changes in BEPS.

SUMMARY OF SECTION A. ON MAIN SUGGESTIONS IN BEPS ACTION 9—CHANGES TO RISK ANALYSIS

This section will discuss the changes of the BEPS in relation to transfer pricing and risk allocation. These changes, and the greater BEPS package, came as a political response[1] to the problems inherent in the international tax system and the increased public attention to multinationals using tax structuring[2] and arbitrage[3] to avoid higher tax bills.[4]

Substantively, this section will look at the origins of transfer pricing rules based on the arm's length principle of Article 9(1) of the OECD Model Tax Convention. This basis on the arm's length principle includes the legal fiction of the separate and independent enterprise,[5] which is explored in-depth. This arm's length principle functioned as a solution to avoid international economic double taxation[6] and provides for tax authorities to grant adjustments of taxable bases.

Delving more into the key transfer pricing process, the section dives into the comparability analysis[7] of how third parties, conducting similar economic activities, price transactions.[8]

Continuing on, this section looks into the theoretical and economic concepts of risk and then the technical analysis of risk in transfer pricing. Following this, the concept of risk management is elucidated.

Having this basis of what risk is, the section continues by showing the changes to risk analysis that have been brought about through BEPS. The essential change is that BEPS Action 9 looks to actual activity and trumps the contracts and intercompany agreements of multinationals. This is done by looking to where economically significant risks have been allocated.

Understanding risk and the changes with BEPS in terms of risk, the section summarizes how risk allocation affects intangibles for taxation purposes.

I. MAIN SUGGESTIONS IN BEPS ACTION 9—CHANGES TO RISK ANALYSIS FROM AN OECD PERSPECTIVE: CONDUCT TRUMPS CONTRACTS

BEPS urges a change to the current transfer pricing rules, because "the existing international standards for transfer pricing rules can be misapplied so that they result in outcomes in which the allocation of profits is not aligned with the economic activity that produced the profits."[9] BEPS Action Plan 9 strives to "ensure that transfer pricing outcomes are aligned with value creation."[10]

It should be noted that BEPS Action Plan 9 also deals with other issues of transfer pricing—that is not the focus of this thesis. This includes a focus on the functions, assets, and risk analysis and how BEPS Action 9 has changed the "functions, risk, assets" ("FAR") analysis as a whole. It first focuses on the concept of assets as the key in economic ownership,[11] then BEPS's recommendation for looking at the people functions governing the assets. The management and key decision-makers of the assets are the keys to the economic ownership, and not so much legal title of the assets. Again, this is not the focus of this thesis but should be delineated as what will not be discussed in detail—but is a large part of the BEPS report on risk allocation.

The basic origin of the arm's length principle is found in Article 9(1) of the OECD and UN Model Tax Convention. Following the interpretation of the OECD Transfer Pricing Guidelines, Article 9(1) requires "that transactions between associated enterprises are priced as if the enterprises were independent, operating at arm's length and engaging in comparable transactions under similar conditions and economic circumstances." Article 9(1) provides for a type of relief of economic double taxation.[12] Although economic double taxation is often hardly relieved, the OECD Model's Article 25 provides for a solution through a mutual agreement procedure.[13]

The expression in Article 9(1) is of a separate and independent enterprise is the basis of the arm's length principle. It is a legal fiction. In economic reality, there are not two independent parties in a transaction but a unified group of wholly owned or majority owned subsidiaries conducting transactions among themselves. Moreover, "even the terms of transactions between independent and unrelated parties are not necessarily fair and reasonable, if the two parties do not have equivalent negotiation powers on a level playing field."[14] However, this is the legal fiction we must follow—as it is the law and international practice.[15] This fiction leads us to the so-called comparability analysis.

The key to a transfer pricing arm's length analysis is the concept of comparability and a comparability analysis. If "the conditions of the transaction are different to those between third parties in comparable circumstances, adjustments to the profits may be needed for tax purposes" by the taxing administrations, and as a result, an accurate pricing can be achieved.[16] Ultimately, this involves a comparability specifically to third parties is key in a comparability analysis.

Historically, transfer pricing has proved effective and efficient for helping prevent double taxation.[17] However, the main problem with transfer pricing thus far is the analysis's "perceived emphasis on contractual allocations of functions, assets and risks,[18] [whereby] the existing guidance on the application of the principle has also proven vulnerable to manipulation." This manipulation can lead to outcomes that do not reflect economic reality. BEPS Action Plan 9 strives to solve the problem with the arm's length principle thus far.

Giammarco Cottani[19] defines risk as volatility meaning that "business outcomes of an enterprise are heavily dependent on how their strategic choices expose them to certain types of volatility, e.g. fluctuations in the upside or downside of any given entrepreneurial direction."[20] Contractual allocation of risk is key for BEPS 8–10; and, Cottani points out that this contractual allocation of risk is normally referred to as the neoclassical economic concept of moral hazard applied in an international tax treaty scenario.[21] Moral hazard in the neoclassical sense is the idea whereby a party insures itself from the probability of failure by shifting the potential of losing—monetary or other—value to another party.[22]

In order to manage risk, it appears key to (1) identify the source of volatility and (2) assess the impact of risk on business activity. To reach an effective risk management, there must exist a uniform definition and categorization of risk.[23] In other words, risk management does not eliminate risk but provides analysis and advice with which to maximize returns while reducing losses—a "risk/return trade-off" scenario.[24]

The BEPS Action points focus on risk specifically and a system to analyze risk. The report defines risks as "the effect of uncertainty on the objectives of the business." Indeed, every action a business takes involves risk. The more risk involved, the higher the expected return will be. BEPS Actions 8–10 provides a six-step approach to analyzing risk: (1) "identification of economically significant risks in the transaction; (2) Contractual assumption of the risks; (3) Functional analysis with respect to risks; (4) Interpretation of Steps 1 through 3; (5) Allocation of risks; and, (6) Pricing of the controlled transaction."

BEPS indicates that a company would not take risk without expecting return.[25] Risk's connection with return on value can be demonstrated by the concept of weighted average cost of capital (WACC) formula.[26] "WACC is the expected rate of return for a company on the basis of the average portion of debt and equity in the company's capital structure, the current required return on equity (i.e., cost of equity), and the company's cost of debt."[27] Given this idea that identifying risk is key to a transfer pricing analysis, multinationals would abuse this strategy by contractually re-allocating risks without any change to business operations. When multinationals abuse[28] the transfer pricing methods, they create distortions in the tax revenue of host countries.[29] BEPS wants to tackle this contractual re-allocation of risk.

To combat artificial contractual re-allocation of risk, the BEPS Report determines[30] when risks are contractually assumed by a party that cannot "exercise meaningful and specifically defined control over the risks, or does not have the financial capacity to assume the risks." Then the tax authorities should re-allocate risks to the party that—in economic reality—"does exercise such control and does have the financial capacity to assume the risks."

Two-Pronged Test of BEPS Action 9 Regarding Risk Allocation

In short, the two prongs of step 5 in the new risk allocation analysis provide for "control over risk" and "whether the party assuming risk . . . has the financial capacity to assume risk"—each with its own definition provided by BEPS—both trump contracts. However, in the end, this two-pronged analysis leads to different results comparing an affiliate within a corporate group and a stand-alone company. But the purpose of the arm's length principle was to lead to the same results when comparing an affiliate within a corporate group and a stand-alone company—even if both companies conduct the exact same actions. Thus, step 5 of the new risk allocation analysis paradoxically takes the cake of the arm's length and eats it as well—creating uncertainty in the fiction of arm's length.

Paragraph 1.65 defines "control over risk." Indicating that risk is to be allocated to the party that is functionally involved "(i) the *capability to make decisions* to take on, lay off, or decline a risk-bearing opportunity, together with the actual performance of that decision-making function and (ii) the capability to make decisions on whether and how to *respond to the risks* associated with the opportunity, together with the actual performance of that *decision-making function*"[31] (emphasis added by author).

The meaning of *assuming risk* is further defined according to Paragraph 1.86 that states that "whether the party assuming risk . . . has the financial capacity to assume risk."[32]

Contractual allocations will only be followed if the functionality test proves the contracts; in other words, contractual allocation may be followed only if the contract allocates the risks to where the OECD wants the risks to be allocated.[33]

II. CONCLUSIONS AND SUMMARY OF CHAPTER 4

This section summarizes the transfer pricing allocation of risk and the changes inherent in BEPS. It also provided theoretical background of risk and risk allocation. The key policy objective that BEPS purportedly still wants transfer pricing risk analysis to look at contracts and then focus on the actual activity. After that analysis, the BEPS paradigm provides for the actual activities—"economic reality"—to trump the contracts.

As will be seen in the summary of the *Medtronic* case, this is not what the U.S. Court does. And, following Hafkenscheid's analysis, this thesis will show that BEPS does not really look into the contracts at all, but BEPS only looks at which entity has the financial capacity to assume risk. In other words, the OECD's BEPS Action Plan on Transfer Pricing only allocates risk—not on contractual bases—but where BEPS wants risk allocated.

NOTES

1. "The Financial Crisis of 2008 and Great Recession that followed have exacerbated income inequality within and between countries. In the aftermath of the economic turbulence, politicians have turned their attention to the twin problems of individual tax evasion and corporate tax avoidance. U.S. legislators enacted the Foreign Account Tax Compliance Act (FACTA), leading to the United States signing a series of Intergovernmental Agreements (IGAs) for the exchange of tax information. The Organization for Economic Co-operation and Development (OECD) developed the Multilateral Agreement for Administrative Assistance in Tax Matters (MAATM) and initiated the Base Erosion and Profit Shifting (BEPS) project to reduce tax evasion and tax avoidance globally." Reuven S. Avi-Yonah and Haiyan Xu, "Evaluating BEPS: A Reconsideration of the Benefits Principle and Proposal for UN Oversight." *Harv. Bus. L. Rev.* 6 (2016): 185.

2. There are "two competing lines of tax cases which deal broadly with uses and limits of anti-tax avoidance doctrines. The source of the conflict suggests that its resolution lies not with the definition of insurance, but with the policies behind general tax doctrines, such as protection of federal tax revenues, promotion of certainty in tax planning, and encouragement of legitimate business transactions. Because the conflict involves fundamental principles, it allows for no precise or uncontroversial resolution." Donald Arthur Winslow, "Tax Avoidance and the Definition of Insurance: The Continuing Examination of Captive Insurance Companies." *Case W. Res. L. Rev.* 40 (1990): 79, 112. *Cf.* Compare with the European Union's definition of tax avoidance. Dennis Weber, *Tax Avoidance and the EC Treaty Freedoms* (2005), 166–235.

3. "Tax arbitrage may be defined as the reciprocal borrowing and lending of money to give at least one party tax-exempt interest income and deductible interest expense." Daniel Shaviro, "Selective Limitations on Tax Benefits." *U. Chi. L. Rev.* 56 (1989): 1189, 1231.

4. "Base erosion and profit shifting affects all countries, not only economically, but also as a matter of trust. BEPS is depriving countries of precious resources to jump-start growth, tackle the effects of the global economic crisis[,] and create more and better opportunities for all. But beyond this, BEPS has been also eroding the trust of citizens in the fairness of tax systems worldwide. The measures [presented in the action reports] represent the most fundamental changes to international tax rules in almost a century: they will put an end to double non-taxation, facilitate a better alignment of taxation with economic activity and value creation, and when fully implemented, these measures will render BEPS-inspired tax planning structures ineffective." *Id.* at 188 fn. 6. *See.* "OECD Presents Outputs of OECD/G20 BEPS Project for Discussion at G20 Finance Ministers Meeting - OECD." Accessed May 29, 2021. https://www.oecd.org/ctp/oecd-presents-outputs-of-oecd-g20-beps-project-for-discussion-at-g20-finance-ministers-meeting.htm.

5. "The proper arm's-length interest rate [or any rate for inter group transactions] to apply to the branch's liabilities can be determined by reference to the rate that would be payable by the permanent establishment if it were a separate independent enterprise, but an adjustment needs to be made to reflect the fact that assets standing behind those liabilities are those of the enterprise as a whole, which would presumably reduce the arm's-length rate." Stephen B. Land, "Treaty Consistency." *Tax Law.* 66 (2012): 113, 120.

6. "Double taxation is a natural consequence of multinational business operation. See Multinational Corporations in World Development, . . . (contending that taxation of foreign-source income often results in double taxation); Organisation for Economic Co-operation & Dev. Comm. on Fiscal Affairs, Transfer Pricing and Multinational Enterprises: Three Taxation Issues 11 (1984) . . . (characterizing double taxation as ordinary occurrence in world of international business).

Lest the reader become alarmed, it is important to note that double taxation is the exception and not the rule. In the vast majority of cases involving both foreign and domestic income, provisions built into national tax laws mitigate or eliminate double taxation. See Julie A. Roin, "The Grand Illusion: A Neutral System for the Taxation of International Transactions." *Va. L. Rev.* 75 (1989): 919, 923–926 (summarizing tax exemptions and tax credit mechanisms for alleviating double taxation); *see* also I.R.C. § 901 (1988) (codifying foreign tax credit). The most common methods for alleviating double taxation are the tax exemption, whereby a country exempts foreign-source income from its cumulative tax base, and the tax credit, which permits a taxpayer to subtract income taxes paid in a foreign country from its domestic tax liability. Roin, supra, at 923–924. A potential third method for alleviating double taxation would be to permit the taxpayer a deduction from profits subject to tax in its country of domicile."

Robert G. Clark, "Transfer Pricing, Section 482, and International Tax Conflict: Getting Harmonized Income Allocation Measures from Multinational Cacophony." *Am. U. L. Rev.* 42 (1993): 1155, 1212 fn. 11.

7. "In any event, the 1968 regulations comprised overall a strong statement of the principle that tax authorities should seek to enforce the arm's length standard through retrospective analysis based on comparables. Moreover, the issuance of the regulations coincided with what appeared at the time to be a definitive judicial adoption of the view that reference to comparables, as opposed to a 'reasonableness' standard, constituted the proper basis of enforcement under the arm's length standard. Thus, the years following the 1968 regulations provided a definitive practical test of a system of enforcement based on comparables." Michael C. Durst and Robert E. Culbertson, "Clearing Away the Sand: Retrospective Methods and Prospective Documentation in Transfer Pricing Today." *Tax L. Rev.* 57 (2003) 37, 58.

8. "Arm's length prices may vary from market to market even for transactions involving the same property or services. Therefore, to achieve comparability, the markets in which the independent and associated enterprises operate must be comparable. To ensure comparability, any differences in the markets should not have a material effect on price unless appropriate adjustments can be made to account for such differences." ¶ 3.03 Guidance for Applying the Arm's-Length Principle, 1998 WL 1038574, 10.

See. OECD Guidelines ¶ 1.55. One economic condition that could pose interesting issues when comparing data from one area to another is relative inflation conditions in the markets. *United States*. See Brooks & Becker, "The Effects of Inflation on Cross-Border Profit Comparisons." *Tax Mgmt. Transfer Pricing Rep.* 7 (June 3, 1998): 77.

9. OECD, OECD/G20 Base Erosion and Profit Shifting Project: Preventing the Granting of Treaty Benefits in Inappropriate Circumstances (2014). For an in-depth analysis of how tax arbitrage and how treaties may be misused "See. e.g., Stef Van Weeghel, *The Improper Use of Tax Treaties: With Particular Reference to the Netherlands and the United States* (1998) . . . ; Philip Baker, *Improper Use of Tax Treaties, Tax Avoidance and Tax Evasion* (2013), http://www.un.org/esa/ffd/tax/2013tmttan/paper9a_baker.pdf." Yariv Brauner, "What the BEPS?" *Fla. Tax Rev.* 16 (2014): 55, 115 fn. 106.

10. *Id.*

11. "The OECD Guidelines do not follow the Section 482 regulations in this regard. Rather, the Guidelines tend to emphasize the importance of economic ownership over legal ownership, particularly in situations involving marketing

intangibles. Moreover, the Guidelines also recognize that for 'legitimate business reasons', related parties may structure their intercompany transactions in a manner that unrelated companies would not contemplate. In that event, the allocation of income attributable to intangibles based on the principles of economic ownership under the OECD Guidelines seems more appropriate than allocation based on legal title. This difference between the Section 482 Regulations and the OECD Guidelines may expose taxpayers to the risk of double taxation and create significant conflict between the United States and the other members of the OECD." James R. Mogle, "The Future of International Transfer Pricing: Practical and Policy Opportunities Unique to Intellectual Property, Economic Substance, and Entrepreneurial Risk in the Allocation of Intangible Income." *Geo. Mason L. Rev.* 10 (2002): 925, 931.

12. Indeed, it is key to note that Article 9 is the only Article in the OECD Model Convention that deals with avoidance of economic double taxation, unlike others such as Article 7 dealing with juridical double taxation. "[T]he OECD Model, apart from article 9, in principle only deals with the prevention of juridical double taxation." F. Debelva and J. Luts, "The European Commission's Proposal for Double Taxation Dispute Resolution: Turning the Tide?" *Bull. Intl. Taxn.* 71 (2017): 5, Journals IBFD.

13. "If there is a dispute [in regards to a transfer pricing adjustment], the solution should be found in the mutual agreement procedure under article 25 of the OECD Model (2014)." O.C.R. Marres, "Interest Deduction Limitations: When To Apply Articles 9 and 24(4) of the OECD Model." *Eur. Taxn.* 56 (2016): 1, Journals IBFD. *See.* Para. 11 *OECD Model: Commentary on Article 9* (2010). *OECD Model Tax Convention on Income and on Capital: Commentary* (July 15, 2014), Models IBFD.

14. Reuven S. Avi-Yonah and Haiyan Xu, "Evaluating BEPS: A Reconsideration of the Benefits Principle and Proposal for UN Oversight." *Harv. Bus. L. Rev.* 6 (2016): 185, 226.

15. Though, there have been calls to replace the current system of transfer pricing: "As the comparability analysis is not practical and feasible as anticipated, we propose the formulary apportionment system based on the single unitary entity principle." Reuven S. Avi-Yonah and Haiyan Xu, "Evaluating BEPS: A Reconsideration of the Benefits Principle and Proposal for UN Oversight." *Harv. Bus. L. Rev.* 6 (2016): 185, 226.

16. "As with the other methods, whether the resale price method produces the most reliable measure of the arm's-length result must be determined under the best method rule and the comparability analysis provisions previously discussed. In terms of functional comparability, a reseller's gross profit provides compensation for performing resale functions related to the product, including an operating profit in return for the reseller's investment of capital and assumption of risks. Thus, comparability under the resale price method is particularly dependent on similarity of functions performed, risks borne, contractual terms, and adjustments to account for the effects of any such differences." What Exempt Organizations Need to Know about the Transfer Pricing Rules, 11 *J. Tax'n Ex. Org.* 217, 226, 2000 WL 1920395, 12. *Compare With.* Matthew 20:1–16 (KJV) Jesus' parable of the workers in the Vinyard: they all got paid the same wage for responding to the same call to work, although each group of workers arrived and started to work at a different time of day. This parable depicts

the open market. Jesus basically took the side of the U.S. Tax Courts that whatever the parties' agree to ex-ante is fair, regardless of how these prices look after the fact, ex-post facto analysis.

17. "Double taxation generally occurs in the context of transfer pricing adjustments, where tax authorities in competing jurisdictions disagree over income allocations attributable to transfer pricing. Transfer pricing adjustment, at income allocation, is the means by which national tax authorities assign market prices to related-party transactions in order to clarify the income attributable to each segment of a multinational corporation, thereby performing the role reserved to the free market in transactions among unrelated parties. When unmitigated double taxation occurs, the taxpayer ordinarily has recourse only to obtain agreement on its behalf between the two countries' tax authorities." Robert G. Clark, "Transfer Pricing, Section 482, and International Tax Conflict: Getting Harmonized Income Allocation Measures from Multinational Cacophony." *Am. U. L. Rev.* 42 (1993): 1155, 1157–1158.

18. "Risk" can be defined as volatility. It is the chances taken by key decision makers for an expected return. G. Cottani, Transfer Pricing, Topical Analyses IBFD (accessed Mar.3, 2017).

19. Advisor, OECD Centre for Tax Policy and Administration.

20. G. Cottani, Transfer Pricing, Topical Analyses IBFD (accessed Mar. 3, 2017).

21. G. Cottani, Transfer Pricing, Topical Analyses IBFD (accessed Mar. 3, 2017). *Compare With.* See Professor Roberts discussing international investment treaties in relation to moral hazard. A. Anthea Roberts, "Triangular Treaties: The Extent and Limits of Investment Treaty Rights." *Harv. Int'l L.J.* 56 (2015): 353, 378.

22. Michael J. Graetz, "Retroactivity Revisited." *Harv. L. Rev.* 98 (1985): 1820, 1841 fn. 82. See, for example, Blume & Rubinfeld, "Compensation for Takings: An Economic Analysis." *Calif. L. Rev.* 72 (1984): 569, 593–597.

23. Cottani has proposed several different types of risk, as a general framework: strategic risks; intellectual capita risks; financial risks; operational risks; and moral hazard risks. G. Cottani, Transfer Pricing, Topical Analyses IBFD (accessed Mar. 3, 2017).

24. G. Cottani, Transfer Pricing, Topical Analyses IBFD (accessed Mar. 3, 2017). *See.* 1.45 and 9.10 of TP Guidelines.

25. "Therefore, referring to the basic functional analysis construct that evaluates related companies in terms of functions performed, risks undertaken, and assets used, those companies employing self-developed valuable intangible assets should be expected to earn above normal returns compared to otherwise comparable companies not possessing valuable intangible assets." ¶ 8.02 Basic Economic Concepts, 1998 WL 1038873, 2.

26. A discounted cash flow (DCF)

> valuation has two steps: first, forecasting future cash flows; and second, discounting those cash flows back to the present. As a starting point, DCF, unlike the Delaware Block Method, targets the correct indicators of value. A share represents a claim on the future cash flows of the company—precisely what DCF is intended to measure. Therefore, DCF is the conceptually correct measure for valuing minority shares in an appraisal proceeding.

In implementing DCF valuation, virtually all courts have adopted a particular manifestation of DCF known as Free Cash Flow (FCF) valuation. There are two problems with this choice that make DCF valuation both inequitable and inefficient. First, the method includes the benefits of interest tax shields in the discount rate, which requires a forecasted capital structure for the company. More specifically, the correct discount rate to use in DCF valuation is the weighted-average cost of capital (WACC). The WACC is a weighted average of the cost of equity and the after-tax cost of debt, in which the weights are the relative amounts of debt and equity in the combined, post-merger company. Most courts have assumed a constant WACC in calculating the present value of cash flows, but this simplifying assumption is correct only when the capital structure of the company is stable over time. If capital structure fluctuates over time, a single WACC is an inaccurate representation of the cost of capital." "Using Capital Cash Flows to Value Dissenters' Shares in Appraisal Proceedings." *Harv. L. Rev.* 111 (1998): 2099, 2105–2106.

27. *John Hancock Life Ins. Co. (U.S.A.) v. C.I.R.*, 141 T.C. 1, 150 (2013).

28. "One of the methods used to confront tax claims from revenue agencies is via transfer pricing because its use is one of the simplest ways to evade taxes." Transfer Pricing in a Global Market, 35 *J. Corp. Tax'n* 17, 17, 2008 WL 193050, 1.

29. "There is an important debate about fundamental tax reform looming, and the problem of homeless income (HI) commonly referred to in the current round of debate as 'base erosion and profit shifting' (BEPS) is at the center of the storm." Bret Wells and Cym Lowell, "Tax Base Erosion: Reformation of Section 482's Arm's Length Standard." *Fla. Tax Rev.* 15 (2014): 737, 738. *Cf.* Indeed, one of the main homeless income and BEPS problems is the concept of transfer pricing and how it can be abused. *See*. "Statement of William J. Sample, Vice President of Worldwide Tax for Microsoft Corporation, Offshore Profit Shifting Hearing (Microsoft & Hewlett Packard), supra note 21, at 30, http://www.hsgac.senate.gov/subcommittees/investigations/hearings/offshore-profit-shifting-and-the-us-tax-code; see also Testimony of Tim Cook, CEO of Apple, Inc., Offshore Profit Shifting Hearing (Apple), supra note 21, at 30 (stating that its cost sharing agreement and tax practices complies fully with all applicable Treasury regulations)." Bret Wells and Cym Lowell, "Tax Base Erosion: Reformation of Section 482's Arm's Length Standard." *Fla. Tax Rev.* 15 (2014): 737, 797 fn. 33.

30. Leading companies look for greater sophistication in their risk assumptions relating to valuations. In an era of heightened volatility, more valuation teams are employing tools such as tornado diagrams or Monte Carlo simulations. Tornado diagrams, for example, are a means of analyzing the potential volatility of individual variables such as oil prices, exchange rates, or finished goods or services selling prices.

A tornado analysis considers one such factor at a time across a range of scenarios. In this way, the process is useful in identifying the discrete issues most likely to have an impact, positive or negative, on performance and, therefore, valuation.

Monte Carlo simulation, by comparison, is a means of analyzing the risks associated with a range of variables. This analysis looks at how variables interact with one another across a swath of randomly generated values and scenarios. Because the analysis looks at correlations between variables and introduces less likely but still possible scenarios, the tool is remarkably useful in helping a company better understand the risk associated with any investment.

V is for Value in Valuation: A Fresh Look at a Transaction Standard, WGL-ACCTALERT VOL 6 NO 153. 2012 WL 10235065, 4.

31. OECD, Aligning Transfer Pricing Outcomes with Value Creation—Actions 8-10 Final Reports, OECD/G20 Base Erosion and Profit Shifting Project (OECD 5 Oct. 2015), International Organizations' Documentation IBFD. Para. 1.65.

32. OECD, Aligning Transfer Pricing Outcomes with Value Creation—Actions 8-10 Final Reports, OECD/G20 Base Erosion and Profit Shifting Project (OECD 5 Oct. 2015), International Organizations' Documentation IBFD. Para. 1.86.

33. R. Hafkenscheid, "The BEPS Report on Risk Allocation: Not So Functional." *Intl. Transfer Pricing J.* 24 (2017): 1, Journals IBFD. *Compare with.* OECD, Aligning Transfer Pricing Outcomes with Value Creation—Actions 8-10 Final Reports, OECD/G20 Base Erosion and Profit Shifting Project (OECD Oct. 5, 2015), International Organizations' Documentation IBFD. Para. 1.65.

Chapter 6

Complication

Compare and Contrast the Policies of the U.S. Precedent as Outlined in Regard to Risk Allocation to BEPS Action 9 Report on Risk Allocation

INTRODUCTION TO CHAPTER 6

In the international framework of international tax, the OECD and the United Nations participate in the concepts of creations of various aspects of law. Indeed, the OECD and UN have similar origins from the end of World War II as well as the aftermath of World War I and the creation of the League of Nations. Realizing the harmful effects of double taxation, the League of Nations itself produced drafts and research around various issues of international taxation.[1] Much of this work aimed to create a framework that countries could adopt to reduce the burden of double taxation in the international scheme. At that time, the graduated income tax was a fairly new concept having been newly introduced around the era of World War I and the 1910s in the United States and Western Europe.

It is worthwhile to partially recapitulate the former discussion on the history of the League of Nations transforming into the OECD and UN. The League of Nations tackled challenges of international taxation producing papers and summaries as well as model treaties. After World War II, the Organisation for European Economic Co-operation (OEEC) picked up the mantel of working on tax issues—among many economic issues. The OEEC worked to ensure economic development in post-War and early Cold War Europe. However, as more countries gained independence from European nations, the UN gained a greater vote. In time, the OECD came into existence focusing on countries that formerly were the focus of the OEEC. The UN paralleled this as a global form.

More specifically, in the context of taxation and international tax development, the OECD has focused on developing rules for the residence countries—that is, predominately the countries where resources go to, such as European countries, the G20, etc. The UN economic tax plan was to set up model tax treaties and do research on source countries—where money is often going from to the residence countries. Even more specifically, in the context of tax treaties models, the UN provides more favorable provisions for the source country to keep and collect more revenue while the OECD focuses on allowing more revenue and income to be allocated to the residence country.

Much of the debate as to which country—that is source or residence country—should gain more tax revenue is based on political reasons. But behind—and sometimes before these political reasons—is the technical and philosophical reasons for taxation. The means and ability to create a system of taxation often relies on substantive rules whether they are contractual systems of Anglo-Saxon common law or the civil law system based in the Napoleonic code.

In response to the "Great Recession" of the late 2000s and the early 2010s, the OECD tried to create a more inclusive framework to address the problems that international taxation had led to. The G20 mandated this and the OECD has tried to create ideas and technical rules to address these issues. The ultimate result was something called the BEPS project. BEPS stands for "base erosion and profit shifting," which is one of the most prevalent problems in tax law and international taxation. The tax base is where income tax begins its calculation. The profits of major multinational corporations are shifted to low-tax jurisdictions.

Within the overall BEPS project, one of the more interesting and ground shaking at the base of the framework of international taxation was Action 9 and its relation to the concepts of transfer pricing. These in a non-explicit manner shifted notions of risk, agency, and legal norms that have a basis in Roman common law. Jurists later codified Roman common law as the Byzantine Corpus Juris Civilis made up of the Code of Justinian, the Digest the Institutes, and the *Novellae Constitutiones*.[2] Even, the rules and such codes were interpreted by Norman common law judges and developed into the modern civil and common law doctrines we know today. The main concepts of law of ancient legal doctrines as they evolved to the modern day suggested that the meeting of the minds—the outward representations of the inward intentions—to assent to an agreement should govern human interaction in part. If such contracts were not relevant, then human interaction would speak for itself, in that contracts would not be needed. In the historical progression, contracts arose as a system of enforcing promises rather than relying on verbal and hand gesture agreements.

There have been critiques of whether or not the Action 9 approach to risk allocation will work. This includes Rutger Hafkenscheid who argues Action 9 is impractical.

This chapter will discuss the policy behind BEPS Action 9 and the changes to risk allocation in favor of actions over contracts. Then, the second section will discuss several examples showing the changes to risk analysis under BEPS Action 9 and the agency implications for risk allocation.

Ultimately, the problems of Action 9 will likely lead to it not being implemented. Moreover, the United States will likely not apply it.

There are diagrams to help in this analysis as well.

POLICY BEHIND BEPS ACTION 9—CHANGES TO RISK ANALYSIS: CONDUCT TRUMPS CONTRACTS

Greater Policy Positions behind BEPS in General and Specific Connections to BEPS

This section will discuss the holistic policy positions behind BEPS with a focus on the specifics of transfer pricing. It has long been known that base erosion and profit shifting has caused problems for revenue agencies of countries to amass money for government expenditures. Whether and how the government is to gather these collected monies is another debate. However, what is certain is that the rule of law dictates that certain amounts of taxable income should be given to the government. Corporations for years have taken advantage of loopholes to pay lower taxes effectively and legally. This is against the spirit of the laws, despite not being against the letter of the law. It could be argued that the laws should be written better. But the purpose was not to have extremely low effective tax rates when the said rates were meant to be at a higher percentage—indeed, the envisioned possible deductions are not likely below half the indicated tax bracket rate.

Indeed, the OECD is the secretariat of the G7 and responded to the G7's request to deal with the 2007–2008 financial meltdown. One of the main causes of the financial crisis—or at least perceived main causes by the public—was that corporations were not paying their "fair share" of taxes. Regardless of the veracity in these claims, the G7 called on the OECD to produce action plans to deal with erosions of taxable bases and profit shifting that would effectively lower taxes. This led to the eponymous Base Erosion and Profit Shifting Action Plans that had initially been indicated.

Much of the world's economy is based out of the United States—thus, U. S. tax regulations are especially important to the whole BEPS project. However, the OECD acted under the assumption that gridlock in the U.S. Congress would effectively negate any prospect of the U.S. changing its tax rules. Therefore, the BEPS initiatives—including the changed rules on transfer pricing—do not expect the United States to change its laws or tax rules. Indeed, BEPS has been structured to solve the world's tax problems without any changes to the U.S. tax rules.[3]

Arm's Length is Here to Stay for Both U.S. and OECD Approaches

The treasury has defended the arm's length principle for years. But the question could be, What is the ALS, and why did the treasury seek to defend it in these terms? The problem for which the ALS attempts to provide the solution may be illustrated by a simple example. Suppose that a product (e.g., computers) is manufactured by a corporation in country A, and then sold to a wholly owned subsidiary of the manufacturer in country B, which proceeds to resell it to unrelated customers. In this common situation, the taxable profit of the subsidiary is determined by three factors: (1) the price at which it resells the computers to the unrelated customers, (2) its expenses other than cost of goods sold, and (3) the price which it pays its parent corporation for the computers. The first two of these factors are governed by market forces outside the control of the parent or the subsidiary. However, because the parent controls the subsidiary, the third factor (the price for which the manufacturer sells the computers to the reseller, or the "transfer price") is wholly within the control of the related parties. Accordingly, the potential for abuse arises because the related parties will seek to increase after-tax profits by manipulating the transfer price. If the effective tax rate in the manufacturer's country is higher, the price will be set as low as possible so as to channel all taxable profit to the reseller. Conversely, if the effective tax rate in the reseller's jurisdiction is higher, the transfer price will be as high as possible, so as to eliminate any taxable profit of the reseller and concentrate the entire profit in the hands of the manufacturer. But for tax considerations, the affiliated parties do not care what the transfer price is, since it merely re-allocates profits within the affiliated group.[4]

The main policy reasons for keeping the ALS are: The most prominent articulation of these policy rationales, consistent with the United States and other OECD member countries, is by the model rules for transfer pricing promulgated by the Organization for Economic Cooperation and Development, the OECD Transfer Pricing Guidelines for Multinational Enterprises and Tax Administrators (the "Guidelines"). The Guidelines function as model rules and all OECD member countries have agreed to incorporate the OECD standards into their own tax administrations. Accordingly, the rationale for ALS articulated in the Guidelines can be considered the generally agreed-upon justification for the use of ALS to set transfer prices.

In describing the role of transfer pricing in MNEs and the associated risk of income distortion, the Guidelines set out an important assumption about the nature of intra-firm prices. "It should not be assumed that the conditions established in the commercial and financial relations between associated enterprises will invariably deviate from what the open market would demand." This critical assumption made by the Guidelines—that the related entities in a single control group related to one another in a way economically analogous to similar unrelated enterprises—indicates that from the standpoint of the Guidelines, ALS is used to set "real" prices. Even where there is no intent on the part of an MNE to minimize or avoid taxes, an adjustment using ALS may be appropriate. The assumption that arms-length prices reflect economic reality of intra-firm transactions, though not made fully explicit in the Guidelines, is the first and most significant justification for the ALS regime. The Guidelines suggest that the structure of MNEs distorts natural prices, even if inadvertently, and that ALS corrects that distortion.

The second stated justification for ALS is closely related to the first. When ALS corrects the price distortions created by intra-firm transactions, it provides "broad parity of tax treatment for members of MNE groups and independent enterprises." The artificial tax advantages produced by MNE transfer pricing would otherwise "distort the relative competitive positions" of the two types of entities. Furthermore, eliminating this artificial competitive advantage promotes the growth of international trade and investment. Similar to the first justification for ALS, the necessary implication of this stated purpose is the assumption that the difference between related entities in an industry and individual entities performing similar productive functions, but independently, is that the related group has the opportunity to distort its tax bill, and thereby gain an artificial advantage over the independent entities. According to the Guidelines, the two scenarios have the same economic reality, but with the potential for different tax consequences, a distortion that ALS corrects. *436 The third stated justification for ALS as the global transfer pricing regime is a functional one. The Guidelines recognize that taxation of MNEs is a global problem requiring collective action. The OECD itself represents collective movement away from tax competition and toward coordination. ALS is a broadly accepted standard, integrated into individual states' tax laws as well as bilateral treaties, including Article 9 of OECD Model Tax Convention. Insofar as ALS is widely and uniformly implemented, its role as a facilitator of collective action is a core justification for its continued use. It is especially useful for avoiding double taxation, which is the central objective of bilateral tax treaties. When one taxing authority makes an adjustment to the income of an entity using ALS, the fact that other tax jurisdictions where the MNE does business allocate income using the same standard reduces the chances of conflicting allocations that lead to double taxation. For these reasons, along with the stated theoretical justifications, the Guidelines express a firm stay-the-course attitude with respect to ALS.[5]

Specific Policy Positions behind BEPS in Connection to Risk Analysis

BEPS Action Plan 9 defines risk management as a party's ability to control transactions that cover risk to the company.[6] Paragraph 1.65 states, "[r]isk assumption means taking on the upside and downside consequences of the risk with the result that the party assuming a risk will also bear the financial and other consequences if the risk materialises." Moreover, risk management does not necessarily mean risk assumption, because a party could assume the risk and contract out the management to someone else. However, *only* contracting allocation of risk is not enough, there must be an assumption of "economically significant risks in a controlled transaction"[7] and the financial capacity to assume such risk that would allow control over those risks, which is to be determined through the framework provided in the Final Report.[8] The policy behind the BEPS methodology is to find the actual economic relations behind intergroup dealings. Again, if actual conduct—actual conduct being the actual economic activity—deviates from the contractual arrangements, then BEPS states that the conduct trumps the contracts.

As an example, BEPS tries to help countries re-write the old taxing rules to provide more uniformity—especially in the aftermath of the world financial crisis starting in 2008—to counter the old arrangements of tax planning.

An example of the changes in BEPS can be examined by comparing a stand-alone company and a subsidiary in a corporate group. For example, a company based in Luxembourg—where people functions, such as management exist; and assets, such as movable capital exist—this company also has a London-based parent whereby financial and investing services are provided for in exchange of the Luxembourg assets.

The risk prior to BEPS is considered to exist in Luxembourg, because the Luxembourg company must make the decision of eventual investment. The U.S. Tax Court would take this approach as well.

However, with the new BEPS regime, the risk is assumed to exist in London, because the people functions—*beispielsweise*, the financiers are individuals making decisions in London.[9]

Rutger Hafkenscheid's Unveiling of BEPS Action 9

Discussing the BEPS Action 9 Report on risk, Rutger Hafkenscheid's article *The BEPS Report on Risk Allocation: Not So Functional* examining the BEPS

Report on Transfer Pricing and risk allocation provides a vital pivot point in comparing BEPS and U.S. Tax Court jurisprudence.

In his article, Hafkenscheid argues that although OECD BEPS Action Plan 9 seems to purport that contractual allocations of risk should still be examined, but he demonstrates that "[i]f a company lacks the functionality, but has the capital to bear risks, the risks and remuneration—according to the OECD—should be allocated to the related party that does have the functionality." Functionality is the key factor and "contractual allocation may be followed only if the contract allocates the risks to where the OECD wants the risks to be allocated."

The OECD seems to be saying that they are still interested in looking at contracts when understanding businesses, but the OECD is not looking at contracts in the risk analysis.

Looking to Actions 8–10 of the BEPS report, at Paragraph 1.60, the new risk analysis is laid as follows:

"The steps in the process set out in the rest of this section for analysing risk in a controlled transaction, in order to accurately delineate the actual transaction in respect to that risk, can be summarised as follows:

1) Identify economically significant risks with specificity (see Section D.1.2.1.1).
2) Determine how specific, economically significant risks are contractually assumed by the associated enterprises under the terms of the transaction (see Section D.1.2.1.2).
3) Determine through a functional analysis how the associated enterprises that are parties to the transaction operate in relation to assumption and management of the specific, economically significant risks, and in particular which enterprise or enterprises perform control functions and risk mitigation functions, which enterprise or enterprises encounter upside or downside consequences of risk outcomes, and which enterprise or enterprises have the financial capacity to assume the risk (see Section D.1.2.1.3).
4) Steps 2-3 will have identified information relating to the assumption and management of risks in the controlled transaction. The next step is to interpret the information and determine whether the contractual assumption of risk is consistent with the conduct of the associated enterprises and other facts of the case by analysing (i) whether the associated enterprises follow the contractual terms under the principles of Section D.1.1; and (ii) whether the party assuming risk, as analyzed under (i), exercises control over the risk and has the financial capacity to assume the risk (see Section D.1.2.1.4).
5) Where the party assuming risk under steps 1–4(i) does not control the risk or does not have the financial capacity to assume the risk, apply the guidance on allocating risk (see Section D.1.2.1.5).

6) The actual transaction as accurately delineated by considering the evidence of all the economically relevant characteristics of the transaction as set out in the guidance in Section D.1, should then be priced taking into account the financial and other consequences of risk assumption, as appropriately allocated, and appropriately compensating risk management functions (see Section D.1.2.1.6)."

Step 5 disregards 2–4, because it says that the contracts will only be followed if the financial capacity to assume the risk is present—otherwise, the intercompany contracts will be disregarded.

Rutger Hafkenscheid indicates that the main problem lies in Step 3 whereby the OECD indicates that arm's length risk allocation is determined by which contracting party *controls* risk. Hafkenscheid points to Paragraph 1.65 that defines "control over risk." Paragraph 1.65 indicates that risk is "to be allocated to the party that is functionally involved":[10]

> (i) the capability to make decisions to take on, lay off, or decline a risk-bearing opportunity, together with the actual performance of that decision-making function and (ii) the capability to *make decisions* on whether and how to *respond to the risks* associated with the opportunity, together with the actual performance of that *decision making* function. (emphasis added by author)[11]

Hafkenscheid clarifies the meaning of assuming risk by is further defined according to Paragraph 1.86 that states that "whether the party assuming risk . . . has the financial capacity to assume risk."[12] Mr. Hafkenscheid shows how the answers to both questions as to who contractually bears the risk and who has the financial capacity to risk lead to the functionality analysis. The disguise of this risk analysis is that "contract [or intercompany agreements] should allocate risks only to the party having the functionality to assume the risks." Hafkenscheid clarifies, "It is therefore not relevant what parties *have* agreed, but rather what they *should have* agreed. Nor is the actual *capitalization* of the related company relevant, but rather the capitalization to which the company can be *assumed* to have *access*, based on its functionality: the OECD defines the financial capacity to assume risk as 'access to funding to take on the risk or lay off the risks.'"[13]

This means that contractual allocations will only be followed if the functionality test proves the contracts; in other words, "contractual allocation may be followed only if the contract allocates the risks to where the OECD wants the risks to be allocated."[14]

EXAMPLE OF POLICY CHANGES IN BEPS ACTION 9—CHANGES TO RISK ANALYSIS—AND THE DICHOTOMY OF THE NEW APPROACH

The stand-alone company will be treated differently than the company in a corporate group. The very concept of the arm's length principle is that companies in a corporate group should be treated the same as stand-alone companies. Note: Persons run each corporate entity. This will be discussed below.

The figures below will demonstrate how the OECD interpretation contradictions the concept of attribution. In this situation, an individual contributes her portfolio investments to a wholly owned company. The stand-alone company has no functionality—according to the OECD—the individual controls the size of the company's assets by contributions and distributions. She also sets the company's risk strategy and level of risk she is willing to take. She controls all the decisions, plans, etc. of the company.

Figures 6.1 to 6.3 illustrate the problem. First, there is an individual managing a bag of money—assets. The individual will be taxed.

Second, the same actions could occur with an individual managing assets, but the square outline over the assets represents the corporate form. This is the case for most stand-alone companies. In this case, the corporate form will be taxed off agency principles where the individual's actions are attributed to the corporate entity as the individual's alter ego.

Third, there is a manager acting out of a company managing assets in a corporate entity, such as in corporate groups with asset managers and investment funds. Traditionally—pre-BEPS and still in the United States through

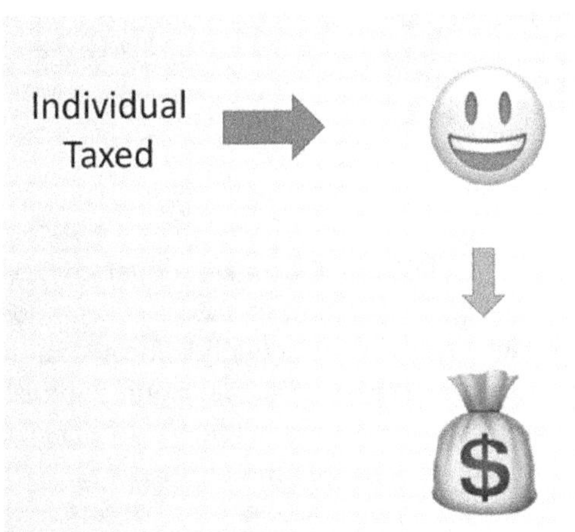

Figure 6.1

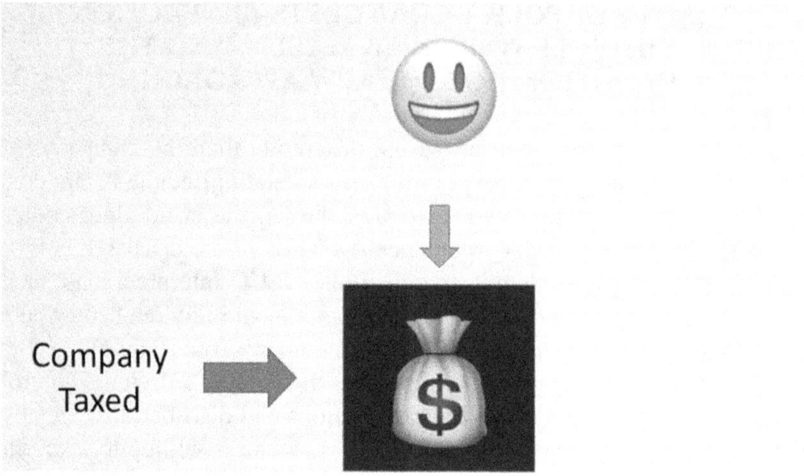

Figure 6.2

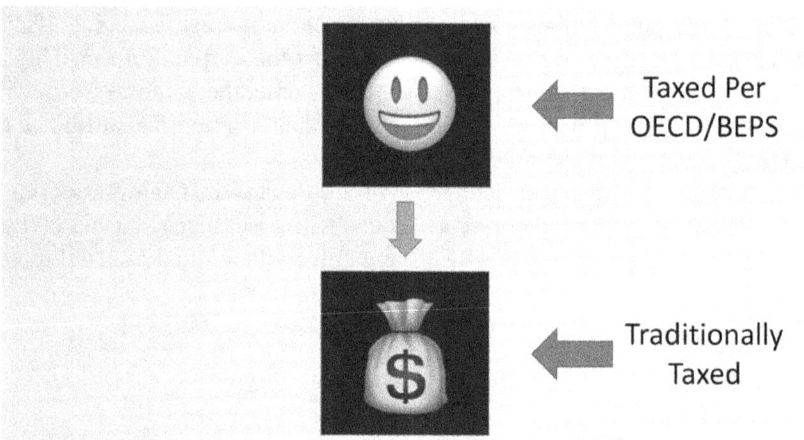

Figure 6.3

the U.S. Tax Court—the location (especially in the international context) of the assets themselves were taxed—the jurisdiction of the assets is where the assets were taxed. This was because risk is contractually allocated to the jurisdiction of the assets. BEPS with the six-step risk allocation approach now states that the place where management is—the jurisdiction of management—where taxation should take place, not the location of the assets.

This will cause a fissure—with a possibility of tax loopholes—assets could be placed outside the United States (in an OECD country following the BEPS risk allocation recommendations) and management within the United States.

The United States will grant taxing rights to the country where the asset is located. The country where the asset is located will grant taxing rights to the United States. In this case; there could be a situation of double non-taxation—the opposite of what was intended under BEPS.

For tax purposes, she is not seen at all, and the company is taxed entirely. Rutger Hafkenscheid points out that the problem with this approach is that:

> The basis of the arm's length principle is that a company is treated as a separate entity for taxation, irrespective of its functionality and of whether it is part of a larger group of companies. This "separate-legal-entity approach" is also the underlying principle of the tax systems applied by all industrialized economies. The separate-legal-entity approach attributes the results of human action to the company as if the company itself had performed these actions. The question is whether the action of the person can be considered to represent the company, i.e., whether the company is bound by it, not whether the company has the functionality to be bound by the representative. In fact, the representation itself forms the functionality. This "attributed functionality" is a fundamental choice underlying the taxation of corporate profits and applies irrespective of which legal form the representation has, e.g. the form of an employment contract, a management agreement, an outsourcing assignment or an agency agreement. It remains completely unclear as to why other forms of representation would have a different result . . . functionality is indeed relevant for determining where the company resides or where it has a taxable presence through a permanent establishment, but the concept is useless for determining transfer prices in related situations.[15]

The problem with this approach is that the OECD denies the concept of agency-principal relations that is a cornerstone of Western legal systems. Hafkenscheid writes:

> The OECD claims that a person with financial capacity to bear business risks would be willing to accept these risks only if that person alone has the functionality to manage the risks. This, however, is in contradiction to economic reality: modern capitalism is built on principal agency relationships in which the capacity to fund investments and manage the risks of those investments is separated. Examples of these principal–agency relationships include investment funds, private-equity funds and listed companies. The separation between risk management and risk assumption is the basis of these relationships. The investment manager has the functionality to control the risks on behalf of and for the account of the investor, but does not assume the risks.
>
> It is by definition the *legal form* of the principal–agency relationship that determines the tax consequences of that relationship. If the relationship takes the legal form of an individual asset management assignment, the assets and

> associated risks are attributed to the investor. If, however, the agency relationship is structured as a fund with legal personality, the assets and associated risks are attributed to the fund entity. Whatever the legal form of the relationship, however (individual asset management assignment or fund), the asset manager managing the risks *never* receives the risk premium that is the remuneration for assuming the risks, whereas this is what the OECD claims that is happening between unrelated parties. That risk premium is either received by the fund (and taxed at the fund level) or by the investor (and taxed at the investor level)."[16]

Indeed, the riskless manager may not get paid enough, but there is a recognizable structure Hafkenscheid mentions exists. Investment firms often get paid whether they make their clients any money or not: this is the plot of *Wolf of Wall Street* for example.[17]

The risk premium may not come in the form of direct management. Usually, risk premium means that, for example, a person will not be going for small proportion gains but only larger proportion gains, so they may still be acting based on that desire for (and reservations about) a premium. In other words, a risk premium is different from a commission.

CONCLUSIONS AND SUMMARY

In summary, simple development of Action 8–10 in regard to transfer pricing is the changing definition of the arm's length principle by reference to the contract being dominated by actual activities.[18]

NOTES

1. For a brief discussion of the history of the international tax regime and the research done by the League of Nations in the 1920s, see Reuven Avi-Yonah, *Advanced Introduction to International Tax Law* (2019), 3–6.

2. Though Roscoe Pound pointed out a twist on this codification of Justinian "we may have to remind the historical and philological Romanist that it was Roman law as codified by Justinian, not the actual law of the Antonines—much less that of Augustus—that became the common law of western Europe." Roscoe Pound, "A Text Book of Roman Law from Augustus to Justinian by W. W. Buckland, M. A., F. B. A., of the Inner Temple, Barrister at Law, Regius Professor of Civil Law in the University of Cambridge, Fellow of Gonville and Caius Co." *Harv. L. Rev.* 26 (1922): 119, 120–121.

3. A unique question is why the OECD and the BEPS project would want the U.S. Tax Court to rule differently?

4. Reuven S. Avi-Yonah, "The Rise and Fall of Arm's Length: A Study in the Evolution of U.S. International Taxation." *Va. Tax Rev.* 15 (1995): 89, 90.

5. Glen Rectenwald, "A Proposed Framework for Resolving the Transfer Pricing Problem: Allocating the Tax Base of Multi-National Entities Based on Real Economic Indicators of Benefit and Burden." *Duke J. Comp. & Int'l L.* 22 (2012): 425, 434–436.

6. The language from the BEPS Final Report states, "(i) the capability to make decisions to take on, lay off, or decline a risk-bearing opportunity, together with the actual performance of that decision-making function, (ii) the capability to make decisions on whether and how to respond to the risks associated with the opportunity, together with the actual performance of that decision-making function."

Moreover, Professors Avi-Yonah and Xu have written that, "Actions 8–10 are the most important part of the BEPS project in addressing related party transactions of MNEs." Reuven S. Reuven S. Avi-Yonah and Haiyan Xu, "Evaluating BEPS: A Reconsideration of the Benefits Principle and Proposal for UN Oversight." *Harv. Bus. L. Rev.* 6 (2016): 185, 225.

7. "Controlled transactions" in this case means transactions within the corporate group between and among subsidiaries.

8. G. Cottani, Transfer Pricing, Topical Analyses IBFD (accessed Mar, 3 2017).

9. This illustrated difference in this hypothetical is between choice was between contractual "will" (intention) terms and some objective/third-party representation (interpretative abstract) of a supposedly observable reality.

10. R. Hafkenscheid, "The BEPS Report on Risk Allocation: Not So Functional." *Intl. Transfer Pricing J.* 24 (2017): 1, Journals IBFD.

11. OECD, Aligning Transfer Pricing Outcomes with Value Creation – Actions 8-10 Final Reports, OECD/G20 Base Erosion and Profit Shifting Project (OECD 5 Oct. 2015), International Organizations' Documentation IBFD. Para. 1.65.

12. *Id.* at Para. 1.86.

13. R. Hafkenscheid, "The BEPS Report on Risk Allocation: Not So Functional." *Intl. Transfer Pricing J.* 24 (2017): 1, Journals IBFD.

14. R. Hafkenscheid, "The BEPS Report on Risk Allocation: Not So Functional." *Intl. Transfer Pricing J.* 24 (2017): 1, Journals IBFD.

15. R. Hafkenscheid, "The BEPS Report on Risk Allocation: Not So Functional." *Intl. Transfer Pricing J.* 24 (2017): 1, Journals IBFD.

16. R. Hafkenscheid, "The BEPS Report on Risk Allocation: Not So Functional." *Intl. Transfer Pricing J.* 24 (2017): 1, Journals IBFD.

17. The story relating to Stratton Oakmont and Jordan Belfort. WOLF OF WALL STREET (Paramount Pictures and Red Granite Productions 2013). *Compare with.* Indeed, not even the fictional plot of *The Firm* with Tom Cruise relating to aggressive tax avoidance structures in The Cayman Islands. THE FIRM (Paramount Pictures 1993).

18. While considering the changes of the definition of arm's length, it is curious to find the origin of the phrase arm's length comes from the concept in waltzing that partners should dance at "arm's length" akin to unrelated parties not "cheek-to-cheek" akin to romantic lovers. Analogously, corporations in a corporate group should

operate as unrelated parties, not romantic lovers. Ben J. M. Terra, Peter J. Wattel, *European Tax Law*, sixth edition (abridged student edition), 2012 Wolters Kluwer Law & Business, page 578, fn. 3. In truth, this definition and name origin is rather bizarre. Is there an implication here about secrecy that is not being stated? Because business partners or corporate subsidiaries do have to act very closely together in order to create products . . . And they have to act in good faith and with relationships of trust between those holding wealth and power to be used by and/or for the benefit of others . . . just as in a Romantic Relationship—as a matter of fact, marital law is much like partnership law . . . when properly applied and interpreted . . .

Chapter 7

The Swerve to the Future[1]

THE QUESTION OF THIS CHAPTER'S THESIS: WILL THE U.S. TAX COURT APPLY ACTION 9 OF OECD BEPS?

The U.S. Tax Court will likely not apply the OECD BEPS Action 9 Recommendation regarding risk allocation for three reasons. (1) Two Constitutional reasons: (a) the Constitutional cavalcade of hierarchy regarding international law in the United States—much less the precedential value of a secondary source, such as OECD reports. (b) The concept of *stare decisis* that is embedded in the common law system of the Anglo-American tradition relies on cases being decided as they have been decided in the past. The tradition of upholding prior precedent is not easily broken—except for egregious reasons, such as regarding slavery.[2]

(2) Given the status of international law and international secondary sources in the United States in addition to the concept of *stare decisis*, the U.S. Tax Court—as all courts in the United States—consistently build on judicial application of law. Four key transfer pricing cases since the 1986 transfer pricing tax reforms in the United States will be shown to support the concept of *stare decisis*.

(3) Finally, the most recent transfer pricing case—Amazon—shows that the court still upholds the prior precedential cases through *stare decisis*. Moreover and perhaps more importantly, in the international context regarding other countries' decision to implement Action 9, had the IRS brought the argument of Action 9 forward, not only would the entire case have been analyzed differently, but the prospect of bringing Action 9's reasoning forward, the IRS would have forfeited all claims to the pricing of the transferred IP to the "empty company"—as will be shown later.

NOTES

1. The title for this chapter comes from *The Swerve* by Stephen Greenblatt that in large part discusses the influence of Lucretius's poem *De rerum natura* (On the Nature of Things—as it is often translated into in English. STEPHEN GREENBLATT, THE SWERVE: HOW THE WORLD BECAME MODERN.

The poem is cited for many interesting instances of atoms and other scientific advancements. But it is often cited for atheistic tendencies.

"For in a season troublous to the state
Neither may I attend this task of mine
With thought untroubled, nor mid such events
The illustrious scion of the Memmian house
Neglect the civic cause.
Whilst human kind
Throughout the lands lay miserably crushed
Before all eyes beneath Religion- who
Would show her head along the region skies,
Glowering on mortals with her hideous face-
A Greek it was who first opposing dared
Raise mortal eyes that terror to withstand
Whence he to us, a conqueror, reports
What things can rise to being, what cannot,
And by what law to each its scope prescribed,
Its boundary stone that clings so deep in Time.
Wherefore Religion now is under foot,
And us his victory now exalts to heaven."

Rather than atheism, this passage says those who support religion are usually hypocritical depending on the situation. Indeed, the atheistic tendencies are not for certain, because as "Lucretius postulates before Christ that all existence on earth is made of atoms that assemble and then on death disperse. The earth in flux takes and uses them for reassembly. The soul and the body are inseparable in life and at death become dispersed atoms. For Lucretius, there is no afterlife for the soul when our eyelids finally close and we become shadows of ourselves." Justice Gregory J. Hobbs, Jr., Poetry, *U. Denv. Water L. Rev.* 18 (2014) 154, 160.

However, Lucretius goes on to say.
"I fear perhaps thou deemest that we fare
An impious road to realms of thought profane;
But 'tis that same religion oftener far
Hath bred the foul impieties of men:
As once at Aulis, the elected chiefs,
Foremost of heroes, Danaan counsellors,
Defiled Diana's altar, virgin queen,
With Agamemnon's daughter, foully slain.
She felt the chaplet round her maiden locks
And fillets, fluttering down on either cheek,

And at the altar marked her grieving sire,
The priests beside him who concealed the knife,
And all the folk in tears at sight of her.
With a dumb terror and a sinking knee
She dropped; nor might avail her now that first
'Twas she who gave the king a father's name.
They raised her up, they bore the trembling girl
On to the altar- hither led not now
With solemn rites and hymeneal choir,
But sinless woman, sinfully foredone,
A parent felled her on her bridal day,
Making his child a sacrificial beast
To give the ships auspicious winds for Troy:
Such are the crimes to which Religion leads.

And there shall come the time when even thou,
Forced by the soothsayer's terror-tales, shalt seek
To break from us. Ah, many a dream even now
Can they concoct to rout thy plans of life,
And trouble all thy fortunes with base fears."

In some sense, this seems to argue that Lucretius is a deist and just does not believe in organized religion.

2. However, consider that in theory, 1772 common law from England came to the United States (although there is no clear rule that supports this). However, in the relatively famous case *Somerset v Stewart* (1772), Lord Mansfield wrote, "The state of slavery is of such a nature that it is incapable of being introduced on any reasons, moral or political, but only by positive law [statute], which preserves its force long after the reasons, occasions, and time itself from whence it was created, is erased from memory. It is so odious, that nothing can be suffered to support it, but positive law. Whatever inconveniences, therefore, may follow from the decision, I cannot say this case is allowed or approved by the law of England; and therefore the black must be discharged." Yet, slavery persisted in the 13 colonies and what eventually became the United States.

Cf.

Indeed, consider that "despite Chief Justice Taney's assertion, slavery had been repudiated within England prior to our Declaration of Independence and prior to the adoption of the United States Constitution through Lord Mansfield's significant opinion in 1772 in *Somerset v. Stewart*. Regardless of its historical inaccuracy, *Dred Scott* announced a constitutional principle that a badge and incident of slavery was that black men (whether they were slaves or not) ". . . had no rights which the white man was bound to respect." By "no rights" the federal constitutional perception meant no rights in the federal court, no rights to equally compete in the labor market, no rights to liberty, *no rights to equality, no rights to justice, no rights to manhood, and black slave women not even having the right to possess their own children. The purpose of the Thirteenth Amendment was not merely abolishing the physical cruelties of slavery, but its purpose was to also eradicate those "badges and incidents of slavery." The Thirteenth Amendment ". . . authorizes Congress not only to outlaw all forms of slavery and involuntary servitude, but also to eradicate the last vestiges and incidents of a society half slave and half free4)4B"B." Surely, if in *Jones, supra*, Congress, through the Thirteenth Amendment can assure equal access to housing, here it can assure equal access to the Courts and ban discrimination in employment. For the denial of equal housing opportunities in *Jones, supra,* was no more a vestige and incident of slavery than the racially invidious discriminatory animus aimed at black plaintiffs in this case." Com. of Pa. v. Local Union No. 542, Int'l Union of Operating Engineers, 347 *F. Supp.* 268, 299–301 (E.D. Pa. 1972), *aff'd sub nom. Com. of Pa. v. Local Union 542, Int'l Union of Operating Engineers*, 478 F.2d 1398 (3d Cir. 1973).

Chapter 8

Reason (1) U.S. Constitutional Policy Regarding International Law and the Concept of *Stare Decisis*

The U.S. Tax Court will not apply the OECD BEPS Action 9 Recommendation regarding risk allocation for three reasons. (1) Two constitutional reasons: (a) the constitutional cavalcade of hierarchy regarding international law in the United States—much less the precedential value of a secondary source, such as OECD reports. (b) The concept of *stare decisis* that is embedded in the common law system of the Anglo-American tradition relies on cases being decided as they have been decided in the past. The tradition of upholding prior precedent is not easily broken—except for egregious reasons, such as regarding slavery.

Constitutional Basis and Framework of the United States: Mixed Monist and Dualist System in the United States Regarding International Law and National Law

There are two prevalent schools of thoughts for interpreting the value of international law in the constitutional frameworks: the dualist and monist approaches.[1]

These frameworks seem to operate independently and dependently of the legal realistic and legal formalistic paradigms, because the dualist and monist theories do not fit into either realism or formalism on their own. In practice, dualism and monism could fit together. However, such a theory would be a synthesis or a complete separation of the two theories.

The monist school of thought "views international and domestic law as together constituting a single legal system."[2] The "classic monistic approach would treat some of the international sources as equal to the municipal sources in resolving the statutory gap or ambiguity. Theoretically, in a monistic system, it is even possible for international sources to override a direct statutory mandate."[3]

Monism "rejects the belief that legal authority in a democracy can only be derived from within the domestic democratic process."[4]

Dualist states "emphasize the difference between national and international law and require the translation of the latter into the former."[5]

The place and value of international law is based on the U.S. Constitution; indeed, "the prevailing view is that for international purposes the United States was a single sovereign state from 1776."[6] Given, that the United States derives its status from the U.S. Constitution, the first chief justice [of the Supreme Court], John Jay, [wrote] "had, by taking a place among the nations of the earth, become amenable to the laws of nations."[7] The constitution gives the "federal government (the President and Senate), not the states, the authority to make treaties."[8]

The constitution itself outlines exactly what place treaties hold in American jurisprudence.[9] However, the constitution does not thoroughly address the value; place; the relation of customary international law in American political institutions and legal framework as a whole; whether customary international law falls at the same level as state or federal law; the relation of treaties to Congress and the constitution; and even whether the president or Congress have a mandate to follow and fulfill the obligations of treaties.[10]

However, the Supreme Court has never considered the status of international law and thus has never declared international law to trump the constitution.[11] Since the 1880s, the Supreme Court and "courts have accepted the equality of statutes and treaties as an established principle.[12] Usually, the Court will apply it to give effect to a later act of Congress inconsistent with an earlier treaty; less frequently they apply it to give effect to a later treaty inconsistent with an earlier act of Congress."[13]

Regarding customary international law in relation to statutes, "[i] 1900, the Supreme Court . . . was prepared to extend [the equality doctrine] to treat customary law and treaties alike, to declare customary international law equal in status to concurrent acts of Congress . . . [It also stated] that a principle of customary international law will not govern if a 'controlling'—that is, a subsequent—act of Congress conflicts with its mandate."[14] This "last-in-time rule is known by the legal maxim *lex posterior derogat priori*."[15]

U.S. TREASURY'S POLICY TOWARD BEPS REGARDING RISK ALLOCATION

Before, analyzing the precedent of the U.S. Tax Court, it is important to see the policy of the treasury—that brings the tax cases against taxpayers before the U.S Tax Court.

The U.S. Treasury's Policy toward international tax has been to support U.S. multinational enterprises through preferential tax treatment of U.S. companies. This includes, the "US tax policy over the last two decades has been to support US multinationals operating outside the United States under more competitive tax conditions than their local competitors."[16]

This policy can be perceived to promote and certainly, "tolerates US multinationals' keeping their foreign profits offshore if not repatriated to the United States, which acts as an incentive to keep foreign profits low taxed by shifting profits from foreign high-tax jurisdictions to foreign low-tax jurisdictions."[17]

Putting this into a greater policy context with a background to the EU State Aid investigations and U.S. Congressional concerns, "on Dec. 1, 2015, the Senate Finance Committee held a hearing on 'International Tax: OECD BEPS and EU State Aid.' At this hearing, treasury deputy assistant secretary of international tax affairs Robert Stack testified that treasury is concerned that the European Commission's investigations and potential decisions:

- appear to disproportionately target U.S. companies;
- potentially undermine U.S. rights under its bilateral tax treaties with EU Member States; ·are taking a novel approach in applying EU State Aid rules and applying that approach retroactively rather than prospectively;
- could give rise to U.S. companies paying EU Member States billions of dollars in tax assessments that may be creditable foreign taxes, resulting in U.S. taxpayers 'footing the bill'; and
- substantively amount to EU taxation of historical earnings that, under internationally accepted standards, no EU Member State had the right to tax."[18]

Following this hearing, a document was formed summarizing the OECD's BEPS project and how it will affect U.S. companies. The report stated that "[i]n the open market, greater returns typically compensate assumption of increased risk. Allocation of profits according to contractual allocation of risks, however, may lead to profit allocations that do not correspond with the activities multinational group entities actually carry out."[19] Following this concern, the BEPS Action Plan "report provides a new analytical framework for analyzing risk and provides that a transaction is not simply delineated by what is set out in a contract. Where necessary, evidence of the parties' actual conduct should supplement the terms of any contract."[20]

The way this method for analyzing risk operates is that the tax authority is first "to assume a risk for transfer pricing purposes the associated enterprise must control the risk (have the capability to decide whether to take on the risk and how to respond to risk) and have the financial capacity to assume the risk (access to funding to take on the risk or to lay off the risk, to pay for the risk mitigation functions, and to bear the consequences of the risk if the risk materializes)."[21] Indeed, where ***management*** is located elsewhere—that is "where an enterprise providing capital does not exercise control over the investment risks that may give rise to premium returns, that enterprise should not expect more than a risk-free return."[22]

INTERNAL REVENUE SERVICE (IRS) ON TRANSFER PRICING AND BEPS

The IRS is a bureau of the U.S. Treasury and acts as the revenue collection agency. The treasury "spent years writing regulations in an attempt to improve application and enforcement of the transfer pricing rules in international transactions."[23] However, "[t]he results, however, create even more problems for both taxpayers and the IRS. Every change in the law affecting international trade means added regulations, further tax rulings, more tax audits and ultimately more litigation, with a corresponding increase in the costs of preparing documentation to demonstrate compliance with the regulations."[24] This complication has led to changes in the "accounting methods used to determine international transfer prices under the new IRS regulations and discusses the problems inherent in applying the regulations."[25] Then, the IRS led to changes involving "documentation requirements of the new transfer pricing regulations and explains why they constitute an onerous burden on businesses."[26]

Fundamentally, "[a]n interesting aspect of the taxing powers of the United States government, is the fact that the IRS Commissioner appears to have the power to choose the best of both worlds, as the Commissioner's view of economic reality dictates."[27] This allows the IRS, "on the one hand, with respect to a contract between two parties, even though there remain obligations to be performed, the Service can determine that the economic reality underlying the transaction is such that the income is deemed received by a party which the Service wishes to tax."[28] This means that "on the other hand, as [seen] in the context of § 482, the Commissioner has the authority indefinitely to review the economic reality underlying a contract to determine if the price, indeed, reflects the economic reality consistent with the commensurate with income standard, regardless of the parties' honest effort to fix contractual obligations at arm's length."[29]

In theory, "the arm's length standard's use of comparable transactions creates a clear legal requirement. For a typical transfer pricing transaction, the Treasury regulations produce a range of results; if the taxpayer can demonstrate its price falls within the permitted range, it can avoid an IRS transfer pricing adjustment. Unfortunately, rapid globalization, the rise of multinational enterprises, and a growing market for intangibles have all but eliminated the 'typical' transfer pricing transaction."[30] Indeed, [i]f the arm's length standard is to serve as the basis for a workable transfer pricing system, functional analysis designed to identify comparable uncontrolled transactions must be successful with sufficient regularity."[31]

However, it is becoming increasingly difficult to compare comparable transactions, but "[u]sing the term 'failure' to describe any legal rule, much less a global legal regime, can tend toward hyperbole. Nevertheless, to the extent that [the arm's length standard] is inadequate to the task it is implemented to fulfill—the allocation of the corporate tax base of MNEs—[the arm's length standard] is a failed doctrine." The main failure "is the disconnect between the assumptions at the core of [the arm's length standard] about the nature of intra-firm transactions and the economic reality of those transactions."[32] Given "the increasing pace of globalization, this disconnect between the assumptions of [the arm's length standard] and the reality of global commerce will only widen, and the use of [the arm's length standard] to allocate global income on a national basis less tenable."[33]

POLICY OF THE U.S. TAX COURT PRECEDENTS REJECTING RISK ALLOCATION

Indeed, looking at the U.S. Tax Court's jurisprudence, it may seem that the decisions ignore the concept of looking at "economic reality" that the OECD proposes. *The policy behind the U.S. Tax Court is that it simply has refused to use extra judicial or international non-binding legal documents to come to a solution.* It is as if the court is applying a textualist[34] approach to interpreting U.S. legal documents. It seems to eschew a statutory level of interpretation following "internationalism" or using scholarly studies of judicial activism. Indeed, the court seems to follow the basic concept in common law of *stare decisis*—established through the use of binding legal documents.[35] *Stare decisis* can be defined in terms of the judiciary as a command "follow syllogistic and logical application of the law as found in the idea of *stare decisis et non quietamovere*, to provide a system of legitimacy and predictability. As the Ninth Circuit Court of Appeals stated, '[s]tare decisis is the policy of the court to stand by precedent; the term is but an abbreviation of stare decisis et non quietamovere—'to stand by and adhere to decisions and not disturb what is settled.'''"[36]

The court seems to apply a formalist theory of interpretation of the U.S. Internal Revenue Code and the Treasury Code that is based on the ordinary meaning of the legal text—and not using secondary sources or international non-binding law for comparison.

EXPLANATION OF THE U.S. TAX COURT'S ADHERENCE TO *STARE DECISIS*

The basic idea of *stare decisis* is that former court precedents will be followed. The concept has its roots in Roman Law and was later conducted by English courts since Anglo-Saxon times.[37]

It has also been upheld by the U.S. Supreme Court several times as the preferred method of deciding decisions.

Although U.S. court cases may sometimes seem like looking into a crystal ball, the courts do have some method. Professor Erwin Chemerinsky's discusses how U.S. courts decisions can seem arbitrary, but in the end, do have some structure.[38] Professor Chemerinsky states, "[a] successful challenge to its legitimacy will lead the Court to provide a more open justification for its rulings, one that more explicitly identifies and defends its value choices. Alternatively, if the U.S. Supreme Court's decision making is actually based on the quest for neutrality, revealing the misguided nature of such a quest facilitates the development of theories of constitutional interpretation."[39]

This explains why the U.S. Tax Court is willing to keep upholding the same rules in decisions as it did in prior cases and not create new rules in conformity with scholarly or international rules.

COMPARING AND CONTRASTING BOTH POLICY APPROACH RESULTS

The stand-alone company will be treated differently than the company in a corporate group. The very concept of the arm's length principle is that companies in a corporate group should be treated the same as stand-alone companies. The new BEPS plans on transfer pricing will lead to different results—and even confusing results. Thus, not only will the U.S. courts be hesitant to apply the BEPS plan on transfer pricing, but so will other courts around the world.

This result is against the goal of BEPS, which is to create rules for countries to follow regardless of whether the United States changes its rules. Now, neither the United States nor other countries will likely have the inclination to change their transfer pricing rules in terms of risk allocation.

This is against the purpose of the arm's length principle, because stand-alone companies and companies in corporate groups will no longer be treated the same.

NOTES

1. See. Antonio Cassese, *International Law in a Divided World* (1986), 15–22. *Cf.* Constitutional Courts and International Law: Revisiting the Transatlantic Divide, *Harv. L. Rev.* 129 (2016): 1362, 1363.

2. Louis Henkin, "The Constitution and United States Sovereignty: A Century of Chinese Exclusion and Its Progeny." *Harv. L. Rev.* 100 (1987): 853, 864 fn. 61.

3. Jonathan Turley, "Dualistic Values in the Age of International Legisprudence." *Hastings L.J.* 44 (1993): 185, 190.

4. Jonathan Turley, "Dualistic Values in the Age of International Legisprudence." *Hastings L.J.* 44 (1993): 185, 190, 205.

5. Filip Spagnoli, "The Globalization of Human Rights Law: Why Do Human Rights Need International Law?" *Tex. Wesleyan L. Rev.* 14 (2008): 317, 333.

6. *See United States v. Maine*, 420 U.S. 515, 520–521 (1975); *United States v. Curtiss-Wright Export Corp.*, 299 U.S. 304, 316 (1936); Morris, "The Forging of the Union Reconsidered: A Historical Refutation of State Sovereignty Over Seabeds." *Colum. L. Rev.* 74 (1974): 1056. For my purposes it does not matter whether between 1776 and 1789 we were thirteen nations or one nation with thirteen parts; all were bound by international law. Either the individual state governments or the Continental Congress (representing "the United States") were responsible internationally. There being no federal or confederated judiciary, only state courts were available to decide questions of international law. *See e.g., Respublica v. De Longchamps*, 1 Dall. 111 (Pa. 1784). Louis Henkin, "The Constitution and United States Sovereignty: A Century of Chinese Exclusion and Its Progeny." *Harv. L. Rev.* 100 (1987): 853, 886.

7. *Chisholm v. Georgia*, 2 U.S. (2 Dall.) 419, 474 (1793). "When the *United States* declared their independence, they were bound to receive the law of nations, in its modern state of purity and refinement." *Ware v. Hylton*, 3 U.S. (3 Dall.) 199, 281 (1796) (Wilson, J.) (emphasis in original). See RESTATEMENT OF THE FOREIGN RELATIONS LAW OF THE UNITED STATES (REVISED), pt. I, ch. 2, introductory note (Tent. Draft No. 6, 1985). Louis Henkin, "The Constitution and United States Sovereignty: A Century of Chinese Exclusion and Its Progeny." *Harv. L. Rev.* 100 (1987): 853, 886 fn. 62.

8. *See id.* art. I, § 10; art. II, § 2, cl. 2. Louis Henkin, "The Constitution and United States Sovereignty: A Century of Chinese Exclusion and Its Progeny." *Harv. L. Rev.* 100 (1987): 853, 886 fn. 64.

9. Louis Henkin, "The Constitution and United States Sovereignty: A Century of Chinese Exclusion and Its Progeny." *Harv. L. Rev.* 100 (1987): 853, 867.

10. Louis Henkin, "The Constitution and United States Sovereignty: A Century of Chinese Exclusion and Its Progeny." *Harv. L. Rev.* 100 (1987): 853, 867.

11. Louis Henkin, "The Constitution and United States Sovereignty: A Century of Chinese Exclusion and Its Progeny." *Harv. L. Rev.* 100 (1987): 853, 869.

12. "*See, e.g., Breard v. Greene*, 523 U.S. 371, 376 (1998) (per curiam); *Reid*, 354 U.S. at 18; *The Chinese Exclusion Cases*, 130 U.S. 581, 600 (1889); *Whitney v. Robertson*, 124 U.S. 190, 194 (1888); *Head Money Cases*, 112 U.S. 580, 599 (1884);

The Cherokee Tobacco, 78 U.S. (11 Wall.) 616, 621 (1870); Restatement (Third)." Vasan Kesavan, "The Three Tiers of Federal Law." *Nw. U. L. Rev.* 100 (2006): 1479, 1635.

13. Louis Henkin, "The Constitution and United States Sovereignty: A Century of Chinese Exclusion and Its Progeny." *Harv. L. Rev.* 100 (1987): 853, 872.

14. Louis Henkin, "The Constitution and United States Sovereignty: A Century of Chinese Exclusion and Its Progeny." *Harv. L. Rev.* 100 (1987): 853, 878.

15. Vasan Kesavan, "The Three Tiers of Federal Law." *Nw. U. L. Rev.* 100 (2006): 1479, 1635.

16. This is especially visible for "[t]hose watching the US Senate Finance Committee Hearings 'International Tax: OECD BEPS & EU State Aid' (www.finance.senate.gov/hearings/international-tax-oecdbeps-and-eu-state-aid) will get the impression that the US Treasury Department's stake in the BEPS Project was foremost and above all about protecting the interests of US multinationals against 'aggressive' tax authorities of other OECD member countries, rather than avoiding profit shifting. See also the interview by BNA with Robert Stack, Deputy Assistant Secretary (International Tax Affairs) US Treasury, available at www.bna.com/videos-m57982058714." R. Hafkenscheid, "The BEPS Report on Risk Allocation: Not So Functional." *Intl. Transfer Pricing J.* 24 (2017): 1, 5, Journals IBFD.

17. A "recent US Treasury White Paper claims that the profits kept offshore are US profits, not foreign profits. US: Treasury Dept., The European Commission's Recent State Aid Investigations of Transfer Pricing Rules (24 Aug. 2016). The present author disagrees. Under Treasury Regulation sec. 1.482-7, a buy-in payment forms the arm's length remuneration for future foreign income generated by the patent that is attributable to the patent existing at the moment of the buy-in. From the moment of the buy-in, the income generated by the patent is the foreign entity's income, i.e. foreign income, not US income—otherwise no arm's length payment would need to be made. If the foreign income is subsequently distributed by the foreign entity to the US parent, the United States will indeed tax these dividends again and give credit for the foreign tax attributable to the foreign profit from which those dividends are paid. The mere fact that the United States grants a credit for foreign tax underscores the fact that the royalties are foreign, not US." R. Hafkenscheid, "The BEPS Report on Risk Allocation: Not So Functional." *Intl. Transfer Pricing J.* 24 (2017): 1, 5, Journals IBFD.

18. Treasury Secretary & Key Lawmakers Weigh in On EU State Aid, Inversions & Tax Reform, 2/18/2016 FTWA ART. 1

19. Background, Summary, And Implications of The OECD/G20 Base Erosion and Profit Shifting Project, 2015 WL 8336616, At *19 *See.* Joint Committee on Taxation, Background, Summary, and Implications of the OECD/G20 Base Erosion and Profit Shifting Project (JCX-139-15), November 30, 2015. This document can also be found on the Joint Committee on Taxation website at www.jct.gov.

20. Background, Summary, And Implications of The OECD/G20 Base Erosion and Profit Shifting Project, 2015 WL 8336616, At *19 *See.* Joint Committee on Taxation, Background, Summary, and Implications of the OECD/G20 Base Erosion and Profit Shifting Project (JCX-139-15), November 30, 2015. This

document can also be found on the Joint Committee on Taxation website at www .jct.gov.

21. Background, Summary, And Implications of The OECD/G20 Base Erosion And Profit Shifting Project, 2015 WL 8336616, At *20 *See*. Joint Committee on Taxation, Background, Summary, and Implications of the OECD/G20 Base Erosion and Profit Shifting Project (JCX-139-15), November 30, 2015. This document can also be found on the Joint Committee on Taxation website at www.jct.gov.

22. Background, Summary, And Implications of The OECD/G20 Base Erosion And Profit Shifting Project, 2015 WL 8336616, At *20 *See*. Joint Committee on Taxation, Background, Summary, and Implications of the OECD/G20 Base Erosion and Profit Shifting Project (JCX-139-15), November 30, 2015. This document can also be found on the Joint Committee on Taxation website at www.jct.gov.

23. Michael Avramovich, "Intercompany Transfer Pricing Regulations Under Internal Revenue Code Section 482: The Noose Tightens on Multinational Corporations." *J. Marshall L. Rev*. 28 (1995): 915, 931. *See*. For an interesting and detailed account of the history of S 482, *see* Jerome R. Hellerstein, "Federal Income Taxation of Multinationals: Replacement of Separate Accounting with "Formulary Apportionment." *Tax Notes Int'l*, Aug. 24, 1993, at 163, available in LEXIS, Taxria Library, TNI file.

24. Michael Avramovich, "Intercompany Transfer Pricing Regulations Under Internal Revenue Code Section 482: The Noose Tightens on Multinational Corporations." *J. Marshall L. Rev*. 28 (1995): 915, 931.

25. Michael Avramovich, "Intercompany Transfer Pricing Regulations Under Internal Revenue Code Section 482: The Noose Tightens on Multinational Corporations." *J. Marshall L. Rev*. 28 (1995): 915, 931.

26. Michael Avramovich, "Intercompany Transfer Pricing Regulations Under Internal Revenue Code Section 482: The Noose Tightens on Multinational Corporations." *J. Marshall L. Rev*. 28 (1995): 915, 931.

27. Karl William Viehe, "The Legal and Economic Realities of Transfer Pricing: An Analysis of the Draft Revenue Procedure on Advance Transfer Price Rulings." *Transnat'l Law* 4 (1991): 1, 5.

28. Karl William Viehe, "The Legal and Economic Realities of Transfer Pricing: An Analysis of the Draft Revenue Procedure on Advance Transfer Price Rulings." *Transnat'l Law* 4 (1991): 1, 5.

29. Karl William Viehe, "The Legal and Economic Realities of Transfer Pricing: An Analysis of the Draft Revenue Procedure on Advance Transfer Price Rulings." *Transnat'l Law* 4 (1991): 1, 5.

30. Sienna C. White, "Cost Sharing Agreements & the Arm's Length Standard: A Matter of Statutory Interpretation?" *Fla. Tax Rev*. 19 (2016): 191, 195. *See*. Reg. § 1.482-1(b)(1).

31. Sienna C. White, "Cost Sharing Agreements & the Arm's Length Standard: A Matter of Statutory Interpretation?" *Fla. Tax Rev*. 19 (2016): 191, 196.

32. Sienna C. White, "Cost Sharing Agreements & the Arm's Length Standard: A Matter of Statutory Interpretation?" *Fla. Tax Rev*. 19 (2016): 191, 196. *Quoting*. Glen Rectenwald, "A Proposed Framework for Resolving the Transfer Pricing Problem:

Allocating the Tax Base of Multi-National Entities Based on Real Economic Indicators of Benefit and Burden." *Duke J. Comp. & Int'l L.* 22 (2012): 425, 436.

33. Sienna C. White, "Cost Sharing Agreements & the Arm's Length Standard: A Matter of Statutory Interpretation?" *Fla. Tax Rev.* 19 (2016): 191, 196. *Quoting*. Glen Rectenwald, "A Proposed Framework for Resolving the Transfer Pricing Problem: Allocating the Tax Base of Multi-National Entities Based on Real Economic Indicators of Benefit and Burden." *Duke J. Comp. & Int'l L.* 22 (2012): 425,436.

34. In explaining various methods of Constitutional interpretation, "[t]he term 'originalism' has been most commonly used since the middle 1980s and was apparently coined by Paul Brest in The Misconceived Quest for the Original Understanding, 60 *B.U. L. Rev.* 204, 204 (1980). Earlier discussions often used the term 'interpretivism' to denote theories that sought to derive meaning from the constitutional text alone ('textualism'), or from the intentions of the originators ('intentionalism'). See, e.g., John Hart Ely, *Democracy and Distrust: A Theory of Judicial Review* 1 (1980) ('interpretivism'); Thomas Grey, Do We Have an Unwritten Constitution?, 27 *Stan. L. Rev.* 703, 706 (1975) ('interpretive model'); H. Jefferson Powell, The Original Understanding of Original Intent, 98 *Harv. L. Rev.* 885 (1985) ('intentionalism'). Current discussions have tended to reject the labels 'interpretivism,' which often embraces nonoriginalist textualism, and 'intentionalism,' which suggests reliance on subjective intentions rather than objective meaning. See Gregory Bassham, *Original Intent and the Constitution* 146 n.3 (1992); Richard B. Saphire, Enough About Originalism, 15 *N. Ky. L. Rev.* 513, 515 n.7 (1988)."

35. Charles Lincoln, "A Structural Etiology of the U.S. Constitution." *J. Legis.* 43 (2016): 122, 131. *See. United States IRS v. Osborne* (*In re* Osborne), 76 F.3d 306, 309 (9th Cir. 1996).

36. Charles Lincoln, "A Structural Etiology of the U.S. Constitution." *J. Legis.* 43 (2016): 122, 131. *See. United States IRS v. Osborne* (*In re* Osborne), 76 F.3d 306, 309 (9th Cir. 1996).

37. The Michigan Supreme Court noted "[t]he doctrine can be traced back to medieval England." *Petersen v. Magna Corp.*, 484 Mich. 300, 387 n. 38 (Mich. 2009).

See also Charles Lincoln, "A Structural Etiology of the U.S. Constitution." *J. Legis.* 43 (2016): 122, 131 fn. 51:

See also Thomas Healy, "Stare Decisis as a Constitutional Requirement." *W. Va. L. Rev.* 104 (2001): 43, 56–62 (hereinafter "Healy"). However, the article itself notes that very few cases were recorded during the Anglo-Saxon period. However, there were many records of Anglo-Saxon and Norman history such as the Anglo-Saxon Chronicle D: Cotton Tiberius B IV (1067), English Historical Documents 150 (David C. Douglass & George W. Greenaway eds., Oxford Univ. Press 2d ed., 1981). Indeed, there are even visual representations, such as the *Bayeux Tapestry*. *See* The Bayeux Tapestry, A Comprehensive Survey (Sir Frank Stenton ed., Phaidon Press rev. ed. 1965).

But earlier Roman law was itself a compilation of cases in digests, which Roman lawyers would reference. Shael Herman, "Legacy and Legend: The Continuity of Roman and English Regulation of the Jews." *Tul. L. Rev.* 66 (1992):

1781, 1797. Even as early as the 1st Century B.C. "Cicero praised his friend, the jurist Servius Sulpicius Rufus for using dialectic and treating law as [a science]," indicating that—much like the modern method of using case law—Romans treated like cases alike. James Gordley, "The Method of the Roman Jurists." *Tul. L. Rev.* 87 (2013): 933, 947 n.73. *See generally Peter Stein, RegulaeIuris: From Juristic Rules to Legal Maxims* (1966).

By 1256 Henry de Bracton wrote of the importance of using past precedent he experienced previously to decide current cases before him, as indicated by his saying, "(i)f any new and unusual matters arise, which have not before been seen in the realm, if like matters arise let them be decided by like since the decision is a good one for proceeding a similibus ad similia." Healy, *supra*, at 56–57.

38. Erwin Chemerinsky, "The Vanishing Constitution." *Harv. L. Rev.* 103 (1989): 43, 61.

39. Erwin Chemerinsky, "The Vanishing Constitution." *Harv. L. Rev.* 103 (1989): 43, 61.

Chapter 9

Reason (2)

Following the Concept of Stare Decisis: *Summary of U.S. Tax Court Precedent on Transfer Pricing Regarding Risk Allocation*

Given the status of international law and international secondary sources in the United States, in addition to the concept of *stare decisis*, the U.S. Tax Court—as all courts in the United States—consistently build on judicial application of law. Four key transfer pricing cases since the 1986 transfer pricing tax reforms in the United States will be shown to support the concept of *stare decisis*.

This section will summarize key transfer pricing of the U.S. Tax Court cases on risk allocation and see whether the post-BEPS era has changed the risk allocation analysis of the U.S. Tax Court. There has been no change in the court's analysis.

The current transfer pricing rules on risk allocation in the United States must be viewed through a historical lens focusing on the precedent interpreting the U.S. Treasury regulations. The key cases are *Veritas* (2009) case, the *Xilinix* (2010) case, the *Altera* (2015) case, the *Medtronic* (2016), and the *Amazon* (2017). Extrapolating a rule out of all these cases seems to indicate that the U.S. Tax Court is following the same paradigm for transfer pricing cases that it had in the past eight years—even over potential alternatives, such as the Commensurate with Income White Paper from Congress in 1988 that the *Medtronic* court did not accept.

In summary, the court first looks into the contracts and then decides what the companies *should* have agreed. And, the court is following the fiction of the arm's length principle consistently.[1]

The *Medtronic* (2016) and *Amazon* (2017) cases would be worthy candidates to show that the U.S. Tax Court is starting to move toward the BEPS approach to risk allocation—as these are the cases that were decided after the introduction of BEPS. But all these cases show the U.S. Tax Court is consistently applying the U.S. Treasury's transfer pricing rules as it did prior to BEPS and after the introduction to BEPS.

It should also be noted that all these cases involve restructurings of corporate groups that transferred ownership of intangibles from a U.S. parent company to a foreign subsidiary. Indeed, this thesis is primarily focusing on risk allocation—not the methods (such as CUP and TNMM), but primarily what methods revolve around risk.

It could be argued that some of these cases—even the *Amazon* case—focus primarily on the cost-sharing agreements or even *Medtronic* that focused primarily on intangibles and the royalty rates, etc. However, this focus on the cost-sharing agreements is not a problem necessarily, because such epiphenomena[2] do not detract from the risk allocation analysis whereby the court first looks into the intercompany contracts and what the companies should have agreed.

This historical analysis is key to understand each subsequent case—as each case builds off the former cases. However, it should be noted that the *Medtronic* and *Amazon* cases are the final culminations of the former cases. Moreover, *Medtronic* and *Amazon* are consistent with prior binding and persuasive precedent and do not chart new grounds toward accepting BEPS.

VERITAS 2009

In *Veritas Software Corp. V. Commissioner*, 133 T.C. 297 (2009), the U.S. Tax Court held that the IRS Commissioner's method of income allocation was arbitrary, capricious, and unreasonable. Moreover, the court held that the comparable uncontrolled transaction method was the best method to use for the payment allocation.

The case dealt with the IRS Commissioner's application of using the income method for calculating a buy-in payment allocation from a subsidiary for a parent's preexisting intangible property. The court found this cost-sharing agreement to be arbitrary, capricious, and unreasonable. This was decided even though the IRS argued that the transfer of the intangibles was exactly the same as a sale. The court decided that the IRS failed in its explanation of the initial value of the transfer of intangibles, and the method did not capture the synergistic value.

The agreements revolved around storage management software that Veritas developed with original equipment manufacturers to be sold through a cost-sharing agreement. This cost-sharing agreement was entered into with one of the foreign subsidiaries. Given this situation, the court found that the comparable uncontrolled transaction method was the best method to determine the buy-in payment.

The court's analysis began with examining the contractual terms, but the court found that there were no significant differences in contractual terms, risks, or property and services provided within the group structure.

This section summarized the key findings of the *Veritas* case. But, the most important aspect was the method of analysis of risk analysis; whereby, the court first looked at the contracts and placed great emphasis on the inter-company contracts that the Veritas group had. The key conclusions are that the U.S. Tax Court focused on the contracts and did not look to whether the subsidiary had control over risk or whether the subsidiary assuming the risk had the financial capacity to assume the risk.

XILINIX 2010

In *Xilinx v. Commissioner*, 598 F.3d 1191 (9th Cir. 2010), the U.S. Federal Court for the Ninth Circuit Court of Appeals decided Xilinx was not required to include value of employees' stock options that were in cost-sharing arrangements with Xilinx's subsidiary under a cost-sharing agreement between companies to develop intangible property.[3]

The court determined that Xilinx was allowed to deduct all the employee's stock options as business expenses. However, the court noted that the U.S Treasury regulations required the controlled parties in cost-sharing agreements to share all costs. These regulations required that the taxable income of the controlled parties be based on whether or not and how other uncontrolled parties would be operating at arm's length. The purpose of the regulation was parity, and the taxpayer would not have had parity with an independent taxpayer if it could not have deducted all the employee's stock options.

This section summarized the key findings of the *Xilinix* case. However, the most important aspect was the method of analysis of risk analysis; whereby, the court first looked at the contracts and placed great emphasis on the inter-company contracts that the Xilinix group had.

The key conclusions are that the U.S. Tax Court focused on the contracts and did not look to whether the subsidiary had control over risk or whether the subsidiary assuming the risk had the financial capacity to assume the risk. This was the same analysis provided for in *Veritas* even though the Ninth Circuit Court of Appeals did not reference this case.

ALTERA 2015

In *Altera v. Commissioner*, 145 T.C. No. 3, Docket Nos. 6253-12, 9963-12 (July 27, 2015), the U.S. Tax Court *en banc* decided again in favor of the taxpayer.[4] A great deal of the case focused on statutory and administrative interpretation—especially in regards to *Chevron* deference as it applies to judicial construction of statutes. However, the key issues in the case involved transfer pricing.

The court examined that the actions of the Altera corporate group-controlled entities entering into "qualified cost-sharing arrangements" to share together in stock-based compensation costs falls under the Administrative Procedure Act (APA). The court further examined that Congress delegated the power to the Treasury—an executive agency—by authorizing the treasury to "prescribe all needful rules and regulations for the enforcement of" the Internal Revenue Code whereby the treasury's enforcement is the final rule of law—including for administration and enforcement of the APA. Thus, adjustments to income—specifically following from the APA and the U.S. transfer pricing regulations—could be sustained only on the basis of the final rule of law—which is allowed, whereby Congress has delegated such power of final rule of law to the treasury.

However, on appeal given that the treasury had the authority to give a final rule of law on administrative proceedings, the U.S. Tax Court found that the treasury's final ruling—requiring that the Altera corporate group controlled entities entering in the qualified cost-sharing agreements to share stock-based compensation costs—lacked any basis in the facts of the case. The court decided that the treasury's ruling lacked basis in the facts of the case, because every indication on the record pointed that the treasury's conclusion—stating that unrelated parties entering into these qualified cost-sharing agreements would share costs—did not reflect economic reality of unrelated parties. In other words, there was no evidence that unrelated companies entering into these qualified cost-sharing agreements would share costs. The treasury never provided evidence to the contrary that unrelated companies entering into these qualified cost-sharing agreements would share costs.

It seems one of the fatal flaws in the treasury's analysis was that the treasury did not examine the taxpayer's intercompany agreements for arm's length cost-sharing agreements—or even other arm's length cost-sharing agreements of tax payers it regulated.[5]

This section summarized the key findings of the *Altera* case. But, the most important aspect was the method of analysis of risk analysis; whereby, the court first looked at the contracts and placed great emphasis on the intercompany contracts that the Altera corporate group had entered into.

The key conclusions are that the U.S. Tax Court focused on the contracts and did not look to whether the subsidiary had control over risk or whether the subsidiary assuming the risk had the financial capacity to assume the risk. This was the same analysis provided for in *Veritas* and *Xilinix*.

MEDTRONIC 2016

Medtronic is likely the most unhelpful case in recent U.S Tax Court history for deciding whether or not the U.S. Tax Court's precedent will be followed because the case was the most fact-intensive transfer pricing case. This means that it is neither helpful nor unhelpful in trying to decide whether or not OECD recommendations of risk allocation will be upheld.

The U.S. Tax Court case decided on June 9, 2016, in *Medtronic, Inc. v. Commissioner*, T.C. Memo No. 2016-112 (2016).[6] The key issue in *Medtronic* was the Medtronic Group agreement for licensing of intangibles used in manufacturing with one of its group members. The price for the licensing of these intangibles and agreements was key for the transfer pricing issue of the *Medtronic* case. If the licensed intangibles were valued at a different rate, then the effective tax liability would change substantially.

In *Medtronic v. Commissioner*, the question before the U.S. Tax Court was whether the IRS had correctly assessed and determined deficiencies in Medtronic's Federal income tax returns for 2005 and 2006. The first issue specifically involved whether "intercompany licenses for intangible property required to manufacture medical device pulse generators (devices and physical therapy delivery devices (leads)) should be reallocated under section 482 to Medtronic US from its Puerto Rican subsidiary, Medtronic Puerto Rico Operations Co. (MPROC)" for the years in question. The second issue involved whether "Medtronic Europe, S.a.r.L (Medtronic Europe) made arm's length payments to Medtronic US or accrued royalties in excess of arm's length to manufacture devices sold to Medtronic USA, Inc. (Med USA), pursuant to a supply agreement."

The court first analyzed the industry background and the Medtronic Group structure. Medtronic had its headquarters in the United States (Medtronic US). Medtronic US owned Medtronic International Technology, Inc. (MITI), another U.S. corporation. MITI owned Medtronic Holding Switzerland GmbH (Swiss Holding). Swiss Holding owned MPROC, Medtronic Europe, and Medtronic Vascular Galway Ltd. based in Ireland (Medtronic Galway). Medtronic Europe, Medtronic Galway, and MPROC checked-the-box[7] to be treated as disregarded entities of the Swiss Holding Company.[8] For U.S. tax purposes, "Swiss Holding conduct[ed] manufacturing in Switzerland, Puerto Rico, and Ireland through manufacturing 'branches.'"

Relevant parts of the Medtronic Group Structure with the transactions at issue in blue:[9]

Then the U.S. Tax Court looked at the relevant intercompany agreements—focusing on Medtronic's licensing, trademarks, and supply agreements.

Before the U.S. Tax Court, Medtronic argued that quality control from the U.S. parent was key in making sure the quality of the products was maintained

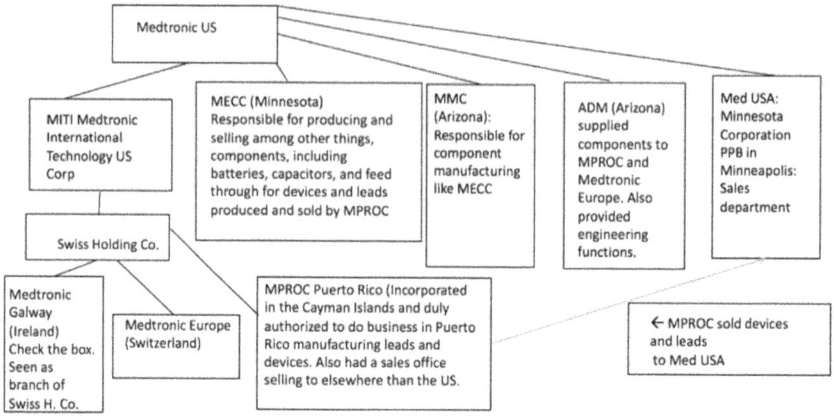

Figure 9.1 Depiction created by author depicting the corporate structure in the *Medtronic* (2016) U.S. Tax Court case. Image initially appeared in author's master's thesis at the University of Amsterdam in 2017.

leading to the main source of revenue. The IRS argued that the sales team created the most revenue for the company. Ultimately, this is a chicken and the egg problem.[10] Without quality at the production level—including research and development and assembly—then the sales team would have nothing to sell. Without the sales team, the best products in the world would not be sold. The question is which one is the significant people functions?

Perhaps it can be said for any shortcomings of the *Medtronic* case that bad facts make bad law. The court followed a modified approach that Medtronic proposed for the comparable uncontrolled profits test with the benchmark of the Puerto Rico branch being the contract manufacturer and the royalty payments from Puerto Rico to the U.S. branch of Medtronic. On the other hand, the IRS wanted the benchmark to be a full-fledged manufacturer using the TNMM method—the CPM method in the United States—but the U.S. Tax Court did not find this method appropriate. In the end, the U.S. Tax Court agreed on adjusted comparables rather than the OECD's comparables. In fact, the adjusted CUP amount is the amount the IRS and Medtronic had agreed on in a previous audit.

Overall, one aspect is clear; the U.S. Tax Court still looks to the contracts to find where risk has been allocated. Ultimately, the contracts reflected economic reality, but the rates did not, thus the court had to adjust the rates.

This section summarized the key findings of the Medtronic case. But the most important aspect was the method of analysis of risk analysis; whereby the court first looked at the contracts and placed great emphasis on the intercompany contracts that the Medtronic Group had. The key conclusions are that the U.S. Tax Court focused on the contracts and did not look to whether the subsidiary had control over risk or whether the subsidiary assuming the risk had the financial capacity to assume the risk. This was the same analysis provided for in *Veritas*, *Xilinix*, and *Altera*.

SUMMARY OF THE U.S. TAX COURT PRECEDENTS AFFECTING RISK ALLOCATION

This chapter summarized the key findings of the *Veritas*, *Xilinix*, and *Altera*, *Medtronic*, and also *Amazon* cases. But the most important aspect was the method of analysis of risk analysis; whereby, the court first looked at the contracts and placed great emphasis on the intercompany contracts. This is especially true in the *Medtronic* and *Amazon* cases. The key conclusions are that the U.S. Tax Court focused on the contracts and did not look to whether the subsidiary had control over risk or whether the subsidiary assuming the risk had the financial capacity to assume the risk. This was the same analysis provided for in *Veritas*, *Xilinix*, *Altera*, *Medtronic*, and *Amazon* cases.

NOTES

1. This legal fiction will be discussed in more detail—but has already been expanded upon in Chapter II.

2. "Epiphenomena" in the sense that it is not essential for the operation or infrastructure of the risk allocation. "Economists start from the presumption that financial activities are epiphenomena, that they create a veil obscuring to superficial observers an underlying reality which they do not affect . . . . [E]conomist[s] can pierce the veil and see that the values of financial assets are just those of the outside assets to which they are ultimately claims, no matter how circuitous the path from the one to the other." Manuel A. Utset, "The Discipline of Institutions and the Disciplining of Banks." *Ann. Rev. Banking* L. 14 (1995): 211, 216. *See.* James Tobin, *Financial Intermediaries*, in The New Palgrave: Finance 35, 41 (John Eatwell et al. eds., 1989).

Alternatively, "[a]ccording to Dworkin, Hart's idea of 'what law is' is fundamentally wrong. That idea is that the sole source of legal obligation in a community is the legal rule, whose validity depends upon its having been adopted according to an identifiable method of legitimation that has been accepted as such by the community's members. This accepted method of legitimation is called a 'rule of recognition,' of which an example is the United States Constitution (p. 21). All other social rules and practices are not properly enforceable by government officials, no matter what moral expectations they create and no matter how stringently they are observed as a matter of custom. Against this rule-oriented position, Dworkin claims that the law is comprised also of principles such as 'no man shall profit by his own wrong,' which regularly figure in judicial decisions and which cannot be dismissed (as they are in the positivist model) as simply extralegal epiphenomena that judges make it a habit to refer to when they are at a loss for proper rules. On the contrary, Dworkin argues, these principles have a constitutive role in any judgment about the validity of a controversial claim of right, such as the claim in *Spartan Steel & Alloys Ltd. v. Martin & Co.* that a plaintiff should be entitled to recover for economic loss following negligent damage to someone else's property (pp. 83–85), or that of the plaintiffs in *Brown v. Board of Education* that there exists a distinctively legal right to attend integrated schools (p. 140)." Peter Gabel, *Taking Rights Seriously by Ronald Dworkin* (Cambridge, MA: Harvard University Press, 1977), pp. Xv, 293. $12.00., *Harv. L. Rev.* 91 (1977) 302, 303–304.

Compare this concept with the "[the] re-orientation of jurisprudential attention to the sort of disciplinary subject who produces all this doctrine, legal theory, and academic argument strikes me as an important enterprise—not the least reason is that it has much more to do with what Law is than the objectivist epiphenomena which routinely go by the name of 'case law,' or 'doctrine,' or even 'legal theory.'" Pierre Schlag, "Foreword: Postmodernism and Law." *U. Colo. L. Rev.* 62 (1991): 439, 448.

3. *Xilinx Inc. v. Comm'r*, 567 F.3d 482, 484 (9th Cir. 2009), rev'd on reh'g, 598 F.3d 1191 (9th Cir. 2010), acq. in result AOD 2010-03.

4. "The Supreme Court explained that 'Chevron deference is appropriate 'when it appears that Congress delegated authority to the agency generally to make rules carrying the force of law, and that the agency interpretation claiming deference was promulgated in the exercise of that authority.'" "Mayo *Found. for Med. Educ. & Research v. United States*, 562 U.S. 44, 57, 131 S.Ct. 704, 178 L.Ed.2d 588 (2011) (quoting *United States v. Mead Corp.*, 533 U.S. 218, 226–227, 121 S.Ct. 2164, 150 L.Ed.2d 292 (2001)). The Supreme Court concluded that when Treasury issues general authority regulations after full notice and comment procedures, these conditions are met and those regulations are therefore entitled to *Chevron* deference. *See id.* at 56–57." *Altera Corp. & Subsidiaries v. C.I.R.*, 145 T.C. 91, 134 (2015).

5. "Lee A. Sheppard, Xilinx and the Future of Transfer Pricing, 123 *Tax Notes* 1295, 1301 (2009) ('There have been several previous attempts to address valuation of intangibles transfers, including the commensurate with income clause, and none of them have worked.')" Andrew Blair-Stanek, "Just Compensation as Transfer Prices." *Ariz. L. Rev.* 58 (2016): 1077, 1138.

6. All facts and analysis of the court came from the *Medtronic, Inc. v. Commissioner*, T.C. Memo No. 2016-112 (2016) unless otherwise indicated.

7. *See.* Professor Clausing's analysis of the effects of "check-the-box" rules and how it undermines CFC rules. Kimberly A. Clausing, "The Effect of Profit Shifting on the Corporate Tax Base." *Tax Notes* 81 (2016): 3. *Compare with.* For a comparison of CFC rule proposals in the European Union. Dennis Weber and Antonio Russo, The CCCTB and Possible Elements of a Technical Outline: The "Switch-Over" Clause, in Common Consolidated Corporate Tax Base 751 (Michael Lang, Pasquale Pistone, Josef Schuch & Claus Staringer eds., 2008).

8. Julian A. Fortuna and Todd D. Radde, "Transfer Pricing Adjustment Challenges Receive Green Light from the Tax Court." *J. Tax'n* 125 (2016): 223, 225, WL 6915865, 4.

9. Image of Medtronic Group structure created by author.

10. Imagine the common hypothetical example of the chairbler craftsman who makes chairs for a living. Indeed, the chairbler could be the best in the world, but if he has no ability to market or sell the chairs, then he will not make money. Subsequently, if his sister can market the chairs, then she will bring in money. But without her brother making the chairs, she will have nothing to sell in this scenario. Who creates the value is a key question in transfer pricing? This is the chicken and egg problem: who creates the monetary value the chairbler craftsman or his sister?

Chapter 10

Reason (3) The U.S. Tax Court Will Not Apply Action 9

Amazon Re-Examined and the IRS's Unwillingness and Inability to Apply OECD's Action 9 Recommendations on Risk Analysis

Finally, the most recent transfer pricing case—Amazon—shows that the court still upholds the prior precedential cases through *stare decisis*. Moreover and perhaps more importantly, in the international context regarding other countries' decision to implement Action 9, had the IRS brought the argument of Action 9 forward, not only would the entire case have been analyzed differently, but the prospect of bringing Action 9's reasoning forward, the IRS would have forfeited all claims to the pricing of the transferred IP to the "empty company"—as will be shown later.

The *Amazon.Com, Inc. v. Commissioner*, 148 T.C. No.8, Docket No. 31197-12 (March 23, 2017) case was decided in favor of the tax payer—just as the four cases in transfer pricing mentioned prior to this were as well.[1] The case revolved around the Amazon.Inc's transfer pricing buy-in payment for an intragroup cost-sharing agreement. The IRS issued a transfer pricing adjustment regarding this buy-in payment. Subsequently, the court found the adjustment to be arbitrary, capricious, and unreasonable.

The court in the *Amazon.Inc* case cited the *Veritas* case to indicate that the IRS's approach of "Aggregation" of various intangibles to determine valuation was not reasonable. The court indicated that there could not be an aggregation of software intangibles as well as the marketing intangibles and trademarks.

Key to the risk analysis, the court indicated that the IRS did not follow its own regulations where the IRS must determine that realistic

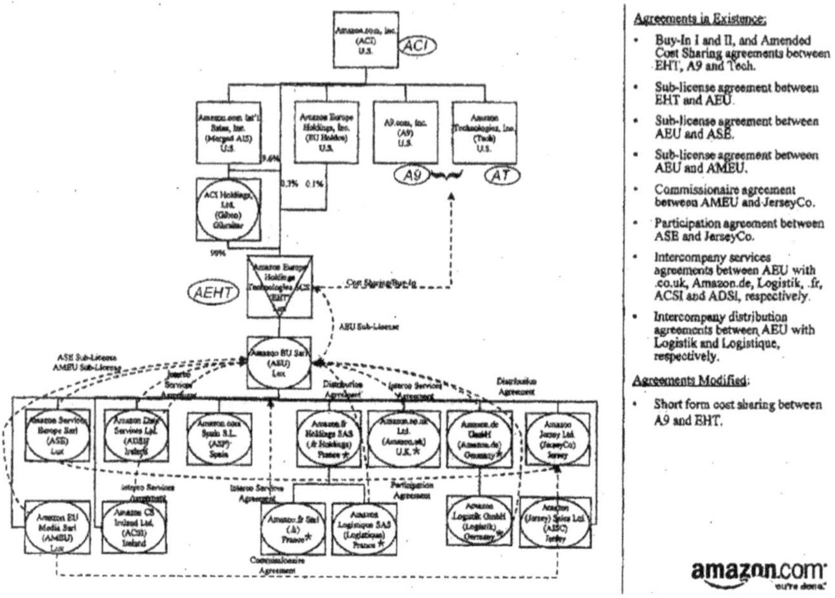

Figure 10.1 Depiction from William Byrnes's article posted on the Wolters Kluwer International Tax Blog. William Byrnes (Texas A&M University Law)/March 24, 2017. *Source*: http://kluwertaxblog.com/2017/03/24/is-amazon-com-inc-the-death-knell-of-the-irs-cost-sharing-agreement-valuation-approach/#_ftn1 (last accessed August 29, 2021)

alternatives exist that would prevent the commissioner from restructuring "the transaction as if the alternative had been adopted by the taxpayer," so long as the taxpayer has actual economic substance. Thus, the court is still looking first at the intercompany agreements and then whether or not the economic substance forms with this reality of the intercompany agreements.

The key in Amazon is that the transfer of intellectual property a company without any functionality, and the IRS did not appear to be any problem that there was no functionality. Had the IRS taken the BEPS approach, and then the IRS would have forfeited any right to tax *Amazon* at all.

In conclusion, this third reason shows the most recent transfer pricing case—Amazon—shows that the court still upholds the prior precedential cases through *stare decisis*. Moreover and perhaps more importantly, in the international context regarding other countries' decision to implement Action 9, had the IRS brought the argument of Action 9 forward, not only would the entire case have been analyzed differently, but the prospect of bringing Action 9's reasoning forward, the IRS would have forfeited all claims to the pricing of the transferred IP to the "empty company"—as will be shown later.

NOTE

1. *Amazon.com Inc & Subsidiaries* (2017) 148 TC No. 8. *Earlier proceedings* at (2016) TC Memo 2016-131, RIA TC *Memo P* 2016-131, 112 CCH TCM 30, *at* P 74,536.00151(25); (2014) TC *Memo* 2014-245, RIA TC Memo P 2014-245, 108 CCH TCM 588, *at* P 74,536.14751(40); *and* (2014) TC *Memo* 2014-149, RIA TC *Memo* P 2014-149, 108 CCH TCM 87, *at* P 4825.05(5).

Chapter 11

Compare and Contrast Current U.S. Precedent to BEPS Action 9 Report on Risk Allocation

INTRODUCTION TO THE DIFFERENT APPROACHES TO RISK ALLOCATION

This chapter compares and contrasts the *Medtronic* case decision to the BEPS Action Plan 9 Report. The pivot of this thesis is based around the concept that BEPS Action Plan 9 purports to still look at contracts, but after a closer examination, it only looks to what entities had the financial capacity to take on risk.

The chapter first focuses on Rutger Hafkenscheid's article *The BEPS Report on Risk Allocation: Not So Functional* that uncovers the veil of disguised focus on risk allocation in BEPS. This includes looking to where Hafkenscheid looks to BEPS to see the diversion.

Finally, the premise that the OECD refuses to look at contracts is set next to the fact that this recent U.S. Tax Court decision has looked and considered contracts and intercompany agreements.

Comparing Hafkenscheid's Analysis of Action 9 to the U.S. Tax Court Jurisprudence

Alternatively, in the *Amazon* case decided by the U.S. Tax Court, "[t]he court's approach in Medtronic was to first review the intercompany agreements and determine if they were all at arm's length,"[1] whereby the court conducts an extensive analysis of the intercompany agreements. This shows, that as opposed to the OECD's BEPS innovative approach, the court still looks at the contracts first. Indeed, although the U.S. Tax Court found that the intercompany contracts represented the actual economic reality, the court still adjusted the royalty rates of the intercompany agreements.[2]

The main difference in the U.S. Transfer Pricing approach for risk allocation is that the United States has expressed—through the U.S. Tax Court—the intention to look at the contracts—and then see if they conform to economic reality. While, on the other hand, the OECD through BEPS has stated in a disguised manner—and as uncovered by Rutger Hafkenscheid—that contracts will only be considered if they are what "should" have been contracted under the functional analysis whereby a party has the control to bear risk and remuneration accordingly.

Fundamental Problem in Risk Allocation Analysis of Action 9 as Compared to the U.S. Tax Court Jurisprudence Regarding Step 5 of the Risk Allocation

The origin of the problem is that legal structure—the contracts, corporate structures, etc.—is actually a form of economic substance. The arm's length principle itself is a legal fiction. Indeed, the acceptance of corporate taxation and the concept of a corporate entity is a legal fiction as well. The corporate entity fiction gained acceptance over a period of time even going back to Sir Edward Coke in the 1612 in the Case of Sutton's Hospital.[3] The U.S. Supreme Court only decided the fundamental right of the government to tax corporations after the passage of the 16th Amendment adopted in 1913 in the *Brushaber v. Union Pacific R. R. Co.* case.[4]

Attribution of human action in a concept is of no meaning without humans in a corporate context. The Step 5 risk analysis negates human attribution to the corporation. Step 5 takes away the fiction of the corporation. A corporation exists without functionality analysis in the context of Step 5.

Overall, the policy behind such decisions will cause confusion and likely double taxation for small and medium size enterprises. Multinational entities will likely—as they are wont— continue in numerous ways to avoid double taxation or even be subject to double non-taxation.

Caption: *The stand-alone company will be treated differently than the company in a corporate group.* The very concept of the arm's length principle is that companies in a corporate group should be treated the same as stand-alone companies. The new BEPS plans on transfer pricing will lead to different results—and even confusing results. Thus, not only will the U.S. courts be hesitant to apply the BEPS plan on transfer pricing, but so will other courts around the world.

In this case, where a manager is acting out of a company managing assets in a corporate entity. Traditionally—pre-BEPS and still in the U.S. through the U.S. Tax Court—the location (especially in the international context) of the assets themselves were taxed—the jurisdiction of the assets is where the assets were taxed (the red circle). This was because risk is contractually allocated to the jurisdiction of the assets. BEPS with the six-step risk allocation approach now states that the place where management is—the jurisdiction of management in the green circle—is where taxation should take place, not the location of the assets.

This is not to say the purpose and goal of BEPS is a bad idea. Richard Wagner writes at the end of Parsifal "*Die Wunde schliesst der Speer nur der Sie schlug*," that is to say, "only the spear [that is the Spear of Destiny] that struck you can heal the wound"[5] As philosopher Slavoj Žižek interpreted the Wagnerian phrase in a social context to mean "the very disintegration of traditional forms opens up the space of liberation."[6] Indeed, the author, Rutger Hafkenscheid,[7] and all others support the idea of avoiding double taxation and preventing double non-taxation. But, it seems that the means to achieve the goal of preventing double non-taxation—and base erosion and profit shifting entirely—is not effectively reached through the risk allocation mechanism as proposed in BEPS, because the tax courts will apply the risk allocation inconsistently. The intellectual appeal of the BEPS proposals is not enough—the transfer pricing methods must be applied consistently.

The policy as exhibited by the U.S. Tax Courts indicates that the court wishes to not follow the BEPS analysis, because it will lead to uncertainty and non-uniform decisions. The U.S. Tax Courts want to apply the U.S. transfer pricing regulations in a consistent manner to avoid legal uncertainty.

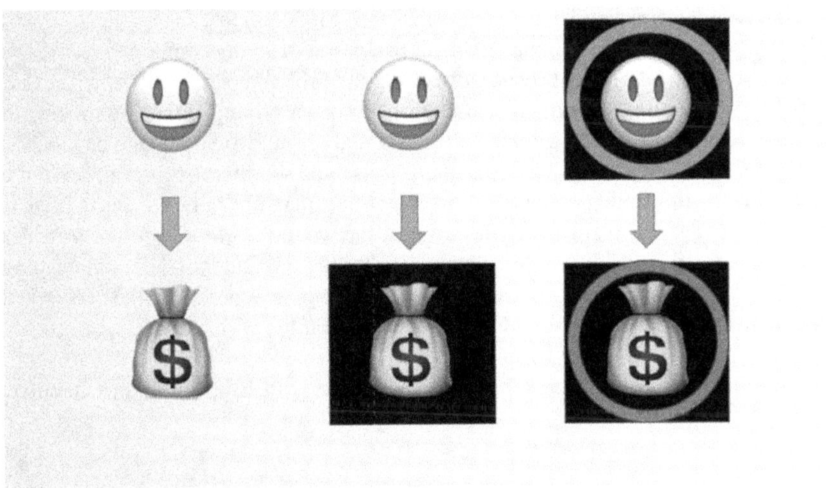

Figure 11.1

NOTES

1. Julian A. Fortuna and Todd D. Radde, "Transfer Pricing Adjustment Challenges Receive Green Light from the Tax Court." *J. Tax'n* 125 (2016): 223, 226 WL 6915865, 6. "Transfer Pricing Cases Update." *J. Int'l Tax'n* 27 (2016): 30, 35, WL 7116202, 6.

2. "The court arrived at a revised royalty rate for the Medtronic-MPROC license agreement of 30% (retail), which was converted to 44% to reflect the wholesale sales of devices. Since Medtronic's lead royalty rate was 15% and was approximately one-half of Medtronic's royalty rate for devices (29%), the court concluded that a reasonable arm's-length royalty rate for leads (22%) would be half of the court calculated royalty rate (44%) for devices." *Id.* at 11.

3. *The Case of Sutton's Hospital*, 77 Eng. Rep. 960 (K.B. 1612). ("[T]he Corporation itself is onely in abstracto, and resteth onely in intendment and consideration of the Law; for a Corporation aggregate of many is invisible, immortal, & resteth only in intendment and consideration of the Law; and therefore cannot have predecessor nor successor. They may not commit treason, nor be outlawed, nor excommunicate, for they have no souls, neither can they appear in person, but by Attorney. A Corporation aggregate of many cannot do fealty, for an invisible body cannot be in person, nor can swear, it is not subject to imbecilities, or death of the natural, body, and divers other cases.")

4. "And, in 1911, in *Flint v. Stone, Tracy Co.*, 220 U. S. 107, a tax upon the business of corporations, measured by the entire net income, was unanimously upheld. In both these decisions, the court distinguished the *Pollock* case on the ground that the tax there discussed was imposed on property because of its ownership, while in these cases it was a tax on the right to use property in a certain way. But the distinction seems more formal than substantial. See 24 Harv. L. Rev. 563." The Income Tax and the Sixteenth Amendment." *Harv. L. Rev.* 29 (1916): 536, 538.

5. The problem can be summarized by a paragraph in an upcoming publication by Alessandro Turina, "The insistence of 'making the problem part of the solution, that is, in this case, trying to reform the international transfer pricing regime by sticking to the arm's length standard by promoting incremental reform would seem to be justified on a deeper level by the acknowledgement—wise and worthy of subscription in the perspective of this author—according to which, ultimately, 'only the spear [that is the Spear of Destiny] that struck you can heal the wound' ('*die Wunde schliesst der Speer nur, der sie schlug*') as the eponymous Protagonist utters while approaching Amfortas to heal him in the last scene of the last Act of Wagner's Parsifal" (Personal Communication with Professor Alessandro Turina, on file with author).

6. Slavoj Žižek, Absolute Recoil 2015.

7. As indicated through personal correspondence with Rutger Hafkenscheid (on file with author).

Chapter 12

The Conclusion and Possible Answers to Chapters 5 through 11

In conclusion, the U.S. Tax Court will not apply the OECD BEPS Action 9 Recommendation regarding risk allocation for three reasons explored in this thesis. The first is the two constitutional reasons: (a) the constitutional hierarchy regarding international law in the United States—much less the precedential value of a secondary source, such as OECD reports. (b) The concept of *stare decisis* that is embedded in the common law system of the Anglo-American tradition relies on cases being decided as they have been decided in the past. The tradition of upholding prior precedent is not easily broken—except for egregious reasons, such as regarding slavery.

(2) Given the status of international law and international secondary sources in the United States in addition to the concept of *stare decisis*, the U.S. Tax Court—as all courts in the United States—consistently build on judicial application of law. Four key transfer pricing cases since the 1986 transfer pricing tax reforms in the United States will be shown to support the concept of *stare decisis*.

(3) Finally, the most recent transfer pricing case—Amazon—shows that the court still upholds the prior precedential cases through *stare decisis*. Moreover and perhaps more importantly, in the international context regarding other countries' decision to implement Action 9, had the IRS brought the argument of Action 9 forward, not only would the entire case have been analyzed differently, but the prospect of bringing Action 9's reasoning forward, the IRS would have forfeited all claims to the pricing of the transferred IP to the "empty company"—as will be shown later.

Thus, this thesis has striven to show that the main differences between the OECD's BEPS transfer pricing analysis and the U.S. Tax Court's approach is and will likely continue to be that U.S. courts still put greater emphasis on the intercompany agreements and contracts than BEPS ultimately does. The

United States will look at the contracts and then see if they conform to economic reality. While, on the other hand, the OECD through BEPS has stated in a disguised manner—and as uncovered by Rutger Hafkenscheid—that contracts will only be considered if they are what "should" have been contracted under the functional analysis, whereby a party has the control to bear risk and remuneration accordingly.

This will cause a possibility of tax loopholes whereby assets are placed outside the United States—in an OECD country following the BEPS risk allocation recommendations—and management will be placed within the United States. The United States will grant taxing rights to the country where the asset is located. The country where the asset is located will grant taxing rights to the United States. In this case, there could be a situation of double non-taxation—the opposite of what was intended under BEPS.

As a point of thought for future research to this analysis,[1] perhaps the main problem with the transfer pricing system is the concept of the separate independent entity underlying the arm's length principle.[2] Perhaps the future holds a formulary apportionment—effectively doing away with the arm's length principle—on an international level as the United States does domestically.[3]

NOTES

1. Author hopes to pursue another degree in the future exploring more avenues of international tax law.

2. Reuven S. Avi-Yonah and Haiyan Xu, "Evaluating BEPS: A Reconsideration of the Benefits Principle and Proposal for UN Oversight." *Harv. Bus. L. Rev.* 6 (2016): 185, 226.

3. Although there are some proposals, such as the European Union's proposed CCCTB that keeps the arm's length principle. Hein Vermeulen and M.F.A Blaauw, "The Tax Treatment of Directly Held Real Estate under the Proposed CCCTB Directive." *Eur. Taxn.* 51 (2011): 12, Journals IBFD.

Chapter 13

Policy Questions for the Future

The OECD adopts a principal of objective behavioral—non-agency—analysis of economic activity, which is impracticable and unworkable. The OECD denies that accurate legal contracts accurately delineate legal relationship.[1] This implies an inherent misrepresentation in corporate business management—the OECD is implying everything created legally is not a representation of the accurate economic model and that substance does not conform to form. The OECD denies the tax implications of principle-agent legal agency relationships as defined by contract law in its transfer pricing recommendations. On the other hand, the U.S. Tax Court still looks to the agency relationships between corporate entities. The U.S. Tax Court follows the correct approach.

Corporate management can be divided between principle and agents. People usually think about management and shareholders, but there are also risk managers and asset managers that can be bifurcated. In terms of management, the bottom of the hierarchy is the managers of the factories. The capital fund managers or the shareholders have all the power—it will be taxed here not at the managers of the factories.[2] The managers at the top of the hierarchy will get the highest level of remuneration. Reliance on contract is the only way that makes sense. Tax is based on legal—rather than equitable—matters.[3] How would one tax equity?

NOTES

1. Lincoln IV, Charles Edward Andrew. Amazon, Medtronic, the OECD on Risk Analysis: Thesis on Transfer Pricing. No. 3fs5x. Center for Open Science, 2017 Advanced LL.M. master's thesis at the University of Amsterdam (abbreviated as

UvA, Dutch: *Universiteit van Amsterdam*) in conjunction with the IBFD (International Bureau of Fiscal Documentation). *See*. Rojo, Luis Durán, and Paul Nina Nina. "The Use of Paragraphs 1.119 to 1.128 of the 2017 OECD Transfer Pricing Guidelines for the Application of Transfer Pricing Rules." *Intertax* 48, no. 6/7 (2020).

2. *Cf.* Contrast with conceptions of corporate residency from the 1906 *De Beers* corporate tax residency case. *See De Beers Consolidated Mines Ltd. v. Howe*, [1906] AC 455, 458 (HL). *See*. Lincoln IV, Charles Edward Andrew. "Is Incorporation Really Better than Central Management and Control for Testing Corporate Residency: An Answer to Corporate Tax Evasion and Inversion." *Ohio NUL Rev.* 43 (2017): 359. "Perhaps the main factors that tipped the scale towards determining that De Beers Co. had residency in the UK were that the meetings in terms of the business's contracts were all in England, the London office controlled the negotiation and signing of contracts, and all majority vote matters were taken care of in London."

3. Elkins, David. "Horizontal Equity as a Principle of Tax Theory." *Yale L. & Pol'y Rev.* 24 (2006): 43.

Chapter 14

Can the System of Money and Debt be a Sanctuary Legally?

Economics and law have long had roots in philosophy from Adam Smith to Hegel. Indeed, Arthur Herman discusses the connection of modern economics to Hegelian thought in his provocative *The Cave and The Light: Plato Versus Aristotle and the Struggles for the Soul of Western Civilization*:

In 1914, Herbert Croly and his friend Walter Lippman set up the magazine that would become Progressivism's mouthpiece, *The New Republic*. That same year, President Wilson set up the centerpiece of the Hegelianization of the American economy, the Federal Reserve Board. From now on, it was believed, the federal government would be able to exercise the same kind of farsighted direction over the economy that central banks enjoyed in England, France, and Germany. That egregious product of self-interested capitalism, the business cycle, with its unpredictable investment booms followed by collapse and unemployment, could be coaxed and prodded "secretly, without legislative enactment or "control, and without the public knowing and caring"—and without resorting to the iron surgery of full-blown communism or socialism. Indeed, membership in the Federal Reserve Bank system would be voluntary.[1]

However, before establishing firm principles of economics and philosophy, a concept of sanctuaries in a legal and literary sense would be more helpful.

In order to embark on the analysis of understanding the concept of sanctuaries in a legal and literary sense, it would be helpful to demonstrate why literature can be of value in interpreting law.

Briefly, the vital reasons using literature as a lens to interpret law is threefold: (1) Law and literature have a historic connection. (2) Literature can improve our understanding of law in terms of understanding the nuances of language and metaphor. Regarding analysis and the subtleties of language, eminent literary critic Harold Bloom wrote that in order to have compelling thought whether in an individual capacity or in the capacity of a Jungian collective conscious, one must utilize memory.[2] Thereafter, the question becomes, what should one commit to memory.[3] To answer, Bloom suggested "[c]ognition cannot proceed without memory, and the Canon is the true art of memory, the authentic foundation for cultural thinking."[4] Here, Bloom refers to the literary Canon from Shakespeare,[5] but also to a lesser extent Plato, Aristotle, Kant, Hegel, and Wittgenstein.[6] (3) Literature can improve our practical understanding of law itself. Regarding literature's specific application to law, Ronald Dworkin, the American legal philosopher and scholar, takes to heart the value of the aesthetic written text to explain how law is like literature: "I propose that we can improve our understanding of law by comparing legal interpretation with interpretation in other fields of knowledge, particularly literature."[7]

In relation to the concept of sanctuaries in a legal and literary sense, an excellent article titled *Liberty to Misread: Sanctuary and Possibility in The Comedy of Errors* closely examines Shakespeare and the law of sanctuary.[8] The article purveys a thesis that sanctuary can be called for in a theatrical tragedy only to be taken off the table of available options in the plot, thereby creating a comedy.[9] The reason the concept of sanctuary is important is because it is the place beyond the reach of governmental power and legal effectiveness of the collection power of monetary instruments.

Indeed, the roots of the right to sanctuary and the right to asylum in churches has roots in medieval English law and tradition as early as the fourth or fifth century BCE during Geoffrey Monmouth's account in *The History of the Kings of England*.[10] Moreover, such laws were present in the time of Shakespeare.

Sanctuary negates the anthropological sense of what is normal without causing a situation of *anomie*. *Anomie*, known as, anthropologically, "normlessness," the uprooting and destabilization of cultural standards often leading to divisions in a community.[11]

In an Hegelian sense of *sublation* through thesis, anti-thesis, and synthesis, there is a proposition of a thesis of normal anthropological existence governed by the modes of culture— that is to say, the lack of sanctuary in a play or possible outcomes.[12] Then the sanctuary negates this state of normalcy.[13] This negation would normally lead to a dysfunctional society following the concept of *anomie* laid out by Émile Durkheim.[14] However, sanctuary exists as one of the exemptions to the rule whereby normal society accepts this exemption, provided by the sanctuary, and the play—that is, the state of affairs—does not descend to chaos.[15]

The author of *Liberty to Misread* argues, "if sanctuary is called forth in the tragedy only to be taken off the table, it can be recruited in comedy as a way to bring forth resolutions and evade disaster."[16] As the article goes on, it seems to lend itself to an anti-thesis:

> *The Comedy of Errors*, the iterations of identity confusion abruptly come to an end when one of the Antipholus and Dromio teams seeks asylum in the "priory" at Ephesus. The resulting sanctuary dispute slows down the action long enough so that the two sets of twins may finally come across one another, allowing for the necessary explanations as well as some surprises. The Abbess is the long-lost wife of Egeon, the unfortunate father of the twins who has been sentenced to death for accidentally violating Ephesian mercantile law. In the end, order is restored, all charges are dropped, and the party enters the abbey to celebrate with a feast.[17]

In the first prong of analysis of this text, if the thesis in this article can be extrapolated, the author states that: sanctuary only can be called for in a tragic work only to be taken off the table of possible outcomes. This means the introduction of sanctuary negates the possibility of tragedy. But such an introduction does not necessarily mean the play or tragedy turns into comedy. Indeed, comedy can be defined in an Aristotelian way as "that which is not tragedy" yet *Liberty to Misread* does not imply this.[18] Indeed, an anti-thesis is implied that sanctuary can be called, rather, in, tragedy to resolve a dispute.

However, if a thesis and anti-thesis exist in Shakespeare's works, particularly here in *Comedy of Errors*; then, a synthesis in Hegelian terms could become apparent. With these theses, the synthesis—in a Hegelian sense—sanctuary can be called for in a tragedy to be taken off the table and yet at the same time resolve a dispute. This may be one of the cornerstones of the Wagnerian ideal of Gesamtkunstwerk,[19] in the sense that there is the ultimate unity of a classical comedy of antiquity and the Shakespearean tragedy.[20]

Yet, this is one part of the entire dialectic. In the second prong of analysis, Shakespeare's work presents an idea of another thesis in comedy—as exemplified from the inchoately subliminally and indirectly expressed idea in *Comedy of Errors*. The thesis is that in comedy, sanctuary can help avoid disaster.[21] In classical antiquity, the existence of a disaster without such a sanctuary to avoid it in a play would be definition of tragedy. The anti-thesis in this scenario would be where the idea of sanctuary can be called forth and not resolve disaster. To explain this anti-thesis can be examined through the lens of how sanctuary can be called forth to resolve disaster yet not resolve at the same time. This *sublated* synthesis seems to be a more accurate reflection of reality. This *sublated* synthesis in a sense maintains "triumph and disaster." That is to say, the synthesis acts to "treat those two imposters the same."[22]

To recapitulate, the first prong this two-part dialectic is of analysis involves a dialectic where the thesis is that sanctuary can be called for in tragedy only to be taken off the table. The anti-thesis in this second prong can be called for in tragedy to resolve a dispute. The synthesis of this first prong is that sanctuary can be called for in tragedy to be taken off the table of possible events and yet at the same time resolve a dispute.

The second prong that starts with a thesis is an inversion of the first prong. This conclusion of the second prong mirrors the conclusion of the first prong. The thesis in the second prong is that comedy acts as a sanctuary to avoid disaster. The anti-thesis provides that sanctuary can be called forth and not resolve disaster. The synthesis is that sanctuary can be called forth to resolve disaster yet not resolve at the same time. This is a more accurate reflection of reality. In a way, it sorts and maintains "triumph and disaster."

Finally, if the first prong in its entirety is the thesis and the second prong is the anti-thesis, then the synthesis is a combination of the two. This would lead to the idea that comedy and tragedy can be one in the same when they most accurately represent reality—and especially law in action. There is both resolve and no resolve. Thus, it is no longer the picturesque world of Shakespeare, but more the modern form where the jurisdiction of greater London is set and the City of London is set as well—contrasting to how it was fading back then.

This thesis of sanctuary is analogous to Slovenian philosopher and cultural critic Slavoj Žižek's interpretation of Beethoven's Ninth Symphony Ode to Joy.[23] According to Žižek, the first part of the music is about the universal fraternity of mankind.[24] According to Žižek, the first part is the sublime beauty with universal adaptability.[25] It is an excellent accolade of expediency. The second part turns into a "carnivalesque" version of the first part.[26] Žižek points out how this second part critiques the first part of the unity and "brotherhood of all mankind."[27] Rather, "in the middle of the movement, after we hear the main melody (the 'joy' theme) in three orchestral and three vocal variations, something unexpected happens that has bothered critics for the last 180 years: at Bar 331, the tone changes totally, and, instead of the solemn hymnic progression, the same 'joy' theme is . . . a conceit borrowed from military music for wind and percussion instruments that 18th-century European armies [used]."[28]

ŽIŽEK AND SHAKESPEARE

At this point, it would be helpful to clearly outline the meaning of "dialectic" in Hegelian terms. Slavoj Žižek's analysis of Shakespeare is a good starting point to provide an example through analogy of the "dialectic."

In Žižek's analysis of Shakespeare's *Troilus and Cressida*, he quotes: "O Madness of Discourse, That Cause Sets Up with and Against Itself!'"[29] Dissecting the passage, Žižek writes, "[i]n the context of the play, these lines refer to Troilus' self-contradicting argumentation when he learns of

Cressida's infidelity: he enumerates arguments for and against what he wants to demonstrate; his reasoning rebels against its own line of argument without seeming to undo itself; and his unreasonableness assumes the appearance of rationality without seeming to contradict itself."[30] This is illustrative of the dialectic, because Troilus' argumentation to himself contradicts himself without seeming that he contradicts himself. This is an example of dialectic because such an argument represents a way to philosophically contradict a state of mind of two opposing sides while also maintaining the initial state of mind.

Žižek writes the concept of dialectic in the case of Troilus is further complicated by, "[a] cause that acts against itself, a reason that coincides with the revolt (against itself) . . . Although these lines refer to feminine inconsistency, they can also be taken as a comment on the secret alliance between the dignity of the Law and its obscene transgression."[31] Žižek elucidates this by stating that "Shakespeare's standard procedure, in his royal chronicles, of supplementing the 'big' royal scenes staged in a dignified way with scenes figuring common people who introduce a comic perspective." In retrospect, it is as if Žižek is describing the concept of sanctuary, "[i]n the royal chronicles, these comic interludes strengthen the noble scenes by way of contrast; in Troilus, however, everyone, even the noblest of warriors, is 'contaminated' by the ridiculing perspective, which invites us to see every character as either blind and pathetic or as involved in ruthless intrigues."[32]

Indeed Žižek writes that "Hamlet's famous 'The time is out of joint; O cursed spite, / That ever I was born to set it right!'—the only way to 'set it right' is to counteract the transgression of Old Order with its inherent transgression, with a crime secretly made to serve the Order. The price to be paid is that the Order which survives is a mockery of itself, a blasphemous imitation of Order."[33]

In relation to the concept of "absolute recoil," in his eponymously titled book *Absolute Recoil*, Žižek explains that, "Hegel uses the term 'absolute recoil' in his explanation of the category of 'ground/reason (*Grund*),' where he resorts to one of his famous wordplays, connecting *Grund* (ground/reason) and *zu Grunde gehen* (to fall apart, literally 'to go to one's ground')."[34]

Žižek quotes a key passage from Hegel's *Science of Logic*, "[t]he reflected determination, in falling to the ground, acquires its true meaning, namely, to be within itself the absolute recoil upon itself, that is to say, the positedness that belongs to essence is only a sublated positedness, and conversely, only self-sublating positedness is the positedness of essence. Essence, in determining itself as ground, is determined as the non-determined; its determining is only the sublating of its being determined. Essence, in being determined thus as self-sublating, has not proceeded from another, but is, in its negativity self-identical essence."[35]

Žižek goes on reasoning that "[t]his is why Graham Priest's answer to Shakespeare's question—'TO BE AND NOT TO BE—THAT IS THE ANSWER'—somehow falls flat, offering a 'synthesis' of being and non-being that obliterates the concrete existential tension of Shakespeare's question: it is better not to be, but even this attempt at radical negation can fail, perhaps it cannot even be achieved, so that we are condemned as undead."[36] Žižek suggests that this means that "what Hamlet discovers in the 'To be or not to be' soliloquy is that annihilation may be impossible—a dimension beyond Heidegger's being-towards-death. The awareness that nothingness is a screen covering up the horror of interminable existence deprives suicide, which appears as the final mastery one can exercise over being, of its function of mastery."[37]

Especially in relation to the concept of Sanctuary and the corollary legal notion of sanctuary, this makes sense, because "[t]o quote Shakespeare's *Troilus and Cressida*, insofar as there is an obvious element of madness involved in seeing ghosts, can the absolute spirit, while engaged in the work of the negative (and this work is the absolute spirit), ever truly say 'my negation has no taste of madness'?"[38]

Indeed,

> [o]ne of the most beautiful cases in literature occurs when, in Shakespeare's *Richard II* (Act 2, Scene 2), Bushy tries to comfort the Queen, worried about the unfortunate King on a military campaign":

Each substance of a grief hath twenty shadows,
Which shows like grief itself, but is not so;
For sorrow's eye, glazed with blinding tears,
Divides one thing entire to many objects;
Like perspectives, which rightly gazed upon
Show nothing but confusion, eyed awry
Distinguish form: so your sweet majesty,
Looking awry upon your lord's departure,
Find shapes of grief, more than himself, to wail;
Which, look'd on as it is, is nought but shadows
Of what it is not.[39]

Concerning Lacanian psychoanalysis, Žižek explains that the preceding quote is an example of the *objet a*. *Objet a* in Lacan's psychoanalytic framework is an unclear object or aspiration that is constantly misrepresented by a person's "desires and fears" onto what exists and does not exist.[40] Žižek explains that "[a] s such, the *objet a* is the strange object which is nothing but the inscription of the subject itself into the field of objects, in the guise of a stain which acquires form only when part of this field is anamorphically distorted by the subject's desire."[41]

The *objet a* in Lacanian psychoanalysis relates to the right of sanctuary in certain physical locations given that "rights serve the same function as the Lacanian notion *objet a*, the object cause of desire."[42] Definitionally, the "*objet a* is the substitute the subject gets when it is subjected to castration upon entering the realm of symbolic mediation. At the same time, however, the *objet a* is also the element that renders all other potential substitutes insufficient. For example, when the child is weaned from the breast and loses its primal object of desire, every other object will be seen as a substitute, as something to fill out this place of the primary lost object."[43] In a psychoanalytic framework, "desire will therefore range from one object to another but will always remain unsatisfied, it will always be a 'desire for something else' insofar as these new objects are seen as substitutes for the first object."[44]

In another book titled *Less Than Nothing: Hegel and the Shadow of Dialectical Materialism,* Žižek further solidifies his argument by pointing to the idea how in Shakespeare's *All's Well That Ends Well* when Diana hides in a room and makes false noises while Helen and Bertram sleep together—further supporting what Žižek calls the "fantasmatic dimension."[45] Žižek points out that in Shakespeare's *As You Like It,* double deception appears again in Orlando's and Rosalind's love story.[46] Rosalind in order to find out whether Orlando's love is true disguises herself as a man—Ganymede.[47] With this disguise, Rosalind—as Ganymede—takes on the personality of Rosalind; that is to say, Rosalind pretends to be Ganymede who in turn is pretending to be herself, Rosalind, while inquiring into Orlando's love of Rosalind.[48] Rosalind in her double disguise goes as far as to ask a friend Celia—but who is disguised as Aliena—to marry Orlando and Rosalind.[49] Žižek analyzes this scene in *Alls' Well that Ends Well* holding that "Rosalind literally feigns to feign to be what she is: truth itself," by staging a double deception whereby marriage can only be asserted through an extramarital affair.[50]

One of the key lessons in Hegel is that opposites are not necessarily incompatible with each other; indeed, the opposites can lead to identity and self-identity. Something, the Universal, can be described through describing its identity, the particulars. In Hegelian terms, the Universal is the essence of the thing, idea, concept, ritual, political party, and so on. The collection of "particulars" leads to the description of the Universal.

Grammatically, to illustrate this, Hegel provides an example that he would not accept "God is God."[51] This is not to say such a statement is not profound, such as the Biblical pronouncement, "I am that I am."[52] Rather "God is . . ." must be followed by descriptive terms, such as "great, eternal, righteous . . . ." Here, God is the Universal; an essence cannot in Hegelian terms be described by itself. The descriptive words and phrases in Hegelian terms are the particulars.

The Hegelian concept of Universal is analogous to Plato's concept of the Forms. In Plato's philosophy, the Forms are described in *The Republic* and *Phaedrus* as "the-things-in-themselves" representing the perfect idea of an object. In Platonic theory, there can be a "perfect" Form of a chair. Manifestations of chairs humans experience in life all partake in that "perfect" form of a chair.[53]

Thus, the Hegelian dialectic can be described as a triad consisting of two particulars and the Universal. For Hegel, the dialectic is when two particulars oppose each other. This does not necessarily mean that opposing particulars are opposite of each other—but the two particulars collide with each other. As the particulars collide, the negative—not necessarily opposite—of the particulars arises. The Universal appears as a negative of the particulars. The Universal is not the opposite of the particulars but can function as both particulars while not being either of them.

What does Žižek's interpretation of Shakespeare have to do with the concept of sanctuary? And, furthermore, what does it have to do with the system of money and debt as a legal sanctuary?

Like economics having a root in philosophy,[54] sanctuary can have a basis in law and the philosophical concepts supporting that law. The concept of sanctuary can arrive as a tragedy as indicated in the law journal article titled *Liberty to Misread: Sanctuary and Possibility in The Comedy of Errors*. The thesis of that article is that sanctuary can be called for in tragedy only to be taken off the table. Indeed, the concept of sanctuary is the place beyond governmental power and the functioning of socially agreed upon monetary instruments—but, in a *sublation* of such a thesis, sanctuary can negate the state of normalcy. Sometimes, this negation could lead to the dysfunction of a society. However, sanctuary can exist as one of the exemptions to the rule where normal society accepts this exemption—thereby not leading to chaos.

Žižek somewhat depicts this idea in an inverted way in *Troilus and Cressida* where a *sublation* occurs in the quote "my negation has no taste of madness"—even though the character is seeing ghosts. Again, Žižek depicts a key aspect of Shakespeare indicating the Lacanian *objet a* exists in "nothing but confusion," that is, confusion as the aspect of chaos.

But the true depiction of Žižek's interpretation of the negation is in Shakespeare's *As You Like It* with a double depiction of deception. Orland loves Rosalind. Rosalind disguises herself as a male and pretends again to be Rosalind—a negation of a negation itself. But even, then, goes a step forward to do a mock ceremony. Rosalind creates a safe sanctuary of a male figure to depict herself. She then marries and creates a fake extramarital affair—the negation of the sanctuary. And, finally, she marries him in real life later in the play. The sanctuary can create chaos, which then creates another safe space.

Like the sanctuary of law, it can create chaos within it, but works to *sublate* itself into a future true sanctuary.

Here, in the triad of Hegelian terms, when the particulars of sanctuary of law and chaos of theatrical tragedy collide, they create a theatrically comedic—that is to say, without a sad ending—artistic work. This theatrically comedic work incorporates the sanctuary of law, the chaos of theatrical tragedy, and the comedic "happy" ending. In this case, the particulars are sanctuary of law and chaos of theatrical tragedy. The Universal is theatrical comedy. Comedy is not the opposite of the particulars but functions as both particulars while not being either of them.

Ultimately, the Hegelian Dialectic is . . . ?[55]

It is important to articulate a clear understanding of Georg Wilhelm Friedrich Hegel's concept of the dialectic. He provided a myriad of examples in his works.

Among Hegel's accessible examples, the concept of quality and quantity provides an informative starting point. For example, in Hegel's *The Logic: Encyclopedia of the Philosophical Sciences*, he writes concerning quality and quantity. He explains that a division of quantity and quality can be separated and commensurable. However, over time certain quantitative changes can lead to qualitative changes.[56] Hegel analyzes this by saying:

> § 108 . . . The identity between quantity and quality, which is found in Measure, is at first only implicit, and not yet explicitly realised. In other words, these two categories, which unite in Measure, each claim an independent authority. On the one hand, the quantitative features of existence may be altered, without affecting its quality. On the other hand, this increase and diminution, immaterial though it be, has its limit, by exceeding which the quality suffers change.

Here, Hegel gives an example of quality and quantity in relation to water—where water turns into ice or steam through incremental changes to quantity that ultimately change the quality of the substance.[57] This is a vital key aspect of his thought and at the same time it exactingly demonstrates the concept of dialectic. He goes on in the next section to further explain:

> § 109 . . . Thus the temperature of water is, in the first place, a point of no consequence in respect of liquidity: still with the increase of diminution of the temperate of the liquid, there comes a point where this state of cohesion suffers a qualitative change, and the water is converted into steam or ice. A quantitative change takes place, apparently without any further significance: but there is something lurking behind, and a seemingly innocent change of

> quantity acts as a kind of snare, to catch a hold of the quality. The antinomy of Measure which this implies was exemplified under more than one garb among the Greeks . . . But if the quantity present in measure exceeds a certain limit, the quality corresponding to it is also put in abeyance. This however is not a negation of quality altogether, but only of this definite quality, the place of which is at once occupied by another. This process of measure, which appears alternately as a mere change in quantity, and then as a sudden revulsion of quantity into quality, may be envisaged under the figure of a nodal (knotted) line.[58]

Indeed, Hegel's theory of the dialectic can be applied to dialectical materialism, logic, and various other fields.[59]

However, of the prime examples of the Hegelian dialectic is Hegel's analysis of history. The greater historical dialectic is a larger representation of what is known in German as the "*Herrschaft und Knechtschaft*" that is variously translated as the "*master-slave*" dialectic or perhaps more accurate to the German as "*Lordship Bondage*" dialectic. This is one of the key ideas in Hegelianism and the concept of the dialectic. In Hegel's *Phenomenology of Spirit*, he writes that "on approaching the other it has lost its own self, since it finds itself as another being; secondly, it has thereby sublated that other, for this primitive consciousness does not regard the other as essentially real but sees its own self in the other."[60]

The two sections above on quality and quantity likely "echoes perhaps the most famous passages he ever wrote—the Lord-Bondsman dialectic in the *Phenomenology*. In this dialectic, two warriors try to subjugate each other. One succeeds and becomes the master, the other the slave. But the master discovers that the other is truly himself. The master is thus reduced to dependency. Likewise, in ratio, Quantum attempts to distinguish itself by expelling the Other, only to find that the Other is as much itself as itself is."[61]

In the same way, quantity may sometimes be altered without affecting quality, such as with the example of boiling water, so too can the "lord" who has subjugated the "bondsman." Subsequently, the lord becomes the bondsman by realizing his dependence on the bondsman.

Moving from the specific lord and bondsman dialectic to the broader philosophy of history, Hegel employs a similar analysis.

In analyzing history, Hegel's dialectic presupposes a rational structure to history and, specifically, political history.[62] Hegel illustrates the dialectic rule by his discussion of a ruler and those who are ruled, the "populace."[63] The rule begins with assertions by the ruler of absolute power.[64] But the ruler's exercise of that power causes resentment in the populace, because the populace sees the ruler exercise freedom.[65] The ruler, sensing a threat from the populace, tries to bring them more firmly under his control.[66] This often begins with simple brutality to force obedience, but there are limits to the effectiveness of force—as there can be in the lord and bondsman dialectic.[67]

In Hegelian terms, a political thesis (the rule that the ruler's authority is absolute) and an antithesis (resistance to the ruler's authority) can exist.[68] At first, the ruler might try to simply suppress the antithesis by forcibly compelling obedience.[69] But, whether as a matter of egocentric psychology or political strategy, the ruler's suppression merely intensifies the popular antithesis—the resistance to the ruler's authority.[70]

The ruler and the populace thus move toward a synthesis.[71] The ruler seeks to bring the populace back under control—in Hegel's terminology, to *inwardize* them—while the populace demands more control.[72]

The ruler thus responds with charters, rights, or laws, which he grants to the populace.[73] This reaffirms the ruler's assertion that his right is absolute, while in fact giving the populace more power.[74]

This synthesis itself lasts for a time but then becomes a new thesis.[75] This, in Hegel's view, keeps going in a spiral, as each new thesis is undercut by a new antithesis.[76] The use of the "spiral" metaphor with Hegel is important: we are not merely going in circles; we are going in circles that bring us closer to the ultimate purpose of history, synthesis (what Hegel calls the "end" of history).[77] This is ultimately the fully equal sharing of power among all.

Historically and since Hegel's lifetime, the Hegelian dialectic has been used and disused in many ways since his writing in the early 1800s.[78] Relatively recently, Francis Fukuyama used a version of the dialectic between a liberal-capitalistic-democracy and communism; in 1989, he argued that the dialectic would resolve itself with a liberal-capitalistic-democracy.[79] In his work, *The End of History* and the *Last Man*, Fukuyama even seems to be suggesting that Hegel's dialectic can apply to "universal rights."[80] Fukuyama acknowledged that history is not a linear progression toward liberal-capitalistic-democracy, but that regressions, even long periods of regressions, occur.[81]

Fukuyama's interpretation of the class of the liberal-capitalistic-democratic world follows the Hegelian paradigm.[82] Essentially, Fukuyama shows two opposite systems clashing with each other.[83] Overtime, systems ebb and flow, much like the ruler giving rights to the populace and then taking rights from the populace.[84] Areas such as stints of communism expanded, but liberal-capitalistic-democracy ultimately took over.[85]

NOTES

1. Indeed, Arthur Herman goes on to say that

> however, the bankers at the Federal Reserve had kept the money flowing into the American economy at a pitch that held interest rates low and kept expanding business and

consumer credit, especially in the stock market. Yet in defiance of all classical economic doctrine, there was no rise in prices.

The business cycle, the dreaded beast of capitalist economies, had finally been tamed—or so it seemed. Economists around the world praised the Federal Reserve. Some even predicted that a "new era" in economics had begun, of continuous prosperity and growth with no threat of crisis or depression. Economic growth without growing pains: it seemed a transformative moment worthy of a Georg Friedrich Hegel or even a Saint Augustine."

Arthur Herman, *The Cave and the Light* (2013). *Cf.* Paul Johnson, *Modern Times* (rev. ed. 1991).

2. This is one of the central themes in is works, but particularly in The Western Canon. Harold Bloom, *The Western Canon: The Books and School of the Ages* (Riverhead Books, 1994).

3. This question of memory and thinking comes up in a televised interview with Charlie Rose and Harold Bloom, The Charlie Rose Show: Interview with Harold Bloom (PBS television broadcast, Dec. 29, 1994).

4. Harold Bloom, *The Western Canon: The Books and School of the Ages* (Riverhead Books, 1994), 86.

5. "Coming after Shakespeare, who wrote both the best prose and the best poetry in the Western tradition, is a complex destiny, since originality becomes peculiarly difficult in everything that matters most: representation of human beings, the role of memory in cognition, the range of metaphor in suggesting new possibilities for language." Harold Bloom, *The Western Canon: The Books and School of the Ages* 30 (Riverhead Books, 1994). *Cf.* Compare for instance what novelists seem to bring into creation. The British writer Evelyn Waugh wrote, "Nothing is more insulting to a novelist than to assume that he is incapable of anything but the mere transcription of what he observes." David Wykes, *Evelyn Waugh: A Literary Life 209-11* (1999). *See.* Charles Edward Linck, Jr., The Development of Evelyn Waugh's Career: 1903–1939 (1962) (PhD Dissertation, University of Kansas).

6. "Yet intelligibility pragmatically transcends its lexicon, and we must remind ourselves that Shakespeare, who scarcely relies upon philosophy, is more central to Western culture than are Plato and Aristotle, Kant and Hegel, Heidegger and Wittgenstein." Harold Bloom, *The Western Canon: The Books and School of the Ages* (Riverhead Books, 1994), 31.

7. Ronald Dworkin, *A Matter of Principle* (1985), 146.

8. Benjamin Woodring, "Liberty to Misread: Sanctuary and Possibility in The Comedy of Errors." *Yale J.L. & Human.* 28 (2016): 319. Though not explicitly mentioned, it seems the author—Woodring—is referring also to Harold Bloom's theory of "Anxiety of Influence" and theory of "misreading." Indeed, misreading is important because as "Bloom argues that for a novice or "ephebe" "to emerge a strong creator, he must constructively misread his most important precursors. If he does not misread them, the ephebe will be trapped in the anxiety of influence." David Cole, "Agon at Agora: Creative Misreadings in the First Amendment Tradition." *Yale L.J.* 95 (1986): 857, 863.

9. Benjamin Woodring, "Liberty to Misread: Sanctuary and Possibility in the Comedy of Errors." *Yale J.L. & Human.* 28 (2016): 319, 323–324.

10. Monmouth wrote that such sanctuary laws existed in England since the fourth or fifth century BCE. He writes of the pre-Saxon, potentially mythological king, Dunvallo Molmuitas "established what the Britons call the Molmutine laws, which are famous among the English to this day. In these, among other things, of which St. Gildas wrote a long time after, he enacted that the temples of the gods, as also cities, should have the privilege of giving sanctuary and protection to any fugitive or criminal, that should flee to them from the enemy." Geoffrey of Monmouth, *History of the Kings of Britain* (Aaron Thompson, J. A. Gilestrans., E.P. Dutton & Co., 1958) (1138–1139). Wikisource contributors, "Six Old English Chronicles/Geoffrey's British History/Book 2," *Wikisource*, https://en.wikisource.org/w/index.php?title=Six_Old_English_Chronicles/Geoffrey%27s_British_History/Book_2&oldid=9052503 (accessed May 29, 2021).

11. Anomie was initially brought up by the anthropologist Émile Durkheim.

> Durkheim described crime as a dysfunctional consequence of the deregulation of norms or a state of anomie. Anomie, or normlessness, was likely to be the greatest when societies were undergoing social and technological change. Durkheim theorized that "disruptions presumably reduce the individuals' sense of belongingness, resulting in anomie at a personal level." He blamed anomie on the disintegration of social norms that occurs due to changes in social institutions caused by transformation of the economic base.

Id. (quoting Mark Abrahamson, "Sudden Wealth, Gratification and Attainment: Durkheim's Anomie of Affluence Reconsidered." *Am. Soc. Rev.* 45 (1980): 49, 49). Michael L. Rustad, "Symposium: Does the World Still Need United States Tort Law? Or Did It Ever?: Torts as Public Wrongs." *Pepp. L. Rev.* 38 (2011): 433, 443 fn. 56.

12. "Just as Foucault argues, the normalizing effect of the label natural or normal conceals a culturally mediated value judgment." Tessa Davis, "Reproducing Value: How Tax Law Differentially Values Fertility, Sexuality & Marriage." *Cardozo J.L. & Gender* 19 (2012): 1, 32.

13. "Asylum is a privilege conferred by a state, not a condition inherent in the . . . one can continue to live as normal a life as possible, then the systematic detention . . . be extradited for whatever reason negates the essence of asylum/sanctuary." *Law and Asylum: Space, Subject, Resistance by Simon Behrman* (2018).

14. Indeed, "[c]hurch burnings constituted martyrdom for the people killed in the violence. Church burnings were equally potent as a violation of a core dominant group taboo against the violation of places of worship as a place of sanctuary. See Theodor Meron, "Crimes and Accountability in Shakespeare." *Am. J. Int'l L.* 92 (1998): 1, 33–35 (noting the legal notions of church sanctuary as reflected in the works of Shakespeare, in this case the legal position of Queen Elizabeth to seek sanctuary against the plotting of Richard III). The common understanding of the sacredness of church space is reflected in the works of modern existentialists as well. See, e.g., Jean Paul Sartre, *The Flies, in No Exit and Other Plays* 49 (Stuart Gilbert trans., 1955) (1943) ('Come, Lead me to Apollo's shrine. We will spend the night there, sheltered from men and flies')." Larry Cata Backer, "Culturally Significant Speech: Law, Courts, Society, and Racial Equity." *U. Ark. Little Rock L. Rev.* 21 (1999): 845, 879 n. 55.

15. Compare with: "Shakespeare is at pains to show in his plays how good men yield to pressure. The episode of the sanctuary, which occurs just before the murder of the princes, closely reflects the chronicles that Shakespeare read, providing an interesting example. Queen Elizabeth, afraid that Richard will murder her children, has taken the young duke of York to a sanctuary under the Lord Cardinal's promise of protection and care (Richard III, II.iv.65-72). On his return to London, Prince Edward, the heir to the throne, is informed by Hastings that his brother York is in a sanctuary and therefore cannot welcome him. Edward does not appear to suspect that anything is amiss and wants his brother to come to him." Theodor Meron, "Crimes and Accountability in Shakespeare." *Am. J. Int'l L.* 92 (1998): 1, 33.

16. Benjamin Woodring, "Liberty to Misread: Sanctuary and Possibility in the Comedy of Errors." *Yale J.L. & Human.* 28 (2016): 319, 323–324.

17. Benjamin Woodring, "Liberty to Misread: Sanctuary and Possibility in the Comedy of Errors." *Yale J.L. & Human.* 28 (2016): 319, 323–324.

18. Indeed, such a definition of opposites would likely not be helpful. Nietzsche argued that opposites do not lead to truth. The definition of something as that which is not is fallacious. Nietzsche argues in the second aphorism of Beyond Good and Evil that belief in "opposites" is the conceit of the metaphysician. Friedrich Nietzsche, *Beyond Good and Evil* (Helen Zimmern trans., 1989) Aphorism 2.

19. *Cf.* Law ramifies itself in fear of the unstable contingencies of its ethical origin and legitimating source. It turns against affirmative beatitude the way the neurotic shrinks in horror from his or her (impermissible) pleasure. The unassimilable excess of desire thus repressed, symptomized in fantasies of recurring trauma, leads to the "undeadness" of law, which is to say, to metaphysical beatitude and mythical violence. At the same time, absent the revelatory authority of contingent justice, Nietzsche's affirmative beatitude risks a "strange fire," a lawless passion--all too familiar fuel for the machinery of fascism's aestheticization of the political. Conversely, if Nietzsche's excess of meaning risks a lawless passion, in the shadow-land of disenchantment law's validity risks exceeding its meaning. This is the condition of Kafka's law in a thoroughly disenchanted world." Richard K. Sherwin, "Law's Beatitude: A Post-Nietzschean Account of Legitimacy." *Cardozo L. Rev.* 24 (2003): 683, 699.

And further compare with the footnote within Sherwin's law review: See, for example, Eric Rentschler, *The Ministry of Illusion* (1996), 21 and Richard K. Sherwin, "Law's Beatitude: A Post-Nietzschean Account of Legitimacy." *Cardozo L. Rev.* 24 (2003): 683, 703 n. 81.

20. "Wagner epitomizes the romantic author, having written singlehandedly both the music and verbal texts for his enormously significant—and simply enormous—works like Tristan und Isolde. Wagner's determination to be solely responsible for the entire authorship of his works comports with the megalomaniacal tendencies for which he is well known. It was also, however, essential to achieving his goal of an aesthetically synthesized Gesamtkunstwerk in which a single author is responsible for all elements of an opera - visual, musical, and dramatic. Charles Cronin, *I Hear America Suing*: Music Copyright Infringement in the Era of Electronic Sound, * First published in 1860, Walt Whitman's 'I Hear America Singing' was a 'paean to American pluralism and personal industry that bore witness to an era before the*

machinery of the music business was first set in motion. By the early twentieth century, 'talking machines' were doing much of America's singing .'" David Suisman, *Selling Sounds: The Commercial Revolution in American Music* 8 (2012), *Hastings L.J.* 66 (2015): 1187, 1220–1221.

21. Indeed, Aristotle in his *Poetics* says that in comedy the bad—variously translated as the ugly and ignoble—could be harmless. Aristotle writes, "Comedy is, as we have said, an imitation of characters of a lower type, not, however, in the full sense of the word bad, the Ludicrous being merely a subdivision of the ugly. It consists in some defect or ugliness which is not painful or destructive. To take an obvious example, the comic mask is ugly and distorted, but does not imply pain." Aristotle, *Poetics* (S.H. Butcher, 2019).

22. This is a reference to Rudyard Kipling's "If" poem. Harry Ricketts, *The Unforgiving Minute: A Life of Rudyard Kipling* (1999).

23. This analysis by Žižek comes from his discussion in The Pervert's Guide to Ideology (Zeitgeist Films et al. 2012).

Consider the influences of Johann Christoph Friedrich von Schiller's influence on Beethoven's work.

> "Schiller's Ode to Joy, as quoted in Beethoven's Ninth Symphony. "Deine Zauber bindet wieder/Was die Mode streng geteilt;/Alle Menschen werden Brüder,/Wo dein sanfter Flügel weilt" (Your magic reunites/What custom strictly divides;/All men become brothers/Wherever your soft wings linger). Ludwig von Beethoven, Symphony No. 9, Opus 125, fourth movement (1824). The words may be found in any respectable recording of the symphony; I have taken them from the notes to Herbert von Karajan, Beethoven 9 Symphonien DGG (1962).

David Luban, "A Theory of Crimes Against Humanity." *Yale J. Int'l L.* 29 (2004): 85, 167 n. 144.

24. This idea is explicitly alluded to and contrasted to in Žižek's discussion of the movie *Clockwork Orange* and its main character—Alex. The Pervert's Guide to Ideology (Zeitgeist Films et al. 2012).

25. However, Žižek's shows how this idea can be conducted by different political movements of divers kinds. The Pervert's Guide to Ideology (Zeitgeist Films et al. 2012).

26. Again, alluding to *Clockwork Orange*'s—Alex. The Pervert's Guide to Ideology (Zeitgeist Films et al. 2012).

27. The Pervert's Guide to Ideology (Zeitgeist Films et al. 2012).

28. "The "Ode to Joy" is more than just a universally popular piece of classical music that has become something of a cliché during the holiday season (especially, oddly, in Japan, where it has achieved cult status). It has also been, for more than a century, what literary theorists call an "empty signifier"—a symbol that can stand for anything. In early twentieth-century France, the Nobel laureate Romain Rolland declared it to be the great humanist ode to the brotherhood of all people, and it came to be called

> the Marseillaise of humanity." In 1938, it was performed as the high point of the Reichsmusiktage, the Nazi music festival, and was later used to celebrate Hitler's birthday. In China during the Cultural Revolution, in an atmosphere of total rejection of European classics, it was redeemed by some as a piece of progressive class struggle.

"Opinion | 'Ode to Joy,' Followed by Chaos and Despair—The New York Times." Accessed May 29, 2021. https://www.nytimes.com/2007/12/24/opinion/24zizek.html. *Cf.* The Pervert's Guide to Ideology (Zeitgeist Films et al. 2012).

29. William Shakespeare, *Troilus and Cressida*, Act v, Scene 2, Line 143. Slavoj Žižek. "Absolute Recoil."

30. Slavoj Žižek, Absolute Recoil 2015.

31. Slavoj Žižek, Absolute Recoil 2015.

32. Slavoj Žižek, Absolute Recoil 2015.

33. Slavoj Žižek, Absolute Recoil 2015.

34. Slavoj Žižek, Absolute Recoil 2015. *See* "G. W. F. Hegel, Science of Logic, Atlantic Heights: Humanities Press International 1989, p. 444." Slavoj Žižek, Absolute Recoil 2015.

35. Slavoj Žižek, Absolute Recoil 2015. *See* "G. W. F. Hegel, Science of Logic, Atlantic Heights: Humanities Press International 1989, p. 444." Slavoj Žižek, Absolute Recoil 2015.

36. Slavoj Žižek, Absolute Recoil 2015.

37. Slavoj Žižek, Absolute Recoil 2015.

38. Slavoj Žižek, Absolute Recoil 2015. *Cf.*

> In common with that particular mode of cultural discourse, Elizabethan drama fulfilled the didactic function of imparting moral education through the device of storytelling. Indeed, Shakespeare's *Troilus and Cressida* pays homage to the Athenian practice of formally reciting Homer's poems in a public ceremony. MacIntyre further notes that the great political philosophers of the latter half of the seventeenth century, Hobbes and Locke, articulated a realistic and "[i]ndividualistic view" of modern society, in which a diverse group of "strangers" actively pursue their interests without constraint. The growth, toward the end of the sixteenth century, of a professional class of lawyers relentlessly pursuing selfish interests at the expense of the communitarian ethos implied by Fortescue and Fulbecke, provided a highly visible target for dramatic satirists. Shakespeare does not readily fall into this category, but the forthright announcement by one of the rebels in The Second Part of King Henry VI upon attaining power, "[t]he first thing we do, let's kill all the lawyers," was probably an accurate reflection of public sentiment concerning the legal profession at the end of the sixteenth century (and any century since).
>
> John Marston, a member of the Middle Temple, mocked the vain affectations and vacuity of common lawyers in *Histrio-Mastix Or, The Player Whipt!*, which Hotson suggests was written as a response to the 1598 performance of Shakespeare's Troilus and Cressida by members of the Middle Temple. The prologue to Marston's play offers a brief parody of Shakespeare's play. In Marston's version, Cressida "Was cleare as is ye Christall streame, that runs along ye street," and Troilus "shakes his furious Speare," an unequivocal reference to the more illustrious of the two dramatists. Shakespeare's poetic vision of a natural order, congruent with Platonic notions of justice and Aristotelian concepts of the common weal, is articulated with great clarity by the character of Ulysses in *Troilus and Cressida.*

Paul Raffield, "A Discredited Priesthood the Failings of Common Lawyers and Their Representation in Seventeenth Century Satirical Drama." *Law & Literature* 17 (2005): 365, 373–374.

39. William Shakespeare, Richard II, Act 2, Scene 2, Lines 14–24.

40. Slavoj Žižek, Absolute Recoil 2015.

41. Slavoj Žižek, Absolute Recoil 2015.

42. Renata Salecl, "Rights in Psychoanalytic and Feminist Perspective." *Cardozo L. Rev.* 16 (1995): 1121, 1133.

43. Renata Salecl, "Rights in Psychoanalytic and Feminist Perspective." *Cardozo L. Rev.* 16 (1995): 1121, 1133.

44. Renata Salecl, "Rights in Psychoanalytic and Feminist Perspective." *Cardozo L. Rev.* 16 (1995): 1121, 1133.

45. Slavoj Žižek, *Less Than Nothing: Hegel and the Shadow of Dialectical Materialism* 2012.

46. Slavoj Žižek, *Less Than Nothing: Hegel and the Shadow of Dialectical Materialism* 2012.

47. Slavoj Žižek, *Less Than Nothing: Hegel and the Shadow of Dialectical Materialism* 2012.

48. Slavoj Žižek, *Less Than Nothing: Hegel and the Shadow of Dialectical Materialism* 2012.

49. Slavoj Žižek, *Less Than Nothing: Hegel and the Shadow of Dialectical Materialism* 2012.

50. Slavoj Žižek, *Less Than Nothing: Hegel and the Shadow of Dialectical Materialism* 2012. *Cf.* "Slavoj Ẑiẑek has argued, post-modernism in a sense precedes modernism. That is, although presented as something new—as a wry, self-conscious and self-referential, critique of modernism—it is too often merely a regression to pre-modern ideas. Naive post-modernism is reactionary—a romantic attempt to reconstruct an imaginary lost pre-modern past." Sense, Sensibility and Smart Contracts: A View From a Contract, 20181004A NYCBAR 13.

51. G.W.F. Hegel, *The Phenomenology of Mind* (William Wallace trans., 1894) § 564.

52. Exodus 3:14. The original Hebrew " אֶהְיֶה אֲשֶׁר אֶהְיֶה" could be variously translated. The middle word, "אֲשֶׁר" is a relativizer that is used to introduce a relative clause often translated as a preposition. The two surrounding words are "אֶהְיֶה," which is a first-person singular future of the verb "הָיָה" which is the infinitive form of the verb "to be."

53. "It was a form of Platonism; just as Plato had regarded particular chairs as manifestations of or approximations to the concept of a chair, Langdell regarded particular decisions on contract law as manifestations of or approximations to the legal concept of contract." Richard A. Posner, "The Decline of Law as an Autonomous Discipline: 1962–1987." *Harv. L. Rev.* 100 (1987): 761, 762.

54. See generally, Adam Smith, *An Inquiry into the Nature and Causes of the Wealth of Nations* 475–476 (Edwin Cannan ed., University of Chicago Press, 1976) (1776). *See*. J. S. MILL, "On the Definition of Political Economy; and on the Method of Investigation Proper to It." *London & Westminster Rev.* 4 (1836): 12.

55. The original version of this section came from an article published by the author. Charles Edward Andrew Lincoln IV, "Hegelian Dialectical Analysis of U.S. Voting Laws." *U. Dayton L. Rev.* 42 (2017): 87, 91. That article itself was an outgrowth of the author's undergraduate senior thesis (formally known as an

independent research and writing project) at Harvard University under the direction of Akiba Covitz—who was then an assistant dean at Harvard Law School.

Much of this chapter's section is taken verbatim from that article, but is significantly altered for this book.

56. "The implication of this is profound. Apparently, numbers are never entirely present, and arithmetic is, to borrow the Derridean phrase, a "philosophy of presence." In effect, every number is "filled in" by the mathematician, so that the ellipsis ("...") is suppressed and the number seems complete. Numbers, Hegel will conclude, are constituted by an absence. Hegel will identify this absence as the very quality of quantity. For Hegel, quantity stands for absolute openness to determination by something external to itself. Quantity has no integrity--no content of its own. Quantity is that which absolutely refuses to define itself. Paradoxically, quantity defines itself precisely when it refuses to define itself. When this pure refusal is isolated, quantity has defined itself after all and has exhibited its true quality." David Gray Carlson, "Hegel's Theory of Quantity." *Cardozo L. Rev.* 23 (2002): 2027, 2028.

57. Georg Wilhelm Friedrich Hegel, *The Logic. Encyclopaedia of the Philosophical Sciences.* 2nd Edition (London: Oxford University Press, §108, 1874).

58. Georg Wilhelm Friedrich Hegel, *The Logic. Encyclopaedia of the Philosophical Sciences.* 2nd Edition (London: Oxford University Press, §108, 1874).

59. Leonard F. Wheat, *Hegel's Undiscovered Thesis-Antithesis-Synthesis Dialectics: What Only Marx and Tillich Understood.* Prometheus (2012).

60. G.W.F. Hegel, *Phenomenology of Spirit*, translated by A.V. Miller with analysis of the text and foreword by J. N. Findlay; Paragraph 179, Pg. 111 (Oxford: Clarendon Press, 1977).

61. David Gray Carlson, "Hegel's Theory of Quantity." *Cardozo L. Rev.* 23 (2002): 2027, 2150 n. 291.

62. Raj Bhala, "Hegelian Reflections on Unilateral Action in the World Trading System." *Berkley J. Int'l L.* 15 (1997): 159, 184 n.93 (noting that Hegel's history is the subject of much debate, but a common formulation concludes Hegel argued a rational structure to history: "Hegel repeats this thesis in his conclusion. . . . (noting that for Hegel, 'world history is not wholly an affair of chance or contingency'; rather 'the history of the world has a rational structure,' and 'this rational structure . . . is the development of freedom') and (stating that 'Hegel considered that the history of the human race is a development from less to greater freedom and from less adequate forms of freedom to freedom in its perfection'") (emphasis omitted) (citations omitted).

63. This process is often referred to as guided by the "Geist." Reginald Leamon Robinson, "The Impact of Hobbes's Empirical Natural Law on Title VII's Effectiveness: A Hegelian Critique." *Conn. L. Rev.* 25 (1993): 607, 661 n.299 (quoting Michael A. Simon: "History for Hegel is an unfolding of the Geist or spirit as it objectifies itself in the world. Spirit actualizes itself by making things happen, and is at the same time conscious of itself. . . . History is the story of the development of human freedom; it is freedom becoming objective, which means that the world is brought into conformity with the rational system of mind. The system of right—that is to say, the law—represents the rational principles that determine the constraints

that operate on what free-willing existents can will at a particular moment of history" (citations omitted).

64. *See* Georg Wilhelm Friedrich Hegel, *The Philosophy of History* (J. Sibree trans., 1956), 43–44.

65. *Id.* at 44.

66. *Id.* at 96.

67. *Id.* at 96–97.

68. Bhala, at 187–188.

69. *Id.* at 187.

70. *Id.*

71. *Id.* at 173, 187–188.

72. This personal interpretation is drawn from part of the Absolute Knowing chapter in *Phenomenology of Spirit*, section 788:

> In revealed religion self-consciousness is aware of itself in pictorial objective form, not as yet *as* self-consciousness. It must cancel this form and become aware of itself in all the forms it has hitherto taken up. They must not merely be forms of self-consciousness for *us*, the phenomenological observers, but for self-consciousness itself. It must see how it has externalized itself in various objects, and in seeing this also canceled the externalization. It must see all its objective forms as itself.

G.W.F. Hegel, *Phenomenology of Spirit* (A.V. Miller trans., 1977) § 788, at 589.

73. Hegel illustrates this point by stating:

> "[W]hat is law [Gesetz] may differ in content from what is right in itself [an sich Recht]." In his view, slavery may be legally valid and yet unjust. Law becomes more consistent with justice insofar as law is a "realization [Verwirklichung]" of "right [Recht]," that is, insofar as law embodies right. Hegel often plays upon the ambiguity of the German word for right, Recht. Recht can mean right in a legal sense, as in having the right to do something, or right as a form of justice, as in to be in the right. Recht can also refer to law, although Hegel uses the word Gesetz as well, which can be translated as "law" or "statute." He does not use the words interchangeably, instead tending to use Gesetz for positive law and Recht for a normative sense of positive law, such as justice. The two come together when Hegel says that "actual legal relationships presuppose laws founded on right [Rechtsgesetz] as something valid in and for itself." Gesetz is distinguishable from Rechtgesetz in that only the latter represents positive law fully consistent with justice. All other varieties of positive laws [Gesetze] embody lesser forms of right [Recht].

Thom Brooks, "Between Natural Law and Legal Positivism: Dworkin and Hegel on Legal Theory." *Ga. St. U. L. Rev.* 23 (2007): 513, 520–521.

74. *See* Francis Fukuyama, *The End of History and the Last Man* (1992) 157–158 (distinguishing a legitimate ruler from a despot in that a legitimate ruler has popular consent, which is often given by the ruler offering rights to life and self-preservation among other rights). This sentiment is also summarized in a recent law review article by Professor Bhala indicating that "[t]he extension of this law [—egalitarian religious benefits to all people—] to both ruler and subject, namely, the idea of a constraint on a ruler other than himself, is a necessary prerequisite toward a consciousness of

freedom on the part of the subject." Bhala, *supra* note 8, at 185. In other words, this aspect of an egalitarian religion conferring "rights" or religious benefits to all people is an instance of a ruler giving up a "monopoly" on religion and having to share it with his subjects. *Id.* at 185–86. This is a precursor to other rights. *Id.* at 186.

75. Bhala, at 188.

76. An *antithesis* does not necessarily imply a negative connotation, but rather an opposite state of affairs from the *thesis.*

77. G.W.F. Hegel, *Elements of the Philosophy of Right* (Allen W. Wood ed., H.B. Nisbet trans., Cambridge Univ. Press, 1991), 26 (explaining "[p]hilosophy forms a circle. It has an initial or immediate point—for it must begin somewhere—a point which is not demonstrated and is not a result. But the starting point of philosophy is immediately relative, for it must appear at another end-point as a result. Philosophy is a sequence which is not suspended in mid-air; it does not begin immediately, but is rounded off within itself" (footnote omitted).

78. For two centuries Hegel was either ignored or vilified by Anglo-American legal scholars. Holmes read Hegel but used him as a foil against which to develop his own theories. There was a general decline of interest in European philosophy with the rise of legal positivism and realism. Moreover, conservative theorists hostile to positivism joined the attack on Hegel for nationalistic reasons in the wake of the World War I. Although Robert S. Summers has suggested that Lon Fuller was influenced by Hegel, Fuller never publicly acknowledged any such influence.

> Richard Hyland uses the search term "Hegel" to demonstrate the ridiculous results of computer assisted research. Finding numerous instances where the term "Hegel" refers to an attorney, judge, or party, Hyland concludes that "the most frequently cited passage about Hegel in American case law" is Judge Learned Hand's paraphrase of William James's comparison of the Internal Revenue Code with Hegel's prose.

Hoffheimer, *supra* note 1, at 825 n.6 (citations omitted).

79. Guyora Binder, "Post-Totalitarian Politics." *Mich. L. Rev.* 91 (1993): 1491, 1493.

80. Fukuyama, *supra* note 20, at 217, 243.

81. Francis Fukuyama, "The End of History?" *Nat'l Interest*, Summer 1989, at 7–18; *see generally* Ari Afilalo and Dennis Patterson, "Statecraft, Trade and the Order of States." *Chi. J. Int'l L.* 6 (2006): 725, 726 n.5 (simplifying Fukuyama's concept in relation to political science: "According to Fukuyama, the liberal democratic model soundly beat fascism and communism because, simply put, it was a better idea. The liberal democratic model had no problem besting the fascist ideology of expansionism and racial superiority. In time, it defeated the Marxist ideology—in part because the growth of a strong and expansive middle class, resulting from (among other factors) the welfare policies of the nation-state, had radically changed the social reality in which Marx wrote. In the end, Fukuyama argued, all good government would be organized along the lines of the liberal democratic model, which would be applied to govern an ethnic or otherwise discrete nation and would protect the rights of minorities" (citation omitted).

82. "Paradigm." Accessed May 29, 2021. http://www.theinfolist.com/php/SummaryGet.php?FindGo=Paradigm. ("Paradigm comes from Greek παράδειγμα (paradeigma), 'pattern, example, sample' from the verb παραδείκνυμι (paradeiknumi), 'exhibit, represent, expose' and that from παρά (para), 'beside, beyond' and δείκνυμι (deiknumi), 'to show, to point out'"). Hegelian dialectic is in every sense a Kuhnian paradigm, applicable to many fields of dynamic social interaction.

83. Jonathan R. Macey and Geoffrey P. Miller, "The End of History and the New World Order: The Triumph of Capitalism and the Competition Between Liberalism and Democracy." *Cornell Int'l L.J.* 25 (1992): 277, 278 ("To understand what Francis Fukuyama means when he says that history has come to an end, one must first understand two things about Fukuyama. First, when Fukuyama says that history is at an end, he means history in the Hegelian or dialectic sense; that is, history as a clash of ideologies. Second, and far more importantly, Fukuyama is a Straussian in the Allan Bloom tradition. Fukuyama's understanding of Hegel (or more precisely, of Alexandre Kojéve, who presented Hegel's arguments about the end of history to the world of political science), leads him to observe that history has ended. Fukuyama's membership in the Straussian cult causes him hopelessly to mischaracterize and misinterpret how world history will unfold in the coming decades" (footnotes omitted).

84. Consider the Political Anthropology of "Gregory Bateson's concept of schismogenesis, which describes the self-amplifying process of divergence: I take an extreme position in reaction to your extreme position, leading you to take a more extreme position, and so on. The polarization feeds on itself as nuanced differences become disagreement, then disapproval, exasperation, and eventually hatred." Glenn Davis Stone, "Biotechnology, Schismogenesis, and the Demise of Uncertainty." *Wash. U. J.L. & Pol'y* 47 (2015): 29, 30. See. Gregory Bateson, *Steps to an Ecology of Mind: Collected Essays in Anthropology, Psychiatry, Evolution, And Epistemology* (University of Chicago Press, 1972), 68–69.

85. *See* FUKUYAMA, *supra* note 20, at 289. Fukuyama's definitive thesis of his work is that the capitalist liberal democracy paradigm is the teleological last, or end form, of political economy; meaning that political economies have reached their end form–teleologically speaking. *See id.*

Conclusion

Gödel, Escher, and Wittgenstein?[1] *The End of Philosophy and Linguistic Analysis of Law*[2]

INTRODUCTION TO INCOMPLETENESS AND LANGUAGE GAMES

Incompleteness specifically refers to the fact that given any system of symbols, there will always be questions that can be formulated in that system that cannot be answered using just the symbols of that system.

An example would be that if a person had a box of objects that she was holding, and an interrogator asked to show the objects in the box which cannot be shown. That would be a paradoxical question with no answer.

Those sorts of questions can always be formulated, and this shows that there are some propositions that will be unresolvable no matter what the premises are of a system.

If one wanted to judge an axiomatic system as David Hilbert did at the turn of the last century[3]—by whether it could have an answer for any question one could ask of it, then one will not be able to make that judgment of some system being more thoroughly "complete" (able to answer questions asked of it) relative to another.

Can this be applied to a system of law and moral judgments?[4] If one perceives law or morality as a propositional system then, yes, it would apply to moral judgments. Many pragmatists do not perceive law as such a propositional system, though. Such pragmatists refer to law with a different approach.

Morality cannot be proved, and everything is subjective intent, including law.[5] So, in the same way, that in the early 1900s, Bertrand Russell's attempts with mathematics were proven futile in *Principia Mathematica*,[6] does this mean that the subjective intent and the philosophical foundations of law are proved futile?

How is Gödel's incompleteness theorem implications for systems as a whole, a problem for morals and law? Nobody has "true" premises to go from? Therefore—it can be said—all our conclusions are subjective. Is this accurate?

Wittgenstein's Pivot

In his *Philosophical Investigations*, when observing a system, Ludwig Wittgenstein somewhat wittily and jokingly remarked how confidently people can make assumptions about systems observed from the outside.[7] Indeed, many assumptions can be taken for granted when describing a system of jurisprudence, mathematics, or even social interactions, such as games. As Wittgenstein[8] comically explained:

> We can easily imagine people amusing themselves in a field by playing with a ball so as to start various existing games, but playing many without finishing them and in between throwing the ball aimlessly into the air, chasing one another with the ball and bombarding one another for a joke and so on. And now someone says: The whole time they are playing a ball-game and following definite rules at every throw. And is there not also the case where we play and—make up the rules as we go along? And there is even one where we alter them—as we go along.[9]

In Wittgenstein's example, persons observing are like the person described standing off to the side observing—and groundlessly imputing to the participants some rigorous system or understanding persons observing believe they must be harboring to make the choices they do. Likewise, they can express what they do to each other in past legal decisions, such as in the conception of *stare decisis*. Wittgenstein is jokingly pointing out people who confidently take for granted such assumptions. Is it not conceivable that judges could be "making it up as they go along"?

THE PROBLEM OF CONSISTENT AND FORMAL SYSTEMS IN WITTGENSTEIN'S "LANGUAGE GAMES" AND GÖDEL'S FIRST INCOMPLETENESS THEOREM

Wittgenstein asks whether any system—regardless of whether it is random or not and no matter the complexity of the system—can follow rules of consistency and formalities?[10] This question arises even if the system is truly "chaotic" or random.[11] This implies that people when observing a system invent rules when no rule or rules really exist.[12] Wittgenstein concedes in his theory of "language games" that there are an infinite number of propositions that exist.[13] Likewise, this infinite number of propositions means that an infinite number of syllogisms can exist. But even with an infinite number of propositions and syllogisms, a system cannot be proven to be truly within a system of consistent formal rules or if we as observe merely ascribe those rules to them.[14]

Gödel's First Theorem considers how classic syllogistic reasoning based on axioms can lead to a truth of all arithmetic numbers and logical systems.[15] Gödel considers that no consistent system of axioms can lead to a truth of a logical and mathematical system.[16] In the alternative, only an inconsistent set of rules—thus, a chaotic and random set of axioms—can explain a system of logic.[17]

Gödel's First Theorem proves Wittgenstein's assertation that observers may attribute systems of formality and consistency to a logical system, but this formality cannot be proven or disproven.

In law, it seems that there is no certain way to prove law is internally consistent or not—much in the same way that mathematics or any other logical system cannot be proven to be consistent and following formal rules.

Legal Formalism

Christopher Columbus Langdell, along with Lon Fuller who continued the tradition, set the foundations for legal formalism. As Black's Law Dictionary indicates legal formalism is "[t]he theory that law is a set of rules and principles independent of other political and social institutions."[18] Legal formalism has been compared to textualism, and "[b]oth textualism and originalism are descendants and close kin to the traditions of legal formalism."[19] This is because "[t]extualism is a constitutional hermeneutic that purportedly explains the proper way of interpreting the Constitution."[20] However, "[r]ather than identifying what the law ought to be, a textualist construes the meaning of the constitutional text itself."[21] For example, Justice Scalia in his *A Matter of Interpretation: Federal Courts and the Law*, "terms the former approach the 'common-law attitude' of the federal judge."[22] However, in response to criticisms of textualism, Justice Scalia had written of formalism stating:

> "Of all the criticisms leveled against textualism, the most mindless is that it is formalist. The answer to that is, of course it's formalistic! The rule of law is about form . . . A murderer has been caught with blood on his hands, bending over the body of his victim; a neighbor with a video camera has filmed the crime and the murderer has confessed in writing and on videotape. We nonetheless insist that before the state can punish this miscreant, it must conduct a full-dress

> criminal trial that results in a verdict of guilty. Is that not formalism? Long live formalism! It is what makes us a government of laws and not of men."[23] Formalism strives to use Aristotelian-based syllogistic and logical thinking to produce legal results.[24]

Although not essential to the context of linguistic interpretation, it is important to note that Scalia's unmentioned Lockean influence that strikingly contrasts with Aristotle's theory of politics. Locke argued to create a government that can guide a polity away from bad intentions no matter what the individual intentions of the members of the government are.[25] In contrast, Aristotle thought a polity may only be good if the governing individuals aimed at the highest good and had good "souls."[26] Here, the metaphysical implications are not immediately relevant. Aristotle thought the best regimes were run by good people, while Locke thought that a government of strong laws—such as the "government of laws and not of men" that Scalia refers to above—was necessary regardless of the individual subjective intent of those governing. This is striking because Scalia arrives at different conclusions from Aristotle while explicitly quoting Aristotle's use of logic.

Legal Formalism Contrasted with Wittgenstein's Language Games

In the *Philosophical Investigations*, Wittgenstein asks, "[b]ut how many kinds of sentence are there? Say assertion, question, and command?—There are countless kinds: countless different kinds of use of what we call 'symbols', 'words', 'sentences'. And this multiplicity is not something fixed, given once for all; but new types of language, new language-games, as we may say, come into existence, and others become obsolete and get forgotten. (We can get a rough picture of this from the changes in mathematics.)"[27] Wittgenstein's statement expresses the idea that almost an infinite amount of language games exists. Indeed, later on in #23, Wittgenstein states that there can be quite a few distinct types of language games that exist. It seems reasonable to assume that there are potentially infinite language games that exist.

Following Wittgenstein's analysis of how many "language games" exist, then there necessarily is an infinite number of propositions that would exist. If so, then following the constraints of legal formalism, there would be an infinite amount of legal syllogisms that could be constructed. If there are infinite legal syllogisms, then there would inherently be contradictory legal syllogisms. This would present an ontological problem within legal formalism, because the adherents of legal formalism argue that legal problems can be resolved through use of syllogistic logic. Yet, if this is true, contradictory legal syllogisms would exist according to Wittgenstein.

Legal Realism

Historically, legal realism has been seen as a response to legal formalism.[28] Indeed, Black's Law Dictionary defines legal realism as "[t]he theory that law is based not on formal rules or principles but instead on judicial decisions deriving from social interests and public policy as conceived by individual judges . . . American legal realism—which flourished in the early 20th century—was espoused by such scholars as John Chipman Gray, Jerome Frank, and Karl Llewellyn . . . The use of policy analysis to resolve a legal problem based on what best promotes public welfare."[29] Brian Leiter has stated, "[t]he paradigm of scholarship established by the [legal] Realists—contrasting what courts say they're doing with what they actually do—is one that has become so much the norm that distinguished scholars practice it without even feeling the need, any longer, to self-identify as Realists."[30] Likewise, legal realism often deals with predictions of legal court conclusions. In fact, "Legal Realism Predictions answer the Holmesian bad man's question: Will a judge (or Service official) who considers this reporting position rule that I owe additional tax and a penalty?"[31]

However, "under the predictive standards as applied to tax law, the more likely than not standard turns legal realism on its head by making the law what the lawyer says it is, since, for purposes of the reliance defense, the lawyer's determination that a position meets the more likely than not standard makes it so."[32]

In another example, "[a]ssessing the challenge that legal realism presents to legal ethics . . . requires that [one] specifically address how lawyers experience indeterminacy in the law and how that experience either affirms or undermines the boundary claim."[33] Once this is addressed, then we must "address . . . whether the law is radically or only marginally indeterminate."[34] Likewise, one "must examine how lawyers actually discover and interpret legal rules."[35] Concurrently, "[w]ith this knowledge, we can then evaluate the traditional model's claim that the bounds of the law meaningfully constrain zealous advocacy."[36]

Overall, legal realism conceives that judges and decision-makers may not always apply straightforward legal formalism but rather make decisions based on policy motivated decisions—sometimes under the guise of legal formalism.[37] Sometimes, you can't have your cake and eat it too.[38]

Legal Realism Contrasted with Gödel's Incompleteness Theorems

As mentioned earlier, Kurt Gödel wrote two Incompleteness Theorems.[39] The first theorem considers how classic syllogistic reasoning based on axioms can lead to a truth of all arithmetic numbers. It "consider[s] how one might try to capture a sophisticated system of classical informal reasoning with a formal system in such a way that the formal system is amenable to a suitable metatheoretical analysis."[40]

This theory shows the limitations of formal systems of logic—including law—because "Gödel's Incompleteness Theorem proves that 'legal, textual, and linguistic demonstrations' must propagate 'propositions (actually, an infinity of them) that can neither be proved nor disproved.'"[41] Furthermore, this is "[b]ecause plausible legal theories support any position in any case, and because an infinite number of indeterminate legal propositions exist, legal formalism is an impossibility."[42]

This is consistent with the legal realistic criticism of the shortcomings of legal formalism, because like the First Theorem of Incompleteness legal formalism is not capable of proving all cases and "truths" of case law based on syllogistic reasoning.

However, formerly, it seems—at any rate—that Wittgenstein's language games seem to clash with legal realism. This clash seems to occur because in theory, there could be an infinite number of propositions that exist based on Wittgenstein's insights in *Philosophical Investigations* #23.[43] Yet in his previous work, Wittgenstein in his *Tractatus Logico-Philosophicus* makes the claim, "every proposition is the result of successive applications of the operation N (ξ) to the elementary propositions."[44]

Despite there are many potential counter-arguments to an infinite number of propositions that exist based on Wittgenstein's insights in *Philosophical Investigations* #23. Indeed, if it is accepted—as a premise—infinite propositions and syllogisms could exist, then that infinite set of formal theories could be incompatible with Gödel's First Incompleteness Theorem. However, there does not seem to be a clear resolution to this clash. A resolution could include a formulation involving a Hegelian sublation[45] or a dialectical synthesis of legal formalism and legal realism.

It would make sense to examine several systems of interpretation. The conclusion here will examine textualism, purposive, and originalism.

Legal Textualism

Justice Scalia argued textualism was not legal formalism.[46] This seems reasonable. Indeed, the two are often categorized differently in legal jurisprudence classes. Black's Law Dictionary definition for legal textualism seems substantially different from legal formalism. It states that legal textualism is "[t]he doctrine that the words of a governing text are of paramount concern and that what they fairly convey in their context is what the text means."[47] Indeed, textualism could be called one of the oldest theories of legal interpretation because of its "emphasis on the primacy of the statutory text and its use of objective tools of construction [which] suggest[s] that much of the methodology is motivated by the long-recognized requirement that laws are legitimately enforced only when their subjects have fair notice of them."[48]

Moreover, "[t]extualism has come to be the dominant theory of statutory interpretation in United States courts," which makes it of primary importance to legal interpretation in the United States.[49] As a basis, "[t]extualism 'ask[s] how a reasonable person, conversant with the relevant social and linguistic conventions, would read the text in context.'"[50] This implies that there is a relevant singular basis for linguistic conventions. Indeed, this is a hotly debated issue.[51] David Foster Wallace's review of Bryan A. Garner's *Dictionary of Modern American Usage* in *Harper's Magazine* in August 2001 outlines the difference between the prescriptivist and descriptivist theories of linguist usage, as well as the political undertones thereof and language's relation to democracy.[52] The prescriptivist theory argues there is a singular standard written English.[53] Such a theory would fall well into the textualist theory of languages.[54] However, the descriptivist theory provides that there is no "standard written English" and dictionaries should aim to describe how language is used.[55] David Foster Wallace seems to sympathize with both but marvels that Bryan Garner's dictionary seems to exist in neither the prescriptivist nor descriptivist theories' camps.[56] Wallace referring to Wittgenstein's language games suggests what matters is communicating with an audience, not necessarily the form it comes to us.[57]

Such definitions are illuminating, but the question remains—what, then, is textualism?[58] This question is phrased in a somewhat parallel formulation of Saint Augustine's formulation "[w]hat, then, is time? I know well enough what it is, provided that nobody asks me; but if I am asked what it is and try to explain, I am baffled."[59] However, in a recent decision in 2018, Judge Thapar, writing for the Sixth Circuit Court of Appeals, had an illuminating discussion on textualism in regards to statutory construction.[60] In analyzing "[s]everal reasons [that] support the idea that canons belong in *Chevron* step one," the court looked to textualist doctrine and the cannons of statutory interpretation.[61] Judge Thapar writes, "[f]irst and foremost, canons can assist a court in determining a statute's meaning."[62] By this point, it seems generally accepted that the premises Judge Thapar lays out are accepted: "[c]anons [of statutory interpretation] that serve this goal can be thought of as 'descriptive'—in contrast to 'normative' canons that are instead designed to favor certain substantive policies."[63] Within the family of descriptive canons, linguistic canons are the strongest species. These canons simply "reflect . . . accepted notions of diction, grammar, and syntax." Black's Law Dictionary (10th ed. 2014)." Indeed, it seems that these are generally accepted principles of statutory interpretation regardless of a textualist predisposition or a purposovist predisposition.[64] Thapar goes on stating that "[e]xamples include the *expressio unius canon* (the expression of one thing implies the exclusion of others); the general/specific canon (a specific provision prevails over a general one if the two are in conflict); and the presumption of consistent usage ("Courts presume that the same words in the same statute mean the same thing.") *In re Jackson Masonry, LLC*, 906 F.3d 494, 501 (6th Cir. 2018); Scalia & Garner, supra, §§ 10, 25, 28. These are all just "ordinary principles that laymen as well as lawyers use to interpret communications." Nelson, "What is Textualism."[65] Here, Judge Thapar connects the generally accepted principles of statutory interpretation with the overall scheme of textualism—essentially stating that there does not seem, at any rate, to be a difference—"accordingly, linguistic canons are just specific applications of the basic goal of interpretation: finding the ordinary meaning of [a] statutory text. These canons clearly and exclusively serve descriptive, rather than normative, purposes. Therefore, they belong in step one, which has the same goal: determining the meaning of the statute."[66] It seems that one fair reading of Judge Thapar's conclusion, in this case, contemplates that "everyone" trying to read a statute starts off as a textualist—in terms of using basic grammatical constructions and the cannons of statutory interpretation to develop meaning. A reader does this without any regard to the legislative history.[67]

The goal, then, for the interlocutor of a statute—at least from a textualist perspective—to read a statute, constitution, regulation, or other similar law without reference to the legislative history, legislative context, or other similar tools.

Legal Textualism Contrasted with Gödel's Incompleteness Theorems

As Scalia indicated, legal textualism "is legal formalism."[68] Such a statement is accurate to an extent. Legal formalism does not focus on the grammatical construction of words as much as legal textualism does. Legal formalism could include grammatical construction, but legal formalism is not predicated on grammatical construction. On the other hand, legal textualism is predicated by grammatical construction.

Returning to the contrast between the prescriptivist and descriptivist theories of language usage, a textualist would fit within the system of the prescriptivist. A textualist uses prescribed rules. But for prescribed rules, the textualist would be subject to any number of descriptivist theories of what the words mean. In a descriptivist world, the system of legal textualism could never provide a full theory of what the words mean. Textualism relies on the axioms of grammatical construction of "standard written English"—or at least the "standard written English" that the judge accepts as the true standard of written English. If a judge relied on a system with any number of "unprovable" and undecided theories of language, the descriptivist judge could come to any number of different conclusions.

Compared to Gödel's incompleteness theorem, legal textualism purports to be a self-sustaining system that in theory could answer any legal question by adhering to strict rules of statutory construction. But no system is self-provable according to Gödel. The axioms of a system must be proved in another system, but those axioms may be provable in a different context. Likewise, the axioms of "standard written English" are not "provable" by any means. They are simply accepted social conventions—what Wittgenstein would call a language game—like the conventions of any of the other theories of statutory and constitutional interpretation— purposivism, realism, formalism, etc.—and if they are simply social conventions, then the rules of grammar are simply defined and described with a descriptivist approach that has gained more influence than other descriptivist approaches. Thus, legal textualism is another type of language game effectively a type of descriptivist approach similar to that of formalism and not dissimilar from purposivism and intentionalism.

Legal Purposivism

One of the potential counter-arguments to using a pure textualist approach arises in purposivism. Perhaps the basis for this critique comes from some formulation of the philosopher David Hume's "is-ought problem"[69] distinguishing just because something is a certain way, does not mean it should or ought to be that way.[70] In his *A Treatise of Human Understanding*, Hume wrote a critique of inductive reasoning:[71]

> I cannot forbear adding to these reasonings an observation, which may, perhaps, be found of some importance. In every system of morality, which I have hitherto met with, I have always remarked, that the author proceeds for some time in the ordinary way of reasoning, and establishes the being of a God, or makes observations concerning human affairs; when of a sudden I am surprised [*sic.*] to find, that instead of the usual copulations of propositions, is, and is not, I meet with no proposition that is not connected with an ought, or an ought not. This change is imperceptible; but is, however, of the last consequence. For as this ought, or ought not, expresses some new relation or affirmation, it is necessary that it should be observed and explained; and at the same time that a reason should be given, for what seems altogether inconceivable, how this new relation can be a deduction from others, which are entirely different from it. But as authors do not commonly use this precaution, I shall presume to recommend it to the readers; and am persuaded, that this small attention would subvert all the vulgar systems of morality, and let us see, that the distinction

> of vice and virtue is not founded merely on the relations of objects, nor is perceived by reason.[72]

In such a way, the interpretation could result in a conclusion and that could lead a reader to say that because the statute *is* a certain way, and thus *ought* to be a separate way.

On the other hand, Black's Law Dictionary defines "purposivism" generally as "[t]he doctrine that texts are to be interpreted to achieve the broad purposes that their drafters had in mind; specif, the idea that a judge-interpreter should seek an answer not only in the words of the text but also in its social, economic, and political objectives."[73] Black's Law Dictionary also provides a citation to the historical development of purposivism stating, "[t]he legal realists — especially Max Radin — raised some of the objections to intentionalism . . . and proposed as an alternative theory a flexible 'mischief' approach to statutory interpretation;" following this proposal, "Professors Henry Hart and Albert Sacks in the 1950s expanded the realists' approach into a 'purposivist' theory of interpretation that seemed as faithful to the principle of legislative supremacy as intentionalism, but without the rigidity and definitional problems of intentionalism."[74]

Historically, purposivism grew out of a contrast with the "plain meaning" approach. Justice Nicholas Conyngham Tindal has one of the earliest articulations of this sentiment in 1844 stating in regards to plain meaning, "the only rule for the construction of Acts of Parliament is, that they should be construed according to the intent of the Parliament which passed the Act."[75] But Sir Nicholas further wrote, "[i]f the words of the statute are in themselves precise and unambiguous, then no more can be necessary than to expound those words in their natural and ordinary sense. The words themselves alone do, in such case, best declare the intention of the lawgiver."[76]

However, this strict application of the plain meaning rule could lead to absurd results.[77] In response to the potential for absurdity, Lord Wensleydale in 1857 wrote, in *Grey v. Pearson* that "[i]n construing . . . statutes . . . the grammatical and ordinary sense of the words is to be adhered to, unless that would lead to some absurdity, or some repugnance or inconsistency with the rest of the instrument, in which case the grammatical and ordinary sense of the words may be modified, so as to avoid the absurdity and inconsistency, but no farther."[78] Some commentators have called Lord Wensleydale's approach, the "Golden Rule."[79]

It seems fair to interpret Lord Wensleydale's approach to the "Golden Rule" as somewhat corollary to the textualist approach—first, one interprets the literal meaning, and then avoids absurd results.[80] This is because there exists, "a basic tenet of statutory construction that where literal application of words of a statute would lead to futile or absurd results, the court may deter from literal textualism."[81] Moreover, the U.S. Supreme Court has held that "no rule of construction necessitates our acceptance of an interpretation resulting in patently absurd consequences."[82] A similar rule has been upheld more recently by the Supreme Court in *Mohasco Corp. v. Silver* (1980).[83]

However, the clearest example of purposivism following closely with the intertwined spectrum of constraints found in textualism finds articulation through Justice Stephen Breyer of the U.S. Supreme Court in 2008 dissenting in *Medellín v. Texas* while critiquing the majority approach because "it [the majority] looks for the wrong thing (explicit textual expression about self-execution) using the wrong standard (clarity) in the wrong place (the treaty language). Hunting for what the text cannot contain, it takes a wrong turn."[84]

The gist is, a reader looks at the statute, uses grammatical and statutes of construction, if the result is good—then the process stops. If the result is not acceptable, then an interpreter must look to the purpose of the statute or the purpose of the legislature in enacting such a statute. This can be difficult.[85]

Legal Purposivism Contrasted with Gödel's Incompleteness Theorems

Legal purposivism seems to share quite a bit with legal realism. Unlike legal textualism and legal formalism, purposivism does not intend to function as a holistic system of interpretation. Rather, purposivism seems to fill in the gaps where the "system" of legal textualism or legal formalism cannot fill in.

Such a theory seems to fall in line with Gödel's incompleteness theorem that a system in itself can be holistic and self-proving. In this sense, legal purposivism is consistent with the legal realism critiquing the shortcomings of legal formalism and legal textualism, because like the First Theorem of Incompleteness, legal formalism is not capable of proving all cases and "truths" of case law based on syllogistic reasoning.

However, Wittgenstein's language games seem to clash with legal purposivism. This clash seems to occur because in theory there could be an infinite number of propositions that exist based on Wittgenstein's insights in *Philosophical Investigations* #23.[86] Yet at the same time, Wittgenstein in his *Tractatus Logico-Philosophicus* makes the claim, "every proposition is the result of successive applications of the operation N (ξ) to the elementary propositions."[87]

Despite there being many potential counter-arguments to an infinite number of propositions that exist based on Wittgenstein's insights in *Philosophical Investigations* #23. Legal purposivism could become a resolution synthesizing legal formalism and legal realism. But it falls short of a complete synthesis of legal formalism and legal realism. However, it does provide a unique option that could create part of a larger synthesis.

Legal Originalism

Originalism tries to find the original meaning intended by the author of a statute or the Constitution—and, uses that meaning in interpreting the statute or constitution. Chief Justice John Marshall in *Marbury v. Madison* (1803) delineated the nature of originalistic inquiry stating:

[T]he constitution organizes the government, and assigns to different departments their respective powers. It [the constitution] may either stop here; or establish certain limits not to be transcended by those departments.

The government of the United States is of the latter description. The powers of the legislature are defined and limited; and that those limits may not be mistaken or forgotten, the constitution is written. To what purpose are powers limited, and to what purpose is that limitation committed to writing; if these limits may, at any time, be passed by those intended to be restrained?

Justice Marshall's interpretation relies on the premise that the U. S. Constitution fundamentally gains its power from the people to the federal government, and then, to the states—not from the people to the states, and then, to the federal government.

Justice Scalia in *Romer v. Evans* agrees with such a conclusion in part in his dissenting opinion by writing, "[s]ince the Constitution of the United States says nothing about this subject, it is left to be resolved by normal democratic means, including the democratic adoption of provisions in state constitutions."[88] Scalia further states that "[t]his Court has no business imposing upon all Americans the resolution favored by the elite class from which the Members of this institution are selected," meaning that the original interpretation of the constitution should be applied as it was originally intended.[89]

Likewise, although Black's Law Dictionary defines originalism as "[t]he doctrine that words of a legal instrument are to be given the meanings they had when they were adopted; specif., the canon that a legal text should be interpreted through the historical ascertainment of the meaning that it would have conveyed to a fully informed observer at the time when the text first took effect,"[90] this definition does seem to encompass Scalia's meaning.

Regarding original intent, Scalia indicated, "[y]ou will never hear me [Scalia] refer to original intent, because as I say I am first of all a textualist, and secondly an originalist. If you are a textualist, you don't care about the intent, and I don't care if the framers of the Constitution had some secret meaning in mind when they adopted its words."[91] Moreover, Bork magnifies Scalia's statement through a specific example of a hypothetical situation, "if someone found a letter from George Washington to Martha telling her that what he meant by the power to lay taxes was not what other people meant, that would not change our reading of the Constitution in the slightest."[92]

Bork says such an "original intent" is irrelevant because "[l]aw is a public act. Secret reservations or intentions count for nothing. All that counts is how the words used in the Constitution would have been understood at the time."[93]

In some sense, this theory of the "intent" of the "lawgiver" is similar to Justice Oliver Wendell Holmes's 1897 Path of Law in which he states that the subjective intent in one's mind is not relevant in contract law but rather the external representation to the other is what is important.[94] Justice Holmes emphasizes that "no one will understand the true theory of contract or be able even to discuss some fundamental questions intelligently until he has understood that all contracts are formal," because the internal—non-formal representations do not matter.[95] Indeed, he goes on to say "that the making of a contract depends not on the agreement of two minds in one intention, but on the agreement of two sets of external signs—not on the parties' having meant the same thing but on their having said the same thing."[96]

Likewise, in ascertaining the secret original intent of the drafters of a law or the Constitution of the United States irrelevant—the importance comes down to finding out how the public would interpret the external representations. At the same time, in some sense, it seems that the origins of originalism and textualism—and perhaps statutory interpretation in general—lies in the same origins of contractual analysis and contract law, in the sense that the internal thoughts or feelings do matter, only the external manifestations.

LEGAL ORIGINALISM CONTRASTED WITH GÖDEL'S INCOMPLETENESS THEOREMS

It has been argued that Wittgenstein's analysis shows that the rules are determinate and the efficacy of originalism is not conserved because "meta-rules do not exist antecedent to the question presented in any individual case."[97] However, in a sense "Wittgenstein must have been saying what has otherwise been advanced by many critics of originalism: that 'the meaning of an expression is the use to which it [was] put,' a formulation poised to fallaciously equate communicative content with purposes or motives."[98] Yet, returning to the definition and connotation of the term "game" "is not fully determined at the time the speaker gives the order; rather, its meaning in context is developed through experience and through practice. If this is Wittgenstein's point, then it seems far more consistent with living originalism than with fidelity to original expected applications."[99]

CONCLUSION ON GÖDEL AND WITTGENSTEIN AS A FORM OF *LEGAL DIALECTICISM:*

Wittgenstein asks whether any system—regardless of whether it is random or not and no matter the complexity of the system—can follow rules of consistency and formalities?[100] This question arises even if the system is truly "chaotic" or random. This implies that people invent rules when none really exist when observing a system. Wittgenstein concedes in his theory of "language games" that there are an infinite amount of propositions that exist. Likewise, this infinite amount of propositions means that an infinite number of syllogisms exist. But even with an infinite amount of propositions and syllogisms, a system cannot be proven to be truly within a system of consistent formal rules or if we as observe merely ascribe those rules to them.

Gödel's First Incompleteness Theorem considers how classic syllogistic reasoning based on axioms can lead to a truth of all arithmetic numbers and logical systems. Gödel considers that no consistent system of axioms can lead to a truth of a logical and mathematical system. In the alternative, only an inconsistent set of rules—thus a chaotic and random set of axioms—can explain a system of logic.

Gödel's First Incompleteness Theorem proves Wittgenstein's assertation that observers may attribute systems of formality and consistency to a logical system, but this formality cannot be proven or disproven.

A DENOUEMENT: UNANSWERED QUESTIONS ON GRAMMATICAL TENSES OF VARIOUS ASPECTS OF LAW

"But as Wittgenstein's Philosophical Investigations proved in the 1950s, words actually have the meanings they do because of certain rules and verification tests that are imposed on us from outside our own subjectivities, viz., by the community in which we have to get along and communicate with other people."

-David Foster Wallace[101]

Overall, legal questions cannot be answered using only theories of interpretation. But insofar as such theories are used—and when such theories are disregarded—grammatical interpretation plays a key role. Whether one uses the textualist approach or the purposovist approach, both approaches are based on how one interprets words. At a basic level, language is successful when it is used to communicate an idea according to David Foster Wallace in the quote above; and, according to Wallace, whether the words are uttered or written "grammatically" only matters insofar as one understands the audience. Even among lexicographers, there are debates about the uses of tenses, meanings of words with in context, and even dictionary definitions. However, key debates within law can come from the tenses and the tenses' certainty and meaning in the context of law.

From the basic simple past aspect, there is a certainty of a grammatical tense. However, compared with the past progressive aspect—which is usually less certain—there is less certainty.

There can be extravagantly subjunctive future conditional. These are interesting types and can be subject to multiple meanings.

From a grammatical perspective, are there diverse ways of explaining the same world and reality? In other words, are there other ways of explaining reality or law? Moreover, do different languages produce diverse ways of interpreting the world with their grammatical and time structures?

The answers to this seem to exist in the questions of what a subject, verb, and object are defined as individuals and in relation to one another—in other words, a social context.

CONCLUSION OF THE DIALECTICAL PATH OF LAW

Thus, anthropology—the area of the social sciences specifically involved with the "exotic" and "apparently inexplicable behavior" of "foreign" peoples—has reached the general conclusion that knowing and understanding the different branches of humanity results in an appreciation for their modes of law.

Governments funded anthropologists to learn about potential adversaries.[102] In all cases, anthropological field workers are at least potential spies that can inform home countries how foreigners act.[103] In the case of a conflict, the government will often debrief individuals who have worked or traveled in an enemy country.[104]

We should ask: What is the truth about humans?[105] What argument is the key to their similarities and differences? At the moment, it appears that all of the ideas discussed are relevant to understanding humanity, even if the positions are contradictory. Social Evolution, Diffusion, the Boasian emphasis on Culture and Cultural Relativity, Functionalism, and Structuralism are all necessary aspects of social theory and law explaining various attempts to understand culture through various interactions in history.

Again, by analogy, moral systems and cultures are ways of interpreting law and what should be done. Here, by analogy, morality and cultures represent the legal theories of legal realism and legal formalism. Those theories are living.[106] The Living Constitution is as much a by-product of English common law that has effectively existed since Anglo-Saxon times—before the 1066 Norman invasion—as is strict legal formalism adhering to pure *stare decisis*.

Like economics having a root in philosophy,[107] sanctuary can have a basis in law and the philosophical concepts supporting that law. The concept of sanctuary can arrive as a tragedy to resolve the play in comedy as illustrated in the law journal article titled *Liberty to Misread: Sanctuary and Possibility in The Comedy of Errors*. One can read the thesis in that article to argue that sanctuary can be called for in tragedy only to be taken off the table. Indeed, as argued in this book, the concept of sanctuary is the place beyond governmental power and the functioning of socially agreed upon monetary instruments—but, in Hegelian terms a *sublation* of such a thesis, sanctuary can negate the state of normalcy. Sometimes, this negation could lead to the dysfunction of a society. However, sanctuary can exist as one of the exemptions to the rule where normal society accepts this exemption—thereby not leading to chaos.

This book has aimed to contribute a single idea—that there could be a new way to interpret law and make legal decisions in any field of law and in any capacity of interpreting law through a theory called *legal dialects* or the *dialectical path of law*.

This theory of the dialectical path of law uses the Hegelian dialectic. The Hegelian dialectic, in short, compares and contrasts two different ideas and shows how they are the same but separate at the same time without the original ideas losing their inherent and distinctive properties —what in Hegelian terms is referred to as the *sublation*. This is not merely a logic game, but a useful tool of analysis.

In demonstrating the use of the dialectical path of law theory, this book uses international tax law and corporate law. This done by taking different aspects of those respective fields of law that seem entirely contradictory and then showing how they are similar—but at the same time without disregarding their key theoretical properties. Specifically, the book examined the dialectics inherent in the OECD's international tax and transfer pricing policy and risk valuation rules compared to the U.S. tax policies as they appear in the U.S. Tax Court, the U.S. Congress, and the U.S. Treasury. However, in order to fully appreciate the development of international tax law, international tax law as such needed to be put into the context of anthropological and sociological theories that led to its development. The anthropological and sociological theories were legal realism operating to interpret the law. But those theories led to a philosophical interpretation of a government, the basis of implementing law, focusing on that of the U.S. Constitution using Plato's theory of the "psyche" or soul as it is variously translated from Ancient Greek. This use of Plato's tripartite conception of the "psyche" can be represented as a type of psychology that serves as the basis of legal realism, but at the same time is based in Plato's use of deductive logic, the basis of legal formalism. Using Plato's conception of the three-part soul as a minor premise to be applied syllogistically to the major premise of the three parts of the U.S. Constitution is legal formalism, Plato's logic. But this formalism extends from the premises of legal realism, the psychological context of law—an example of the Hegelian dialectical sublation.

Next, the book puts the two theories of legal realism and formalism into action comparing the U.S. Tax Court's interpretation of risk to the OECD's interpretation of risk. This is the ultimate synthesis of what the book aims to demonstrate—that shifting notions of risk and agency law are at the basis of international taxation, one of the most advanced areas and frontiers of law that is constantly changing.

Thereafter, the book examined the development of law from contracts to corporate law— even in the context of law and literature—in order to illuminate international tax law's dialectical path in history and conceivably predict its future path and end. Next, the book defines the Hegelian dialectic and shows that this theory of the legal dialectical path of law is based in Hegel's theory of dialectics. Finally, the book concludes by showing how inherently the definitions as provided by the proponents of legal formalism and legal realism, the theories themselves do not logically account entirely for their own premises. This inherent contradiction represents the Hegelian dialectic and represents an inherent answer, or sublation, of the two theories of legal formalism and legal realism being turned inside out. This book proposes the *sublation* of formalism and realism is the theory of the dialectical path of law. This means despite over a century of differences between legal realism and legal formalism that the indispensable properties of the two theories are shown to be the same in the dialectical path of the law. The book ends with final questions about further research in grammatical, and not merely linguistic, analysis of law.

NOTES

1. An incongruous juxtaposition on the title of the title Gödel, Escher, Bach: an Eternal Golden Braid (1979) by Douglas Hofstadter while acknowledging the creative influence Hofstadter's book had on this author's thinking.

2. The idea for this chapter came from an article that is currently a work in progress to be published on a similar subject, but is expected to be published after this book is published.

3. Clark A. Remington, "Llewellyn, Antiformalism and the Fear of Transcendental Nonsense: Codifying the Variability Rule in the Law of Sales." *Wayne L. Rev.* 44 (1998): 29, 41.

> "Bertrand Russell and Alfred North Whitehead undertook the systematic construction of mathematics in their *Principia Mathematica* in such a way that troubling inconsistencies would be avoided. Even if they were successful in banishing inconsistencies from their system, a matter that was itself unclear, they raised doubts about its completeness. These questions inspired the mathematician David Hilbert to issue the following challenge to the world's mathematicians (as described by Douglas Hofstadter): 'to demonstrate rigorously--perhaps following the very methods outlined by Russell and Whitehead--that the system defined in *Principia Mathematica* was both *consistent* (contradiction-free), and *complete* (i.e., that every true statement of number theory could be derived within the framework drawn up in *P.M.*).' This challenge 'occupied the minds of many of the greatest mathematicians in the world during the first thirty years of this century.'"

Id. (citations omitted).

4. Indeed, law is often critiqued on moral grounds—if such is true, then is law a system of morals?

5. *Cf.* "Brown and Greenberg also confuse the idea of subjectivity with that of vagueness and assume these two ideas to be one. See id. at 1457–1458. They conclude that human insight is necessary to resolve legal disputes, id. at 1485, a deduction with which I do not quibble. They reach this conclusion because they believe that the task of identifying "good" arguments is non-algorithmic. Id. at 1482. This thesis too is unremarkable, and I share it, but Brown and Greenberg embrace it without rejecting the truth of strong artificial intelligence (AI). See id. at 1460–1462 (pretermitting conclusion as to tenability of strong AI). Strong AI holds that all mental processes and attributes consist of complicated algorithms and, if not for the practical difficulties of doing so, could be exactly reproduced by a computer program. See PENROSE, supra note 30, at 17–18. If the proponents of strong AI are correct, which I doubt, then the question of deciding which argument is "good" is indeed algorithmic. See, for example, Daniel C. Dennett, *Consciousness Explained* (1991); cf. SEARLE, supra note 42, at 43–57 (arguing that the failings of strong AI and other attempts to define human cognition as a physical phenomenon result from their refusal to acknowledge that "consciousness" and "intelligence" have "an ineliminable subjective ontology"). David R. Dow, "Gödel and Langdell-A Reply to Brown and Greenberg's Use of Mathematics in Legal Theory." *Hastings L.J.* 44 (1993): 707, 726 n. 73.

6. "At the turn of the century, some thirty years before Gödel developed these theorems, the mathematician David Hilbert had asked whether it could be proved that the axioms of arithmetic are consistent-that is, whether the finite number of logical steps based upon those axioms could ever lead to contradictory results. Some ten years after Hilbert posed the question, Bertrand Russell and Alfred Whitehead published the first volume of Principia Mathematica, which endeavored to prove that all pure mathematics can be derived from a small number of fundamental logical principles. The Principia failed in this quest; it also did not answer Hilbert's question." David R. Row, "Gödel's Theorem addressed the system described in the Principia. David R. Dow, Gödel and Langdell-A Reply to Brown and Greenberg's Use of Mathematics in Legal Theory." *Hastings L.J.* 44 (1993): 707, 713–714.

7. Ludwig Wittgenstein, *Philosophical Investigations* #83.

8. Despite having an incredibly fascinating biography and life, the specifics of his life are not key for the analysis for purposes of this chapter. For a thorough biography, see James Carl Klagge, *Wittgenstein: Biography and Philosophy* (2001).

9. Ludwig Wittgenstein, *Philosophical Investigations* #83.

10. Ludwig Wittgenstein, *Philosophical Investigations* #201. In the text of this section, Wittgenstein writes:

"This was our paradox: no course of action could be determined by a rule, because every course of action can be made out to accord with the rule. The answer was: if everything can be made out to accord with the rule, then it can also be made out to conflict with it. And so there would be neither accord nor conflict here.

It can be seen that there is a misunderstanding here from the mere fact that in the course of our argument we give one interpretation after another; as if each one contented us at least for a moment, until we thought of yet another standing behind it. What this shews is that there is a way of grasping a rule which is not an interpretation, but which is exhibited in what we call 'obeying the rule' and 'going against it' in actual cases.

Hence, there is an inclination to say: every action according to the rule is an interpretation. But we ought to restrict the term 'interpretation' to the substitution of one expression of the rule for another."

11. A corollary of Ludwig Wittgenstein, *Philosophical Investigations* #201.

12. An interpretation of Ludwig Wittgenstein, *Philosophical Investigations* #201.

13. Ludwig Wittgenstein, *Philosophical Investigations* #201.

14. This refers back to the demonstration that David Hilbert conducted mentioned earlier in this chapter. "David Hilbert [1862–1943], in his study of the axioms sustaining Euclidean geometry published in 1899, argued that the whole system is built on twenty-one unproven statements from which all the other claims of Euclidean geometry can be deduced. In fact, the only difference between a theorem and an axiom is that axioms are accepted as true, while theorems have to be proven true by deriving them from the initial axioms." Giuseppe Dari Mattiacci, "Gödel, Kaplow, Shavell: Consistency and Completeness in Social Decision-Making." *Chi.-Kent L. Rev.* 79 (2004): 497, 520 n. 24.

15. This footnote in an excellent law review succinctly explains Gödel's First and Second Theorems.

> More precisely, Gödel's first theorem states that "For suitable L [which stands for formal system or logic that is able to treat natural numbers and their addition and multiplication], there are undecidable propositions in L; that is, propositions F such that neither F nor <<nondisplaybe symbol>> F is provable.

Giuseppe Dari Mattiacci, "Gödel, Kaplow, Shavell: Consistency and Completeness in Social Decision-Making." *Chi.-Kent L. Rev.* 79 (2004): 497, 520 n. 40.

16. "Euclidean geometry, for example, was believed to be consistent because its theorems are true of space. Non-Euclidean geometries (which are false of our daily experience) were considered consistent because theorems could be mapped into theorems of Euclidean geometry.33 Hence, if no contradiction emerges in the latter, the former must also be free of antinomies. However, the observation that no

contradiction has arisen yet is not sufficient to conclude that no contradiction exists; thus, the consistency of Euclidean geometry needs to be proved. Moreover, proving the consistency of a system by reference to another system only transfers the problem from one system to the other and does not provide any final solution. The only way to prove with absolute certainty that a system is free of contradictions is to construct a proof of such a claim within the system itself." Giuseppe Dari Mattiacci, "Gödel, Kaplow, Shavell: Consistency and Completeness in Social Decision-Making." *Chi.-Kent L. Rev.* 79 (2004): 497, 511–512.

17. "Gödel's results were later refined by Rosser, supra note 39. The original formulation referred to ω-inconsistency, that is to the following case: it is possible to prove a certain property of numbers in a general way and, at the same time, it is possible to prove that number 1 does not have the property, number 2 does not have the property, and so forth for all numbers. A certain property is proved in general and disproved for each of its occurrences. Simple inconsistency is a slightly different concept, as it implies that a property is proved and disproved in a general fashion at the same time. If a system is inconsistent, it is also ω-inconsistent, while the opposite is not necessarily true. Further developments were due to Alonzo Church [1903-1995], Stephen Kleene [1909-1994], and Alan Turing, supra note 29. In particular, S. C. Kleene, "General Recursive Functions of Natural Numbers." *Mathematische Annalen* 112 (1936): 727, provides a third (after Gödel and Rosser) approach to prove Gödel's first theorem." Giuseppe Giuseppe Dari Mattiacci, "Gödel, Kaplow, Shavell: Consistency and Completeness in Social Decision-Making." *Chi.-Kent L. Rev.* 79 (2004): 520 n. 47.

18. Legal formalism was espoused by such scholars as Christopher Columbus Langdell and Lon Fuller. Legal Formalism, *Black's Law Dictionary* (11th ed. 2019).

19. Daniel S. Goldberg, "I Do Not Think It Means What You Think It Means: How Kripke and Wittgenstein's Analysis on Rule Following Undermines Justice Scalia's Textualism and Originalism." *Clev. St. L. Rev.* 54 (2006): 273, 278.

20. *Id.*

21. Daniel S. Goldberg, "I Do Not Think It Means What You Think It Means: How Kripke and Wittgenstein's Analysis on Rule Following Undermines Justice Scalia's Textualism and Originalism." *Clev. St. L. Rev.* 54 (2006): 273, 278.

22. *Id.* (citation omitted).

23. Antonin Scalia, *A Matter of Interpretation: Federal Courts and the Law* (1997), 25.

24. Richard A. Posner, *How Judges Think* (2008), 41.

25. "For Aristotle, good regimes have rulers dedicated to the common good, while bad ones have rulers who use their positions to further their private interest. For Locke and Montesquieu there is no such distinction. A good regime has the proper institutional structures for satisfying while containing the selfish men who make it up, while a bad one does not succeed in doing this. Selfishness is presupposed; men are not assumed to be as they ought to be, but as they are." Allan Bloom, *The Closing of the American Mind: How Higher Education Has Failed Democracy and Impoverished the Souls of Today's Students* (1987), 178.

26. Allan Bloom, *The Closing of the American Mind: How Higher Education Has Failed Democracy and Impoverished the Souls of Today's Students* (1987), 178.

27. Ludwig Wittgenstein, *Philosophical Investigations* #23.

28. H. L. A. Hart, *The Concept of Law* (2d ed. YEAR) Hart, H. L. A. (1961). *The Concept of Law* (2nd ed. / with a postscript edited by Penelope A. Bulloch and Joseph Raz.) (Oxford: Clarendon Press). Ch.VII; *see* Brian Leiter, "American Legal Realism," in Martin P. Golding and William A. Edmundson, eds., *The Blackwell Guide to the Philosophy of Law and Legal Theory* (Oxford: Blackwell, 2005), 50. *Cf. See generally* Neil Duxbury, *Patterns of American Jurisprudence*. (New York: Oxford University Press, 1995), ch. 2.

29. Legal Realism, *Black's Law Dictionary* (11th ed. 2019).

30. Brian Leiter, "American Legal Realism." in *The Blackwell Guide to the Philosophy of Law and Legal Theory* (Martin P. Golding and William A. Edmundson eds., 2005), 60.

31. Bradley T. Borden and Sang Hee Lee, "Boundaries of the Prediction Model in Tax Law's Substantial Authority." *Tax Law.* 71 (2017): 33, 43.

32. Scott A. Schumacher, "Macniven v. Westmoreland and Tax Advice: Using "Purposive Textualism" to Deal with Tax Shelters and Promote Legitimate Tax Advice." *Marq. L. Rev.* 92 (2008): 33, 73.

33. David B. Wilkins, "Legal Realism for Lawyers." *Harv. L. Rev.* 104 (1990): 468, 477.

34. *Id.*

35. *Id.* at 478.

36. *Id. See generally* Gwen Thayer Handelman, "Law and Order Comes to "Dodge City": Treasury's New Return Preparer and IRS Practice Standards." *Wash. & Lee L. Rev.* 50 (1993): 631.

37. *Cf.* Justice Stevens in 1984 in one of his dissents wrote:

> Some students of the Court take for granted that our decisions represent the will of the judges rather than the will of the law. This dogma may be the current fashion, but I remain convinced that such remarks reflect a profound misunderstanding of the nature of our work. Unfortunately, however, cynics—parading under the banner of legal realism—are given a measure of credibility whenever the Court bases a decision on its own notions of sound policy, rather than on what the law commands.

Trans World Airlines, Inc. v. Franklin Mint Corp., 466 U.S. 243, 282–283 (1984).

38. "Unfortunately, when called upon to remember this famous quotation, some people flounder about and get it backwards by saying, 'You can't have your cake and eat it, too.' To which the response is 'Of course, you can.' You can have it and then eat it. What you can't do is eat it and then still have it." James D. Maugans, "The Grammatical Lawyer." *Prac. Law.*, July 1991, at 11.

39. The biography of Kurt Gödel's life—despite being supremely interesting—is not important for the analysis of this chapter. For an interesting biography on Gödel's life, see John Dawson, *Logical Dilemmas: The Life and Work of Kurt Gödel* (Wellesley, MA: A. K. Peters, 2005).

40. Mike Townsend, "Implications of Foundational Crises in Mathematics: A Case Study in Interdisciplinary Legal Research." *Wash. L. Rev.* 71 (1996): 51, 108.

41. Mark R. Brown and Andrew C. Greenberg, "On Formally Undecidable Propositions of Law: Legal Indeterminacy and the Implications of Metamathematics." *Hastings L.J.* 43 (1992): 1439, 1441 (citation omitted).

42. *Id.*; *see* Douglas R. Hofstadter, *Gödel, Escher, Bach: An Eternal Golden Braid* (1979).

43. Wittgenstein, *Philosophical Investigations* #23.

44. This idea is supported in Wittgenstein's earlier philosophical thought. Ludwig Wittgeinstein, Tractatus Logico-Philosophicus 6.001 *Cf.* However, Wittgenstein's philosophical thought changed. Consider the counter argument to the idea that every proposition is the result of successive applications of the operation N to the elementary propositions:

> The Tractatus relied on what has been called the picture theory of meaning, in which the logical simples of reality exist in a strict isomorphism with the essential elements of language. In short, this concordance between the atomistic parts of reality and the basic elements of language allowed language to "picture" reality. In the years immediately prior to 1929, Wittgenstein became dissatisfied with many of the consequences of this view. In particular, he became convinced that its handling of color and color gradations was unsatisfactory.

Bruce A. Markell, "Bewitched by Language: Wittgenstein and the Practice of Law." *Pepp. L. Rev.* 32 (2005): 801, 807.

45. Indeed, in "discussing Hegel's continuation of Aristotelian metaphysics, Derrida writes: "Nature is the Idea outside itself. . . Space is the abstract universality of this Being-outside-itself. Nature, as 'absolute space'. . . not in relation to itself, knows no mediation, no difference, no determination, no discontinuity. It corresponds to what the Jena Logic called ether: the element of ideal transparency, of absolute indifferentiation, of undetermined continuity, of absolute juxtaposition, that is, the element without interior relations." In the Hegelian scheme, the self-identical transcendental origin constitutes itself and its outside-it-self through sublation by self-negation)." Michael Dignan, "Of Experimentology: A Genealogical Deconstruction of Invention in Patent Law's Enablement Requirement." *Wake Forest J. Bus. & Intell. Prop. L.* 18 (2017): 40, 56 n.115.

46. Posner, *supra* note 11.

47. Textualism, *Black's Law Dictionary* (11th ed. 2019).

48. Note, "Textualism as Fair Notice." *Harv. L. Rev.* 123 (2009): 542, 542.

49. Note, "Preemption as Purposivism's Last Refuge." *Harv. L. Rev.* 126 (2013): 1056, 105.

50. *Id.* (citation omitted).

51. Bryan A. Garner, "Making Peace in the Language Wars." *Green Bag* 2d 7 (2004): 227.

52. *See generally* David Foster Wallace, "Tense Present: Democracy, English, and the Wars over Usage." *Harper's Mag.*, Apr. 2001.

53. Wallace describes the prescriptivist adherents as "SNOOT" Bryan A. Garner, "If You Care About Language, Consider Yourself a SNOOT." *Student Law*, Nov.

2006 (citing Wallace's Harper's Magazine as it appears in David Foster Wallace, Consider the Lobster (2005)).

54. David Foster Wallace, "Tense Present: Democracy, English, and the Wars over Usage." *Harper's Mag.*, Apr. 2001, at 39.

55. David Foster Wallace, "Tense Present: Democracy, English, and the Wars over Usage." *Harper's Mag.*, Apr. 2001, at 39.

56. David Foster Wallace, "Tense Present: Democracy, English, and the Wars over Usage." *Harper's Mag.*, Apr. 2001, at 40.

57. David Foster Wallace, "Tense Present: Democracy, English, and the Wars over Usage." *Harper's Mag.*, Apr. 2001, at 47.

58. Inspiration for this question comes from an excellent book Eva Brann, *What, Then, Is Time?* (1999).

59. *Arangure v. Whitaker*, 911 F.3d 333, 340 (6th Cir. 2018).

60. *Id.*

61. *Id.* at 340.

62. *Id.* (citing Caleb Nelson, "What is Textualism?" *Va. L. Rev.* 91 (2005): 347, 383–386).

63. *Id.* at 393–94; see also *Black's Law Dictionary* (10th ed. 2014); Jonathan D. Urick, "Note, Chevron and Constitutional Doubt." *Va. L. Rev.* 99 (2013): 375, 409.

64. *Arangure v. Whitaker*, 911 F.3d 333, 340 (6th Cir. 2018).

65. *Arangure v. Whitaker*, 911 F.3d 333, 340 (6th Cir. 2018).

66. *Arangure v. Whitaker*, 911 F.3d 333, 340 (6th Cir. 2018).

67. *Cf.* Indeed, "although textualists criticize purposivism as involving a fruitless search for subjective legislative intent, that characterization may reflect the fact that textualism originated in reaction to the Court's traditional (and perhaps anachronistic) understanding of purposivism. As Hart and Sacks took pains to demonstrate in their influential Legal Process materials, one can also plausibly cast purposivism as an objective framework that aspires to reconstruct the policy that a hypothetical 'reasonable legislator' would have adopted in the context of the legislation, and not the search for a specific policy that Congress actually intended to adopt." John F. Manning, "What Divides Textualists from Purposivists?" *Colum. L. Rev.* 106 (2006): 70, 76.

68. Antonin Scalia, *A Matter of Interpretation: Federal Courts and the Law* (1997). 25.

69. Sometimes referred to as Hume's guillotine. "If there is one intellectual debate that rivals in sterility and repetitiveness the jurisprudential quest for the essence of law, it is the perennial attempt by moral philosophers to disassemble, or at least circumvent, Hume's Guillotine." James Boyle, "Modernist Social Theory: Roberto Unger's Passion." *Harv. L. Rev.* 98 (1985): 1066, 1071, 1072. (book review) Others refer to this formulation as "Hume's law" Campbell Brown. See. "Two Versions of Hume's Law." *J. Ethics & Soc. Phil.* 9 (2015): 1.

70. In this sense, "Hume sought to teach us not that there is no truth about how we ought to live, but that (as a matter of empirical observation) deductive logic is not what moves us from factual premises to conclusions about how we ought to live." David Schmidtz, "Bastiat and the Origins of Political Economy." *Geo. J.L. & Pub. Pol'y* 15 (2017): 835, 843.

71. James Boyle, "Modernist Social Theory: Roberto Unger's Passion." *Harv. L. Rev.* 98 (1985): 1066, 1071, 1076 (book review):

> This is made particularly obvious if one contrasts Hume's moral skepticism with his critique of causation and inductive reasoning. The "problem of induction"—that no amount of prior experience can give us logical grounds for predicting the future—was potentially just as debilitating to the empiricist/scientific project as Hume's Guillotine has been to moral reasoning. But in the absence of lived experience to which it could be connected, the problem of induction remained as merely a philosophical brain-teaser that empiricists warned us to ignore, for without induction "science is impossible."

Id.

72. David Hume, *Treatise of Human Nature* (1739) § 3.1.1. In this section, Hume generally critiques inductive reasoning. *Cf.* "'We'll never survive!' 'Nonsense. You're only saying that because no one ever has.'" William Goldman, *The Princess Bride: S. Morgenstern's Classic Tale of True Love and High Adventure* (1973); *The Princess Bride* (20th Century Fox).

73. Purposivism, *Black's Law Dictionary* (11th ed. 2019).

74. William N. Eskridge Jr. and Philip P. Frickey, "Statutory Interpretation as Practical Reasoning." *Stan. L. Rev.* 42 (1990): 321, 332–33 (citations omitted). As found in Purposivism, *Black's Law Dictionary* (11th ed. 2019).

75. *Sussex Peerage Case* (1844) 11, Clark & F. 85, 103, 109, 8 Jur. 793.

76. *Id.* Even the United States Supreme Court has found this to be persuasive authority citing to the *Sussex Peerage Case*. *See Donnelly v. United States*, 228 U.S. 243, 273 (1913):

> One of the exceptions to the rule excluding it is that which permits the reception, under certain circumstances and for limited purposes, of declarations of third parties, made contrary to their own interest; but it is almost universally held that this must be an interest of a pecuniary character; and the fact that the declaration alleged to have been thus extrajudicially made would probably subject the declarant to a criminal liability is held not to be sufficient to constitute it an exception to the rule against hearsay evidence. So it was held in two notable cases in the House of Lords,—*Berkeley Peerage Case* (1811) 4 Campb. 401;(1811) 4 Campb. 401; *Sussex Peerage Case* (1844) 11, Clark & F. 85, 103, 109, 8 Jur. 793, recognized as of controlling authority in the courts of England.

Id.

77. An excellent example recounts how an absurd result came up in an election impersonation case:

> In the English election of 1868, a man named Chappell exercised his right to vote. He then did so a second time, this time under another name. The name however, belonged to a dead man. Chappell was charged with impersonating a person entitled to vote. The problem for the court was in construing the words 'a person entitled to vote.'

The impersonated voter was dead. He was not entitled to vote. Chappell therefore was acquitted. The case illustrates a certain approach to legal interpretation that dominated nineteenth-century judicial practice and that was related to the emerging philosophy of legal positivism. According to the positivist approach, what matters in judicial interpretation is the pure word of law; no extra-legal considerations ought to be taken into account, such as, in this instance, the desirability of discouraging electoral fraud. The sole meaning of the law, then, is to be derived from the word of the law itself. This approach originates, in part, from the work of Jeremy Bentham, who in the late eighteenth century sought to rid the law of the 'pernicious fictions' by which it had been infected by legal commentators of the English common law tradition. The law's meaning and authority, he argued, ought to be grounded not in obscure myths and customs, but in the transparency and precision of the text of the law. It is the textuality of the law, however, which tends to disrupt the claim to certainty of law-as-Logos. The word of law, in the case of Whitely v. Chappell, is haunted by a ghost in the electoral machine with which the court cannot rationally deal. That the judgment in the case did not meet the 'justice' of the circumstances was accepted by all of the judges who acknowledged that the word of the law was incompetent to deal satisfactorily with this uncanny event: 'I regret that we are obliged to come to the conclusion that the offence charged was not proved; but it would be wrong to strain words to meet the justice of the present case, because it might make a precedent and lead to dangerous consequences in other cases.' To take the law at its word in this instance, then, is to allow the impersonator of the deceased to go free and to traumatize the law with the uncanny phenomenon of the dead man voting." Sue Chaplin, "'Written in the Black Letter' the Gothic and/in the Rule of Law." *Law & Literature* 17 (2005): 47, 49.

78. *Grey v. Pearson*, 6 H. of L. Cas. 106; Wigram on Extrinsic Evidence, §§ 10–14; 1 Jarman on Wills, 6th Am. ed., 413. *See.* Wills—Construction—Varying Technical Words, 10 *Harv. L. Rev.* 66 (1896). Indeed, historically, "[t]he 'golden rule,' text infra at note 351, is usually traced to Grey v. Pearson, 6 H.L.C. 61, 10 Eng. Rep. 1216 (H.L.1857), quoted infra note 351." Hans W. Baade, "The Casus Omissus: A Pre-History of Statutory Analogy." *Syracuse J. Int'l L. & Com.* 20 (1994): 45, 94.

79. "A second version of formalism is the Golden Rule of statutory interpretation. The Golden Rule differs from the Literal Rule in that under the Golden Rule the plain meaning of a statute should not be followed if its leads to an absurd result. Thus, under the Golden Rule, a court should depart from the literal text of a statute if the text is ambiguous or the literal meaning would create an absurd result." R. Randall Kelso, "Statutory Interpretation Doctrine on the Modern Supreme Court and Four Doctrinal Approaches to Judicial Decision-Making." *Pepp. L. Rev.* 25 (1997): 37.

80. The United States Eleventh Circuit Court of Appeals has wrote that a standing rule of statutory interpretation requires that "plain language will not be followed to the point of absurdity." *Clark v. Riley*, 595 F.3d 1258, 1266 (11th Cir. 2010).

81. *In re Friesenhahn*, 169 B.R. 615, 637 (Bankr. W.D. Tex. 1994).

82. *United States v. Brown*, 333 U.S. 18, 27, 68 S.Ct. 376, 380, 92 L.Ed. 442 (1948). See. *In re Friesenhahn*, 169 B.R. 615, 637 (Bankr. W.D. Tex. 1994).

83. *Mohasco Corp. v. Silver*, 447 U.S. 807, 818, 100 S.Ct. 2486, 2493, 65 L.Ed.2d 532 (1980). See. *In re Friesenhahn*, 169 B.R. 615, 637 (Bankr. W.D. Tex. 1994).

84. *Medellin v. Texas*, 552 U.S. 491, 562, 128 S. Ct. 1346, 1389, 170 L. Ed. 2d 190 (2008).

85. As the Supreme Court of New Mexico wrote in discussing such difficulties, it "may be difficult in some circumstances to determine which of two laws can be characterized as specific and which can be characterized as general. However, this difficulty does not preclude application of the rule or signal that such an inquiry would be futile. As with the interpretation of all statutes, courts should resort to traditional means of ascertaining legislative intent." *State v. Cleve*, 1999-NMSC-017, ¶ 28, 127 N.M. 240, 251, 980 P.2d 23, 34.

86. Wittgenstein, *Philosophical Investigations* #23.

87. This idea is supported in Wittgenstein's earlier philosophical thought. Ludwig Wittgeinstein, Tractatus Logico-Philosophicus 6.001 *Cf.* However, Wittgenstein's philosophical thought changed. Consider the counter argument to the idea that every proposition is the result of successive applications of the operation N to the elementary propositions:

> The Tractatus relied on what has been called the picture theory of meaning, in which the logical simples of reality exist in a strict isomorphism with the essential elements of language. In short, this concordance between the atomistic parts of reality and the basic elements of language allowed language to "picture" reality. In the years immediately prior to 1929, Wittgenstein became dissatisfied with many of the consequences of this view. In particular, he became convinced that its handling of color and color gradations was unsatisfactory.

Bruce A. Markell, "Bewitched by Language: Wittgenstein and the Practice of Law." *Pepp. L. Rev.* 32 (2005): 801, 807.

88. *Romer v. Evans*, 517 U.S. 620 (1996).

89. *Romer v. Evans*, 517 U.S. 620 (1996).

90. Originalism, *Black's Law Dictionary* (11th ed. 2019).

91. Speech at CUA, 14 October 1996.

92. Bork, *The Tempting of America*, 144.

93. Bork, *The Tempting of America*, 144.

94. Oliver Wendell Holmes Jr., "The Path of the Law." *Harvard Law Review* 10 (1897): 457.

95. Oliver Wendell Holmes Jr., "The Path of the Law." *Harvard Law Review* 10 (1897): 457.

96. Oliver Wendell Holmes Jr., "The Path of the Law." *Harvard Law Review* 10 (1897): 457.

97. "My thesis is two-pronged: (1) because meta-rules, like any other rules, are indeterminate, the picture of constitutional interpretation that relies on meta-rules to constrain judicial discretion is mistaken; and (2) assuming arguendo that Wittgenstein's analysis shows that rules are actually determinate, the efficacy of textualism-originalism is still not preserved because meta-rules do not exist antecedent to the question presented in any individual case. The first premise seems a stronger claim to me insofar as it challenges the determinacy and meaning of all rules. Accordingly, I will call the first argument the 'strong thesis' and the second argument the 'weak thesis.'" Daniel S. Goldberg, "I Do Not Think It Means What You Think It Means: How Kripke and Wittgenstein's Analysis on Rule Following Undermines Justice Scalia's Textualism and Originalism." *Clev. St. L. Rev.* 54 (2006): 273, 274–275.

98. Jonathan Gienapp, "Historicism and Holism: Failures of Originalist Translation." *Fordham L. Rev.* 84 (2015): 935, 947. *See generally*. Lawrence B. Solum, "Intellectual History as Constitutional Theory." *Va. L. Rev.* 101 (2015): 1111.

99. Jack M. Balkin, "The American Constitution as 'Our Law'." *Yale J.L. & Human.* 25 (2013): 113, 145.

100. As outlined in Wittgenstein's "notorious paragraph" discussing the problems in Bertrand Russell's *Principia Mathematica* and Gödel's Incompleteness Theorems where a system can prove a proposition or not and what such a proof would mean and what a corollary of a *reductio ad absurdum* would mean as well. Ludwig Wittgenstein, *Remarks on The Foundations of Mathematics* Part I, Appendix I (G.H. von Wright, R. Rhees & G.E.M. Anscombe eds., G.E.M. Anscombe trans., rev. ed. 1983) § 8.

101. David Foster Wallace, "Tense Present: Democracy, English, and the Wars over Usage." *Harper's Mag.*, April 2001, at 407 (discussing "dictionary wars" among the various conservative and liberal ideologies while reviewing Bryan A. Garner's Modern English Usage dictionary).

102. "Anthropologists as Spies | The Nation." Accessed May 29, 2021. https://www.thenation.com/article/archive/anthropologists-spies/.

103. *Id.*

104. *Id.*

105. In the Bible Pilate asks Jesus, "Τί ἐστιν ἀλήθεια;" translated "what is truth?" (King James version) *Cf.* "Jesus said, 'My kingdom is not of this world. If it were, my servants would fight to prevent my arrest by the Jews. But now my kingdom is from another place.' 'You are a King, then!' said Pilate. Jesus answered, 'You are right in saying I am a king. In fact, for this reason I was born, and for this I came into the world, to testify to the truth. Everyone on the side of truth listens to me.' 'What is the truth?' Pilate asked." James B. Johnston, Esq., "The Bridge Connecting Pontius Pilate's Sentencing of Jesus to the New Jersey Death Penalty Study Commission's Concerns over Executing the Innocent: When Humans Beings with Inherently Human Flaws Determine Guilt or Innocence, and Life or Death." *Rutgers J. L. & Religion* 10 (2009): 15 fn. 118. "In Pilate and Jesus, Giorgio Agamben argues that Pontius Pilate never formally condemned Jesus of Nazareth. 'The traditional interpretation of Jesus' trial . . . must be revised,' he urges, because 'there has not been any judgment in a technical sense.' In Agamben's telling, Pilate's non-judgment is the original truth of Jesus's death that has been covered over by tradition. This is an intriguing hypothesis, but Agamben's use of sources in arguing it is highly irregular. This article offers a critique of the legal and philological argumentation of Pilate and Jesus. In the process, it revisits an ancient—and still actual—controversy surrounding the Roman trial of Jesus and demonstrates that Pilate did sentence Jesus, pro tribunali, to death on a cross." D. L. Dusenbury, "The Judgment of Pontius Pilate: A Critique of Giorgio Agamben." *J.L. & Religion* 32 (2017): 340.

These Biblical analyses are helpful because they can be representations of cultural systems. *See.*

> Jordan B. Peterson, *Maps of Meaning: The Architecture of Belief* (1999) (drawing from neuropsychology, anthropology, and mysticism to argue, in part, how religious, ethnic,

and other cultural systems help to regulate human emotion and experience); see also Tseming Yang, "Race, Religion, and Cultural Identity: Reconciling the Jurisprudence of Race and Religion." *Ind. L.J.* 73 (1997): 119, 127–28 (viewing membership in a cultural group as providing a normative "scaffold" for meaning-creation)." Murad Hussain, "Defending the Faithful: Speaking the Language of Group Harm in Free Exercise Challenges to Counterterrorism Profiling."

Yale L.J. 117 (2008): 920, 969.

106. "It may be that at Yale Law School, which Tushnet attended between 1966 and 1969, the flame of legal realism was kept alive, especially because the identification of Yale with legal realism during the 1920s and 1930s is what propelled Yale into the first rank of law schools.) The legal realists, Tushnet explained, demonstrated the indeterminacy of legal doctrine, which meant that rules and precedents could be manipulated to produce often contradictory legal outcomes. The result was, the realists argued, that the explanation for these outcomes must be sought outside of the system of legal doctrine, in the sociology of power." Morton J. Horwitz, "Mark Tushnet, Legal Historian." *Geo. L.J.* 90 (2001): 131, 131–132.

Cf. "Law does not escape these social forces. The recent literature is replete with articles by scholars attempting to discover, impose, clarify, and defend meaning in the law. Indeed, a recent scholarly movement holds that 'interpretive communities' or 'communities of meaning' are, if not the most important factor in legal judgment and interpretation, at least a key element. Yet, contrasting notions about the relevant meanings, and how to determine them, abound. Are we to be persuaded by strict constructionists or context-dependents? Should we be concerned with adjudication or interpretation? Is legal formalism alive in new forms or has deconstruction irretrievably scattered the pieces? Is social life about community, freedom, order, equality—or something else? There is little consensus on what our core values and meanings ought to be, or even how we are to arrive at them." Jean Stefanck, "The Law Review Symposium Issue: Community of Meaning or Re-Inscription of Hierarchy?" *U. Colo. L. Rev.* 63 (1992): 651, 652.

107. See generally, Adam Smith, *An Inquiry Into the Nature and Causes of the Wealth of Nations* 475–476 (Edwin Cannan ed., University of Chicago Press, 1976) (1776). *See.* J. S. Mill, "On the Definition of Political Economy; and on the Method of Investigation Proper to It." *London & Westminster Rev.* 4 (1836): 12. *Cf.* Robin Paul Malloy, "Invisible Hand or Sleight of Hand? Adam Smith, Richard Posner and the Philosophy of Law and Economics." *Kan. L. Rev.* 36 (1988): 209.

Bibliography

"Anglo-Saxon Chronicle," 1067 AD, version D, (B. L. Cott, Tiber B. iv).

"Anthropologists as Spies | The Nation." Accessed May 29, 2021. https://www.thenation.com/article/archive/anthropologists-spies/.

"Catastrophe" used here in the Ancient Greek sense of "cata" and "strophe," meaning under turned or overturning. Oxford English Dictionary (2d ed. 1989).

"Constitutional Courts and International Law: Revisiting the Transatlantic Divide," *Harv. L. Rev.* 129 (2016): 1362, 1363.

"G. W. F. Hegel, Science of Logic, Atlantic Heights: Humanities Press International 1989, p. 444." Žižek, Slavoj. Absolute Recoil 2015.

"Grodt & McKay Realty, 77 T.C. at 1237–1238 (internal citations omitted); see also Anschutz, 664 F.3d at 324–25." *Id.*

"Henry George Liddell, Robert Scott, An Intermediate Greek-English Lexicon, Λογ ιστικός." Accessed May 19, 2021. http://www.perseus.tufts.edu/hopper/text?doc=Perseus%3Atext%3A1999.04.0058%3Aentry%3Dlogistiko%2Fs.

"Henry George Liddell, Robert Scott, An Intermediate Greek-English Lexicon, Θυμοειδής." Accessed May 19, 2021. http://www.perseus.tufts.edu/hopper/text?doc=Perseus%3Atext%3A1999.04.0058%3Aentry%3Dqumoeidh%2Fs.

"Holmes, Privilege, Malice, and Intent," *Harv. Law Rev.* 8 (1894): 1, 7.

"Human Rights: An Examination of Universalism and Cultural Relativism: Journal of Comparative Social Welfare: Vol 22, 23-36 No 1." Accessed May 18, 2021. https://www.tandfonline.com/doi/abs/10.1080/17486830500522997.

"Immanuel Kant, The Philosophy of Law 15 (W. Hastie trans., Edinburgh: T. & T. Clark, 1887). This is a translation of Kant's Metaphysische Anfangsgrunde der Rechtslehre (1796), also translated as The Metaphysical Elements of Justice." *Id.* at fn. 29.

"Is the Federal Reserve Truly Independent from Executive Pressure?" Kevin Morrissey, IV. *Executive Influence on the Federal Reserve, Rev. Banking & Fin. L.* 38 (2018) 37, 47.

"Justice Scalia's Textualism and Originalism," *Clev. St. L. Rev.* 54 (2006): 273, 278.

"Note, Preemption as Purposivism's Last Refuge," *Harv. L. Rev.* 126 (2013): 1056, 105.
"Note, Textualism as Fair Notice," *Harv. L. Rev.* 123 (2009): 542, 542.
"Obama Signs Health Care Overhaul into Law - The New York Times." Accessed May 19, 2021. https://www.nytimes.com/2010/03/24/health/policy/24health.html.
"Obama to Appeal Immigration Ruling to Supreme Court - The New York Times." Accessed May 19, 2021. https://www.nytimes.com/2015/11/11/us/politics/supreme-court-immigration-obama.html.
"OECD Presents Outputs of OECD/G20 BEPS Project for Discussion at G20 Finance Ministers Meeting - OECD." Accessed May 29, 2021. https://www.oecd.org/ctp/oecd-presents-outputs-of-oecd-g20-beps-project-for-discussion-at-g20-finance-ministers-meeting.htm.
"Opinion | 'Ode to Joy,' Followed by Chaos and Despair - The New York Times." Accessed May 29, 2021. https://www.nytimes.com/2007/12/24/opinion/24zizek.html.
"Plato, Republic, Book 4, Section 439d." Accessed May 19, 2021. http://www.perseus.tufts.edu/hopper/text?doc=Perseus%3Atext%3A1999.01.0167%3Abook%3D4%3Asection%3D439d.
"Plato, Republic, Book 4, Section 439e." Accessed May 19, 2021. http://www.perseus.tufts.edu/hopper/text?doc=Perseus%3Atext%3A1999.01.0168%3Abook%3D4%3Asection%3D439e.
"The Fifth Circuit Court of Appeals Rules Against Obama's Executive Actions on Immigration: The Atlantic." Accessed May 19, 2021. https://www.theatlantic.com/politics/archive/2015/11/fifth-circuit-obama-immigration/415077/.
"The Income Tax and the Sixteenth Amendment," *Harv. L. Rev.* 29 (1916) 536, 538.
"Three Approaches to Law and Culture Symposium: The Future of Legal Theory: Essay 96 Cornell Law Review 2010-2011."
"Transfer Pricing in a Global Market," *J. Corp. Tax'n* 35 (2008): 17, 17, WL 193050, 1.
"U.S. Reports: Otis v. Parker, 187 U.S. 606, 609 (1903)." n.d. Image. Library of Congress, Washington, D.C. 20540 USA. Accessed May 16, 2021. https://www.loc.gov/item/usrep187606/.
"Using Capital Cash Flows to Value Dissenters' Shares in Appraisal Proceedings," *Harv. L. Rev.* 111 (1998): 2099, 2105–2106.
"V is for Value in Valuation: A Fresh Look at a Transaction Standard," *WGL-ACCTALERT* 6, no 153 (2012): WL 10235065, 4.
"What Exempt Organizations Need to Know About the Transfer Pricing Rules," *J. Tax'n Ex. Org.* 11 (2000): 217, 226, WL 1920395, 12.
"Wills - Construction - Varying Technical Words," *Harv. L. Rev.* 10 (1896): 66.
¶ 14.11 International Transactions Involving Intangible Assets Among Related Parties (International Transactions), 1998 WL 1038740, 9.
¶ 18.09 INDIAN TAX CONSIDERATIONS FOR U.S. INVESTMENTS, U.S. Tax. Foreign Cont. Bus. ¶ 18.09.
¶ 3.03 Guidance for Applying the Arm's-Length Principle, 1998 WL 1038574, 10.
¶ 8.02 Basic Economic Concepts, 1998 WL 1038873, 2.

26 U.S.C.A. § 316 (West)

60 Am. Jur. 2d Patents § 925.

A Better Way: Our Vision for a Confident America, GOP TAX REFORM TASK FORCE (November 30, 2016), https://abetterway.speaker.gov/_assets/pdf/ABetterWay-Tax-PolicyPaper.pdf [perma.cc/G6B3-YMT3].

Abrahamson, Mark. "Sudden Wealth, Gratification and Attainment: Durkheim's Anomie of Affluence Reconsidered," *Am. Soc. Rev.* 45 (1980): 49, 49.

Ackerman, Bruce. "The Living Constitution," *Harv. L. Rev.* 120 (2007): 1737, 1754–1755.

Adams, Francisco Gonzáles-Hermosillo. "El Sometimiento Del Señorío Indígena de Cholula Ante la Corona Española," *Signos históricos* 3 (2001): 6.

Adler, Matthew D. "Expressive Theories of Law: A Skeptical Overview," *University of Pennsylvania Law Review* 148, no. 5 (2000): 1363–1501, 1376. https://doi.org/10.2307/3312747.

Advising Small Businesses (2016).

Alaszewski, Andy. "Anthropology and Risk: Insights into Uncertainty, Danger and Blame from Other Cultures: A Review Essay," *Health, Risk & Society* 17, no. 3–4 (2015): 205–225, 205–210.

Allaire, Yvan, and Mihaela E. Firsirotu. "Theories of Organizational Culture," *Organization Studies* 5, no. 3 (1984): 193–226, 195.

Allen, Francis. "Rostow: Is Law Dead?" *Michigan Law Review* 70, no. 4 (1972): 766–772; Rostow, *The Rightful Limits of Freedom in a Liberal Democratic State: Of Civil Disobedience*, in id. at 60–66.

Allen, Jessie. "A Theory of Adjudication: Law as Magic," *Suffolk University Law Review* 41 (2007): 773, 755.

Altera Corp. & Subsidiaries v. C.I.R., 145 T.C. 91, 134 (2015).

Amazon.com Inc & Subsidiaries (2017) 148 TC No. 8. *Earlier proceedings* at (2016) TC Memo 2016-131, RIA TC *Memo P* 2016-131, 112 CCH TCM 30, *at* P 74,536.00151(25); (2014) TC *Memo* 2014-245, RIA TC Memo P 2014-245, 108 CCH TCM 588, *at* P 74,536.14751(40); *and* (2014) TC *Memo* 2014-149, RIA TC *Memo* P 2014-149, 108 CCH TCM 87, *at* P 4825.05(5).

Ambrose, Meg Leta. "Lessons from the Avalanche of Numbers: Big Data in Historical Perspective," *Journal of Law & Policy for the Information Society* 11 (n.d.): 201, 232.

Anglo-Saxon Chronicle D: Cotton Tiberius B IV (1067), English Historical Documents 150 (David C.).

Arangure v. Whitaker, 911 F.3d 333, 340 (6th Cir. 2018).

Aristotle, De Anima 412a1-413a10 (W.D. Ross ed., 1956) (defining psuche as the active organization of a body that has life, potentially, or dunamei).

Aristotle, Ethica Nicomachea, supra note 13, at 1105b20-28.

Aristotle, Poetics (S.H. Butcher, 2019) 9.

Arulanantham, Ahilan T. "Breaking the Rules?: Wittgenstein and Legal Realism," *Yale L.J.* 107 (1998): 1853, 1869–1871.

Ashforth, Blake E. and Fred Mael. "Social Identity Theory and the Organization," *Academy of Management* 14 (1989): 20, 20.

Ault, Hugh J. "Some Reflections on the OECD and the Sources of International Tax Principles," *Tax Notes Int'l* 70 (2013): 1195.

Austin, John. *The Province of Jurisprudence Determined* (1832), reprinted in John Austin, *The Province of Jurisprudence Determined and The Uses of the Study of Jurisprudence* 132 (Noonday, 1954).

Avi-Yonah, Reuven S. "The Structure of International Taxation: A Proposal for Simplification," *Tex. L. Rev.* 74 (1996): 1301, 1303.

Avi-Yonah, Reuven S. and Haiyan Xu. "Evaluating BEPS: A Reconsideration of the Benefits Principle and Proposal for UN Oversight," *Harv. Bus. L. Rev.* 6 (2016): 185, 226.

Avi-Yonah, Reuven S. and Haiyan Xu. "Evaluating BEPS: A Reconsideration of the Benefits Principle and Proposal for UN Oversight," *Harv. Bus. L. Rev.* 6 (2016): 185.

Avi-Yonah, Reuven S. and Haiyan Xu. "Evaluating BEPS: A Reconsideration of the Benefits Principle and Proposal for UN Oversight," *Harv. Bus. L. Rev.* 6 (2016): 185, 225.

Avi-Yonah, Reuven. *Advanced Introduction to International Tax Law* (2019) 3–6.

Avramovich, Michael. "Intercompany Transfer Pricing Regulations Under Internal Revenue Code Section 482: The Noose Tightens on Multinational Corporations," *J. Marshall L. Rev.* 28 (1995): 915, 931.

Baade, Hans W. "The Casus Omissus: A Pre-History of Statutory Analogy," *Syracuse J. Int'l L. & Com.* 20 (1994): 45, 94.

Backer, Larry Cata. "Culturally Significant Speech: Law, Courts, Society, and Racial Equity," *U. Ark. Little Rock L. Rev.* 21 (1999): 845, 879 n. 55.

Bagwell, Marvin N. "Unsettling Mortgage Law: Implications for Practitioners and title Insurers: Can't Live Without Air: Title Insurance and the Bursting of the Real Estate Bubble," *Pace L. Rev.* 30 (2009): 180, 200–201.

Bak, Thomas. "Power-Law Distributions and the Federal Judiciary," *Jurimetrics* (2006): 139–160, 141–142.

Baker, Philip. Improper Use of Tax Treaties, Tax Avoidance and Tax Evasion (2013), http://www.un.org/esa/ffd/tax/2013tmttan/paper9a_baker.pdf. Brauner, Yariv. "What the BEPS?," *Fla. Tax Rev.* 16 (2014): 55, 115 fn. 106.

Balkin, Jack M. "The American Constitution As "Our Law"," *Yale J.L. & Human.* 25 (2013): 113, 145.

Bandura, Albert. "Social Cognitive Theory: An Agentic Perspective." *Annual Review of Psychology* 52, no. 1 (2001): 1–26, 22–23.

Banta, Natalie M. "Substantive Due Process in Exile: The Supreme Court's Original Interpretation of the Due Process Clause of the Fourteenth Amendment," *Wyo. L. Rev.* 13 (2013): 151, 179.

Barbarians at the Gate (Glenn Jordan 1993).

Barker, William B. "An International Tax System for Emerging Economies, Tax Sparing, and Development: It Is All about Source," *U. Pa. J. Int'l L.* 29 (2007): 349, 360–361.

Barker, William B. "An International Tax System for Emerging Economies, Tax Sparing, and Development: It Is All about Source," *U. Pa. J. Int'l L.* 29 (2007): 349, 389 fn. 3.

Barker, William B. "Optimal International Taxation and Tax Competition: Overcoming the Contradictions," *Nw. J. Int'l L. & Bus.* 22 (2002): 161, 182–183.

Barnard, Alan and Jonathan Spencer. *Encyclopedia of Social and Cultural Anthropology* (1996) 213.

Barrett, Stanley R. *Culture Meets Power* (2002).

Baskin & Miranti, supra note 68, at 69; Chatfield, supra note 65, at 79–80.

Bassham, Gregory. *Original Intent and the Constitution* 146 n.3 (1992).

Bateson, Gregory. *Steps to an Ecology of Mind: Collected Essays in Anthropology, Psychiatry, Evolution, and Epistemology* (University of Chicago Press, 1972) 68–69.

Baudrillard, Jean. *The Precession of the Simulacra, in Simulacra and Simulation* (Sheila Faria Glaser trans., University of Michigan Press, 1997) (1981).

Beck, Randy. "The Faith of the "Crits": Critical Legal Studies and Human Nature," *Harv. J.L. & Pub. Pol'y* 11 (1988): 433.

Bederman, David J. *The New International Law in an Old Age of Indeterminacy The Shield of Achilles: War, Peace, and the Course of History* by Philip Bobbitt (New York: Alfred A. Knopt, 2002), pp. Xxxiii, 919. (Fnd1), *Tex. L. Rev.* 81 (2003) 1521, 1533–1534.

Beebe, Barton, and Jeanne C. Fromer. "Are We Running Out of Trademarks: An Empirical Study of Trademark Depletion and Congestion," *Harv. L. Rev.* 131 (2017): 945, 975.

Beethoven, Ludwig von. Symphony No. 9, Opus 125, fourth movement (1824).

Beiser, Frederick C. *German Idealism: The Struggle against Subjectivism, 1781–1801* (Harvard University Press, 2002).

Belier, Wouter W. *Decayed Gods: Origin and Development of Georges Dumézil's "Ideologie Tripartie"* (1991) 17–20.

Benedict, Ruth. *The Chrysanthemum and the Sword: Patterns of Japanese Culture* (1967) 450–454.

Berkeley Peerage Case (1811) 4 Campb. 401; (1811) 4 Campb. 401; *Sussex Peerage Case* (1844) 11, Clark & F. 85, 103, 109, 8 Jur. 793.

Bernard, H. Russell et al. "The Construction of Primary Data in Cultural Anthropology," *Current Anthropology* 27 (1986): 382, 383–384.

Bhala, Raj. "Hegelian Reflections on Unilateral Action in the World Trading System," *Berkley J. Int'l L.* 15 (1997): 159, 184 n.93.

Binder, Guyora. "Post-Totalitarian Politics," *Mich. L. Rev.* 91 (1993): 1491, 1493.

Biography Editors. "Franz Boas." Biography. Accessed May 18, 2021. https://www.biography.com/scientist/franz-boas.

Birmingham, Robert. "Proving Miracles and the First Amendment," *Geo. Mason L. Rev.* 5 (1996): 45, 60.

Black, Bernard and Reinier Kraakman. "A Self-Enforcing Model of Corporate Law," *Harv. L. Rev.* 109 (1996): 1911, 1981 n. 42.

Black's Law Dictionary (11th ed., 2019).

Blackstone, William. *Commentaries on the Law of England 18* (William Draper Lewis ed., 1902).

Blair-Stanek, Andrew. "Just Compensation as Transfer Prices," *Ariz. L. Rev.* 58 (2016): 1077, 1138.

Blaut, Morris J. *The Colonizer's Model of the World: Geographical Diffusionism and Eurocentric History* (2012) 7.

Bloom, Allan. *The Closing of the American Mind: How Higher Education Has Failed Democracy and Impoverished the Souls of Today's Students* (1987) 178.

Bloom, David T. "The Legal Underpinnings of the Global Foreign Exchange Market," *NC Banking Inst.* 23 (2019): 27, 28.

Bloom, Harold. *The Western Canon: The Books and School of the Ages* 30 (Riverhead Books, 1994).

Bloom, Harold. *The Western Canon: The Books and School of the Ages* (Riverhead Books, 1994) 31.

Blume, Lawrence and Daniel L. Rubinfeld, "Compensation for Takings: An Economic Analysis," *Calif. L. Rev.* 72 (1984): 569, 593–597.

Board of Governors of the Federal Reserve System. "Federal Reserve Board - Federal Reserve Banks." Accessed May 20, 2021. https://www.federalreserve.gov/aboutthefed/federal-reserve-system.htm. *See.* Bulman-Pozen, Jessica. "Our Regionalism," *U. Pa. L. Rev.* 166 (2018): 377, 442.

Bobonich, Christopher. "Persuasion, Compulsion, and Freedom in Plato's 'Laws'," in *Plato* (Gail Fine ed., Oxford: Oxford University Press, 2000) 884.

Boettke, Peter J., and Daniel J. Smith. "Federal Reserve Independence: A Centennial Review," *The Journal of Prices & Markets* 1, no. 1 (2012): 2013, 31–48.

Bolson, Andrew. "Lessons from an Outlier What Young Lawyers Can Learn from the Story of Joe Flom," *N.J. Law.*, August 2013, at 57 fn. 2.

Bolson, Andrew. "Lessons from an Outlier What Young Lawyers Can Learn from the Story of Joe Flom," *N.J. Law.*, August 2013, at 57.

Borden, Bradley T. and Sang Hee Lee. "Boundaries of the Prediction Model in Tax Law's Substantial Authority," *Tax Law* 71 (2017): 33, 43.

Bork, R. *The Tempting of America: The Political Seduction of the Law* (New York: The Free Press, 1990) 144.

Bowie, Fiona. *The Anthropology of Religion* (2000) 18.

Boyd, Robert and Peter J. Richerson. *Culture and the Evolutionary Process* (1988) 288–290.

Boyle, James. "Modernist Social Theory: Roberto Unger's Passion," *Harv. L. Rev.* 98 (1985): 1066, 1071, 1076 (book review).

Boyle, James. "Modernist Social Theory: Roberto Unger's Passion," *Harv. L. Rev.* 98 (1985): 1066, 1071, 1072 (book review).

Boyle, James. "Thomas Hobbes and the Invented Tradition of Positivism: Reflections on Language, Power, and Essentialism," *University of Pennsylvania Law Review* 135, no. 2 (1987): 383–426, 391.

Brann, Eva. *What, Then, Is Time?* (1999).

Brauner, Yariv. "Treaties in the Aftermath of Beps," *Brook. J. Int'l L.* 41 (2016): 973, 1041 fn. 50.

Brauner, Yariv. "Treaties in the Aftermath of BEPS," *Brook. J. Int'l L.* 41 (2016): 973, 1041 fn. 51.

Brauner, Yariv. "Value in the Eye of the Beholder: The Valuation of Intangibles for Transfer Pricing Purposes," *Va. Tax Rev.* 28 (2008): 79, 82.

Brauner, Yariv. "Value in the Eye of the Beholder: The Valuation of Intangibles for Transfer Pricing Purposes," *Va. Tax Rev.* 28 (2008): 79, 83.

Brauner, Yariv. *What the BEPS?* (Univ. of Fla. Coll. of Law, Legal Studies Working Paper No. 15-40, 2014), http://ssrn.com/abstract=2408034.

Breard v. Greene, 523 U.S. 371, 376 (1998) (per curiam).

Brest, Paul. "The Misconceived Quest for the Original Understanding," *B.U. L. Rev.* 60 (1980): 204, 204.

Brick, Howard. *Cold War Social Science* (2012) 157.

Briggs, Donald C. and Marvin Alisky. *Historical Dictionary of Mexico* (1981).

Briscoe, Virginia Wolf. "Ruth Benedict Anthropological Folklorist," *The Journal of American Folklore* 92, no. 366 (1979): 445–476.

Britannica, T. Editors of Encyclopaedia. "Code of Justinian." *Encyclopedia Britannica*, August 27, 2019. https://www.britannica.com/topic/code-of-justinian.

Britannica, T. Editors of Encyclopaedia. "Lewis Henry Morgan." *Encyclopedia Britannica*, December 13, 2020. https://www.britannica.com/biography/lewis-henry-morgan.

Brooks, Thom. "Between Natural Law and Legal Positivism: Dworkin and Hegel on Legal Theory," *Ga. St. U. L. Rev.* 23 (2007): 513, 520–521.

Brown, Campbell. See. "Two Versions of Hume's Law," *J. Ethics & Soc. Phil.* 9 (2015): 1.

Brown, Mark R. and Andrew C. Greenberg. "On Formally Undecidable Propositions of Law: Legal Indeterminacy and the Implications of Metamathematics," *Hastings L.J.* 43 (1992): 1439, 1441 (citation omitted).

Brumann, Christoph. "Writing For Culture: Why a Successful Concept Should Not Be Discarded," *Current Anthropology* 40, no. S1 (1999): S1–S27, 5.

Burris, Donald S. "From Tragedy to Triumph in the Pursuit of Looted Art: Altmann, Benningson, Portrait of Wally, Von Saher and Their Progeny," *J. Marshall Rev. Intell. Prop. L.* 15 (2016): 394, 434.

Burrough, Bryan and John Heylar, *Barbarians at the Gate: The Fall of RJR Nabisco* (1990).

Byrne, Donna M. "Locke, Property, and Progressive Taxes," *Neb. L. Rev.* 78 (1999): 700, 724–725.

Byrnes, IV, William. *Byrnes' Analysis of the 200+ page Amazon Decision. Is it the Death Knell of the Income Method and Inclusion of Employee Stock Compensation for Cost Sharing Agreement Valuation?* Kluwer International Tax Blog. "Byrnes' Analysis of the 200+ Page Amazon Decision. Is It the Death Knell of the Income Method and Inclusion of Employee Stock Compensation for Cost Sharing Agreement Valuation?," March 24, 2017. http://kluwertaxblog.com/2017/03/24/is-amazon-com-inc-the-death-knell-of-the-irs-cost-sharing-agreement-valuation-approach/.

Caistor, Nick. *Mexico City: A Cultural and Literary Companion* (2000) 4–6.

Calloway v. Comm'r, 691 F.3d 1315, 1327 (11th Cir. 2012).

Carlson, David Gray. "Hegel's Theory of Quantity," *Cardozo L. Rev.* 23 (2002): 2027, 2150 n. 291.

Carlson, David Gray. "Hegel's Theory of Quantity," *Cardozo L. Rev.* 23 (2002): 2027, 2028.

Carneiro, Robert L. "Herbert Spencer as an Anthropologist," *The Journal of Libertarian Studies* 5, no. 2 (1981): 153–210, 182–183.

Carrillo, Jo. "Disabling Certitudes: An Introduction to the Role of Mythologies of Conquest in Law," *U. Fla. JL & Pub. Pol'y* 12 (2000): 13, 31 fn. 24.

Cassese, Antonio. *International Law in a Divided World* (1986) 15–22.

Castillo, Susan. "Colonial Encounters in New World Writing, 1500-1786. Performing America - ProQuest," 2006, 23–24. https://www.proquest.com/openview/a21a4fcf513a2219cc30b944cb5751e8/1?pq-origsite=gscholar&cbl=27448.

Caudill, David S. "Freud and Critical Legal Studies: Contours of a Radical Socio-Legal Psychoanalysis," *Ind. L.J.* 66 (1991): 651, 658–659.

Chaplin, Sue. ""Written in the Black Letter" the Gothic and/in the Rule of Law," *Law & Literature* 17 (2005): 47, 49.

Chapman v. C.I.R., 107 T.C.M. (CCH) 1433 (T.C. 2014).

Chapman, Robert. *Archaeologies of Complexity* (2003) 6.

Chemerinsky, Erwin. "The Vanishing Constitution," *Harv. L. Rev.* 103 (1989): 43, 61.

Chevron, U.S.A., Inc. v. NRDC, Inc., 467 U.S. 837, 844 (1984).

Childe, V. Gordon. "Social Evolution in the Light of Archaeology," *The Australian Journal of Anthropology* 4, no. 1 (1948): 175, 177.

Chisholm v. Georgia, 2 U.S. (2 Dall.) 419, 474 (1793).

Chodorow, Nancy. *Family Structure and Feminine Personality*, reprinted in *Feminism in the Study of Religion* (Darlene Juschka ed., Continuum, 2001), 81, 81–105.

Christians, Allison D. "Tax Treaties for Investment and Aid to Sub-Saharan Africa A Case Study," *Brook. L. Rev.* 71 (2005): 639, 660.

Cicero, *De legibus*, 1.18, at 316-17 (Clinton Walker Keyes trans., 1928).

Cicero, *De Republica* (Cambridge, MA: Loeb Classical Library, 1928), 3.22.33.

Claeys, Gregory. "The" Survival of the Fittest" and the Origins of Social Darwinism," *Journal of the History of Ideas* 61, no. 2 (2000): 223–240, 227.

Clark v. Riley, 595 F.3d 1258, 1266 (11th Cir. 2010).

Clark, Robert G. "Transfer Pricing, Section 482, and International Tax Conflict: Getting Harmonized Income Allocation Measures from Multinational Cacophony," *Am. U. L. Rev.* 42 (1993): 1155, 1212 fn. 11.

Clark, Robert G. "Transfer Pricing, Section 482, and International Tax Confilct: Getting Harmonized Income Allocation Measures from Multinational Cacophony," *Am. U. L. Rev.* 42 (1993): 1155, 1157–1158.

Clark, Robert. "The Last of the Iroquois: History and Myth in James Fenimore Cooper's: "The Last of the Mohicans"," *Poetics Today* 3, no. 4 (1982): 115–134.

Clausing, Kimberly A. "The Effect of Profit Shifting on the Corporate Tax Base," *Tax Notes* 81 (2016): 3.

Clifford, Michael. "Hegel and Foucault: Toward a History without Man," *Clio* 29, no. 1 (1999): 1. Gibbon, Edward. *The Decline and Fall of the Roman Empire*, Chapter 38 General Observations on the Fall of the Roman Empire in the West.

Cohen, Lawrence. "003: Introduction to Social/Cultural Anthropology | Anthropology." Accessed May 18, 2021. https://anthropology.berkeley.edu/003-introduction-sociocultural-anthropology-0.

Cole, David. "Agon at Agora: Creative Misreadings in the First Amendment Tradition," *Yale L.J.* 95 (1986): 857, 863.

Com. of Pa. v. Local Union No. 542, Int'l Union of Operating Engineers, 347 F. Supp. 268, 299–301 (E.D. Pa. 1972), *aff'd sub nom. Com. of Pa. v. Local Union 542, Int'l Union of Operating Engineers*, 478 F.2d 1398 (3d Cir. 1973).

Compare with the European Union's definition of tax avoidance. Weber, Dennis. *Tax Avoidance and The EC Treaty Freedoms* (2005) 166–235.

Conley, John M. and William M. O'Barr. "Back to the Trobriands: The Enduring Influence of Malinowski's Crime and Custom in Savage Society," *Law & Social Inquiry* 27, no. 4 (2002): 847–874, 858.

Conn, Steven. *History's Shadow: Native Americans and Historical Consciousness in the Nineteenth Century* (The University of Chicago Press, 2004), 215.

Connelly, Andrew James. *Counting Coconuts: Patrol Reports from the Trobriand Islands, Part I: 1907-1934* (2007) 9.

Cook, Derek and Jennie K. Martin. "Oil and Gas Basics Understanding the Sticks to Avoid Stones and Broken Bones," *Tex. B.J.* 76 (2013): 319.

Cottani, G. Transfer Pricing, Topical Analyses IBFD (accessed 3 Mar. 2017). *See.* 1.45 and 9.10 of TP Guidelines.

Cottani, G. Transfer Pricing, Topical Analyses IBFD (accessed 3 Mar. 2017).

Cottrol, Robert J. "Normative Nominalism: The Paradox of Egalitarian Law in Inegalitarian Cultures - Some Lessons from Recent Latin American Historiography," *Tulane Law Review* 81 (2007): 891–892 (noting that such an article needs a basis in definition of culture as a premise for use throughout the article).

Covitz, Akiba. "The Soul of the Polity: Beginnings of American Constitutional Thought," n.d. Accessed May 16, 2021. https://repository.upenn.edu/dissertations/AAI9926112/.

Crito 46 B (one of the passages which the Christian apologists used to prove that Socrates knew the λόγος), *Theaetetus* 186 C ἀναλογίσματα πρός τε οὐσίαν καὶ ὠφέλειαν, and *Laws* 644 D. Aristotle *Eth.* 1139 a 12 somewhat differently.""

Cudahy, Hon. Richard D. "Retail Wheeling: Is This Revolution Necessary?," *Energy L. J.* 15 (1994): 351, 356.

Daloz, Jean-Pascal. "Elite Distinction: Grand Theory and Comparative Perspectives," *Comparative Sociology* 6, no. 1–2 (2007): 27–74, 27–28.

Daly, Martin et al. "Kinship: The Conceptual Hole in Psychological Studies of Social Cognition and Close Relationships," in *Evolutionary Social Psychology* (Jeffry A. Simpson and Douglas T. Kenrick eds., Lawrence Erlbaum Associates, Inc., 1997).

Dane, Perry. "Jurisdictionality, Time, and the Legal Imagination," *Hofstra L. Rev.* 23 (1994): 1, 94.

Dane, Perry. "Jurisdictionality, Time, and the Legal Imagination," *Hofstra L. Rev.* 23 (1994): 1, 94.

Davenport, William. "Nonunilinear Descent and Descent Groups," *American Anthropologist* 61 (1959): 557, 560.

Davis, Kingsley and Wilbert E. Moore. "Some Principles of Stratification: A Critical Analysis: Reply," *American Sociological Review* 18, no. 4 (1953): 394–397, 247–248.

Davis, Tessa. "Reproducing Value: How Tax Law Differentially Values Fertility, Sexuality & Marriage," *Cardozo J.L. & Gender* 19 (2012): 1, 32.

Dawkins, Richard. *The Selfish Gene* 192 (1989).

Dawson, John. *Logical Dilemmas: The Life and Work of Kurt Gödel* (Wellesley, MA: A. K. Peters, 2005).

De Beers Consolidated Mines Ltd. v. Howe, [1906] AC 455, 458 (HL).

Debelva, F. and J. Luts, "The European Commission's Proposal for Double Taxation Dispute Resolution: Turning the Tide?," *Bull. Intl. Taxn.* 71 (2017): 5, Journals IBFD.

Dennett, Daniel C. *Consciousness Explained* (1991).

Dharmapala, Dhammika. *Base Erosion and Profit Shifting: A Simple Conceptual Framework* (Univ. of Chi. Law Sch. Coase-Sandor Inst. for Law & Econ., Working Paper No. 703, 2015), http://ssrn.com/abstract=2497770.

Dharmapala, Dhammika. *What Do We Know About Base Erosion and Profit Shifting? A Review of the Empirical Literature* (Univ. of Chi. Law Sch., Coase-Sandor Inst. for Law & Econ., Working Paper No. 702, 2014), http://ssrn.com/abstract =2373549.

Dignan, Michael. "Of Experimentology: A Genealogical Deconstruction of Invention in Patent Law's Enablement Requirement," *Wake Forest J. Bus. & Intell. Prop. L.* 18 (2017): 40, 56 n.115.

Dimock, Wai Chee. "Rethinking Space, Rethinking Rights: Literature, Law, Science," *Yale J.L. & Human.* 10 (1998): 487, 493–494.

Dimock, Wai Chee. "Tenth Anniversary Symposium: New Direction: Rethinking Space, Rethinking Rights: Literature, Law, Science," *Yale J.L. & Human.* 10 (1998): 487, 493–494.

Doernberg, Richard L. "The U.S.-India Income Tax Treaty: Breaking New Ground in Taxing Services Income from Licensing Technology," *Tax Law.* 44 (1991): 735.

Donnelly v. United States, 228 U.S. 243, 273 (1913):

Dumézil, Georges. *Archaic Roman Religion* (1966) 585.

Dumézil, Georges. *Archaic Roman Religion* (Baltimore: Johns Hopkins University Press, 1970).

Dumézil, Georges. *Flamen-Brahman* (1935).

Dumézil, Georges. *Mitra-Varuna: An Essay on Two Indo-European Representations of Sovereignty* (Derek Coltman trans., 2d ed. 1988).

Durst, Michael C. and Robert E. Culbertson. "Clearing Away the Sand: Retrospective Methods and Prospective Documentation in Transfer Pricing Today," *Tax L. Rev.* 57 (2003): 37, 58.

Dusenbury, D. L. "The Judgment of Pontius Pilate: A Critique of Giorgio Agamben," *J.L. & Religion* 32 (2017): 340.

Duxbury, Neil. *Patterns of American Jurisprudence* (New York: Oxford University Press, 1995), ch. 2.

Dworkin, Ronald. *A Matter of Principle* (1985) 146.

Economic Cooperation Act of 1948 (62 Stat. 137).

Edwards, Impact. Phil. *The Reason Every Meme Uses That One Font*, VOX (July 26, 2015), http://www.vox.com/2015/7/26/9036993/meme-font-impact [https://perma.cc/k2dr-xw3E].

Edwards, Linda H. "Once Upon a Time in Law: Myth, Metaphor, and Authority," *Tenn. L. Rev.* 77 (2009): 883, 916.

Elkins, David. "Horizontal Equity as a Principle of Tax Theory," *Yale L. & Pol'y Rev.* 24 (2006): 43.

Ellickson, Robert C. and Charles Dia. "Thorland, Ancient Land Law: Mesopotamia, Egypt, Israel," *Chi.-Kent L. Rev.* 71 (1995): 321, 375.

Elliott, John Huxtable. *Imperial Spain 1469-1716* (2002) 17.

Elwell, Frank W. "Marvin Harris on the Universal Structure of Soceities." *Socio-Cultural Systems*. Accessed May 18, 2021. http://www.faculty.rsu.edu/users/f/felwell/www/theorists/essays/harris1.htm; *see also* Taylor, Steve. *The Madness of Materialism, Psychol. Today* 55 Accessed May 18, 2021. https://www.psychologytoday.com/blog/out-the-darkness/201203/the-madness-materialism.

Ely, John Hart. *Democracy and Distrust: A Theory of Judicial Review* 1 (1980) ("interpretivism").

Encountering Jung: Jung on Mythology 39–40 (Robert A. Segal ed., 1998).*English Historical Documents*, 2nd ed., Vol. 2 (David C. Douglass and G. W. Greenaway eds., London: Oxford University Press, 1981).

Eskridge Jr., William N. and Philip P. Frickey. "Statutory Interpretation as Practical Reasoning," *Stan. L. Rev.* 42 (1990).

Esq., *Ruminations Mighty Oaths*, Vt. B.J., Spring 2005, at 17, 2005.

Ewen, Stuart. *All Consuming Images: The Politics of Style in Contemporary Culture* (1999) 4.

Filmer, Paul, Chris Jenks, Clive Seale, and David Walsh. "Developments In Social Theory," *Researching Society and Culture* 2 (2004): 33–46, 33.

Fisher, Bruce D. "The Ethical Consumer: A Rejecter of Positive Law Arbitrage," *Seton Hall L. Rev.* 25 (1994): 230, 245.

Flaherty, John P., and Maureen E. Lally-Green. "The European Union: Where is it Now," *Duq. L. Rev.* 34 (1995): 923, 930.

Fletcher Cyc. Corp.

Flood, Robert and Peter Garber. *Speculative Bubbles, Speculative Attacks and Policy Switching* (1994).

Ford, Richard Thompson. "Bourgeois Communities: A Review of Gerald Frug's City Making," *Stanford Law Review* 56 (2004 2003): 231, 232.

Fortuna, Julian A. and Todd D. Radde, "Transfer Pricing Adjustment Challenges Receive Green Light from the Tax Court," *J. Tax'n* 125 (2016): 223, 225 WL 6915865, 4.

Fortuna, Julian A. and Todd D. Radde. "Transfer Pricing Adjustment Challenges Receive Green Light from the Tax Court," *J. Tax'n* 125 (2016): 223, 226 WL 6915865, 6. Transfer Pricing Cases Update, 27 *J. Int'l Tax'n* 30, 35, 2016 WL 7116202, 6.

Foster, Sydney. "Should Courts Give Stare Decisis Effect to Statutory Interpretation Methodology?," *Geo. L.J.* 96 (2008): 1863.

Frazer, James G. *The Golden Bough: A Study in Magic and Religion* 412 (abr. ed. 1940).

Frazer, James George. *The Golden Bough* (1922).

Frazer, Sir James. *The Golden Bough* (1922).

Fred, Spier. "How Big History Works: Energy Flows and the Rise and Demise of Complexity," *Social Evolution & History* 4, no. 1 (2005): 30, 49.

Freud, S. "The Ego and the Id," in 19 *The Standard Edition of the Complete Psychological Works of the Complete Psychological Works of Sigmund Freud* (J. Strachey ed. 1951) 3.

Freud, Sigmund. The Ego and the Id (1923), in *The Standard Edition of the Complete Psychological Works of Sigmund Freud* (James Strachey ed. and trans., 1961) 3, 25.

Fried, Michael S. "The Evolution of Legal Concepts: The Memetic Perspective," *Jurimetrics J.* 39 (1999): 291, 292.

Fried, Michael S. "The Evolution of Legal Concepts: The Memetic Perspective," *Jurimetrics J.* 39 (1999): 291, 300–301.

Frost, Tom. "Agamben's Sovereign Legalization of Foucault," *Oxford J Legal Studies* 30, no. 3 (2010): 545.

Frye, Northrop. *Anatomy of Criticism* 136 (1957)

Fukuyama, Francis. "The End of History?," *Nat'l Interest*, Summer 1989, at 7–18; *see generally* Afilalo, Ari and Dennis Patterson. "Statecraft, Trade and the Order of States," *Chi. J. Int'l L.* 6 (2006): 725, 726 n.5.

Fukuyama, Francis. *The End of History and the Last Man* (1992).

Gabel, Peter. *Taking Rights Seriously by Ronald Dworkin* (Cambridge, MA: Harvard University Press, 1977), pp. Xv, 293. $12.00., *Harv. L. Rev.* 91 (1977) 302, 303–304.

Garbarino, Carlo and Giulio Allevato, "The Global Architecture of Financial Regulatory Taxes," *Mich. J. Int'l L.* 36 (2015): 603, 648.

Garbarino, Merwyn S. *Sociocultural Theory in Anthropology: A Short History* (1983) 32–34.

Garnaat, Maxwell M. The Republic of Virtue: The Republican Ideal in British and American Property Law, *Cornell Int'l LJ* 51 (2018): 731, 735.

Garner, Bryan A. "Making Peace in the Language Wars," *Green Bag* 2d 7 (2004): 227.

Garner, Bryan A. *If You Care About Language, Consider Yourself a SNOOT, STUDENT LAW*, Nov. 2006 (citing Wallace's Harper's Magazine as it appears in David Foster Wallace, Consider the Lobster (2005)).

Geertz, Clifford and Michael Banton. *Religion as a Cultural System* (1966) 1.

Geertz, Clifford. *Works and Lives: The Anthropologist as Author* (1988) 56–57.

Geoffrey of Monmouth, *History of the Kings of Britain* (Aaron Thompson, J. A. Gilestrans., E.P. Dutton & Co. 1958) (1138-39). Wikisource contributors, "Six Old English Chronicles/Geoffrey's British History/Book 2," *Wikisource*, https://en.wikisource.org/w/index.php?title=six_old_english_chronicles/geoffrey%27s_british_history/book_2&oldid=9052503 (accessed May 29, 2021).

Gershenhorn, Jerry. *Melville J. Herskovits and the Racial Politics of Knowledge* (2004) 93–94.

Ghizoni, Sandra Kollen. *Reserve Bank Organization Committee Announces Selection of Reserve Bank Cities and District Boundaries*, FED. RES. HIST., http://www.federalreservehistory.org/events/detailview/16.

Ghosh, Abhik. *Cultural Evolution* (2007) 16; see Peter Laska, *Left Curve* (2000) 24.

Gienapp, Jonathan. "Historicism and Holism: Failures of Originalist Translation," *Fordham L. Rev.* 84 (2015): 935, 947.

Gil, Paul. *What Is a "Meme"? What Are Examples of Modern Internet Memes?*, ABOUT TECH, http://netforbeginners.about.com/od/weirdwebculture/f/what-is-an-internet-meme.htm [http://perma.cc/lfg4-nmjn]. Videos and graphic images like the "Rickroll," *Rickroll*, KNOW YOUR MEME, http://knowyourmeme.com/memes/rickroll [https://perma.cc/wze7-q9m3], the "Numa Numa Guy," *Numa Numa*, KNOW YOUR MEME, http://knowyourmeme.com/memes/numa-numa [https://perma.cc/y4mx-rjg4].

Gluck, Abbe R. "Imperfect Statutes, Imperfect Courts: Understanding Congress's Plan in the Era of Unorthodox Lawmaking," *Harv. L. Rev.* 129 (2015): 62, 63.

Gluck, Abbe R. "The States as Laboratories of Statutory Interpretation: Methodological Consensus and the New Modified Textualism," *The Yale Law Journal* (2010): 1750–1862, 1754.

Gluck, Abbe R. "The States as Laboratories of Statutory Interpretation: Methodological Consensus and the New Modified Textualism," *The Yale Law Journal* (2010): 1750–1862, 1754 fn. 8.

Goldberg, Daniel S. "I Do Not Think It Means What You Think It Means: How Kripke and Wittgenstein's Analysis on Rule Following Undermines Justice Scalia's Textualism and Originalism," *Clev. St. L. Rev.* 54 (2006): 273, 274–275.

Goldman, William. *The Princess Bride: S. Morgenstern's Classic Tale of True Love and High Adventure* (1973).

Gonzalez, Carlos E. "Reinterpreting Statutory Interpretation," *NCL Rev.* 74 (1995): 585, 586.

Gordley, James. "The Method of the Roman Jurists," *Tul. L. Rev.* 87 (2012): 933, 947 fn. 73 (2013).

Gordley, James. "The Method of the Roman Jurists," *Tul. L. Rev.* 87 (2013): 933, 947 n.73.

Graetz, Michael J. "Retroactivity Revisited," *Harv. L. Rev.* 98 (1985): 1820, 1841 fn. 82.

Graetz, Michael J. and Michael M. O'Hear. "The "Original Intent" of U.S. International Taxation," *Duke L.J.* 46 (1997): 1021, 1023.

Grande, Albert. "Education as a Natural Right," *John's J. Legal Comment* 21 (2006): 53, 53–56.

Green, Leon. "The Negligence Issue," *The Yale Law Journal* 37, no. 8 (1928): 1029–1047, 1043.

Greenblatt, Stephen. *The Swerve: How the World Became Modern.*

Greenfield, Patricia M. "Three Approaches to the Psychology of Culture: Where do They Come From? Where Can They Go?" *Asian Journal of Social Psychology* 3 (2000): 223, 228.

Gregory, Kathleen L. "Native-View Paradigms: Multiple Cultures and Culture Conflicts in Organizations," *Administrative Science Quarterly* 28 (1983): 359, 359–376.

Grey v. Pearson, 6 H. of L. Cas. 106; Wigram on Extrinsic Evidence, §§ 10-14; 1 Jarman on Wills, 6th Am. ed., 413.

Grey, Thomas C. "Holmes and Legal Pragmatism," *Stan. L. Rev.* 41 (1989): 787, 861.

Grey, Thomas. "Do We Have an Unwritten Constitution?," *Stan. L. Rev.* 27 (1975): 703, 706 ("interpretive model").

Grinberg, Itai. "The New International Tax Diplomacy," *Geo. L.J.* 104 (2016): 1137, 1140.

Grinberg, Itai. *Breaking BEPS: The New International Tax Diplomacy*, Geo. L. J. (forthcoming), http://ssrn.com/abstract=2652894.

Grofman, Bernard and Janet Landa. *Social Networks* (1983) 347–348.

Grossman, Lewis A. "Langdell Upside-Down: James Coolidge Carter and the Anticlassical Jurisprudence of Anticodification," *Yale J.L. & Human.* 19 (2007): 149, 150.

Guthrie, W.K.C. *A History of Greek Philosophy* (Cambridge Univ. Press, 1962) 419–434.

Hackney, James R. "The Intellectual Origins of American Strict Products Liability: A Case Study in American Pragmatic Instrumentalism," *The American Journal of Legal History* 39, no. 4 (1995): 443, 445.

Hackney, James R. "The Intellectual Origins of American Strict Products Liability: A Case Study in American Pragmatic Instrumentalism," *The American Journal of Legal History* 39, no. 4 (1995): 443, 445.

Hafkenscheid, R. "The BEPS Report on Risk Allocation: Not so Functional," *Intl. Transfer Pricing J.* 24 (2017): 1, Journals IBFD.

Halberstam, Daniel. "Of Power and Responsibility: The Political Morality of Federal Systems," *Virginia Law Review* (2004): 731–834, 740.

Hamburger, Philip A. "Natural Rights, Natural Law, and American Constitutions," *Yale Law Journal* (1993): 907–960.

Hamilton, Neil, and Jeff Maleska. "Helping Students Develop Affirmative Evidence of Cross-Cultural Competency," *Scholar: St. Mary's Law Review on Race and Social Justice* 19 (2017 2016): 187, 197.

Handelman, Gwen Thayer. "Law and Order Comes to "Dodge City": Treasury's New Return Preparer and IRS Practice Standards," *Wash. & Lee L. Rev.* 50 (1993): 631.

Hanke, Lewis. *Bartolomé De Las Casas: An Interpretation of His Life and Writings* (2013) 6.

Hansmann, Henry. "How Close Is the End of History?," *J. Corp. L.* 31 (2006): 745, 749.

Harris, Marvin. *The Rise of Anthropological Theory* (1968).

Harris, Marvin. *Theories of Culture in Postmodern Times* (1999) 46–47.

Hart, H. L. A. *The Concept of Law* (2d ed. Year) Hart, H. L. A. (1961). *The Concept of Law* (2nd ed. / with a postscript edited by Penelope A. Bulloch and Joseph Raz.) (Oxford: Clarendon Press). Ch.VII; *see* Leiter, Brian. "American Legal Realism," in *The Blackwell Guide to the Philosophy of Law and Legal Theory* (Martin P. Golding and William A. Edmundson eds., Oxford: Blackwell, 2005) 50.

Hawkes, Christopher. *Archeological Theory and Method: Some Suggestions from the Old World* (1954) 155–168.

Head Money Cases, 112 U.S. 580, 599 (1884); *The Cherokee Tobacco*, 78 U.S. (11 Wall.) 616, 621 (1870); Restatement (Third).

Healy, Thomas. "Stare Decisis as a Constitutional Requirement," *W. Va. L. Rev.* 104 (2001): 43, 56–62. *Petersen*, 484 Mich. at 314.

Healy, Thomas. "Stare Decisis as a Constitutional Requirement," *W. Va. L. Rev.* 104 (2001): 43, 56–57.

Healy, Thomas. "Stare Decisis as a Constitutional Requirement," *W. Va. L. Rev.* 104 (2001): 43, 56–62.

Hegel, G.W.F. *Elements of the Philosophy of Right* (Allen W. Wood ed., H.B. Nisbet trans., Cambridge Univ. Press, 1991) 26.

Hegel, G.W.F. *Phenomenology of Spirit* (A.V. Miller trans., 1977) § 788, at 589.

Hegel, G.W.F. *Phenomenology of Spirit*, translated by A.V. Miller with analysis of the text and foreword by J. N. Findlay; Paragraph 179, Pg. 111 (Oxford: Clarendon Press, 1977).

Hegel, G.W.F. *The Phenomenology of Mind* (William Wallace trans., 1894) § 564.

Hegel, Georg Wilhelm Friedrich. *The Logic. Encyclopaedia of the Philosophical Sciences*. 2nd Edition (London: Oxford University Press. §108. 1874).

Hegel, Georg Wilhelm Friedrich. *The Philosophy of History* (J. Sibree trans., 1956) 43–44.

Hegeman, Susan. *Patterns for America: Modernism and the Concept of Culture* (1999) 9.

Helferich, Gerard. *Stone of Kings: In Search of the Lost Jade of the Maya* (2012) 330.

Hellerstein, Jerome R. "Federal Income Taxation of Multinationals: Replacement of Separate Accounting with Formulary Apportionment," *Tax Notes Int'l*, Aug. 24, 1993, at 163, available in LEXIS, Taxria Library, TNI file.

Helvering v. F. & R. Lazarus & Co., 308 U.S. 252, 255, 60 S. Ct. 209, 210–11, 84 L. Ed. 226 (1939).

Henkin, Louis. "The Constitution and United States Sovereignty: A Century of Chinese Exclusion and Its Progeny," *Harv. L. Rev.* 100 (1987): 853, 886 fn. 62.

Henshilwood, Christopher S., Curtis W. Marean, Philip Chase, Iain Davidson, Clive Gamble, Trenton W. Holliday, Richard G. Klein et al. "The Origin of Modern Human Behavior: Critique of the Models and Their Test Implications," *Current Anthropology* 44, no. 5 (2003): 627–651, 636.

Herman, Arthur. "The Cave and the Light (2013). *Cf.* Paul Johnson," *Modern Times* (rev. ed. 1991).

Herman, Shael. "Legacy and Legend: The Continuity of Roman and English Regulation of the Jews," *Tul. L. Rev.* 66 (1991): 1781, 1797.

Herman, Shael. "Legacy and Legend: The Continuity of Roman and English Regulation of the Jews," *Tul. L. Rev.* 66 (1992): 1781, 1797.

Hermann, Donald H. J. "Phenomenology, Structuralism, Hermeneutics, and Legal Study: Applications of Contemporary Continental Thought to Legal Phenomena," *U. Miami L. Rev.* 36 (1982): 379, 390–391.

Hershovitz, Scott. "Wittgenstein on Rules: The Phantom Menace," *Oxford J. of Leg. Stud.* 22 (2002): 619, 639–640.

Heylighen, Francis and Klaas Chielens. "Evolution of Culture, Memetics," in *Encyclopedia of Complexity and System Science* 3205, 3205 (Robert Meyers ed., 2009).

Hildabrand, Clark. "The Geographic (Un)representativeness of the Federal Reserve Board of Governors," *Yale L. & Pol'y Rev.* 34 (2015): 155, 185 n. 2014.

Hilligan, Marion and Nelson P. Miller. "Don Petersen & Chris Hastings, SYMPOSIUM ISSUE: World Views Collide: A Dialogue on State-Authored Embryonic Stem-Cell Research, Human Enhancements, Physician-Assisted Suicide and the Value of Life: Superhuman-Biotechnology's Emerging Impact on the Law," *T.M. Cooley L. Rev.* 24 (2007): 1, 25–26.

Hinkle, Thornton M. "Magna Charta," *Yale L.J.* 8 (1899): 262, 264–265.

Hinsley, Curtis M. "Scott Michaelson. The Limits of Multiculturalism: Interrogating the Origins of American Anthropology. xxviii+ 245 pp., bibl., index. Minneapolis: University of Minnesota Press, 1999. $49.95." (2003).

Hirshman, Linda R. "The Virtue of Liberality in American Communal Life," *Mich. L. Rev.* 88 (1990): 983, 1000–1001.

History of Cuba. "Bartolomé De Las Casas." Accessed May 18, 2021. http://www.historyofcuba.com/history/oriente/LasCasas.htm.

Hobbs, Jr., Justice Gregory J. "Poetry," *U. Denv. Water L. Rev.* 18 (2014): 154, 160.

Hobbs, Patrick E. "Entity Classification: The One Hundred-Year Debate," *Cath. U. L. Rev.* 44 (1995): 437, 441.

Hockett, Robert. "The Deep Grammar of Distribution: A Meta-Theory of Justice," *Cardozo L. Rev.* 26 (2004): 1179, 1190–1191 (2005).

Hofstadter, Douglas R. *Gödel, Escher, Bach: An Eternal Golden Braid* (1979)—Hofstede, Geert. "The Cultural Relativity of the Quality of Life Concept," *Academy of Management Review* 9, no. 3 (1984): 389–398, 389.

Holmes, Jr., Oliver Wendell. "The Path of the Law," *Harvard Law Review* 10 (1897): 457.

Holmes, Jr., Oliver Wendell. *The Common Law* (Mark DeWolfe Howe ed., Harvard Univ. Press, 1963) (1881).

Holmes, Oliver Wendell. "The Path of the Law," *Harvard Law Review* 110, no. 5 (1997): 991–1009.

Horwitz, Morton J. and Mark Tushnet. "Legal Historian," *Geo. L.J.* 90 (2001): 131, 131–132.

Hume, David. *Treatise of Human Nature* (1739) § 3.1.1.

Hussain, Murad. "Defending the Faithful: Speaking the Language of Group Harm in Free Exercise Challenges to Counterterrorism Profiling," *Yale L.J.* 117 (2008): 920, 969.

IBFD, Glossary, Technical Assistance Fees. Accessed September 27, 2016 at 6:07 PM.

In re Friesenhahn, 169 B.R. 615, 637 (Bankr. W.D. Tex. 1994).

In regards to gift giving cultures. Malinowski, Bronislaw. *Argonauts of the Western Pacific* (Routledge, 1961) (1922) 72–76.

Inglehart, Ronald and Christian Welzel. *Modernization, Cultural Change, and Democracy: The Human Development Sequence* (Cambridge University Press, 2005), 47, 47–48.

Jakobson, Roman, and Franz Boas. "Franz Boas' Approach to Language," *International Journal of American Linguistics* 10, no. 4 (1944): 188–195.

James Adam, "The Republic of Plato, Book 4, Section 439E." Accessed May 19, 2021. http://www.perseus.tufts.edu/hopper/text?doc=Perseus%3Atext%3A1999.04.0094%3Abook%3D4%3Asection%3D439e.

James, Allison. *Handbook of Ethnography* (2001) 246–257.

Jefferson, Thomas. *Jefferson's Manual of Parliamentary Practice* (1801), reprinted in Rules of the House of Representatives, H.R. Doc. No. 279, 99th Cong., 2d Sess. (1987).

Jinks, Derek P. "Essays in Refusal: Pre-Theoretical Commitments in Postmodern Anthropology and Critical Race Theory," *Yale L.J.* 107 (1997): 499, 499–500.

Jogarajan, Sunita. "Stamp, Seligman and the Drafting of the 1923 Experts' Report on Double Taxation," *World Tax J.* 5 (2013): 368.

John Hancock Life Ins. Co. (U.S.A.) v. C.I.R., 141 T.C. 1, 150 (2013).

Johnson v. United States, 135 S. Ct. 2551, 2562 (2015).

Johnson, George. *A Fire in the Mind: Science, Faith, and the Search for Order* 308–16 (1996).

Johnston, James B. "The Bridge Connecting Pontius Pilate's Sentencing of Jesus to the New Jersey Death Penalty Study Commission's Concerns over Executing the Innocent: When Humans Beings with Inherently Human Flaws Determine Guilt or Innocence, and Life or Death," *Rutgers J. L. & Religion* 10 (2009): 15 fn. 118.

Joint Committee on Taxation, Background, Summary, and Implications of the OECD/G20 Base Erosion and Profit Shifting Project (JCX-139-15), November 30, 2015. This document can also be found on the Joint Committee on Taxation website at www.jct.gov.

Jung, C.G. *The Archetypes and the Collective Unconscious 4-5* (R.F.C. Hull trans., Princeton Univ. Press 2d ed., 1980) (1934).

Justice Crucified: The Story of Sacco and Vanzetti by Roberta Strauss Feuerlicht (New York: Mcgraw-Hill Book Co., 1977), pp. Xviii, 480. $15.00., 92 *Harv. L. Rev.* 781 (1979).

Kampelman, Max M. "Entering New Worlds: A Challenge," *Colum. J. Transnat'l L.* 32 (1995): 457, 458.

Kant, Immanuel. *Critique of Pure Reason* (1781).

Kant, Immanuel. *Prolegomena to Any Future Metaphysics [1783]* (Lewis W. Beck ed. and trans., Bobbs-Merrill: Indianapolis, 1985).

Kar, Robin Bradley. "The Deep Structure of Law and Morality," *Tex. L. Rev.* 84 (2006): 877, 903.

Kar, Robin Bradley. "Western Legal Prehistory: Reconstructing the Hidden Origins of Western Law and Civilization," *U. Ill. L. Rev.* (2012).

Karajan, Herbert von. Beethoven 9 Symphonien DGG (1962).

Karlan, Pamela S. "Foreword: Democracy and Disdain, The Supreme Court 2011 Term," *Harv. L. Rev.* 126 (2012): 1–45, 5.

Kelso, R. Randall. "Statutory Interpretation Doctrine on the Modern Supreme Court and Four Doctrinal Approaches to Judicial Decision-Making," *Pepp. L. Rev.* 25 (1997): 37.

Keohane, Robert O. "Reciprocity in International Relations," *International Organization* (1986): 1–27.

Kerpel, Diana Magaloni. *The Colors of the New World: Artists, Materials, and the Creation of the Florentine Codex* (2014) 55.

Kesavan, Vasan. "The Three Tiers of Federal Law," *Nw. U. L. Rev.* 100 (2006): 1479, 1635.

Kirk, Jerome and Marc L. Miller. *Reliability and Validity in Qualitative Research* (1986) 35.

Klagge, James Carl. *Wittgenstein: Biography and Philosophy* (2001).

Kleene, S. C. "General Recursive Functions of Natural Numbers," *Mathematische Annalen* 112 (1936): 727.

Kocourek, Lezioni Di Filosofia Del Diritto. by Giorgio Del Vecchio. Città Di Castello, Società Anonima Tipographica "Leonardo Da Vinci", *1930. Pp. IV, 351, Yale L.J.* 40 (1931) 1129, 1130.

Koepping, Klaus-Peter. *Fieldwork and Footnotes: Studies in the History of European Anthropology* (1995) 75.

Komter, Aafke. "Gifts And Social Relations: The Mechanisms of Reciprocity," *International Sociology* 22, no. 1 (2007): 93–107, 96.

Kuper, Adam. *Anthropology and Anthropologists: The Modern British School* (3rd ed. 1996), 1–34.

Land, Stephen B. "Treaty Consistency," *Tax Law* 66 (2012): 113, 120.

Law and Asylum: Space, Subject, Resistance by Simon Behrman (2018).

Law, David S. "Constitutional Archetypes," *Tex. L. Rev.* 95 (2016): 153, 160–161.

Layton, Robert. *An Introduction to Theory in Anthropology* (1997) 38.

Leaf, Murray J. *Pragmatism and Development: The Prospect for Pluralist Transformation in the Third World* (1998) 20.

LeDuc, André. "Making the Premises about Constitutional Meaning Express: The New Originalism and Its Critics," *BYU J. Pub. L.* 31 (2016): 111, 199.

Leiter, Brian. "Legal Realisms, Old and New," *Valparaiso University Law Review* 47, no. 4 (2014): 67–81, 949–950.

Leiter, Brian. "American Legal Realism," in *The Blackwell Guide to the Philosophy of Law and Legal Theory* (Martin P. Golding and William A. Edmundson eds., Wiley, 2005) 60.

Leonard, Thomas C. "Origins of the Myth of Social Darwinism: The Ambiguous Legacy of Richard Hofstadter's Social Darwinism in American Thought," *Journal of Economic Behavior & Organization* 71, no. 1 (2009): 37–51, 39.

Lesser, Alexander. "Evolution In Social Anthropology," *Southwestern Journal of Anthropology* 8, no. 2 (1952): 134–146, 135.

Lessig, Lawrence. 1998. "The New Chicago School," *The Journal of Legal Studies* 27 (S2): 661–691, 662. (noting that this adaptation is based in the concept of "trust" whereby "[t]he ultimate effect of the law is to provide entrustors with incentives to enter into fiduciary relationships, by reducing entrustors' risks and costs of preventing abuse of entrusted power, and of ensuring quality fiduciary services."); *see generally* Reich-Graefe, Rene. "Deconstructing Corporate Governance: The Mechanics of Trusting," *Delaware Journal of Corporate Law* 38 (2013): 103, 190.

Leviathan, Thomas Hobbes. Chapter xxiv of the Nutrition and Procreation of a Commonwealth.

LeVine, Robert A. and Karin Norman. "The Infant's Acquisition of Culture: Early Attachment Reexamined in Anthropological Perspective," *The Psychology of Cultural Experience* (Carmella C. Moore and Holly F. Mathews eds., Cambridge University Press, 2001), 83–104.

Levinson, Sanford. "Taking Law Seriously: Reflections on "Thinking Like a Lawyer"," *Stan. L. Rev.* 30 (1978): 1071, 1109 fn. 126.

Lévi-Strauss, Claude. *Structural Anthropology* (1963) 35–36.

Lévi-Strauss, Claude. *Structural Anthropology* (C. Jacobson and B. Schoepf trans., 1963).

Lewis, Andrew D. "The Ever-Protruding Stick in the Bundle: The Accommodation of Groundwater Rights in Texas Oil and Gas," *Tex. A&M L. Rev.* 2 (2014): 79, 86–87.

Lewis, Diane. "Anthropology and Colonialism," *Current Anthropology* 14 (1973): 581, 586–588.

Lewis, Herbert S. et al. *Current Anthropology* (2001) 381–406.

Liddell & Scott's famous lexicon in legal secondary sources: Clark, Randall Baldwin. "Platonic Love in a Colorado Courtroom: Martha Nussbaum, John Finnis, and Plato's Laws in Evans v. Romer," *Yale J. L. & Humanities* 12 (2000): 1, 5–6.

Linck, Alice E. Meyer. *The Psychological Basis of Hazlitt's Criticism* (1960) (Ph.D. Dissertation, University of Kansas).

Linck, Jr., Charles Edward. The Development of Evelyn Waugh's Career: 1903-1939 (1962) (Ph.D. Dissertation, University of Kansas).

Lincoln IV, Charles Edward Andrew. "Hegelian Dialectical Analysis of US Voting Laws," *U. Dayton L. Rev.* 42 (2017): 87, 111 fn. 31.

Lincoln IV, Charles Edward Andrew. "Is Incorporation Really Better than Central Management and Control for Testing Corporate Residency: An Answer to Corporate Tax Evasion and Inversion," *Ohio NUL Rev.* 43 (2017): 359.

Lincoln IV, Charles Edward Andrew. "Hegelian Dialectical Analysis of U.S. Voting Laws," *U. Dayton L. Rev.* 42 (2017): 87, 91.

Lincoln IV, Charles Edward Andrew. *Amazon Inc., BEPS, and the New Method of Risk Allocation Comparing U.S. Jurisprudence and OECD Approaches to Risk Allocation in the Post-BEPS Era of Transfer Pricing*, University of Amsterdam LL.M. Thesis for Advanced Masters in International Tax Law Final Version – July 27, 2017 Supervisors: Hein Vermeulen And Rutger Hafkenscheid.

Lincoln IV, Charles Edward Andrew. Amazon, Medtronic, the OECD on Risk Analysis: Thesis on Transfer Pricing. No. 3fs5x. Center for Open Science, 2017.

Lincoln IV, Charles Edward Andrew. *Are International Tax Treaties Compatible with Controlled Foreign Corporation (CFC) Rules? A Technical and a Political History Approach for a Normative Result*, A Thesis Submitted in partial fulfillment of the requirements of the degree of Master of Laws in Tax at Boston University by Charles Edward Andrew Lincoln IV Adviser: Richard T. Ainsworth (2018). On file with author.

Lincoln IV, Charles Edward Andrew. *Can Sovereign Nations Achieve Uniformity of Transnational Tax Laws?*, A Thesis Submitted in partial fulfillment of the requirements of the degree of Master of Laws in Tax at Boston University by Charles Edward Andrew Lincoln IV Adviser: Richard T. Ainsworth (2018). On file with author.

Lincoln, Charles E. "The Chronology of Chichen Itza: A Review of the Literature," in *Late Lowland Maya Civilization: Classic to Postclassic*, ed. Jeremy A. Sabloff and E. Wyllys Andrews V (Albuquerque: University of New Mexico Press, 1986), 141–156.

Lincoln, Charles E. *Ethnicity and Social Organization at Chichen Itza, Yucatan, Mexico.* (PhD. dissertation, Department of Anthropology, Harvard University) Advisors Mathews, Peter, and Gordon R. Willey. (1990).

Lincoln, Charles Edward. *Ethnicity and Social Organization at Chichen Itza, Yucatan, Mexico*. Harvard University, 1990. (PhD. dissertation, Department of Anthropology, Harvard University) Advisors Mathews, Peter, and Gordon R. Willey. (1990).

Lincoln, Charles. "A Brief Historical Sketch of an Anthropological Analysis of the Development of International and Comparative Law," *Fla. Coastal L. Rev.* 19 (2019): 221.

Lincoln, Charles. "A Structural Etiology of the US Constitution," *J. Legis.* 43 (2016): 122.

Lincoln, Charles. "A Structural Etiology of the US Constitution," *J. Legis.* 43 (2016): 22.

Lincoln, Charles. "A Structural Etiology of the US Constitution," *J. Legis.* 43 (2016): 122, 131. *See. United States IRS v. Osborne* (*In re* Osborne), 76 F.3d 306, 309 (9th Cir. 1996).

Lincoln, Charles. "A Structural Etiology of the US Constitution," *J. Legis.* 43 (2016): 122, 131.

Lincoln, Charles. "A Structural Etiology of the US Constitution," *J. Legis.* 43 (2016): 122, 131 fn. 51.

Lind, Douglas. "Constitutional Adjudication as a Craft-Bound Excellence," *Yale Journal of Law & the Humanities* 6 (1994): 353, 363–365 (emphasis added by author).

Lind, Timothy Christian. *The Movement of Gift: Owning, Giving and Sharing in Religious Perspective* (2004) 43.

Linda M. Beale, "Congress Fiddles While Middle America Burns: Amending the Amt (and Regular Tax)," *Fla. Tax Rev.* 6 (2004): 811, 820–821.

Lipshaw, Jeffrey M. "The Epistemology of the Financial Crisis: Complexity, Causation, Law, and Judgment," *S. Cal. Interdis. L.J.* 19 (2010): 299, 314 fn. 53.

Littleton, Scott C. *The New Comparative Mythology: An Anthropological Assessment of the Theories of Georges Dumézil* (1973).

Litvak, Kate. "Monte Carlo Simulation of Contractual Provisions: An Application to Default Provisions in Venture Capital Limited Partnership Agreements," *Cornell L. Rev.* 98 (2012): 1495, 1496.

Lobban, Richard A. "Pigs and Their Prohibition." *International Journal of Middle East Studies* 26, no. 1 (1994): 57–75, 58.

López, Kimberle S. *Latin American Novels of the Conquest: Reinventing the New World* (2002) 44.

Lowie, Robert H. "Edward B. Tylor," *American Anthropologist* 19, no. 2 (1917): 262–268.

Luban, David. "A Theory of Crimes Against Humanity," *Yale J. Int'l L.* 29 (2004): 85, 167 n. 144.

Lucretius: On the Nature of Things (H. A. J. Munro trans.), reprinted in 12 Great Books of the Western World (Robert Maynard Hutchins ed., 1952) 1, 12.

Lupher, David A. *Romans in a New World: Classical Models in Sixteenth-Century Spanish America* (2006) 55.

Macey, Jonathan R. and Geoffrey P. Miller. "The End of History and the New World Order: The Triumph of Capitalism and the Competition Between Liberalism and Democracy," *Cornell Int'l L.J.* 25 (1992): 277, 278

MacFarlance, Philip J. "The IMF's Reassessment of Capital Controls after the 2008 Financial Crisis: Heresy or Orthodoxy," *UCLA J. Int'l L. Foreign Aff.* 19 (2015): 167, 180.

Machiavelli, Niccolo. *The Prince* (Luigi Ricci and E.R.P. Vincent trans.), reprinted in *Social and Political Philosophy: Readings from Plato to Ghandi* (John Somerville and Ronald E. Santoni eds., 1963), 123.

Macintyre, Martha. "Warfare and the changing context of 'Kune'on Tubetube," *The Journal of Pacific History* 18, no. 1 (1983): 11–34, 11–12.

Mackay, Charles. *Extraordinary Popular Delusions and the Madness of Crowds* 1–97 (1980).

Macklin, Ruth. *Against Relativism: Cultural Diversity and the Search for Ethical Universals in Medicine* (1999) 44.

Madden, M. Stuart. "Myth, Folklore, and Ancient Ethics," *Cumb. L. Rev.* 37 (2006): 43, 58–59.

Madden, M. Stuart. "The Graeco-Roman Antecedents of Modern Tort Law," *Brandeis LJ* 44 (2005): 865, 90.

Makarius, Raoul, Harumi Befu, Gertrude E. Dole, Louis C. Faron, Stevan Harrell, Sue-Ellen Jacobs, Edmund Leach et al. "Ancient Society and Morgan's Kinship Theory 100 Years After [and Comments and Reply]," *Current Anthropology* 18, no. 4 (1977): 709–729, 709–711.

Malinowski, Bronislaw. *Theories of Man and Culture* (1973) 272.

Malkan, Jeffrey. "Literary Formalism, Legal Formalism," *Cardozo Law Review* 19 (1997): 1393, 1417.

Malloy, Robin Paul. "Invisible Hand or Sleight of Hand? Adam Smith, Richard Posner and the Philosophy of Law and Economics," *Kan. L. Rev.* 36 (1988): 209.

Manhire, Jack. "Tax Compliance as a Wicked System," *Florida Tax Review* 18 (2016): 235, Texas A&M University School of Law Legal Studies Research Paper No. 16-29.

Mann, Susan. "The Universe and the Library: A Critique of James Boyd White as Writer and Reader," *Stan. L. Rev.* 41 (1989): 959, 965.

Manning, John F. "Separation of Powers as Ordinary Interpretation," *Harv. L. Rev.* 124 (2010): 1939, 2004 (2011).

Manning, John F. "What Divides Textualists from Purposivists?," *Colum. L. Rev.* 106 (2006): 70, 76.

Marbury v. Madison, 5 U.S. (1 Cranch) at 180.

Marcos, Cristina, and Sarah Ferris. "House Votes to Repeal ObamaCare | TheHill." Accessed May 19, 2021. https://thehill.com/policy/healthcare/231638-house-votes-to-repeal-obamacare.

Markell, Bruce A. "Bewitched by Language: Wittgenstein and the Practice of Law," *Pepp. L. Rev.* 32 (2005): 801, 807.

Markovits, Richard S. "On the Economic Efficiency of Using Law to Increase Research and Development: A Critique of Various Tax, Antitrust, Intellectual Property, and Tort Law Rules and Policy Proposals," *Harv. J. on Legis.* 39 (2002): 63, 92.

Markovits, Richard S. "Why Kaplow and Shavell's "Double-Distortion Argument" Articles Are Wrong," *Geo. Mason L. Rev.* 13 (2005): 511, 619 n. 152.

Marres, O.C.R. *Interest Deduction Limitations: When to Apply Articles 9 and 24(4) of the OECD Model*, 56 Eur. Taxn. 1 (2016), Journals IBFD. *See*. Para. 11 *OECD Model: Commentary on Article 9* (2010). *OECD Model Tax Convention on Income and on Capital: Commentary* (15 July 2014), Models IBFD.

Matheson, Thornton. "Financial Sector Taxation and the Ongoing Financial Crisis," *Taxing the Financial Sector: Financial Taxes, Bank Levies and More* 203 (Otto Marres and Dennis Weber eds., 2012).

Matthew 20:1-16 (KJV).

Mattiacci, Giuseppe Giuseppe Dari. "Gödel, Kaplow, Shavell: Consistency and Completeness in Social Decision-Making," *Chi.-Kent L. Rev.* 79 (2004): 520 n. 47.

Maugans, James D. "The Grammatical Lawyer," *Prac. Law.*, July 1991, at 11.

Mautner, Menachem. "Three Approaches to Law and Culture," *Cornell L. Rev.* 96 (2011): 839, 841–844.

Mayo Found. for Med. Educ. & Research v. United States, 562 U.S. 44, 57, 131 S.Ct. 704, 178 L.Ed.2d 588 (2011).

Mazur, Orly. "Transfer Pricing Challenges in the Cloud," *B.C. L. Rev.* 57 (2016): 643, 693.

Mead, Margaret and Franz Boas. *Coming of Age in Samoa* (1973) 55.

Medellin v. Texas, 552 U.S. 491, 562, 128 S. Ct. 1346, 1389, 170 L. Ed. 2d 190 (2008).

Medtronic, Inc. v. Commissioner, T.C. Memo No. 2016-112 (2016).

Mehrotra, Ajay K. "Lawyers, Guns, and Public Moneys: The U.S. Treasury, World War I, and the Administration of the Modern Fiscal State," *Law & Hist. Rev.* 28 (2010): 173, 183.

Meron, Theodor. "Crimes and Accountability in Shakespeare," *Am. J. Int'l L.* 92 (1998): 1, 33.

Merrill, Thomas W. "Judicial Deference to Executive Precedent," *Yale L.J.* 101 (1992): 969.

Meyer, Linda. "" Nothing We Say Matters": Teague and New Rules," *The University of Chicago Law Review* 61, no. 2 (1994): 423–492, 460.

Michaelsen, Scott. *The Limits of Multiculturalism: Interrogating the Origins of American Anthropology* (U of Minnesota Press, 1999).

Miles, Thomas J., and Cass R. Sunstein. "The New Legal Realism," *U. Chi. L. Rev.* 75 (2008): 831, 851 n. 21.

Mill, J. S. "On the Definition of Political Economy; and on the Method of Investigation Proper to It," *London & Westminster Rev.* 4 (1836): 12.

Millán-Zaibert, Elizabeth. "Frederick Beiser: German Idealism. The Struggle against Subjectivism, 1781-1801," (2004).

Mogle, James R. "The Future of International Transfer Pricing: Practical and Policy Opportunities Unique to Intellectual Property, Economic Substance, and Entrepreneurial Risk in the Allocation of Intangible Income," *Geo. Mason L. Rev.* 10 (2002): 925, 931.

Mohasco Corp. v. Silver, 447 U.S. 807, 818, 100 S.Ct. 2486, 2493, 65 L.Ed.2d 532 (1980). See. *In re Friesenhahn*, 169 B.R. 615, 637 (Bankr. W.D. Tex. 1994).

Monaghan, Henry Paul. "Stare Decisis and Constitutional Adjudication," *Columbia Law Review* 88, no. 4 (1988): 723–773, 749–752.

Montesquieu, *The Spirit of the Laws* (Thomas Nugent trans., Hafner Pub. 1949) (1748) bk. XI, ch. 6, at 152.

Moore, Alexander. *Cultural Anthropology: The Field Study of Human Beings* (1998) 272.

Moore, Randy. *Creationism in the United States* (1998) 486–507.

Morris, Richard B. "The Forging of the Union Reconsidered: A Historical Refutation of State Sovereignty Over Seabeds," *Colum. L. Rev.* 74 (1974): 1056.

Morriss, Andrew P. "Codification and the Right Answers," *Chi.-Kent L. Rev.* 74 (1999): 355.

Musgrave, Richard A. and Peggy B. Musgrave. *Public Finance in Theory and Practice* 303 (3rd ed., 1980).

Mutén, Leif L. Double Taxation Conventions Between Industrialised and Developing Countries, in Double Taxation Treaties Between Industrialised and Developing Countries; *OECD and Un Models, A Comparison* 3 (Kluwer Law and Tax'n Pubs., 1990).

National Archives. "Executive Orders Disposition Tables," August 15, 2016. https://www.archives.gov/federal-register/executive-orders.

Nat'l Fed'n of Indep. Bus. v. Sebelius, 132 S. Ct. 2566, 2580.

Navarri, Máximo José Rodríguez. *La Conquista de Méjico* (2016) 56.

Neiburg, Federico and Marcio Goldman. *Anthropology and Politics in Studies of National Character* (1998) 65.

Nelson, Caleb. "What is Textualism?," *Va. L. Rev.* 91 (2005): 347, 383–386.

Nietzsche, Friedrich. *Beyond Good and Evil* (Helen Zimmern trans., 1989) Aphorism 2.

Nonet, Philippe. "What is Positive Law?" *The Yale Law Journal* 100, no. 3 (1990): 667–699, 667–668.

Northrop, F.S.C. "Law, Language and Morals," *Yale L.J.* 71 (1962): 1017, 1028. *See.* "Chapter I. the General Concept of Rights," *Stan. L. Rev.* 58 (2006): 2000, 2006.

Nourse, Victoria. "Toward a Due Foundation for the Separation of Powers: The Federalist Papers as Political Narrative," *Tex. L. Rev.* 74 (1995): 447, 521 fn. 330.

Nussabaum, Martha. "The Supreme Court: 2006 Term: Foreword: Constitutions and Capabilities: "Perception" against Lofty Formalism," *Harv. L. Rev.* 121 (2007): 4, 34.

Nussbaum, Martha C. Commentary on Aristotle, De Motu Animalium 271, 363–364 (Martha Craven Nussbaum trans., 1978) (discussing Aristotle, De Motu Animalium 702a30-31, 703b29-32).

Nussbaum, Martha C. *Poetic Justice: The Literary Imagination and Public Life* 53–72 (1995).

Nuzzo, Angelica. "Reflective Judgment, Determinative Judgment, and the Problem of Particularity," *Wash. U. Jurisprudence Rev.* 6 (2013): 7, 21.

Obiora, L. Amede. "Reconstituted Consonants: The Reach of A "Common Core" Analogy in Human Rights," *Hastings Int'l & Comp. L. Rev.* 21 (1998): 921, 955 fn. 13.

OECD Draft Handbook on Transfer Pricing Risk Assessment (OECD 2013). Discussing who is in the best position to assess risks and by what methodology.

OECD Guidelines ¶ 1.55. One economic condition that could pose interesting issues when comparing data from one area to another is relative inflation conditions in the markets. *United States.* See Brooks & Becker, "The Effects of Inflation on Cross-Border Profit Comparisons," *Tax Mgmt. Transfer Pricing Rep.* 7 (June 3, 1998): 77.

OECD Model Convention, Art. 12.2.

OECD, Aligning Transfer Pricing Outcomes with Value Creation – Actions 8-10 Final Reports, OECD/G20 Base Erosion and Profit Shifting Project (OECD 5 Oct. 2015), International Organizations' Documentation IBFD.

OECD, Aligning Transfer Pricing Outcomes with Value Creation – Actions 8-10 Final Reports, OECD/G20 Base Erosion and Profit Shifting Project (OECD 5 Oct. 2015), International Organizations' Documentation IBFD. Para. 1.65.

OECD, OECD/G20 Base Erosion and Profit Shifting Project: Preventing the Granting of Treaty Benefits in Inappropriate Circumstances (2014).

Ogbu, John U. "Cultural Discontinuities and Schooling," *Anthropology & Educ. Quarterly* 13 (1982): 304, 290–307.

Oosterhuis, Paul W. "The Evolution of International Tax Policy-What Would Larry Say," *Ohio NUL Rev.* 33 (2007): 1, 2–3.

Organisation for Economic Co-operation & Dev. Comm. on Fiscal Affairs, *Transfer Pricing and Multinational Enterprises: Three Taxation Issues* 11 (1984).

Originalism, *Black's Law Dictionary* (11th ed. 2019).

Orlove, Benjamin S. "Ecological Anthropology," *Annual Review of Anthropology* 9, no. 1 (1980): 235–273.

Ouchi, William G. and Alan L. Wilkins. "Organizational Culture," *Annual Review of Sociology* 11 (1985): 457, 458, 461–464, 471.

Overby, Brooke. "Contract, in the Age of Sustainable Consumption," *J. Corp. L.* 27 (2002): 603, 626.

Palen, Ronen. "Money Matters: The Law, Economics, and Politics of Currency: International Financial Centers: The British-Empire, City-States and Commercially Oriented Politics," *Theoretical Inq. L.* 11 (2010): 149, 154.

Palencia-Roth, Michael. "The Conquistadors: First-Person Accounts of the Conquest of Mexico. Edited and Translated by Particia de Fuentes. New World Encounters. Edited by Stephen Greenblatt," *Comparative Civilizations Review* 35, no. 35 (n.d.) (1997): 1, 7.

Palincsar, A. Sullivan. "Social Constructivist Perspectives on Teaching and Learning," *Annual Review of Psychology* 49, no. 1 (1998): 345–375, 345, 354.

Pascale Saint-Amans who is leading the OECD's tax division through the BEPS era. "On BEPS," see, e.g., Saint-Amans, Pascal and Rafaelle Russo. "The BEPS Package: Promise Kept," *IBFD Bulletin for International Taxation* 70 (2016): 4.

Patterson, Dennis. "Wittgenstein and Constitutional Theory," *Tex. L. Rev.* 72 (1994): 1837, 1851.

Payne v. Tennessee, 501 U.S. 808, 827, 737–738 (1991).

Perillo, Joseph M. "Exchange, Contract and Law in the Stone Age," *Ariz. L. Rev.* 31 (1989): 17 25–26.

Personal correspondence with Rutger Hafkenscheid (on file with author).

Petersen v. Magna Corp., 484 Mich. 300, 314 (Mich. 2009).

Petersen v. Magna Corp., 484 Mich. 300, 387 n. 38 (Mich. 2009).

Petersen, Glenn. "Indigenous Island Empires: Yap and Tonga Considered," *Journal of Pacific History* 35, no. 1 (2000): 5–27, 27.

Peterson, Jordan B. *Maps of Meaning: The Architecture of Belief* (1999).

Phillips, Jim, and Bradley Miller. "" Too Many Courts and Too Much Law": The Politics of Judicial Reform in Nova Scotia, 1830—1841," *Law and History Review* 30, no. 1 (2012): 89–133, 91.

Piaget, Jean, *Structuralism* (2015) 67.

Piantadosi, Steven T. "Zipf's Word Frequency Law in Natural Language: A Critical Review and Future Directions," *Psychonomic Bull. & Rev.* 21 (2014): 1112.

Pinto, Dale. "" Conservative" and" Radical" Alternatives for Taxing E-Commerce (PART 1)," *Journal of International Taxation* 16, no. 8 (2005).

Pistone, Pasquale. General Report, in The Impact of the OECD and UN Model Conventions on Bilateral Tax Treaties 2 (Michael Lang et al. eds., 2012).

Plato, *The Republic of Plato* (Allan Bloom ed. and trans., 2d ed. 1991).

Plato, *Timaeus* (Robin Waterfield trans., Oxford: Oxford University Press, 2008).

Popper, Karl R. *The Open Society and Its Enemies* (2012) 77–79.

Portilla, Miguel León. *Bernardino de Sahagún: First Anthropologist* (2012) 33.

Portilla, Miguel León. *Native Mesoamerican Spirituality: Ancient Myths, Discourses, Stories, Doctrines, Hymns, Poems from the Aztec, Yucatec, Quiche-Maya and Other Sacred Traditions* (1980) 26.

Portilla, Miguel León. *The Broken Spears: The Aztec Account of the Conquest of Mexico* (2006) 44.

Posner, Richard A. "The Decline of Law as an Autonomous Discipline: 1962-1987," *Harv. L. Rev.* 100 (1987): 761, 762.

Posner, Richard A. *How Judges Think* (2008) 41.

Pouncy, Charles R. P. "Contemporary Financial Innovation: Orthodoxy and Alternatives," *SMU L. Rev.* 51 (1998): 505.

Pound, Roscoe. "Fifty Years of Jurisprudence," *Harv. L. Rev.* 51 (1937): 777, 582 fn. 129 (1937).

Pound, Roscoe. "A Text Book of Roman Law from Augustus to Justinian by W. W. Buckland, M. A., F. B. A., of the Inner Temple, Barrister at Law, Regius Professor of Civil Law in the University of Cambridge, Fellow of Gonville and Caius Co," *Harv. L. Rev.* 26 (1922): 119, 120–121.

Pound, Roscoe. "Mechanical Jurisprudence," *Columbia Law Review* 8 (1908): 605, 606.

Powell, H. Jefferson. "The Original Understanding of Original Intent," *Harv. L. Rev.* 98 (1985): 885.

Pradeau, Jean-Francois. *Plato and the City* (University of Exeter Press, Exeter, 2002) 129.

Prakash, Saikrishna, and Steven D. Smith. "How to Remove a Federal Judge," *Yale LJ* 116 (2006): 72, 87–88.

Priel, Dan. "The Place of Legitimacy in Legal Theory," *McGill Law Journal / Revue de Droit de McGill* 57, no. 1 (2011): 1–35, 29–30.

Raffield, Paul. "A Discredited Priesthood the Failings of Common Lawyers and Their Representation in Seventeenth Century Satirical Drama," *Law & Literature* 17 (2005): 365, 373–374.

Ragsdale Jr, John W. "The Rise and Fall of the Chacoan State," *UMKC L. Rev.* 64 (1995): 485, 528.

Rectenwald, Glen. "A Proposed Framework for Resolving the Transfer Pricing Problem: Allocating the Tax Base of Multi-National Entities Based on Real Economic Indicators of Benefit and Burden," *Duke J. Comp. & Int'l L.* 22 (2012): 425, 434–436.

Reich-Graefe, Rene. "Deconstructing Corporate Governance: The Mechanics of Trusting," *Delaware Journal of Corporate Law* 38 (2013): 103, 124–125 (stating that law, social norms, and linguistics are intertwined in a unique way).

Reid, 354 U.S. at 18.

Remington, Clark A. "Llewellyn, Antiformalism and the Fear of Transcendental Nonsense: Codifying the Variability Rule in the Law of Sales," *Wayne L. Rev.* 44 (1998): 29, 41.

Renfrew, Colin. *Archaeology and Language: The Puzzle of Indo-European Origins* (1990) 13.

Renteln, Alison Dundes. *International Human Rights: Universalism Versus Relativism* (2013) 77–79.

Rentschler, Eric. *The Ministry of Illusion* (1996) 21 and Sherwin, Richard K. "Law's Beatitude: A Post-Nietzschean Account of Legitimacy," *Cardozo L. Rev.* 24 (2003): 683, 703 n. 81.

Report on Double Taxation Submitted to the Financial Committee by Professors Bruins, Einaudi, Seligman, and Sir Josiah Stamp, League of Nations Doc. E.F.S. 73.F.19 (1923).

Respublica v. De Longchamps, 1 Dall. 111 (Pa. 1784).

Rev. Rul. 72-183, 1972-1 C.B. 213 (1972).

Revenue Act 1928, s 601, 26 U.S.C. s 611, 26 U.S.C.A. Int. Rev. Acts, page 456.

Revenue Act of 1962, Hearings Before the Committee on Finance, U.S. Senate, 87th Cong. 2d Sess., on H.R. 10650, pt. I, p. 447–448; see also S. Rep. No. 87-1881, at 3662 (Dissenting Views).

Rhonheimer, Martin. "Natural Law as a Work of Reason: Understanding the Metaphysics of Participated Theonomy," *Am. J. Juris.* 55 (2010): 41, 47, 50.

Richards, Janet and Mary Van Buren. *Order, Legitimacy, and Wealth in Ancient States* (2000) 3–6.

Ritter, Henning. "The Ethnological Revolution: On Marcel Mauss," *Comparative Civilizations Review* 22, no. 22 (1990): 2.

Robert, H. *Robert's Rules of Order Newly Revised* (1970). Levmore, Saul. "Parliamentary Law, Majority Decisionmaking, and the Voting Paradox," *Virginia Law Review* (1989): 971–1044.

Roberts, Anthea. "Triangular Treaties: The Extent and Limits of Investment Treaty Rights," *Harv. Int'l L.J.* 56 (2015): 353, 378.

Robertson, Robin. *Jungian Archetypes, Jung, Gödel and the History of Archetypes* 186 (1995).

Robinson, Reginald Leamon. "The Impact of Hobbes's Empirical Natural Law on Title VII's Effectiveness: A Hegelian Critique," *Conn. L. Rev.* 25 (1993): 607, 661 n.299.

Roin, Julie A. "The Grand Illusion: A Neutral System for the Taxation of International Transactions," *Va. L. Rev.* 75 (1989): 919, 923–926.

Rojo, Luis Durán, and Paul Nina Nina. "The Use of Paragraphs 1.119 to 1.128 of the 2017 OECD Transfer Pricing Guidelines for the Application of Transfer Pricing Rules," *Intertax* 48, no. 6/7 (2020).

Romer v. Evans, 517 U.S. 620 (1996).

Rorty, Richard. The World Well Lost, *in* Consequences of Pragmatism, supra note 12, at 3, 1415.

Rosenblatt, Daniel. "An Anthropology Made Safe for Culture: Patterns of Practice and the Politics of Difference in Ruth Benedict," *American Anthropologist* 106, no. 3 (2004): 459–472.

Rosenzweig, Adam H. "Building a Framework for a Post-BEPS World," *Tax Notes Int'l* 74 (2014): 1077; Vann, Richard J. "Policy Forum: The Policy Underpinnings of the BEPS Project--Preserving the International Corporation Income Tax," *Can. Tax J.* 62 (2014): 433; Ault, Hugh J. et al. Base Erosion and Profit Shifting: A

Roadmap for Reform (Bos. Coll. Law Sch., Working Paper No. 324, 2014), http://ssrn.com/abstract=2459646.

Rotman, Leonard I. "Debunking the "End of History" Thesis for Corporate Law," *B.C. Int'l & Comp. L. Rev.* 33 (2010): 219, 272 fn. 45.

Rotman, Leonard I. *Debunking the "End of History"* Rotman, Leonard I. "Debunking the End of History Thesis for Corporate Law," *BC Int'l & Comp. L. Rev.* 33 (2010): 219.

Row, David R. "Gödel's Theorem Addressed the System Described in The Principia. David R. Dow, Gödel and Langdell-A Reply to Brown and Greenberg's Use of Mathematics in Legal Theory," *Hastings L.J.* 44 (1993): 707, 713–714.

Rustad, Michael L. "Symposium: Does the World Still Need United States Tort Law? Or Did It Ever?: Torts as Public Wrongs," *Pepp. L. Rev.* 38 (2011): 433, 443 fn. 56.

Ryang, Sonia. *Chrysanthemum's Strange Life: Ruth Benedict in Postwar Japan* (2002) 87–116.

Salecl, Renata. "Rights in Psychoanalytic and Feminist Perspective," *Cardozo L. Rev.* 16 (1995): 1121, 1133.

Saphire, Richard B. "Enough About Originalism," *N. Ky. L. Rev.* 15 (1988): 513, 515 n.7.

Sartre, Jean Paul. *The Flies, in No Exit and Other Plays* 49 (Stuart Gilbert trans., 1955) (1943)

Savage-Rumbaugh, Sue et al. "The Emergence of Knapping and Vocal Expression Embedded in a Pan/Homo Culture," *Biology and Philosophy* 19 (2004): 541.

Scalia, Antonin. *A Matter of Interpretation: Federal Courts and the Law* (1997) 25.

Schauer, Frederick. "Constitutional Positivism," *Conn. L. Rev.* 25 (1993): 797, 799.

Scheibler, Ingrid. "Gadamer, Heidegger, and the Social Dimensions of Language: Reflections on the Critical Potential of Hermaneutical Philosophy," *Chi.-Kent L. Rev.* 76 (2000): 853, 888.

Schlag, Pierre. "Foreword: Postmodernism and Law," *U. Colo. L. Rev.* 62 (1991): 439, 448.

Schmidtz, David. "Bastiat and the Origins of Political Economy," *Geo. J.L. & Pub. Pol'y* 15 (2017): 835, 843.

Schnoor, Britta A. "International Law, the Power of the Purse, and Speaking with One Voice: The Legal Cacophony Created by Withholding US Dues from the United Nations," *Iowa Law Review* 92, no. 3 (2007): 1133, 1138–1139.

Schumacher, Scott A. "Macniven v. Westmoreland and Tax Advice: Using "Purposive Textualism" to Deal with Tax Shelters and Promote Legitimate Tax Advice," *Marq. L. Rev.* 92 (2008): 33, 73.

Schwartz, Andrew W. "No Competing Theory of Constitutional Interpretation Jutifes Regulatory Takings Ideology," *Stan. Envtl. L.J.* 34 (2015): 247, 25.

Schwidetzky, Walter D. "The Partnership Allocation Rules of Section 704(b): To Be or Not to Be," *Va. Tax Rev.* 17 (1998): 707, 739.

Scuillo, Nick J. "Žižek/Questions/Failing," *Willamette L. Rev.* 47 (2011): 287, 325 n. 55.

Sear, Rebecca and Ruth Mace. "Who Keeps Children Alive? A Review of the Effects of Kin on Child Survival," *Evolution and Human Behavior* 29 (2008): 1, 5–15.

Sense, Sensibility and Smart Contracts: A View From a Contract, 20181004A NYCBAR 13.

Sewell Jr., William H. "A Theory of Structure: Duality, Agency, and Transformation," *American Journal of Sociology* 98, no. 1 (1992): 1–29, 8.

Sewell Jr., William H. "A Theory of Structure: Duality, Agency, and Transformation," *American Journal of Sociology* 98, no. 1 (1992): 1–29, 1, 7, 12 (1992).

Shackleton, R. "Montesquieu." *Encyclopedia Britannica*, February 6, 2021. https://www.britannica.com/biography/Montesquieu.

Shakespeare, William. Richard II, Act 2, Scene 2, Lines 14–24.

Shakespeare, William. *Troilus and Cressida*, Act v, Scene 2, Line 143. Slavoj Žižek. "Absolute Recoil."

Shaviro, Daniel. "Selective Limitations on Tax Benefits," *U. Chi. L. Rev.* 56 (1989): 1189, 1231.

Shaviro, Daniel. *The Crossroads Versus the Seesaw: Getting a 'Fix' on Recent International Tax Policy Developments* (N.Y. Univ. Sch. of Law, Pub. Law & Legal Theory Research Paper Series, Working Paper No. 15-20, 2015), http://ssrn.com/abstract=2605144.

Shaviro, Daniel. The Financial Transactions Tax Versus (?) the Financial Activities Tax 21-22 (N.Y.U. Law and Econ. Working Papers, Working Paper No. 292, Mar. 2012), http://lsr.nellco.org/nyu_lewp/292.

Shepard, Hon. Randall T. and Douglas Fivecoat, "Indiana's Supreme Court in the Civil War: How Can the Constitution Be Unconstitutional?," *Res Gestae*, April 2006, at 29, 32.

Shepard, Paul. *Limited Wants, Unlimited Means* (1998) 33.

Sheppard, Lee A. "Xilinx and the Future of Transfer Pricing," *Tax Notes* 123 (2009): 1295, 1301.

Sherwin, Richard K. "Law's Beatitude: A Post-Nietzschean Account of Legitimacy," *Cardozo L. Rev.* 24 (2003): 683, 699.

Sherwin, Robert T. "# HaveWeReallyThoughtThisThrough: Why Granting Trademark Protection to Hashtags Is Unnecessary, Duplicative, and Downright Dangerous," *Harv. JL & Tech.* 29 (2015): 455, 493 n. 195.

Sitaraman, Ganesh. "Economic Structure and Constitutional Structure: An Intellectual History," *Tex. L. Rev.* 94 (2015): 1301, 1315.

Sitmaartensdijk, Jan and Yfke Nijland. *Operatie Black Tulip: De uitzetting van Duitse burgers na de oorlog* (Amsterdam: Boom, 2009).

Skaar, *Permanent Establishment: Erosion of a Tax Treaty Principle* (Netherlands: Aspen Publishers, 1991).

Slanski, Kathryn E. "The Law of Hammurabi and Its Audience," *Yale J.L. & Human.* 24 (2012): 97, 98–99.

Slocum, Brian G. "Overlooked Temporal Issues in Statutory Interpretation," *Temp. L. Rev.* 81 (2008): 635, 637–1638.

Smith, Adam. *An Inquiry into the Nature and Causes of the Wealth of Nations 475-76* (Edwin Cannan ed., University of Chicago Press, 1976) (1776).

Smith, Adam. *An Inquiry into the Nature and Causes of the Wealth of Nations 475-76* (Edwin Cannan ed., University of Chicago Press, 1976) (1776).

Smith, N. *A Commentary to Kant's 'Critique of Pure Reason'* 363–381 (1918).
Smith, Steven D. "Believing like a Lawyer," *BCL Rev.* 40 (1998): 1041, 1111–11112 (1999).
Smith, Steven D. "Law as Language," *Mercer Law Review* 63 (2011): 891, 893.
Sokol, D. Daniel. "Competition Policy and Comparative Corporate Governance of State-Owned Enterprises," *B.Y.U. L. Rev.* 2009 (2009): 1713, 1812 fn. 28.
Solum, Lawrence B. "Intellectual History as Constitutional Theory," *Va. L. Rev.* 101 (2015): 1111.
Somerset v Stewart (1772).
Spagnoli, Filip. "The Globalization of Human Rights Law: Why Do Human Rights Need International Law?," *Tex. Wesleyan L. Rev.* 14 (2008): 317, 333.
Speech at CUA, 14 October 1996.
Spencer, Herbert. *A Plea for Liberty: An Argument Against Socialism and Socialistic Legislation* (Murray, 1891) 15–17.
Spencer, Herbert. *Social Statics* (1851) 19–20.
Staszewski, Glen. "The Dumbing Down of Statuary," *B.U.L. Rev.* 95 (2015): 209, 217–219.
State v. Cleve, 1999-NMSC-017, ¶ 28, 127 N.M. 240, 251, 980 P.2d 23, 34.
Statement of William J. Sample, Vice President of Worldwide Tax for Microsoft Corporation, Offshore Profit Shifting Hearing (Microsoft & Hewlett Packard), supra note 21, at 30, http:// www.hsgac.senate.gov/subcommittees/investigations/hearings/offshore-profit-shifting-and-the-us-tax-code; see also Testimony of Tim Cook, CEO of Apple, Inc., Offshore Profit Shifting Hearing (Apple).
Stauder, Jack. *The "Relevance" of Anthropology to Colonialism and Imperialism* (1974) 29–51.
Stefanck, Jean. "The Law Review Symposium Issue: Community of Meaning or Re-Inscription of Hierarchy?," *U. Colo. L. Rev.* 63 (1992): 651, 652.
Stein, Harry. "America Can Still Do Big Things: Dispelling the Fiscal Hysteria That Thwarts Good Public Policy," *Harv. L. & Pol'y Rev.* 11 (2017): 141, 153.
Stein, Peter. *Regulae Iuris: From Juristic Rules to Legal Maxims* (1966).
Stern, Bernhard J. "Concerning the Distinction between the Social and the Cultural," *Social Forces* 8, no. 2 (1929): 264–1271.
Stinchcombe, Arthur L. "Social Structure and Organizations," *Handbook of Organizations* (James G. March ed., 1965) 142, 142–193.
Stocking Jr, George W. "Franz Boas and the Culture Concept in Historical Perspective 1," *American Anthropologist* 68, no. 4 (1966): 867–882, 867.
Stone, Glenn Davis. "Biotechnology, Schismogenesis, and the Demise of Uncertainty," *Wash. U. J.L. & Pol'y* 47 (2015): 29, 30.
Storey, E. A., and Terry L. Jones. "Diffusionism in Archaeological Theory," *Polynesians in America: Pre-Columbian Contacts with the New World* (2011).
Suisman, David. "Selling Sounds: The Commercial Revolution in American Music 8 (2012)," *Hastings L.J.* 66 (2015): 1187, 1220–1221.
Sunstein, Cass R. "Must Formalism Be Defended Empirically?," *U. Chi. L. Rev.* 66 (1999): 636, 638.

Super, Charles M. and Sara Harkness. "The Developmental Niche: A Conceptualization at the Interface of Child and Culture," *International Journal of Behavioral* 9 (1986): 545, 547.

Sussex Peerage Case (1844) 11, Clark & F. 85, 103, 109, 8 Jur. 793.

Sweeney, Joseph C. "The Just War Ethic in International Law," *Fordham Int'l LJ* 27 (2003): 1865, 1903.

Sylla, Richard. "Economy of Supplying Money to a Growing Economy: Monetary Regimes and the Search for an Anchor to Stabilize the Value of Money," *Theoretical Inq. L.* 11 (2010): 1, 23.

Sylla, Richard. "Economy of Supplying Money to a Growing Economy: Monetary Regimes and the Search for an Anchor to Stabilize the Value of Money," *Theoretical Inq. L.* 11 (2010): 1, 23.

Tarin, G. Boyd. "The Bank for International Settlements: Keeping A Law Profile?," *Transnat'l Law.* 5 (1992): 839, 851–852.

Taylor, Cliff. "Chances of US Tax Reform High under Donald Trump, PwC Says." The Irish Times. Accessed May 29, 2021. https://www.irishtimes.com/business/economy/chances-of-us-tax-reform-high-under-donald-trump-pwc-says-1.2944744.

Taylor, Steve. "The Madness of Materialism," *Psychol. Today* 55 Accessed May 18, 2021. https://www.psychologytoday.com/blog/out-the-darkness/201203/the-madness-materialism; *see Cultural Materialism,* All About Philosophy, Accessed April 13, 2018, https://www.allaboutphilosophy.org/ cultural-materialism.htm.

Terra, Ben J.M. and Peter J. Wattel. *European Tax Law*, sixth edition (abridged student edition). Wolters Kluwer Law & Business, 2012, page 578, fn. 3.

The Bayeux Tapestry, *A Comprehensive Survey* (Sir Frank Stenton ed., Phaidon Press rev. ed. 1965).

The Bayeux Tapestry, A Comprehensive Survey (Sir Frank Stenton ed., New York: Phaidon, 1957).

The Case of Sutton's Hospital, 77 Eng. Rep. 960 (K.B. 1612).

The Charlie Rose Show: Interview with Harold Bloom (PBS television broadcast, Dec. 29, 1994).

The Chinese Exclusion Cases, 130 U.S. 581, 600 (1889).

The Civil Code of the State of New York (pt. 1), 2 Alb. L.J. 385, 385 (Nov. 19, 1870).

The Federalist No. 47, at 301 (James Madison) (Clinton Rossiter ed., 1961).

The Firm (Paramount Pictures 1993).

The Iliad of Homer 14:28-30 (Richmond Lattimore trans., 25th reprint ed. 1976) (1951).

The Liddell & Scott's A Greek-English Lexicon defines the word as, "ψυχή ψύχω I.breath, Lat. anima, esp. as the sign of life, the life, spirit." "Henry George Liddell, Robert Scott, An Intermediate Greek-English Lexicon, Ψυχή." Accessed May 19, 2021. http://www.perseus.tufts.edu/hopper/text?doc=perseus%3atext%3a1999.04.0058%3aentry%3dyuxh%2f.

The Pervert's Guide to Ideology (Zeitgeist Films et al. 2012).

The Princess Bride (20th Century Fox).

The Twelve Federal Reserve Districts, FED. RES. BOARD, http://www.federalreserve.gov/otherfrb.htm (providing a map of the current districts and noting that "the Board of Governors revised the branch boundaries of the System in February 1996").

This is a reference to Rudyard Kipling's "If" poem. Ricketts, Harry. *The Unforgiving Minute: A Life of Rudyard Kipling* (1999).

This is especially visible for "[t]hose watching the US Senate Finance Committee Hearings 'International Tax: OECD BEPS & EU State Aid' (www.finance.senate.gov/hearings/international-tax-oecdbeps-and-eu-state-aid) will get the impression that the US Treasury Department's stake in the BEPS Project was foremost and above all about protecting the interests of US multinationals against "aggressive" tax authorities of other OECD member countries, rather than avoiding profit shifting. See also the interview by BNA with Robert Stack, Deputy Assistant Secretary (International Tax Affairs) US Treasury, available at www.bna.com/videos-m57982058714." Hafkenscheid, R. "The BEPS Report on Risk Allocation: Not So Functional," *Intl. Transfer Pricing J.* 24 (2017): 1, 5, Journals IBFD.

Thompson, Julio A. *Essays on Kelsen.* Edited by Richard Tur and William Twining (New York: Oxford University Press, 1986), pp. VIII, 345. $44.00, 86 *Mich. L. Rev.* 1470, 1474 fn. 9 (1988).

Tobin, James. "Financial Intermediaries," in *The New Palgrave: Finance* 35, 41 (John Eatwell et al. eds., 1989).

Tolstoy, Leo. *War and Peace, Epilogue*, pt. II (Rosemary Edmonds trans., Greenwich House 1982) (1868).

Tomlins, Christopher. "Revolutionary Justice in Brecht, Conrad, and Blake," *Law & Literature* 21, no. 2 (2009): 185–213, 188.

Tooby, John and Leda Cosmides. *The Adapted Mind: Evolutionary Psychology and the Generation of Culture* (1995) 24.

Tooker, Elisabeth. "The Structure of the Iroquois League: Lewis H. Morgan's Research and Observations," *Ethnohistory Tucson, Ariz* 30, no. 3 (1983): 141–154.

Townsend, Mike. "Implications of Foundational Crises in Mathematics: A Case Study in Interdisciplinary Legal Research," *Wash. L. Rev.* 71 (1996): 51, 108.

Trans World Airlines, Inc. v. Franklin Mint Corp., 466 U.S. 243, 282–283 (1984).

Treasury Secretary & Key Lawmakers Weigh in On EU State Aid, Inversions & Tax Reform, 2/18/2016 FTWA ART. 1.

Tribe, Laurence. "Equal Dignity: Speaking It's Name," *Harv. L. Rev. F.* 129 (2015): 16, 16.

Turley, Jonathan. "Dualistic Values in the Age of International Legisprudence," *Hastings L.J.* 44 (1993): 185, 190.

Turner, Jonathan H., and Alexandra R. Maryanski. "Is 'Neofunctionalism' Really Functional?" *Sociological Theory* 6, no. 1 (1988): 110–121, 1120–1112.

Turner, Terence. "Anthropology and Multiculturalism: What is Anthropology that Multiculturalists Should Be Mindful of It?" *Cultural Anthropology* 8, no. 4 (1993): 411–429 (1993); *see also* Gumperz, John J., and Stephen C. Levinson. "Rethinking Linguistic Relativity," *Current Anthropology* 32, no. 5 (1991): 613–623, 614.

Tylor, Edward B. "On a Method of Investigating the Development of Institutions; Applied to Laws of Marriage and Descent," *The Journal of the Anthropological Institute of Great Britain and Ireland* 18 (1889): 245–272.

U.S.C.A. § 543 (West).

Udell, Collin O'Connor. "Parading the Saurian Tail: Projection, Jung, and the Law," *Ariz. L. Rev.* 42 (2000): 731, 776.

United Nations Dep't of Economic and Social Affairs, United Nations Model Double Taxation Convention Between Developed and Developing Countries viii (2001).

United Nations, Commentary on the Articles of the 1980 United Nations Model Double Taxation Convention Between Developed and Developing Countries 2 (Jan. 1, 1980).

United States IRS v. Osborne (In re Osborne), 76 F.3d 306, 309 (9th Cir. 1996).

United States v. Brown, 333 U.S. 18, 27, 68 S.Ct. 376, 380, 92 L.Ed. 442 (1948).

United States v. Curtiss-Wright Export Corp., 299 U.S. 304, 316 (1936).

United States v. Maine, 420 U.S. 515, 520–521 (1975).

United States v. Mead Corp., 533 U.S. 218, 226–227, 121 S.Ct. 2164, 150 L.Ed.2d 292 (2001).

United States v. Nixon, 418 U.S. 683, 703–705 (1974).

Updike, John. Roger's Version 23–24 (1986).

Urick, Jonathan D. "Note, Chevron and Constitutional Doubt," *Va. L. Rev.* 99 (2013): 375, 409.

Utset, Manuel A. "The Discipline of Institutions and the Disciplining of Banks," *Ann. Rev. Banking L.* 14 (1995): 211, 216.

Valauri, John T. "Dialectical Jurisprudence: Aristotle and the Concept of Law," *Drexel Law Review* 3 (2010): 415, 420.

Vermeulen, Hein and M.F.A Blaauw. "The Tax Treatment of Directly Held Real Estate under the Proposed CCCTB Directive," *Eur. Taxn.* 51 (2011): 12, Journals IBFD.

VerSteeg, Russ. "A Contract Analysis of the Trojan War," *Ariz. L. Rev.* 40 (1998): 173, 192.

VerSteeg, Russ. "Early Mesopotamian Commercial Law," *U. Tol. L. Rev.* 30 (1999): 183, 212–213.

Viehe, Karl William. "The Legal and Economic Realities of Transfer Pricing: An Analysis of the Draft Revenue Procedure on Advance Transfer Price Rulings," *Transnat'l Law.* 4 (1991): 1, 5.

Viehe, Karl William. "The Legal and Economic Realities of Transfer Pricing: An Analysis of the Draft Revenue Procedure on Advance Transfer Price Rulings," *Transnat'l Law.* 4 (1991): 1, 5.

Vlasic, Mark V. and Helga Turku. Countering IS's Theft and Destruction of Mesopotamia, World Policy Blog, (July 7, 2015, 8:55 AM), http://www.worldpolicy.org/blog/2015/07/07/countering-is%E2%C80%99s-theft-and-destructionmesopotamia.

Wald, Eli. "The Rise and Fall of the Wasp and Jewish Law Firms," *Stan. L. Rev.* 60 (2008): 1803, 1812.

Walker, George A. "Financial Crisis-U.K. Policy and Regulatory Response," *Int'l Law.* 44 (2010): 751, 751–752.

Wallace, David Foster. "Tense Present: Democracy, English, and the Wars over Usage," *Harper's Mag.*, April 2001.

Walsh, James J. *Education of the Founding Fathers of the Republic: Scholasticism in the Colonial Colleges* (1970) 104–105.

Ware v. Hylton, 3 U.S. (3 Dall.) 199, 281 (1796) (Wilson, J.) (emphasis in original). See Restatement of the Foreign Relations Law of the United States (Revised), pt. I, ch. 2, introductory note (Tent. Draft No. 6, 1985).

Weaver, William G. "Richard Rorty and the Radical Left," *Virginia Law Review* (1992): 729–757.

Weber, Dennis and Antonio Russo. "The CCCTB and Possible Elements of a Technical Outline: The "Switch-Over" Clause," in *Common Consolidated Corporate Tax Base* 751 (Michael Lang, Pasquale Pistone, Josef Schuch and Claus Staringer eds., 2008).

Weeghel, Stef Van. *The Improper Use of Tax Treaties: With Particular Reference to The Netherlands and The United States* (1998).

Weiner, Annette B. "Cultural Difference and the Density of Objects," *American Ethnologist* 21, no. 2 (1994): 391–403, 394–395.

Wells, Bret and Cym Lowell, "Tax Base Erosion: Reformation of Section 482's Arm's Length Standard," *Fla. Tax Rev.* 15 (2014): 737, 797 fn. 33.

Wells, Bret and Cym Lowell. "Tax Base Erosion: Reformation of Section 482's Arm's Length Standard," *Fla. Tax Rev.* 15 (2014): 737, 745.

Wells, Catharine Pierce. "Langdell and the Invention of Legal Doctrine," *Buff. L. Rev.* 58 (2010): 551, 618 fn. 152.

West, Patrick C. *Theory of Liberty, Legitimacy and Power* (2013) 216.

Westbrook, David A. "Liberal Environmental Jurisprudence," *UC Davis L. Rev.* 27 (1993): 619, 712 fn. 161.

Wheat, Leonard F. *Hegel's Undiscovered Thesis-Antithesis-Synthesis Dialectics: What Only Marx and Tillich Understood* (Prometheus, 2012).

White, Leslie A. "Energy and the Evolution of Culture," *American Anthropologist* 45, no. 3 (1943): 335–356, 350.

White, Leslie A. "Energy and the Evolution of Culture." *American Anthropologist* 45, no. 3 (1943): 335–356, 350.

White, Sienna C. "Cost Sharing Agreements & the Arm's Length Standard: A Matter of Statutory Interpretation?," *Fla. Tax Rev.* 19 (2016): 191, 196. *Quoting*. Rectenwald, Glen. "A Proposed Framework for Resolving the Transfer Pricing Problem: Allocating the Tax Base of Multi-National Entities Based on Real Economic Indicators of Benefit and Burden," *Duke J. Comp. & Int'l L.* 22 (2012): 425, 436.

Whitney v. Robertson, 124 U.S. 190, 194 (1888).

Wikipedia contributors, "Otto von Bismarck," *Wikipedia, The Free Encyclopedia*, https://en.wikipedia.org/w/index.php?title=Otto_von_Bismarck&oldid=1023682217 (accessed May 20, 2021).

Wildgen, Wolfgang. *The Paleolithic Origins of Art, Its Dynamic and Topological Aspects, and the Transition to Writing* (2004) 111–112.

Wilkins, David B. "Legal Realism for Lawyers," *Harv. L. Rev.* 104 (1990): 468, 477.

Winslow, Donald Arthur. "Tax Avoidance and the Definition of Insurance: The Continuing Examination of Captive Insurance Companies," *Case W. Res. L. Rev.* 40 (1990): 79, 112.

Wittgenstein, Ludwig. *Philosophical Investigations* (G.E.M. Anscombe and R. Rhees eds., G.E.M. Anscombe trans., 1972) § 201.

Wittgenstein, Ludwig. *Philosophical Investigations* (Oxford: Basil Blackwell, 1968).

Wittgenstein, Ludwig. *Remarks on the Foundations of Mathematics Part I*, Appendix I (G.H. von Wright, R. Rhees and G.E.M. Anscombe eds., G.E.M. Anscombe trans., rev. ed. 1983) § 8.

Wittgenstein, Ludwig. *Remarks on the Philosophy of Psychology*, 2 vols., ed. G.H. von Wright and Heikki Nyman, trans. C.G. Luckhardt and M.A.E. Aue (Chicago: University of Chicago Press, 1980), II:190.

Wittgenstein, Ludwig. *Remarks on Frazer's Golden Bough at vi* (Rush Rees ed. and A.C. Miles trans., 1979).

Wittgenstein, Ludwig. *Tractatus Logico-Philosophicus* (Routledge, 2013) § 2.022. Later, Wittgenstein came to regret such statements.

Wittgeinstein, Ludwig. *Tractatus Logico-Philosophicus* 6.001.

Wittgenstein, On Certainty.

Wittgenstein, *Philosophical Investigations* #23.

Wittgenstein, Philosophical Remarks.

Wittgenstein, *The Blue Book*, 5.

Wolff, Mark J. "Failure of the International Monetary Fund & World Bank to Achieve Integral Development: A Critical Historical Assessment of Bretton Woods Institutions Policies, Structures & Governance," *Syracuse J. Int'l L. & Com.* 41 (2013).

Woodring, Benjamin. "Liberty to Misread: Sanctuary and Possibility in the Comedy of Errors," *Yale J.L. & Human.* 28 (2016): 319.

Wright, Gary A. "Origins of Food Production in Southwestern Asia: A Survey of Ideas," *Current Anthropology* 12, no. 4/5 (October 1, 1971): 447–477. https://doi.org/10.1086/201233.

Wright, Kent and Jacques De Saint Victor. *La Premiere Contre-rèvolution (1789-1791)* (Paris: Presses Universitaires De France, 2010), pp. 504. é30 (Isbn 978-2-130-57077-6), 30 *Law & Hist. Rev.* 319, 320–321 (2012).

Wykes, David. *Evelyn Waugh: A Literary Life* 209–11 (1999).

Xilinx Inc. v. Comm'r, 567 F.3d 482, 484 (9th Cir. 2009), rev'd on reh'g, 598 F.3d 1191 (9th Cir. 2010), acq. in result AOD 2010-03.

Yang, Tseming. "Race, Religion, and Cultural Identity: Reconciling the Jurisprudence of Race and Religion," *Ind. L.J.* 73 (1997): 119, 127–128.

Yoffee, Norman. *Myths of the Archaic State: Evolution of the Earliest Cities, States, and Civilizations* (2005) 23, 93.

Yoshino, Kenji. "The City and The Poet," *Yale LJ 114* (2005): 1835, 1842–1843.

Yoshino, Kenji. "The City and the Poet," *Yale L.J.* 114 (2005): 1835, 1842.

Young, Michael W. *Malinowski: Odyssey of an Anthropolgist* (Yale Univ. Press, 2004), 1884–1920 xx.

Youngstown Sheet & Tube Co. v. Sawyer, 343 U.S. 579, 647 (1952).
Zelinsky, Wilbur. "The Hypothesis of the Mobility Transition," *Geographical Review* (1971): 219–249, 219.
Žižek, Slavoj. *Absolute Recoil* (2015).
Žižek, Slavoj. *Absolute Recoil: Towards A New Foundation of Dialectical Materialism* (2015).
Žižek, Slavoj. *Less Than Nothing: Hegel and the Shadow of Dialectical Materialism* (2012).
Žiẑek, Slavoj. *Less Than Nothing: Hegel and the Shadow of Dialectical Materialism* (2012.)
Žižek, Slavoj. *Welcome to the Desert of the Real* 2 (2002).

Index

About the Author

Charles Lincoln is currently a PhD student at the University of Groningen (abbreviated as UG; Dutch: *Rijksuniversiteit Groningen*, abbreviated as *RUG*) studying international tax law in the field of business law, European Law, and tax law under the umbrella of the research program of Protecting European Citizens and Market Participants. Charles received a master's degree in tax law LL.M. (Latin: *Magister Legum* or *Legum Magister*) from Boston University in May 2018. Charles also received an advanced LL.M master's degree in international tax law from the University of Amsterdam (abbreviated as UvA, Dutch: *Universiteit van Amsterdam*) in October 2017. He also graduated from Texas A&M University School of Law in May 2016 with a J.D. In May of 2013, he received a bachelor's degree in government from Harvard University.

www.ingramcontent.com/pod-product-compliance
Lightning Source LLC
LaVergne TN
LVHW011810200926
848484LV00005B/1135
9781793632258